DARE T~~O~~ ~~DREAM~~

Kevin Perkins has proved himself one of Australia's best journalists, writers and biographers.

Regarded by his colleagues as the reporters' reporter, he "covered the waterfront" as an investigative journalist and hard-hitting columnist on various Sydney metropolitan newspapers for almost 40 years - and as a news executive for 20 of those years.

Noted for his meticulous research and flair with stories of human interest, Perkins is the author of several best-selling books, including biographies of famous English bodyline bowler Harold Larwood, Prime Minister Sir Robert Menzies, gambler Big Bill Waterhouse, legendary trainer Tommy Smith and woman in a man's world, Gai Waterhouse.

Also by Kevin Perkins

THE LARWOOD STORY, with Harold Larwood
IN MY SHOES, with Elaine Fifield
MENZIES, LAST OF THE QUEEN'S MEN
THE GAMBLING MAN
THE HEART CAN WAIT
TJ THE MIDAS MAN
AGAINST ALL ODDS - GAI WATERHOUSE

Kevin Perkins

DARE TO DREAM

The Life and Times of a Proud Australian

First published 2001 by Golden Wattle Publishers
Level 6, 77 Castlereagh Street, Sydney
ABN 91 092 526 906

National Library of Australia
Cataloguing-in-Publication Data

Perkins, Kevin
Dare to Dream - The Life and Times of a Proud Australian

ISBN 0 646 39467 3

Cover Design: Simon Leong Design, Sydney
Cover Photo: Emigrant Joseph John Alam, trudging off on his first day as a
hawker in 1890 after being rejected by mine workers at Wallsend in the
Hunter Valley of NSW

Distributed by Gary Allen Pty Ltd

Printed in Australia by Griffin Press

For two women who understood -
Ngaire, who suggested this book;
Cynthia, who gave it a title.

All men dream but not equally.   Those who dream by night in the dusty recesses of their minds, wake in the day to find that it was vanity; but the dreamers of the day are dangerous men, for they may act their dream with open eyes, to make it possible.

-Lawrence of Arabia (Seven Pillars of Wisdom)

AUTHOR'S FOREWORD

JUAN Antonio Samaranch, President of the International Olympic Committee, was in Sydney in 1993 on a mission.

Was Sydney worthy of the 2000 Games?

Brisbane had lost out to Barcelona and Paris for the 1992 Games and Melbourne, with its superior sporting facilities to Sydney, was already beaten for the 1996 Games by Atlanta, Athens and Toronto.

Now Sydney, with only the Darling Harbour complex to prove it could build huge facilities, was bidding for 2000.

Nick Greiner, then NSW Premier, had committed funds to build stadiums for athletics and swimming at Sydney's Homebush Bay area. Some work had begun there, but it was still a wasteland and a dump when Samaranch came to town.

Premier Greiner said he would not have bid for 2000 without Darling Harbour. It was all Sydney had in the ground then to back its claims. Beijing was looking more attractive.

As Samaranch was escorted around Darling Harbour by Rod McGeoch, chief executive of the Sydney Olympic Bid, the President enthused over its colourful world-standard facilities for entertainment, cultural and social activities - important facets for an influx of Games visitors.

Samaranch also noted its vast indoor arenas, knowing that 70 per cent of all Olympic sports would be held indoors.

Finally he turned to Rod McGeoch and said: "I think Darling Harbour is fantastic. I find it much more impressive than Sydney's Olympic plans for Homebush Bay."

In that defining moment, the powerful IOC President decided that Sydney would be the 2000 Olympics front runner. A few months later, he announced the IOC decision: "...and the winner is - *Syd-eney.*"

In the opinion of many insiders who strived to gain the 2000 Games for Australia, including the Minister-in-Charge, Bruce Baird, Sydney would not have won without Darling Harbour.

One man above all others was responsible for creating Darling Harbour - and winning the right for Australians to stage the "best Games ever," as Samaranch triumphantly described them at the closing ceremony.

Tom Hayson was that man, a proud and remarkable Australian.

I hope you enjoy reading his life story (and this first inside account of how Darling Harbour grew out of his imagination and enthusiasm), as much as I enjoyed writing it.

Sydney, July 2001. KEVIN PERKINS

INTRODUCTION

THIS is the human interest story of one man's struggle for acceptance in the land of his birth, and his courage and determination to succeed.

Tom Hayson was born into a desperately poor migrant family in a small bush town as a second generation Australian. He had to battle to overcome adversity.

The story takes us through the three exciting careers he carved out until, by sheer grit, persistence and ability he climbed his personal mountain and reached remarkable heights of achievement.

Hayson earned respect the hard way, just as his family did before him. His forebears, Christian Lebanese, came here as poor immigrants in 1886.

They were among those early Christians who fled Lebanon not only to seek a better way of life but also to escape religious persecution from their then Turkish Muslim occupiers.

This country, with its White Australia policy from around that time, was a very different place then compared with today. The dominant Anglo-Saxon population was generally hostile or indifferent towards the Lebanese, Greeks, Italians, Chinese and the other small numbers of "foreign" migrants. And not for migrants of that period were the wonderfully generous benefits and conditions available to newcomers in the great social experiment taking place today.

Such beneficial conditions were undreamed of then. For all migrants there were no social advantages like those enjoyed by today's ethnic population, no medical benefits, no dole, no support groups, no anti-discrimination laws. It was a case of work or perish.

But the Haysons, or Jacobs as they were known then, made it as good Australians. They did it by assimilating, by going out into the community and mixing with ordinary Australians, by working hard, marrying Australians, integrating into Australian culture and as a result, were accepted and made welcome.

Dare to Dream is not a political book or a history of migration, although it touches on Australia's changing social pattern over the years as Hayson's human story unfolds. But somewhere in the tale there might just be a clue as to why today's Great Experiment is showing cracks and tensions.

All Tom Hayson ever wanted was to be recognised as a good Australian. For his contribution to the land that he loves, many prominent people have already stood up and declared him to be a *great* Australian.

By the way, it wasn't President Kennedy but Lebanon's greatest poet, Kahlil Gibran, who coined the phrase: "Think not what your country can do for you but what you can do for your country." President Kennedy simply pinched the line.

It could well have been written for Tom Hayson.

Sydney, August, 2001. KEVIN PERKINS

TABLE OF CONTENTS

1. The Phoenician Connection 1

2. Lure of the Unknown 7

3. Aliens in a Foreign Land 13

4. The Kindly Nuns of Cowshit Flat 23

5. The "Different" Bush Kid 30

6. A Gentleman of the Fourth Estate 45

7. The World's Most Adventurous Broadcaster 77

8. Foreign Correspondent 96

9. "I am Real Estate" 123

10. Hero Smithy and Hard Lessons 131

11. The Golden Gate 147

12. Boomerang 156

13. Sex Shops and Ladies of the Night 168

14. Doing a Hayson 180

15. Darling Harbour...the drama begins 192

16. James Rouse, Master Planner 207

17. The Girl in the Red Bikini 222

18. Barbarians inside the Gate 229

19. Not so Tender Process 244

20. The Battle of Darling Harbour 254

21. "The Duke" Takes a Bow 284

22. Taking Darling Harbours to the World 299

23. Vision versus Commercialism 307

24. The Resurgence 332

25. Thoughts of a Dinkum Aussie 341

26. Striking Olympic Gold 357

Epilogue 367

1

THE PHOENICIAN CONNECTION

At first glance the tiny village of Aitou high up in the mountains of North Lebanon seemed an unlikely place.

Static and barren, it gave every indication of existing in a time warp where life ground inexorably on and nothing much had changed for centuries.

Life in Aitou was simple, basic and hard. The men were peasants, mostly illiterate, tilling the sparse soil on the rocky hillsides to scratch out a living.

In earlier days here villagers carried soil on their backs from more fertile areas lower down the mountains to create gardens for growing fruit, vegetables and crops.

The people of Aitou had no great ambitions or expectations. Their one overriding desire was to survive.

They had about them an air of resignation, a calm acceptance of fate, a feeling they could not rise above their present oppressed lifestyle - a condition developed and endured over time.

Their country had long been a region of Syria in the Ottoman Empire. Lebanon had been part of Syria throughout its history, except during the Crusades. More recently the Turks had dominated this land for over 300 years, hounding the early Christians who had sought refuge in the wild and inaccessible mountains of North Lebanon rather than abandoning their faith.

The Aitou villagers might have been peasants, downtrodden and trapped by circumstances but most of them had strong character, born of

1

a history written in blood and forged through generations of surviving successive persecutions and sufferings over the centuries.

The village was so languid and unprepossessing it defied anyone imagining a humble man from here might soon begin a journey that would end ultimately in one of his grandsons achieving an international reputation in far-off Australia for astute deal making and visionary entrepreneurship, exciting the admiration of the world.

The sequence of events was destined because two young men here did not fit the prevailing stereotype that accepting oppression was inevitable.

They were looking beyond their narrow existence in this atmosphere of poverty, religious fear and desperation over the future, believing there had to be a better life beyond the mountains and the sea. They yearned for a chance in the New World, in either America or Australia.

A hundred or so villagers from North Lebanon had already fled this poverty and religious intolerance for the bright promise of other continents. The stories of their success had begun trickling back. And the two Aitou men were now contemplating joining the vanguard of this first wave of emigration.

Tannous and his brother Josef felt a quiet pride in their heritage which went back far beyond Christianity, descending them from the once mighty Phoenicians.

They knew from stories handed down through generations that their Phoenician heritage was one of adventure, trail-blazing trade and brisk business enterprise.

As they sat talking one day under clear blue skies on the family's small plot of land in the village, the brothers pondered their uncertain future while recalling the tumultuous past. Tannous and Josef had no doubt about the quality of current village life.

Taxes were still high and controls tight even though with the intervention of the French after a civil war twenty years earlier, the people of North Lebanon had gained a special status for their historic homeland as a province within the Ottoman system.

But it had made little difference to village life. Only religion and the comfort of family unity gave hope and meaning to the people's dreary, monotonous lifestyle. Villagers were still little more than vassals.

The family bonds of Tannous and Josef Elhessen and the other Aitou peasants were emotionally strong, like their attachment to the land and the pull of religion. Family, church and village dominated their existence.

Their loyalties did not go beyond the village. Nor did they feel any sense of national identity. All aspects of their identity such as religion, customs, dress or even the food they produced was local in character, not national.

Political awareness was unheard of and still a long way off.

Like the rest of the village, the brothers followed the Maronite Catholic faith established by the ascetic Syrian monk St John Maroun who had preached in the Syrian desert and died there in the year 410. The ordinary people and hierarchy of the Maronite church later fled the rich plains of Syria after it converted to Islam and settled in the rugged mountains of North Lebanon with other Christian sects to escape further persecution.

Religion was a powerful force in the rest of Lebanon too, just as it was generally in the Middle East, where not only Christianity but also Islam and Judaism were born.

Tannous and Josef knew Christianity had been alive and well along the Lebanese coastline from the very first century. Like other Aitou villagers they were steeped in the history of Lebanon's religious past, their forefathers passing down tales of the early Lebanese as the first in the world after the people of Israel to receive the word of Jesus.

Disciples of Jesus travelled from Israel to adjacent Lebanon to spread the word and early adherents of the new religion made their way to Lebanon after being scattered in Palestine. Adopted there after its birth in Palestine, Christianity then spread to Rome and beyond.

Jesus himself travelled through south Lebanon, as described in one of 70 Bible references to this ancient land. Saint Paul converted many pagans in the old Lebanese seaside towns of Tyr, Sidon, Byblos, Tripoli and Beirut. Saint Peter visited Lebanon on his way to Rome, naming one of his disciples, Saint John Mark from Jerusalem, while in Byblos.

But the brothers knew that just as religion had given Lebanon its special character, it also brought division. They worried over these tensions, never knowing when some religious dispute might flare or a Turk might force them out of his way or abduct a pretty Lebanese village girl.

Their fears were real. Although Aitou was solidly Maronite Catholic, the Lebanese Christians elsewhere in the country were divided into 15 other different Christian faiths, among them the Melkites or Greek

Catholics, Greek Orthodox, Armenian Orthodox, Armenian Catholics, Syrian Catholics, Protestants, Syrian Orthodox and Chaldeans.

Lebanon was a Christian island in a vast Muslim sea, the only Christian country in the Arab world. The brothers knew enough to realise this was the real problem and the cause of festering trouble.

Even the Lebanese Muslims were split, into Sunnis and Shiites, following a dispute in the seventh century over who should become their caliph after the death of the prophet Muhammad. The Druze, a fiercely independent group, then broke away as an offshoot of the Shiites, and there were also smaller factions.

The Turks had sparked tension and strife between the Christians and Muslims in Lebanon after invading the Arab world and adding Syria to their Ottoman Empire in 1517. They ruled the conquered people according to their religions, not by local laws where they lived in the Empire.

Tannous and Josef had learned from their parents how these tensions had simmered. To reduce crowding in their villages, many Maronite Christians moved from their mountain strongholds to coastal plains in the south, where Druze feudal lords traditionally lived. At the same time large numbers of Druze moved to mountain areas.

As the Maronites tried to break the grip of Druze landholders, civil war erupted in 1858, ending two years later with the Druze massacring 12,000 Maronites and destroying at least 60 villages. Turkish soldiers stood idly by while Christians were slaughtered.

It was at this point that France had intervened to keep the peace, obtaining for Lebanon a limited form of independence from the Turks.

The feud caused enormous damage to village economies. Silk crops were destroyed and many villagers had little in the way of goods to barter for food. Crippling diseases like typhus and typhoid spread rapidly.

But in the wake of international attention over the Druze atrocities, a great social and cultural change took place in Lebanon as the influence of Western nations was felt for the first time.

A period of prosperity followed. The United States, France and other European nations established numerous schools and church missions in Lebanon, enabling students to study the values and customs of the West.

The fine American and Jesuit Universities of Beirut grew out of this trend. Foreign languages were taught in the mission schools and the Lebanese education system took on many aspects of the West. This benefited the cities and big towns, but villages like Aitou mostly remained uneducated.

Western culture also permeated the rigid Lebanese way of life in other ways. Beirut and Tripoli soon became world famous for their French-oriented nightclubs and casinos where patrons raged all night. Sex, booze and voluptuous belly dancers were par for the course in this new freewheeling atmosphere.

Suddenly Lebanon emerged as the modern cultural melting pot mingling East with West, and as the Arab world's window to the West, posing questions of national identity that would go unresolved.

Lebanon had always geographically been at the crossroads of East and West. A small country on the eastern shore of the Mediterranean bounded by Syria and Israel, it measured only 200 km long and 100 km across at its widest point.

It had absorbed a long succession of Mediterranean cultures, the Phoenicians toppling earlier peoples and ruling from about 1200 years before Christ, establishing dominant trading and cultural centres in the Lebanese ports of Tyre, Sidon and Byblos.

After the Phoenicians faded away a wave of invasions came from the Sumerians, Babylonians, Egyptians, Assyrians, Persians, Greeks, Romans, Arabs, Crusaders, Mamluks and the Ottomans.   Later came the French.

The white Caucasian element remained strong in this incredible ethnic and cultural mix, especially in the coastal towns.

Ironically, it was the result of the "modern" Western influences which now so concerned the two brothers from Aitou.

The winds of industrial change which had blown into Lebanon from other parts of the world had altered the traditional economic and social pattern of this ancient land and its people forever.

Owing to the leap forward in land and sea transport, particularly through the Suez Canal opening in 1869, European goods appeared in Lebanese bazaars.

The trickle became a flood as manufactured goods from England and France and other parts of Europe saturated Lebanese markets.

Once more the effect on village economies was disastrous. Handicrafts such as silk making and dyeing could no longer compete with the manufactured imports and many people could not subsist using the only skills they knew.

Handlooms stopped weaving cloth and bartering, the main means of business transaction, began to crumble. Unprepared, without resources, villagers flocked to the cities searching for work. Families, the backbone of Lebanese society which had held fast for centuries, began to break up, eroding traditional values and challenging old conservative ideas.

Many lowly village workers found themselves exploited in the cities and pushed to the bottom of the economic barrel as a new type of businessman and professional person developed among the recently educated classes.

Tannous and Josef Elhessen and their family were among those seriously affected by this economic revolution, which also disrupted village networking.

On the day they sat under the clear blue skies talking for hours about their future, they looked down to the Mediterranean far below and nodded in agreement.

The only good thing about Aitou now seemed to be the road leading out of it.

2

LURE OF THE UNKNOWN

THE Elhessens were an old family who went back as far as anyone could remember and beyond. No records were kept but folklore passed down from ancestors said they were much older than the village itself.

The family farmed several acres in a basically rocky area where they lived in a stone house hewn from local material. Their forebears had chipped away at the rocks to make flat areas for gardens.

They kept a few goats for milk and cheese, grew grapes from which they made their own alcoholic arrack and a little red wine, planted enough vegetables for their own use and also tended olive and apricot trees.

Their main income had derived from silk made from their own silk worms. This had been bought in the village by merchants' agents for sale to Lebanese in the cities or exported from Beirut. But imported cloth had killed off the market.

Even seasonal work harvesting local corn and wheat crops was now hard to find in more fertile areas just below the village. The family had relied on this work to pay their debts. They bought their provisions on trust from the stores and when the farmers sold their crops and paid the harvesters, they paid the storekeepers.

The Elhessen family supplemented their meagre income by producing charcoal, a popular form of heating for warmth and cooking.

To do so, Tannous and Josef Elhessen went out into the bush and cut green oak sticks which they piled high to a point at the top. Then, covering the pile with soil, they burned the sticks slowly from the base for up to a month.

It was hard, patient work, especially in winter when the village was mostly under snow from January until March and sometimes April.

The Elhessen brothers loved the dry climate with its four distinct seasons. In summer the sky was the brightest blue with no unseasonable rain.

Aitou clung to a sloping ridge of the Makmel Mountains in the main Lebanon Mountain chain, about 90 kilometres north of Beirut and 1500 metres above the Mediterranean. The Makmels rose to the highest point in the Middle east, more than 3000 metres.

The country took its name from these mountains, the old Aramaic word *laban* meaning white. Originally they were called the White Mountains because the peaks were capped with snow almost all year.

They were also known as the Phoenician Mountains, for this was where the Phoenicians lived and cut the famous cedars for trading and building the ships in which they ventured beyond the known world.

King David once used this renowned cedar to build his Temple of Solomon in Jerusalem, and the Egyptians made their ships from this most famous tree in the world.

Cedars still stood a little higher up the mountains, nestling darkly under the peaks, some of them thousands of years old. Aitou lay on one of the old mountain routes to the cedars.

Nobody was prouder of their Phoenician ancestry than the brothers.

Some of the older village men still wore the baggy flowing garments said to have been favoured by the Phoenicians. These amazing seafarers were known to have contributed so much to civilisation - even the alphabet by which the world learned to read and write.

The brothers were sad at the prospect of leaving their mountain retreat which they regarded as beautiful. Rocky it may have been but the landscape generally was green, with many deep gorges, valleys, waterfalls and springs. The porous limestone of the mountains, although providing thin soil, created many underground springs, allowing irrigation in the slopes below Aitou where the terraced hills stood out as a scenic monument to the ingenious tillers of the past.

The great cedar forests of earlier days had been almost entirely wiped out for lumber, but other trees were still plentiful - oaks, pines, firs, cypresses and junipers. And in the rainy season the hills were ablaze with brilliant wild flowers - scarlet anemones, hollyhocks, poppies, iris and cyclamen.

The beauty the brothers saw in North Lebanon was due to its naturalness, not something shaped by human hand. Their mountains were wild and unspoiled. While walking in the hills they found grass, trees, shrubs and other natural vegetation in abundance.

The water in streams and springs was pure. They loved the gentle gurgle of running water, the timeless essence of the place.

They knew their surroundings intimately, including where the early Christians had hidden to escape the Muslim conquerors and where the Maronites dug in with the Crusaders, confronting and defeating the Turks.

They had several times visited one favourite hiding place just below Aitou, the Valley of the Saints, where Christians had hidden in inaccessible caves on sheer cliff sides reached only by ladders.

Tannous and Josef finally decided.

They would leave Aitou at once. To stay was to wait for some kind of tragedy to take place.

The year was 1886. Tannous Yacob Elhessen was 22, Josef 20. Only Josef was married, to a girl named Rachel from the Maronite village of Kfarsghab. Rachel had given birth to a son named Diab. It was agreed that Rachel and her son would accompany them to the new land.

The brothers had a sister, Sarah, and a younger brother called Bechara the Dumb, a mute by birth although physically sound. Sarah, Bechara and their parents would stay behind in Aitou.

They had agonised over whether to go to America because they knew of several men from other villages who had already shown the way by travelling there. But others from neighbouring villages had gone to Australia in the first exodus from Lebanon that began in the 1860s after the Druze massacre, and had written home. Australia seemed a good place.

Tannous and Josef had heard of Australia as youths, following the gold rush fever of the 1850s. They no longer thought the streets were paved with gold. But they were excited by the tales drifting back of fortunes made at the diggings as the cry of "rush-ho" went up, attracting thousands of foreigners to the new Eldorado.

They knew they would not be stubbing their toes on gold nuggets glistening in the dust but understood on the grapevine that there was money to be made in Australia for those prepared to work. Gold was also

9

the reason California had beckoned but somehow they felt less apprehensive about Australia.

Tannous, on hearing that Australia was hot and dry, told Josef they might never see anything like their colour-splashed homeland again.

They told everybody they would miss the comforting simplicity and intimacy of village life.

In the environment they knew so well the whole village regarded itself as one family, everyone feeling love for one another. If someone fell seriously ill, most of the village visited. And if a villager died, every man went unshaven for 40 days as a mark of respect and the women wore black for that period.

This characteristic caring for others in times of death, sickness or hardship even extended to the borrowing of money. Documents were never exchanged. To avoid embarrassing the borrower, a person lending money never did it publicly. He went to one side so nobody noticed.

To demonstrate the trust involved, an Aitou man wanting to borrow money once could not give or suggest any security. He had never borrowed before. So he plucked a hair from his moustache. "Here," he told the lender, "take this as a deposit. When I return the money you can give me back my hair."

The Lebanese family unit, now under threat, had formed its characteristic strength in earlier days when the people needed to protect themselves against persecuting invaders. The friendliness and hospitality for which the Lebanese people were already known, originated in this time of early hardship. The oppressed and forlorn could always find succour here.

The Elhessen brothers had learned from their parents the virtue of patience. Handed down from earlier generations, this quality came from the endurance of having to live for so long under an invader's heel.

Everyone in Aitou went to church. Anyone who said he or she did not believe in Jesus was the odd one out. Folklore in the village claimed that religion had not mattered until the Turks divided the people of Lebanon through their religion, taking sides and pitting one faith against another.

The Aitou church where the brothers worshipped had a notice board for village announcements. If someone died or a former villager returned, the priest posted a notice and rang the church bell.

Hell, something had happened! People tumbled out into the dusty streets to see what was going on.

For weddings, the whole village turned out because it was said there was a bride in every house. Festivities centring on the house of the bride lasted four nights, with lots of music and dancing. Marriages were arranged but if a boy and girl did not like each other, parents would not force the ceremony.

Religious festivals such as Assumption Day and The Way of the Cross were conscientiously observed. The priests occupied a strong position in the social and justice side of village life too, sometimes taking part in disputes. But first the village head, appointed by the Turkish Government, dealt with complications.

The church was a centre of fun as well as devotion. On the Sunday before Lent the villagers gathered near the church and made whoopee.

Aitou was noted for its sweet red wine. The roisterers would roll a huge container into place, everyone emptied a jar of wine into it and someone beat a big drum while the crowd danced and caroused. A favourite dance was the *dabkah*.

Life in the village would have remained tolerable except for the poverty which now reached a new low phase.

Most people were kept poor through paying taxes, a system strictly enforced by the Turks or their administrators. First the collectors asked for Turkish money. If that could not be produced, they asked for food such as grain.

But living standards varied. One family became wealthy by capitalising on the system. Appointed from outside Lebanon as mediators in Aitou between the Turkish Government and the poor and uneducated villagers, they helped with paperwork such as reading and answering letters. At the business end they asked the village how much they owed the government, then paid the taxes and later collected it from the people, charging interest.

Tannous and Josef would never have decided to leave unless overtaken by grinding poverty.

To earn the money to pay for their journey they had to strike a canny deal.

They borrowed money from a villager in return for allowing him to work the family's four or five acre farm for 30 years, negotiating for their parents and Bechara the Dumb to live there still and use some of the land.

When the time to depart arrived, the brothers and Josef's wife Rachel said goodbye to numerous villagers before making their tearful farewells with the family. Their mother, sensing she was seeing her loving sons for the last time, insisted on going with them as far as Tripoli where they hoped to get aboard a vessel. It was closer than Beirut.

To own a donkey in Aitou then was akin to anyone in the world today sporting a Rolls but they managed to borrow one for Mrs Elhessen to ride to Tripoli and back. When she set off on the donkey she had Rachel's little son Diab seated in front. The others walked.

Old man Elhessen and Bechara stood and watched them go out of sight down the hill to the north towards the Mediterranean, waving slowly to the last.

For a day they walked down the mountains through rough passes and rocky tracks until they reached the coastal plain and Tripoli. Here next morning Tannous and Josef said their last emotional goodbyes to their mother as they found their way on to a tramp steamer to Port Said in Egypt.

With little more than the clothes they stood up in, they embarked there on the French steamer *Australian* bound for Sydney, wretchedly poor migrants leaving behind a rich ethnic history and carrying only hope and memories of their family and homeland, not knowing where their journey might lead them.

3

ALIENS IN A FOREIGN LAND

"YOUR name. Name? What's your name?"

The immigration official on the wharf at Sydney Cove had difficulty being understood when the Elhessen brothers, one with wife and child, disembarked from the *Australian* after a hot, meandering five-week journey from Port Said.

He was Anglo-Saxon and couldn't speak Arabic. They couldn't speak English. But they'd practised for this moment with a passenger on board who knew some English.

"Youssef Yacob," said the younger brother, following the Lebanese custom of leaving out his surname and using his second Christian name taken from the Bible.

"Joseph Jacob? All right," said the official. "You're Joe Jacob."

Tannous answered similarly: "Tannous Yacob."

"Tom or Tony?" asked the official, wanting none of this Arab stuff. "Tom? Right. You're Tom Jacob."

That's how the Elhessen boys were officially inducted into their new land, as aliens from Syria which still refused to recognise Lebanon's separate identity, claiming it was part of Greater Syria. It would be more than 30 years before North Lebanon was joined with the rest of Lebanon including the coastal towns of Beirut and Tripoli and the Bekaa Valley to become the State of Greater Lebanon, and not until independence from France in World War 11 that "Lebanese" would finally replace "Syrian."

At the time, federation of the separate Australian colonies was still a few years off and customs and immigration functions were something of a

13

hit or miss affair compared to the more formal arrangements later under the new Commonwealth.

The "Jacob" brothers were confused and bewildered by their introduction to a way of life that was totally foreign. And the situation would not change quickly for them or the friends they had made on the trip out from the old country.

In Port Said they had found several other Lebanese bound for Sydney and joined them on the steamer. They included four sisters, the Hashems, from a Christian enclave near Beirut, due to link up with Lebanese friends who had already emigrated to Sydney.

As the vessel chugged its way over the equator to Sydney by way of Bombay, Canton, Hong Kong, Singapore and Darwin, the unattached Tannous had plenty of time to break the ice with the Hashem girls. He became infatuated with one, Philomena, and at journey's end he pledged to see her again, no matter what.

He and Joseph, although they paid for their passage and travelled steerage - because there was no cheaper class - also did menial jobs on board to help pay their way.

The group was lucky to make it to Australia without incident.

Some Lebanese emigrants of the period were victims of unscrupulous middle men or shipping agents who extracted the most money they could for the longest trip, then sent them off to wherever the first steamer took them. Some hopefuls, thinking they were bound for America, ended up in Australia, and vice versa.

In Sydney, the Jacob boys found their way to the inner working class suburb of Redfern, fast becoming a haven for Lebanese arrivals as Carlton was in Melbourne. They knew they would find help here from countrymen already settled in.

Several Lebanese, or Syrians as they were called, had already set themselves up in business in Redfern and, like the Greeks and Italians before them, were willing to help their own kind.

Tannous and Josef's immediate need was to find work. That was potentially difficult as they had no skill apart from farming a small holding of family land. Physically they looked different which for a start tended to make them unwelcome. They could not speak the language, were strangers viewed with suspicion and distrust and were shunned by the general community because it was felt they would take the jobs of Australians.

Social service benefits or any form of government handout did not exist. The stark reality was that if they didn't earn by the sweat of their brow or by some business activity, they would starve.

As a first line of inquiry, they sought guidance from the local Catholic priest at Redfern.

Without hesitation they turned to hawking, the self-employed enterprise for which the first wave of Lebanese immigrants to Australia would become universally known. In this period the majority of the first generation of Lebanese immigrants to the United States, South America and Africa also set out as hawkers, best described as the earliest form of door-to-door travelling salesmen.

Hawking was a simple and uncomplicated occupation, requiring little capital, no special skill in English except a few basic phrases, turnover could be quick for those prepared to work hard, enabling the ambitious and energetic among them who dreamed of owning their own small businesses to save enough money to succeed eventually. In a philosophical way it also appealed to their Phoenician heritage to be independent and involved in trade.

But more importantly, Australians looked on hawking as being a lowly means of livelihood beneath their dignity. Luckily this attitude generated less hostility towards the newcomers because it was felt they would not take Australian jobs.

In addition, the Lebanese gained more acceptance from Australians than most other ethnic groups because it soon became apparent they were far less likely to "steal" local white women and interbreed with them. In short, the first Lebanese intake was seen as not so inclined to water down the white European race.

More than any other group they tended to wait until they could afford to bring out wives or sweethearts from their homeland.

This belief would hold the line against criticism for a while, at least until the numbers of hawkers increased.

Other ethnic migrants had already introduced hawking to Australia, in particular Chinese, Indian, Jewish and Afghan traders. But it was the Lebanese who would make an industry of it.

None was poorer than the ordinary Lebanese migrant, nor more willing to work laboriously at the task.

When "Tom" and "Joe" began hawking towards the end of 1886, they obtained their merchandise from small Lebanese traders who had just started in business. With little money the brothers had to think and act on a small scale, carrying a limited range of merchandise in a swag over their backs on a short stick as they went from door to door around the suburbs of Sydney.

Hawking, the "service industry" run by itinerants and centred on Redfern, was still in its infancy. But, in the space of about two years, this poor man's form of commerce suddenly mushroomed as upper class Lebanese businessmen like J.G. Malouf, Stanton and Aziz Melick, Naser Abdullah, George Dan and the Coorey Brothers established warehouses and factories in Redfern, some opening branch outlets in other parts of Australia.

Mr Malouf, educated at the American University in Beirut, arrived in Sydney in 1888 and set up right away as a draper and merchant in Elizabeth Street, Redfern.

Stanton Melick, another well-to-do Lebanese businessman to arrive in 1888, immediately became a leading Redfern warehouseman and manufacturer. So did Mr Dan, in 1890, employing 100 Australians in his factory and carving a reputation for generosity to the poor and needy of the area.

The Jacob brothers barely made a living at first, although toiling for long hours. Unable to speak English or read signs, they walked everywhere, finding their way by following the train line to various suburbs.

Fortunately, while still struggling to survive, they were befriended by Stanton Melick who had the Christian faith in common with them, although he was Greek Orthodox. Their friendship followed a pattern in which village or religious relationships from the old country often determined where the hawkers obtained supplies.

Melick gave Tannous and Josef (only the Australians called them Tom and Joe), goods on consignment, allowing credit until they could afford to repay him. In this way they broke through the poverty barrier, each graduating to pushing a handcart from door to door. Mellick did the same for scores of others.

New arrivals were thus given a start by established businessmen, instructed for a day or two on how to set prices and what basic phrases to use, handed the merchandise and sent on their way.

It soon became obvious as hawking numbers increased that Sydneysiders, and Melburnians too, could buy their needs in the existing city retail shops. That meant hawkers had to move to country areas. The Jacob boys slowly hawked their way up to northern and north-western NSW towns.

Their lives were lonely and primitive. Like other hawkers, they were separated from their friends, church and family for months at a time. Often they did not see another Syrian hawker for months while on the road, a factor in their becoming "Australianised" more readily than if they had mixed only with their own countrymen.

Tannous, who had fallen in love with Philomena Hashem, did not see her for months on end when he went bush, but she promised to wait for him. Josef, too, was separated from Rachel and their son Diab for long periods.

They became welcome visitors to outlying sheep and cattle stations, exchanging news and gossip.

Their idealistic goal was the same as with most other hawkers - to buy a small business or start a shop in some country town where they would not be competing with a fellow countryman.

Advancing from humble foot slogging salesman to owner of a drapery or clothing store was important to these pioneer settlers of the bush because it meant they had put their roots down and could truly call Australia home. In specially fitted-out horse drawn carts and later in old broken-down trucks, hawkers visited desolate farms and communities in NSW, Victoria, South Australia and Queensland selling a wide range of goods including haberdashery, clothes and boots.

By World War 1 the Lebanese hawker would be a common sight on the vast country landscape, with Lebanese drapery or clothing stores sprinkled throughout towns in the eastern states and South Australia.

Some fell by the wayside, unable to endure the physical and psychological rigours of such an isolated, demanding life. Others, in a tribute to determination and hard work, saved up and brought their wives and families out from Lebanon often after waiting patiently for several years.

Many sagas of the hardship and handicaps overcome by these enterprising individuals were documented in historical archives.

Stories of hawkers walking for months to find a suitable town to trade in were commonplace. The Nader family who emigrated in 1895 walked from Sydney to Cootamundra, starting a migration of Lebanese to the area. Another family took six months to walk to Toowoomba, selling along the way.

The Jacob brothers and other early Lebanese businessmen in Australia gave meaning to the Arab proverb: "trade will lead a man far."

But along the way they had to endure many personal and emotional hardships because of their ethnic differences.

When Redfern was dubbed Little Syria due to the large number of Lebanese businessmen and residents there, it was more than a colourful description. The name had racist connotations.

Feelings among the overwhelming white Anglo-Saxon population were generally against the immigrants, either through fear of losing jobs or because of plain xenophobia. Their slightly swarthy complexions and distinctive features such as hooked noses set them apart at once.

Race was not an issue earlier in colonial Australia when the Anglo-Saxons and Celts formed the status quo. But the gold rush immigration of the 1850s had brought a dramatic change in attitudes.

At first the flood of immigrants from various countries was generally welcomed by the isolated colonials- even with this influx, 92.5 per cent of the non-indigenous population in 1862 was either born in the British Isles or the Australian colonies.

But the Chinese working the gold fields had aroused resentment.

A national racist policy had its origin in this period when white miners clashed violently with Chinese diggers on the Buckland River and at Bendigo in Victoria in the late 1850s, at Lambing Flat in NSW in 1861 and at Clunes in Victoria in 1873, where five coach loads of Chinese brought in as strike breakers over a wages issue were set upon and stoned, even by white women.

That resulted in a rash of colonial legislation to restrict Chinese immigration. Race would be enmeshed with politics from this time, co-inciding with a burst of Australian nationalism and the move to nationhood.

In 1888 the Inter-Colonial Council Conference decided to restrict entry of all Chinese to Australia except in a few categories such as merchants and tourists. *White Australia* was on its way with the first debate on Asians, to be revisited a century later following comments by a flame-haired Queensland politician, Pauline Hanson.

Australia was not alone then among immigrant states in adopting a racist policy. The United States and Canada did the same.

A *Melbourne Punch* publication in 1888 under the heading of "The Yellow Gulf Stream," showed Uncle Sam off-loading an evil looking stream of Chinese from the United States to a sinking Australia. For many years *The Bulletin's* original masthead carried the words "Australia for the White Man and China for the Chows," later changing to "Australia for the White Man."

Leading NSW and Victorian politicians of the time declared there was no place for "Asiatics or coloureds" in the future Australia.

The early Lebanese who emigrated to Australia around the time of the Jacob brothers, although generally referred to as Syrians, were officially categorised as coming from Turkey "or other countries in Asia."

Politicians in the NSW Parliament grouped them as "aliens" or "coloured hawkers" but in particular and erroneously as "Turks," "Arabs," "Afghans," "Hindus," "Assyrians" or "Asiatics."

They first appeared as Syrians in NSW census records in 1891 but as representing "the Syrian and Indian hawker nuisance."

Tannous, his brother and other Syrians who regarded themselves as Lebanese, were unhappy over being categorised in this way and especially as Asiatics, maintaining that as Lebanese from the Mediterranean area they were Caucasians, whites or Europeans.

But public opinion was hardening against them. In 1893 the NSW Premier Mr Dibbs circularised other colonial Premiers asking them to take action against "the influx of coloured races, Syrians, Afghans, Hindus and others."

Other politicians called for legislation to stop these "inferior races" whose liberty to gain employment was "unjust to Australian citizens and demoralising to society."

Warming to the issue in the NSW Legislative Assembly, the member for West Macquarie in 1895 drew attention to a matter of "urgent public importance" - the spineless attitude of the government in opposing legislation to exclude aliens from the colony. He then proposed a bill to bar all Syrians, Japanese, Javanese and Kanakas, all of whom were "lower than the lowest of Chinese" and who "could not be assimilated to the conditions of the working population of the colony."

The situation in Redfern in 1895 was highlighted in the excellent book, *Phoenician Farewell - Three Generations of Lebanese Christians in Australia,* in which author Dr Jim McKay quoted the MLA for Redfern as complaining:

"...we see all around us an insidious invasion of people that are gradually creeping up on us, sapping away the character of the British race from which we are descended. ...Now in the Redfern electorate we have a Syrian town where not only Syrian but Hindus are gradually forcing the white population out...In my district it is practically impossible for white people to live anywhere near the people to whom I refer....white people do not care to reside anywhere close to them. Some couple of hundred of them are now settled in my electorate, and they are forcing away from two streets all the white population who reside there."

Politicians continued to call for the hawking licences of "inferior Syrians" to be cancelled and their immigration stopped.

Intriguingly, a major complaint against them was that they "terrorised helpless women in isolated areas and forced them to buy their goods."

It was not generally until 1901 in Australia that in immigration terms they were separately categorised as Syrians - and more than 50 years later before they would be officially recognised as Lebanese.

That was the difficult environment in which Tannous and Joseph Jacob plied their trade and tried to settle into their new land.

Small wonder they and other Lebanese hawkers kept mostly to themselves and worked tirelessly to establish a future. But it had the effect of making many feel inferior.

Apart from congregating around Redfern in Sydney and Carlton in Melbourne, those pioneer immigrants did not form ghettoes with Arabic environments, mainly because the itinerant nature of their employment took most of them to country areas where they mixed with Australians rather than with their own race.

Most of them took on Australian cultural ways instead of sticking to their old habits and customs, although family groups banded together for birthdays, weddings and other special occasions and assisted one another in looking after children. They also met at church and for picnics.

After three years of hawking up and down inland NSW, returning to Sydney only to stock up on supplies or to celebrate festive occasions like Christmas, Tannous had saved enough money to marry Philomena. They wed according to Latin rites in St Vincent's Catholic Church in Redfern -

at that stage the Eastern rite Maronites had not yet built their St Maroun church there.

The newlyweds rented a house in Redfern from where they would raise a large family of five boys and two girls. The eldest boy was named Frederick Thomas Jacob. He would play a role in the destiny that was preordained in Aitou.

Tannous continued hawking to support his family, not seeing them for long intervals as he worked the country areas, saving small amounts of money as he waited to buy his own business.

Two years after his marriage, showing his love for and commitment to his new homeland, Tannous became a naturalised citizen on May 9, 1892 in the 39th year of the reign of Queen Victoria, giving him all the rights of a natural born British citizen.

To further show the mysteries of record keeping in those days, his name was recorded as Tannous Sacomb Elhessen.

Meanwhile, the pressure to curb Syrians and other so-called "Asiatics" continued unabated.

After Federation and the first Federal election in 1901, the Labor Party sought immediate legislation for a "white Australia."

Conservative Prime Minister Edmund Barton readily agreed, calling for the prevention of "an influx of that class and race of persons who ought to be kept without the limits of a white Australia or a civilised Commonwealth."

The Labor Party's view was clearly put in Parliament by its leader, John Watson, who said: "The objection I have to the mixing of the coloured people with the white people of Australia...lies in the main in the possibility and probability of racial contamination."

Senator George Pearce, a senior Labor figure, said in that Parliamentary debate that the supply of low cost immigrant labour was only "a minor objection." The chief objection, he said, was "entirely racial." Others too spoke in favour of the need for a "unity of race."

Apart from the Chinese, who worked zealously and sent their money home, the hard-working Kanakas from the cane fields of Queensland were singled out for special attention.

White workers passionately opposed all forms of immigration which they feared would threaten their jobs, especially from non-whites whom they thought would work for lower wages and accept poorer living standards.

The upshot was the new Federal Government's Immigration Restriction Act of 1901, aimed at placing "certain restrictions" on immigration and to provide "the removal from the Commonwealth of prohibited immigrants." It restricted prostitutes, criminals and most people contracted to do manual labour, ending the employment of Pacific Islanders.

The outright exclusion of anyone who was non-white was averted only by pressure from the British Government, concerned that its strategic interests in the Far East would be affected, especially in relations with Japan.

A compromise was found in the use of a written dictation test by Australian immigration officials in a language unknown to an undesirable immigrant applicant, enabling them to bar him or her on the ground of illiteracy. The Act required the migrant to "write out a dictation test and sign in the presence of an officer a passage of 50 words in length in an European language directed by the officer."

Most sections of the Australian community welcomed the White Australia policy. Prime Minister Billy Hughes would describe it some years later as "the greatest thing we have achieved."

In this inhospitable atmosphere Tannous and Philomena knew that if their first born, Frederick, and his Lebanese bride of the future and their other children wished to succeed and be happy, they would have to forget the old ways of their ancestors and fully embrace the Australian way of life.

4

THE KINDLY NUNS OF COWSHIT FLAT

ABOUT the time Tannous Jacob married Philomena Hashem in Sydney, two Christian families were on board a steamer out of Beirut, travelling fourth class and bound for Melbourne.

Fate decreed that the Beirut families and the Jacob family formerly of Aitou, would be united.

Oddly the Beirut group consisted of two brothers who had married two sisters. Kanin Joseph Nader was married to Amelia Saleeba, sometimes known as Jamelia, and John Nader was the husband of Sarah Saleeba, sometimes called Janita. All were Maronites.

The eldest brother, Kanin Nader, had three daughters, Etena, Annisy and Mary, born in Beirut between 1879 and 1888. John Nader did not have any children.

They decided to travel to Australia for the same reason as most other Lebanese immigrants - they were wretchedly poor, there seemed no chance of improving their lot by staying and they hoped to establish a better future for their families. A desire to escape from Turkish oppression was also a factor.

They were met in Port Melbourne in late 1890 by some earlier Lebanese settlers who had established themselves there in the clothing business. Their inability to speak English created an immediate barrier, but they weathered the difficult initial adjustment period by speaking to Lebanese contacts in their native Arabic.

The Naders quickly learned it was not a good time to have come to Melbourne, then in depression. At the time the city had a population of about half a million, even after thousands had left for country areas trying to find work.

The brothers, both of small stature, began at once as foot hawkers in order to live. But they could see it was too tough in the city, no matter how many hours they put in. John Nader left his wife in Melbourne for sporadic periods while he walked to Victorian towns, looking like the typical Australian "swaggie" with his worldly goods over his shoulder on a stick.

Kanin, dealing with the established Lebanese warehousing firm of Latoof and Callil - the Melbourne counterpart of Sydney's Stanton Melick - managed to arrange financial backing and emerged as a small shopkeeper selling fancy goods in Little Lonsdale Street in the heart of the city.

Another daughter was born to Kanin and Amelia in 1895. They named the baby Mary Lavina, often called Mulveena. Two years later their fifth daughter, Ada, was born. In that same year, 1897, John and Sarah Nader had their first child, Catherine, nicknamed Tepti.

Kanin ceased trading in fancy goods in 1896, finding it too hard to stay afloat while paying back borrowings. But in 1897 his wife, despite having five young daughters to care for and helping in the family business as well as taking it upon herself to communicate with other Lebanese families, turned up in Little Lonsdale Street as a grocer. She kept the shop open for two years.

As in Sydney the Melbourne suppliers staked many hawkers to a wagon, horse and stock. They were sent out into the Victorian countryside hawking from farm to farm, displaying their wares from special drop-down sides of the wagon. But in this period those venturing out from Melbourne were hit by severe droughts and their horses died from dehydration.

As a result they became aware that the Murray River bordering NSW was a splendid permanent source of water. Albury and its surrounds emerged as an attractive base. John Nader through his travels was one of those to quickly realise it.

Rather than continue the unequal struggle in Melbourne, Kanin decided that Albury offered a better prospect and just before the turn of the century he and John moved their families there.

Other Lebanese families had already settled in, beginning in the 1880s. Before the Naders, earlier arrivals were a Mr Sarroff, B. Abicare, S.M.

Abikhair, followed by the Elias family, A.M. Abikhair, the Salamy family, Mary Haddad, and Messrs Galleti and David. In time these and later Lebanese arrivals would contribute substantially to the commercial and civic life of the district.

But of all the ethnic groups who came to Australia just before and after the turn of the century, the Lebanese were the poorest. Those who came to Albury were no exception. Hawking was their salvation and for some, after a period of hard work and perseverance as they gradually built up a bank, they later followed the traditional path into shopkeeping and wholesale supplying.

Albury developed because of the mighty Murray.

A settler built a hut and store on a bank of the river in 1836, and the town grew from that. A few buildings sprang up on the river site and as more settlers moved into that area, later to be known as Wodonga Place, the commercial centre moved to higher ground to Townsend Street, gradually encroaching north until Dean Street became the main street.

The area down by the river flats where the town began was generally called South Albury. When the Naders came to Albury, this part of the town had market gardens down near the river, a tannery which had been built in 1867, brick kilns, flour mills, a soap factory and a joss house where the local Chinese met and worshipped. Several dairies existed on the rich river flats and cows roamed freely.

Many people simply called it The Flat, but it was also known as Irishtown because of the number of Irish Catholics living there.

This was the desperately poor end of town. Locals, including those who lived there, colloquially called it Cowshit Flat due to the numerous cow pats and the depressing quality of life there.

Other residents looked down on those living there, regarding it as the lower end of the social and residential spectrum.

The poor lived here in tents, in dwellings that were little better than humpies or other poor quality houses.

When the Naders arrived they were directed to this part of the town, as were other hapless Lebanese before them. One of those was Mrs Rose Elias who came to Albury in 1894 with her two young children and a new baby after the untimely death of her husband, Joseph. She had waited patiently in Beirut with her two baby sons for eight years after Joseph emigrated to Australia, until he had saved enough money to send for her. The reunion was happy but short, with a third son, Joe, being only six months old when the family breadwinner died at Nambucca Heads in NSW.

Rose, showing the enterprise for which the Lebanese were noted, wasted no time on bemoaning the absence of organised social services. She leaped right in and started a drapery business - not in the main business precinct but by pushing a pram laden with shoe laces, pins, camphor, stockings, socks, needles, cottons, buttons and other goods.

Mrs Elias wheeled the pram around the Albury area for more than 10 years until her health failed. Later, two of her sons, Joe and Alf, started an ice works, bringing summer relief with frozen water to a town that had not yet even heard of refrigerators.

On his 95th birthday, Joe would tell how, when delivering blocks of ice which customers placed in kerosene tins and covered with sacks, he didn't have the heart to charge some people because they were so poor.

The Nader families lived for some time in Cowshit Flat, also more politely known to some as Poverty Row.

Nuns associated with the new St Patrick's Church in Albury used to visit Cowshit Flat every Saturday, providing manna from heaven in the form of soup and other food for the destitute families who had no alternative to living there in tents and rough abodes.

The nuns came to the area in 1868 and the church was built four years later. Some of those who lived down on the Flat helped make the bricks for the church.

Around the time the Naders arrived, Albury and the surrounding area was suffering from extremes of weather. A mice plague hit the district, then a plague of grasshoppers caused widespread loss to crops. People were kept away from the Albury Show because the Murray flooded to more than 16 feet above its summer level, then came a drought.

Sir Henry Parkes visited the town and addressed a large audience on Federation. The Glee Club was advertising for "good fresh voices," the Dramatic Club was revived, a skating rink was opened and the Salvation Army was fined for causing a racket by marching nightly through the streets singing and playing brassily, without seeking permission. Eventually the Salvos were given the nod but conditions were imposed by the council.

The Albury Hospital decided not to take any more patients until finances improved and a hotelier offered to donate £5 if his brother publicans did the same because "their business sent more patients to the hospital than any other."

Kanin and John Nader, although battling financially, wanted to show their civic spirit to this cause. They joined with members of the Abikhair family to help in the hospital's plight. Kanin donated seven shillings and seven pence and John, seven shillings and sixpence, making a total of £10 with the Abikhairs' contribution. This gesture by the local Syrian Christians merited an item in the *Albury Border Post* on January 5, 1900, under the heading "A Handsome Donation."

The Nader men would spend the rest of their lives in Albury as hawkers. John, who was only 5 feet 4 inches tall, had a hunched back and was troubled by arthritis and only with difficulty could he wield the hand barrow which he trundled to Mate's Corner each day to sell fruit and vegetables. At a later stage he upgraded to an old Chev truck custom built as a hawker's van with display shelves down the outer sides. The van sides were hinged, lifting up to form a roof and down to form a counter.

Kanin was even shorter than his brother. He too was stooped, barely able to push his heavy cart and, being a foreigner and coming from the wrong side of the tracks, was taunted and teased by schoolchildren.

His wife Amelia, who befriended the beleaguered Mrs Rose Elias, was remembered as a frail, genteel lady with skin like ivory. She had a lovely disposition and was never known to raise her voice.

Lavina took after her mother in looks. A pretty girl, her features were more European than Lebanese. Her style, the way she dressed and did her hair, were more Anglo-Saxon than Lebanese and from her early teenage years, she preferred the company of Anglo-Saxon girls to those from her own ethnic background and sought them out.

It appeared that she was deeply affected by remarks passed about the impoverished circumstances in which the family first lived at Albury, and at racist jibes in her early school days. These did not cease even when the family's lot improved and they moved into a house in Hume Street, Albury, closer to the town centre.

After she left school at 15, Lavina worked for about five years from 1910 in Abikhair's drapery store, founded in 1907 by old hawker-cum-shopkeeper Saad Abikhair, in Olive Street on the periphery of Albury's shopping centre. Later her younger sister Ada joined her.

The shop was as typical a well-stocked haberdashery as could be found anywhere in the world, dimly lit, cluttered with an extraordinary array of goods, displayed on stacked shelves as high as the ceiling. Name it and if customers couldn't find it anywhere else, Abikhair's would have it.

Their goods included hats, silk stockings, scarves, lace gloves, bolts of the finest cloth, flowers for hats or dresses, handkerchiefs, flannel undershirts, morning dress and mourning apparel, work trousers, underwear, socks, gloves, shirts, braces, arm bands, cuff links, skeins of wool, corsets, children's toys, blankets, saucepans, aprons, tea towels, men's bowler hats, heavy rolls of linen and calico...

Customers did not browse, each one was *served*. No bright lights here, just naked bulbs. Although well stocked with ready-made clothing, the store also carried materials in an unmanufactured state so customers could make their own garments. And although lay-bys were encouraged, credit was never given.

In an old worldly way, the store's layout and goods were clearly divided into male and female categories. The menswear and ladies wear sections were diagonally opposite each other, with their own separate entrances and window displays.

But it was in women's millinery and foundation garments that Abikhairs specialised, boasting of the number of ladies they fitted out with hats and corsets for the Melbourne Cup. As a thriving haberdashery that no longer exists in the modern gaudy and neon-lit sales outlets of today, it was humble but superb.

Lavina soon reached the high standard required of Abikhair's sales assistants, being both efficient and discreet. As she went about her work, keeping her inner thoughts to herself, she couldn't help noticing how the Abikhairs, like most of the rest of Albury's Syrian families, kept largely to themselves, inter-marrying and forming business partnerships with one another rather than with the Anglo-Saxons.

Their capacity for hard work and meticulous attention to business were legendary. The story was told that as old Saad Abikhair lay dying in Albury Hospital, the family gathered around his bed and someone said to him: "We're all here, Saad." The old draper's eyes flickered as he breathed his last words: "Who's minding the shop?"

Although they would be respected for their enterprise and civic efforts, they were still regarded as different by the wider Anglo-Saxon community. Even when naturalised, they would remain Syrian in the eyes of the town.

Lavina would instinctively remember her feelings from those days.

Tannous Jacob had finally realised his ambition.

By sacrificing most pleasures and by skimping and saving while based in Redfern, he and Philomena had managed to buy a general store business in the town of Barraba in the North-West Slopes of NSW. With further saving, they bought the property itself and the house at the rear.

Most of their family including Frederick, the eldest, still lived in Sydney. Working as a clerk, Frederick was thinking about marriage. The Lebanese still married strictly into their own at that time, with families, feeling like outsiders, clinging to one another. Children were shepherded and protected by the parents.

So the word went out among family members and friends in the Jacob circle that a handsome young man was seeking a bride...and the scene was set for an arranged marriage in the Lebanese style. The Nader family heard of this through a friend and responded with Lavina in mind. Tannous travelled from Barraba to Albury to talk to Kanin and Amelia, saying he had a good business, there was also a future in the town for the couple and their children if they married, that Lavina would be safe and protected because Frederick was a nice young man. Tannous was told Lavina was a sweet girl, and a virgin.

At that time Lavina was spending time with her elder married sister Annisy, at the hamlet of Burrawang near Bowral in the Southern Highlands of NSW. A meeting was arranged between the two young people and the moment Frederick spotted Lavina, he was smitten. Lavina liked him too.

They were married on November 21, 1917, in St Paul's Catholic Church in Moss Vale near Bowral. Lavina was 22, Frederick 21. The couple went to Barraba to live, assisting in running the general store. They would have five children.

The second born, Thomas Clement Jacob, was named after his grandfather Tannous in honour of his leaving the village of Aitou 34 years before to start a new life. Young Tom was delivered by local medico Dr Phipps on April 15, 1920 in the Alice Street house owned by his grandparents at the rear of their store in Queen Street, Barraba.

Old Tannous had no desire to go back to Lebanon. But dreamily he wondered if the characteristics of a long and venturesome heritage going back centuries might somehow resurface in the genes of this second generation Australian boy named after him.

5

THE "DIFFERENT" BUSH KID

THE youthful years for young Tom Jacob in the country town of Barraba should have been the happiest and most carefree of his life.

The town in the 1920s with a population of about 1,000 and hundreds more in the district, was the centre of a friendly and close-knit community, producing top quality beef, wool and fat lambs, with gold mining and gemstones.

It lay between the larger towns of Tamworth and Narrabri, about 500 kms north-west of Sydney, amid undulating hills and pleasing rural scenery, not far from mountain peaks and the Horton Falls and Valley. The area was ideal for bush walking and exploring, with attractive gardens, a Chinese market garden and fruit trees galore.

Best of all the Manilla River ran through the town, providing many suitable water holes for swimming and fishing. A boy could lose himself here along the river bank, lying in the hot sun, fishing, boating and dreaming.

The first settlers came to Barraba around 1830 after the explorer Alan Cunningham crossed the Manilla River on his way to discovering the Darling Downs in Queensland and on returning to Sydney reported on the rich lands he passed through. Cobb and Co coaches serviced the town until the railways came in 1907.

Queen Street, the town's main thoroughfare, was lit at night by kerosene lamps until 1915 and its noonday starkness was softened in the year Tom Jacob was born there when the local council began planting shady peppercorn trees, each one patriotically commemorating an Australian soldier killed in World War 1.

In Tom's childhood years in the town, the water supply was somewhat rudimentary, although effective. The town centre was supplied with the life-giving fluid after it was pumped from the river into a large overhead storage tank. In every sense the town's prosperity depended on the elements. In drought, everyone including the shopkeepers suffered.

Barraba was a typical sleepy little rural town, although for its size it had a good range of services and amenities, including sport, even a brass band.

Apart from stock and agricultural topics, little seemed to arouse people's excitement. Locals still talked of the red letter day in the town's history when the NSW Governor, Sir Harry Rawson, visited to open the first Barraba Show in 1904.

The one dramatic event that still animated Barraba folk was the murder of the town's only bank manager, William McKay, in the Commercial Bank on the afternoon of April 18, 1884 when an attempted holdup by two "bushrangers" went horribly wrong.

Tethering two magnificent horses to the rail outside, the bandits donned masks, drew their guns and held up Mr McKay, only to shoot him dead when he refused to hand over the contents of the open safe, panicking after the manager's wife screamed for help.

They mounted and rode off. Later in the bush police arrested two men, John Cummings, a shearer's representative and Alec Lee, alias Joseph Anderson, a Danish sailor who had arrived in Australia a few years earlier. They were found guilty at a sensational trial and hanged in Tamworth Jail.

Cummings, about to stand as a political candidate, repeatedly protested his innocence and Lee told the court Cummings was not at the bank holdup. And later, a convicted robber and housebreaker, Bert Osborne, claimed *he* had shot the manager.

Was Cummings innocent? Was there a third man at the stickup? These and other questions by any visitor to Barraba could spark a debate or punchup until the beer ran out.

The old Commercial Bank became the Victoria Hotel. As a curious kid, Tom Jacob sneaked into the hotel to see the hole where one of the bullets had passed through a door.

Tom had a loving family-oriented childhood, cared for by his mother and father who managed the general store and "spoiled" by his grandparents, all of whom lived in the house behind the store.

When he was six or seven, his grandparents left the store to his father and returned to Sydney, buying a house in Rawson Street, Auburn. Tom visited them twice a year on school holidays.

As he grew he became a Huck Finn type of youngster, getting up to any mischief he could with his mates. Stealing fruit from the many trees that townspeople normally kept in those days was a specialty. Hardly a small orchard in the district escaped their attention.

A prime target for their plundering ways was a Chinese market gardener on a bank of the Manilla River not far from Tom's home. They called him Pong Suey. Many times Tom and two or three pals laughed at this venerable old man as they sat in his tree gorging on mulberries, ignoring him as he implored them in a strange sing-song dialect to leave his fruit alone, before jumping down and fleeing.

They enjoyed Pong Suey's juicy sugar melons too. Tom or one of his friends would grab a melon or two and if Pong Suey confronted him with a big stick, he would toss the melons in the river and run. A mate waiting in the shallows further downstream would pluck the melons out and they feasted on them at a pre-arranged hideout.

That was seen as normal good clean fun for country boys. The challenge was to be chased, then outrun the pursuer. Often they had to run the gauntlet of angry farmers or orchardists who fired on them with saltpetre pellets from 10-gauge shotguns. Sometimes Tom painfully picked saltpetre out of his arse and legs after failing to make a quick enough getaway.

He had the same average intelligence, enjoyed the same fun and joined in the same escapades as his young peers. He looked and acted the same. But increasingly at school he was treated differently.

Yet the only difference he could see in himself from his Anglo-Saxon mates was a slight variation in physical appearance. Tom's skin was olive white while the bodies of nearly all the others at school in places where the sun had not reached, were a slightly pinkish white inherited from their English, Scottish, Welsh or Irish forebears.

Tom's eyes were hazel like many of the others. The only other subtle difference was that his dark hair accentuated the slightly swarthy nature of his skin.

He told himself he was born in Australia, just like his father, and he felt just as much at home as an Australian boy as any of his Anglo-Saxon friends and fellow pupils.

He could not understand why, and found it hurtful, that some playmates who were friendly one minute could turn so quickly the next and taunt him with racial insults.

It could happen in a dispute over a simple game of marbles. "You dago" they might suddenly say. "You bloody wog - go back home where you came from. Go back to the desert."

In a fist fight with another boy one day at the Barraba public school, Tom was getting the better of the exchange when his opponent, a "pure" Australian boy, suddenly yelled at him: "You black bastard. We don't want you here, you black bastard."

It hurt him deeply, more than any physical pain. That day when he went home he rolled back his shirt sleeves and lifted up his short trousers and looked closely at his skin. Then he peered into a mirror. "I'm not black," he said aloud to himself, "I'm almost as white as they are." Whenever he was called names, he would invariably look in the mirror.

It was always the same. Whenever other kids wanted to sting him, they resorted to racial vilification. It was usually "dago," "wog," wop," "reffo" or "go back to your tent, you Arab." Sometimes it was "Eye-tie" or even "Jew boy." Anything that could hurt.

Tom would learn many years later that three cousins of his, Elaine, Olga and John Nasser, received the same treatment at school in Sydney more than 20 years later. Their grandmother was one of the Hashem girls from Beirut. Elaine and Olga had olive skins and black hair, John had fair skin with blue eyes. As the girls played a piano duet at a Cleveland Street public school concert, with John turning over the sheet music, they heard someone in the audience say loudly: "Look at the white dago turning the pages for the two black dagoes."

The name calling had started in earnest when Tom was eight. He was tagged "Licorice" and his younger brother Claude was called "Chocolate." Abbreviated, this became Lic and Choc.

From that first day when he was branded with the name because of his olive skin, and whenever he thought about it in the future, the humiliation and embarrassment he felt from that nickname as a child would resurface, even well into adult life.

He never understood how young minds could think up such hurtful things to say to their playmates. One small boy from a poor family was called "Worm," and another "Maggot." Although young Tom thought that was awful, he didn't regard it as insulting as the names they called him based on the colour of his skin.

From about the age of seven Tom was constantly reminded that he, his brothers and sisters were different to other children who were the offspring of the town's overwhelming Anglo-Saxon population.

Barraba at the time had about 12 other residents of non-English speaking backgrounds. A Greek family owned the milk bar and Italians had the main restaurant. They had the same olive white skin colouring as Tom. Children from those families were also called "dagoes" and" wogs" at school but they seemed to weather it better than Tom.

Some of the other ethnic kids would call back names that were just as hurtful, or immediately raise their fists. But Tom was inclined to take it and almost slink away. He had a breaking point where he was forced into an angry response, but mostly he was inclined to just let it go. Deep within him it hurt and his sensitive nature was such that although he didn't respond, he knew he could never treat the person who offended him in the same warm and friendly way again. He simply retired more into himself.

The ethnic children and most of their families found comfort in one another's company and an "us versus them" culture developed generally. Strangely, apart from fits of name calling, the two groups mingled well at school and play.

It played on his mind so much that he convinced himself the Greek and Italian children were more accepted than him, that more barbs were directed at him than the others.

Whenever the kids went on school outings such as playing football in nearby towns like Glen Innes, they travelled on the back of a truck. Maybe he imagined it but it seemed the teachers would load all the Anglo-Saxon kids first and he would always be last with the teacher saying "hey, young Jacob, hop on." Unconsciously he would be standing back, intimidated, thinking the others were looking down on him.

The name calling, particularly "black bastard," had made him feel inferior. The feeling would remain deeply ingrained in his psyche. The nicknames he'd been called and the shame he felt as the target would be kept pent up inside him, hidden from others until late in his life when he could finally come to terms with them and unburden himself.

As a boy trying to escape this sense of inferiority he would often get away on his own, walking for miles around the country roads outside Barraba or along the Manilla River banks, staying away for hours.

Tom would sit on the river bank fishing and thinking. His habit was to take a piece of meat from his mother's ice box, cut it into small pieces and tie one to a length of string which he attached to a stick, dangling it in the water close to the bank. He caught crayfish called cray bobs, which people said tasted a bit like lobster. Tom sometimes sat there until it was dark or until his parents sent someone to look for him.

He loved being near the profuse wattle trees, admiring the fluffy yellow blooms of this Australian floral emblem and enjoying their delicate perfume.

While on his walks or in solitary riverside reveries, Tom studied animals, the horses and cattle and the birds. He marvelled at how the colourful array of birdlife, unless disturbed, sat calmly in the wattle trees or foraged close by as if keeping him company, and he envied their ability to flit or soar to freedom beyond the horizon.

They were, he mused, better companions than some of his school associates. His thoughts in these quiet moments would be the reason why on growing up he wore ties with bird and animal motifs - they didn't care about his ethnic background or his colour.

Even then, as young as he was, he grappled with the reality and effect of racial prejudice, although not fully understanding it.

Years later he would articulate his feelings in this way: "If you have an olive skin, you don't know where the hell you are, whether black or white. You sit on a dividing line. You don't know which side to push yourself on to. At times I've felt ashamed that I've wanted to push myself more on to the white side than the black. At other times I've tried to compensate by going more to the black side. You can't help feeling this way because you're in between."

Sometimes as he lay awake at night Tom overheard his parents talking about the discrimination against them. He heard his father say the Anglo-Saxons rarely invited them into their homes. Farmers who came into their shop were courteous and friendly but never invited them to social functions like a woolshed dance. He heard his mother say to his father one night: "You know why they don't invite us? Because we're not one of them. " And Tom wondered what his mother meant.

A few days later Tom said to his mother: "Mum, why aren't we one of them? We live here too." Lavina said: "Well, we're not exactly the same. We come from a country that is different. And as a result, this sort of thing happens. We're strangers here but we shouldn't be different. The only thing we can do is to be friendly with them, even if it hurts occasionally."

Sometimes after a particularly upsetting name-calling incident at school, when he was called nigger or something else beyond the normal dago or wog, Tom came home crying to his mother. Lavina felt the anguish of his hurt. She would wipe away his tears, put her arms around him and say: "Sticks and stones may break my bones, but names will never hurt me. Say that over and over to yourself and you won't feel so bad about it."

"But why do they keep calling me black when I'm not?" he would ask.

His mother went to great pains to talk to him and her approach was always along the same lines.

"Don't take any notice," she'd say. "You must remember this is their country, we've come from another country and they think we're going to take something from them. When they realise we're just the same as them and we just want to live and work quietly and mind our own business, they'll stop calling you names and we'll be left in peace."

Not only children were responsible for the racial insults. Often they repeated to Tom what their parents had told them about the "wogs" in Barraba. A woman living nearby one day told her children they were not to play or mix with "those Jacob dagoes."

Lavina, throwing aside her usual courteous manner, marched straight to the woman's house and angrily upbraided her for her ignorance.

Tom's father, suddenly fearing a possible smalltown backlash from customers in his shop, asked Lavina what she'd said. "It's none of your business," she replied. "But I told her exactly what I thought of her."

The outburst in front of the children was unusual for Lavina, who always educated them to respect their father as head of the house. Although a strong character, she subjugated herself to uplift the family, building up the children if their feelings were wounded and always giving her husband credit when he gave his opinion.

"Son," she would say to Tom whenever his father chastised him, "everything your father says is right. You will remember this one day when you become a father. Your father is a good father and although what he tells you now may seem wrong, later on in life you will appreciate what he is saying to you."

Frederick Jacob was a gentle, sensitive man and only a little over five feet tall. As a clerk he was not a good businessman, lacking promotional flair and imagination. Lavina, on the other hand, was highly imaginative. Everything she did was for her children and, within the limits of her parochial environment and motivated by ethnic differences, she always pushed and encouraged them to strive in order to better themselves.

Although she tried not to show it, Tom knew he was her favourite. And it pleased her that he always went to the St John's Catholic Church and had a Christian indoctrination.

She toiled hard. In those days there were no appliances like refrigerators, washing machines or even gas stoves. The dunny was outside, outback bush style and the night carter or "honey cart" called regularly. Lavina cooked in pots on a wood fuel stove, where she also heated a solid flat iron to iron the clothes. To wash the clothes, she boiled a big copper container over a wood fire. She seemed always to be cooking, ironing, sewing or mending.

Tom's father was a naturally talented musician. He played the violin with such soulfulness he could almost make it weep. He taught Tom to play violin and father and son were also in the Barraba Brass Band where Tom played the cornet. Music could be the means of moving young Tom to tears or flights of fancy.

An example of the boy's sensitivity was seen one day when he tried to show his mates how swiftly the pigeons in his loft could fly. He had built the loft himself, watching the pigeons lay their eggs and breed, and he adored a blue hen more than any other. He tied a piece of strong twine to one of the hen's legs, hoping to guide it in flight. The bird flew out of the loft at great speed and was in full flight when he pulled on the twine. To his horror he pulled out the bird's leg. It died soon after.

With his mates gathered around, Tom gave his favourite pigeon a royal burial. With tears trickling down, he laid the bird to rest in a grave on a special cleared plot of ground, then played the hymn *Nearer My God to Thee* on his cornet. The instrument felt part of him, the sound pouring out his emotion. In his prayers, he vowed never to take the life of any creature again.

Tom loved the occasional holiday visits to his grandparents' rambling old home in Auburn, Sydney. It had a big covered verandah on two sides in the Australian colonial style.

The main thing he liked was the olive tree old Tannous had planted in the back garden. Tannous would sit under the tree with him and tell him stories that excited his imagination.

"I come from a land that has millions and millions of olive trees," Tannous would begin.

"What land?" young Tom would ask.

"Lebanon, where the seed for this olive tree came from. Where I was born and grew up. There are cedars up in the mountains. The Cedars of Lebanon. The best known trees in the world. Thousands of years old..." And he would tell the earnest youngster about life in Lebanon and describe the scenery, at times breaking into Arabic to show how the people spoke.

Sometimes he'd pluck an olive from the tree and ask Tom to look at it closely. Then he'd wax philosophically. "See that green? Wherever you see the green of that olive, remember there are three things you should value in life above everything else. Green, because where there is green there is water and life. The second is women. Always respect them. The third is always be true to yourself, like a tree."

"How do you mean true to yourself?" asked Tom.

"Well, you should align yourself to a tree. If you do that son, it means you have to work, because that's what the tree does. A seed or an acorn goes into the ground and eventually you get an olive tree or an oak. A lot of work creates a beautiful tree."

Tom would go with the old man while he played draughts in a public park. At weekends Tannous would fill Tom's pockets with peanuts and take him to Sydney's Domain park to hear all the spruikers on various subjects, telling him he felt very much at home among all the nationalities there. The world was bigger in Sydney.

It was Tannous who told Tom that in the year he was born, 1920, great change had come to the land of their fathers. Lebanon had finally thrown off the harsh invaders. After the Turks were defeated in the Great War, he explained, France was awarded Syria under what they called a mandate and from that had created the State of Greater Lebanon by joining North Lebanon with lands in the coastal areas like Beirut. Although under mandate to France and still not independent, Lebanon now had its own identity and a new flag with a green cedar as its emblem.

Young Tom didn't know where Tannous got all this information because he still couldn't read or write English and the newspapers had to be read to him.

Tannous's tales so fired Tom's curiosity and imagination that he would leave their home in Auburn and walk to the main artery of Parramatta Road and watch all the cars go by. This was different, exciting, unpredictable. Where were they going? Tom wished he could travel too. Sydney is where I want to be, he mused. He stayed away so long that several times the police were called to find him.

When Tom told Tannous of his unhappiness at school because of the names they called him, the old man advised him not to worry and said chuckling with pride and mischief: "Don't forget, we Lebanese have added the lovely texture of olive colouring to the pink paleness of many Anglo-Saxon Australians."

To inspire Tom and show him the value of determination and perseverance, Tannous told him the story of Lebanese emigrant Joseph John Alam, who was related to Tom because Alam had married a sister of Tom's grandmother - another one of the Hashem girls.

Before the turn of the century, in 1890, Joe was hired by the owners of a small coal mine at Wallsend, near Newcastle in the Hunter Valley of NSW. But he lasted only an hour. The other miners went on strike, declaring "we don't want a dago working with us."

The next day Joe Alam was on the road with a full swag of goods, supported by a strap across one shoulder. A relative took a photo of him as he trudged off on his hawking mission.

Joe soon took his family to the growing town of Dubbo in central western NSW to avoid competing with other Lebanese in the Newcastle area. Building up his savings in pennies like other Lebanese hawkers, he acquired a small shop which became Dubbo's largest general store - and the Alam family later achieved renown for their contribution to the area.

"Remember," Tannous told Tom, "don't be upset. You can do good things like Joe Alam. Our family goes back to the Phoenicians. We are thousands of years old..."

Each time Tom went home after staying with his grandparents, he asked his mother about Lebanon. But she always firmly turned him and the rest of the family off the subject. She hated to be thought of as Syrian or Lebanese.

"We are not from Arab people, "she often said. "The Arabs are mostly Muslims but we are Christians - we come from a mixture of invaders from the Western world and the ancient Phoenicians. But you don't have to think about that because it's too far back and complicated. Just think of yourselves as Australians."

Tom could not understand then why his mother would not talk about the family's ethnic background, or why she appeared to have turned against her own ethnic people. But later he would realise it was no doubt due to the slurs hurled at her in her poor childhood and her desire to protect her children from similar hurt and to integrate them into Australian society.

As a family they talked about their background but Lavina made no bones about the fact that she was strongly pro-British and Anglo-Saxon Australian in everything she did, except in food, often cooking Lebanese dishes like cabbage rolls, stuffed marrows, tabbouleh and kibbi - a minced meat with wheat speciality.

She did so to please her husband, who still hankered for things Lebanese. "When we have enough money," he sometimes said, "we'll go back and see what the old country is like now."

Lavina would say at once: "Never. There is no old country for me. This is my country, Australia. This is your country, Australia. You were born here and so was I."

Then she would turn to the children: "I want you all to remember this. You are Australian, you are not Lebanese. Tom, look at your young friend Patrick. His parents were born in Ireland but he was born here. He is not Irish, he's Australian."

Normally a gentle person, this was the one area in which Lavina was the dominant partner. Frederick would have liked some Arabic spoken within the family, but she would not hear of it. Lavina never went to any Lebanese functions arranged by friends or relatives, so the children didn't.

Sometimes young Tom, his curiosity aroused by Tannous, tried to start a detailed discussion. "Yes mum," he might say, "I know I'm an Australian, but didn't our family come from a place called Lebanon? Where's that?"

"That's another story," his mother would reply, "and that chapter is closed. When you come to this country, you accept it for what it is. If you want to succeed and you want this country to grow and prosper and you want the people here to stop calling you names, then you have to be one of them."

Lavina, with her lovely auburn hair and fair to olive skin, on looks alone could easily have been regarded as Anglo-Saxon when not in a Lebanese setting. She only ever wanted to be classed as an Australian.

Tom had wondered what Lebanon and the people there would be like. But his mother's attitude made a big impression on him. He decided he wanted to be a good Australian and do something special when he grew up. Gradually he put aside his curiosity about his ethnic past and where the family came from, and Lebanon for now was a closed subject due to his mother's influence.

In school Tom was tops at English but an ordinary student at other things. He developed a croup and then played on his mother's affection by coughing unnecessarily so he could wag school, spending the time to explore the nearby bush. He convinced himself he had an affinity with trees, slapping his hands against them and believing he could feel their strength.

A passionate reader, he would go into the local newsagency and buy a booklet or magazine and, being short of money, would pinch one or two others and pop them up his jumper. Never comics which were the juvenile craze then, but publications on faraway places.

He had a fantastic imagination and would often go down by the river and lay on his back, gazing up through the trees into the sky, wondering what was beyond the horizon, what was out there among the stars.

He yearned to travel to strange places. He borrowed a friend's bicycle and explored all around Barraba. When told not to do something, he would try to do it, no matter how outlandish. Tom was a difficult boy, at times hard to control.

What made Tommy run?

He needed to prove he was not inferior. I can see it in their eyes, he told himself, as pure white adults and youths look me up and down registering the colour of my skin against their milky white. They think I'm inferior. Second class.

Then to lift himself he would say: I'm just as good as they are. No, I'm better.

But he knew he would have to prove it. To be accepted, to stop them saying go back to your tent in the desert you bloody Arab, he knew he would always have to be presentable, well dressed and go one better than those taunting him.

The injustice of it all, the hurt of it, although overwhelming at the time, would hone his mind and motivate him, shaping the future.

An ambition to achieve was born out of a feeling of inadequacy for the accident of birth in having an olive skin in a predominant white society.

Frederick Jacob tried to hang on to the store when the world depression hit in 1929 and the Australian economy struck rock bottom. But it was a losing battle.

Tom as a kid of 11 in 1931 would always remember feeling ashamed and depressed to see his father, trying to shift stock, practically giving it away with a big sign out front saying "all goods must be sold regardless of price."

Barraba, like other towns, was hard hit by the depression which began with plummeting world commodity prices making Australian primary produce uneconomic. When the Government could no longer borrow money overseas, living standards suddenly fell as national income declined and towns like Barraba relying on sheep, cattle and agriculture were among the first to suffer.

At least one third of the nation's breadwinners were thrown out of work, and the word "depression" left a searing scar on the nation's conscience. People survived on government relief only by doing physical work.

After Tom's father sold out, just managing to clear his debts, he took the family to the industrial city of Newcastle. They were so poor he had to do relief work on the roads to pay the rent and buy meagre amounts of food.

Here in their rented house in the suburb of Hamilton, Tom was introduced to some forms of "modern" living, a flush toilet which he had to be shown how to use, and a gas water heater in the bathroom. His mother showed him how to start the flame with a match and the heater lit with such a whoomp he was frightened to use it again.

Tom went to Newcastle Junior High School but when it came to his ethnic background, little had changed. Some of the boys would say "here comes the wog" and he hated it, once again feeling he was not accepted by his peers.

He tried to join in everything, cricket and football. If he tackled another player a bit hard or stopped his progress, he was called a bloody dago. Tom knew this was more in anger than anything else, but he also knew what was in their minds - it was always a question of black or white.

He tried to help his mother by taking a paper run, illegally jumping on and off trams in bare feet to sell newspapers. Some conductors turned a blind eye as long as he kept out of their way but others threatened to kick him, saying "get off you bloody little dago." Sometimes he skinned his knees when misjudging the leap off a moving tram.

Tom could see his parents were having difficulty coming to grips with their grim new situation, in clothing, feeding and educating their five children. They could not afford to buy him shoes, but that was of no consequence in the struggle to survive. He observed his father's fatigue from digging up roads, the concern in his mother's eyes. Even the taunts now seemed to take more effect because the family was so poor.

Tom thought he'd help his parents by running away and making some money. He knew he was a good talker and after reading a book about the art of selling, he decided he would get a job as a salesman.

He was just 13. He confided to a young Anglo-Saxon school friend who lived a few streets away: "I'm leaving home to make my fortune to help mum and dad." With little thought his friend said: "I'll come with you." They "jumped the rattler" by climbing on board a train without tickets and ended up at Currabubula, near Tamworth in northern NSW.

Sleeping out under the stars they survived by scrounging food in shops, especially from a warm-hearted Italian fruiterer, by saying they came from very poor families and their parents had no food in the house. A butcher gave them a few chops and sausages, which they cooked on a roadside fire.

After five days they began to wilt. That night they came upon a woolshed dance and from the darkness listened to the lively music from a piano accordion, drums and violin, watching everyone enjoying themselves.

They felt homesick. Tom said: "If you want to go home, I'll go home."

Next day they jumped on a south-bound train but were detected by the guard who threw them off at the next station, threatening to call the police.

They found their way to the Hume Highway and hitched a ride with a motorist who stopped a long way down the road after going past them. They soon knew why - he was intoxicated, sipping from a bottle of whisky and his car, an old rattletrap Studebaker, had no brakes. He could stop only by changing down through the gears.

After a hair-raising ride, they made it to Newcastle and home that night. The police had been alerted. Tom's parents were so relieved to see him they said little by way of reproach, greeting him with open arms. His friend wasn't so lucky, receiving a thrashing.

What's more, his parents came around to Tom's parents early next morning and abused them, blaming Tom for leading their son astray.

"You're nothing but a bunch of bloody dagoes," said the angry father, "keep your son away from our boy, you wogs."

And adding the time honoured insult in what was then a racist country, "why don't you go back to the desert where you came from?"

Tom would never forget it. But he still harboured thoughts of doing something new and exciting and making a fortune.

After almost three years in Newcastle, Tom's parents told him the best news imaginable: "We're moving to Sydney."

6

A GENTLEMAN OF THE FOURTH ESTATE

TOM Jacob finished his education in Sydney by gaining his Intermediate Certificate at Stanmore Commercial High School. But it was no flash pass, just the basic 4 Bs, although he usually excelled in English.

He simply didn't study. Instead, he voraciously read newspapers and magazines especially about exotic places like India. He felt for the underdog, studying faces in the street, reading all he could about non Anglo-Saxons in Australia, Aborigines, Greeks, Italians, Jews.

As soon as he left school at 15 he acquired an "s" on the end of his name. *Tom Jacobs.* His father, who had found work spasmodically as a clerk again, decided the name Jacob sounded too Jewish, and although he had nothing against members of the Jewish race, he felt that in a desperate employment period with the effect of the Depression still rampant, a less ethnic-sounding name might be more acceptable in finding a job. Some areas like Maitland in NSW still had unemployment of up to 60 per cent.

Shortly before, in 1934, ethnic harmony and the jobs issue in Australia were severely jolted by race riots in Kalgoorlie where two people were killed. A largely Anglo-Saxon and Celtic mob attacked and destroyed an Italian and Slav miners' camp, renewing images of the attacks on Chinese miners in the 1860s.

As a young journalist I once met an Australian man by arrangement in the Sportsman's Bar of the old Australia Hotel in Sydney (where a barmaid often entertained patrons by balancing two middies of beer on her ample boobs). The man described the depth of racist feelings that existed still in the period leading up to World War 11.

He and a friend noticed a sign outside an Italian barber's shop near Sydney's Central Railway, advertising for a barber's assistant. Underneath were the words "no Australian need apply."

Outraged, the man and his friend defecated in a brown paper bag, called and asked the Italian barber about the job. When he said he would not employ an Australian, they hit him over the head with the foul-smelling substance, leaving him somewhat deterred and the worse for wear, so to speak. The man who took this direct action was still proudly retelling the story in the Sportsman's Bar in the late 1950s.

The only job young Tom Jacobs could find after searching desperately for several months was a clerk's in an iron foundry in suburban Marrickville. It was the last job he should have taken, bristling as he was with ambition and ideas and dreams to do big things. Also, he wasn't a figures man.

Wearing his only pair of shoes and his one suit which he kept for church, the eager intelligent lad was keen to learn and make a good impression. And he was grateful too, thrilled to think that now he could help his family make ends meet.

All went well in the first week. Mostly he stayed in his glass-partitioned office learning about files and invoices, occasionally venturing out amid the din, dust and heat of the foundry floor to get the feel of things.

In the second week when he walked on to the floor a young worker of about 20, tall and solidly built with bulging muscles, put down the lump of hot iron he was hammering. "Hey," he called.

Smiling, ready to please, Tom went over to him.

"What's an Arab doing here in a collar and tie pushing a pen?" the fellow sneered. "Can't do real work. Too proud to get among the sweat and toil, eh? You bloody dagos are all the same."

The only person of non-Anglo Saxon background at the foundry, Tom had prayed something like this would not happen.

Stung, he retorted: "You're only fit for heavy labouring work."

The tormentor, bigger and stronger, suddenly lashed out, crunching his knuckles into Tom's face, knocking him down. He got up and they fought. Others stopped it, but not before one wild haymaker broke Tom's nose.

He quit a few days later, vowing to work only for himself in future.

What hurt most was not the smashed nose and trickling blood but the rejection, the non acceptance that had so often wounded him emotionally for somehow being "different," although he was born and bred in this land, belonged to it in every way and was immensely proud of the fact.

Economic necessity required him to find a job immediately to help his family but work, in the local idiom of the time, was as scarce as the proverbial rocking horse manure. He resorted to the only thing he could think of, although it revived ghosts and spectres of the past.

To do so took a great leap in courage. He knew that with his non-English background, although he was Australian in every sense, he ran the risk of being classified as a wog or an Arab. But he had no choice.

Grandfather Tannous fitted him out with a big battered old suitcase he'd once used, told him how to obtain the licence and supplies, and he turned back the clock nearly 60 years to his family's desperate, humble start in Australia by taking to the road.

Not wishing to be seen hawking around Petersham in the inner western suburbs where he lived with his family, he walked to nearby Enfield and even the hawkers' heartland of Redfern, then to other adjacent suburbs.

All these areas were pretty well "hawked out" and after winding himself up each day for the effort of knocking on the doors of whole streets, he received a rebuff nine times out of 10. Then someone took pity on him and suggested he call at petrol garages instead of homes.

He took a map of Sydney, divided it into suburbs in his general area, noted where the garages were and began systematically calling. He hit paydirt right away. Young mechanics gathered around, saying "what have you got in there?"

He opened the suitcase, nearly as big as himself, displaying socks, shoe laces, razor blades, shaving cream, hair cream and ties for sixpence each, singlets, boxer shorts, hankies.

On his third visit to a garage at Newtown, a mechanic asked: "Got any Frenchies?"

He didn't know what the fellow was talking about but said: "No, but I'll bring you some next time."

Returning to the Redfern warehouse supplying him - he arrived on foot with his suitcase, others came in trucks - he asked if they had "Frenchies." Yes, how many? "I'll have half a dozen," said unsophisticated Tom.

The salesman laughed lewdly. "We sell 'em by the gross, mate. You know, there's lots of jig-a-jig going on in this town."

Tom sold the gross in a week. And he would do a roaring trade with young fornicators, many of whom bought for their mates as well because in those coy days before sexual freedom they were too embarrassed to ask for rubber goods in a chemist shop if women were behind the counter.

Tom discreetly labelled his rubber goods as prophylactics. French letters, not French ties, were the order of the day!

His best sales spot for lecherous young blokes was a garage in Enfield.

While waiting for them to take their lunch break, he'd sit in a jacaranda tree in a corner of the Enfield school grounds while classes were in, eating sandwiches his mother had prepared in a brown paper bag. He liked to be alone and felt people would stare at him if he ate in the street. Sometimes those walking by spotted him and asked what he was doing up there.

"Having my lunch," he'd say with unassailable logic.

The question of his ethnicity often came up.

A mechanic would say: "Where'd you come from?" "Sydney."

"Yes, but where did your mother and father come from?"

Eventually he'd have to say Lebanon. "Arab, eh?"

"No," Tom would say, "I'm not an Arab. I come from a country surrounded by Arabs, but I'm not one of them."

Then he'd mull over all the reasons why he wasn't an Arab. What about all the Caucasians who went through Lebanon, the Crusaders and the French? These were the sorts of things that went through the mind of a person who was "different."

If they asked him whether he was Greek or Italian he'd quickly say yes, trying to avoid explanation. He knew the Greeks and Italians were still largely looked upon as second class citizens, although more accepted than Arabs or Syrians.

He felt for the Arabs too because he was aware Australians looked down on them routinely as cheats and persons of inferior status just because they were Arabs. It was just that he regarded himself as coming from a Lebanese background rather than Arab and he wanted to be accepted as Caucasian.

He was growing up in a world where he had to continually justify himself because of his heritage. But instead of feeling proud, he was trying to hide his ethnicity.

It shamed him that he was not standing up for his Lebanese background.

He knew he was denying his own people by saying he had Greek or Italian blood in him, and it hurt, but he thought he could do little else in the prevailing atmosphere. Often when he said he was Greek or Italian, people would say: "Oh that's good. We don't want too many of those bloody Arabs coming into this country."

Privately Tom felt he was not just of Lebanese background, but *Christian* Lebanese. And he held the Christian values dearly, especially those setting out right from wrong. The principle of not doing anything wrong was important to him because in his simple form of faith he believed that one day he would have to stand before his Maker, and would not be able to hide anything.

Tom loved the city newsreels, which ran continuously until late at night. He sat there entranced, watching over and over the glimpses of life and events from various parts of the world. Then he saw a film called *A Message from Reuter* starring Edward G. Robinson, showing how the famous newsagency developed from sending messages by carrier pigeon.

That did it. He knew at once what he wanted. Tom dreamed about being a reporter, seeing himself travelling the world, involved in life, interviewing famous people. In between hawking, he haunted the newspaper inquiry desks especially *The Sun*, an afternoon paper then in the city centre in Elizabeth Street just around the corner from Martin Place, asking if there were any jobs for reporters.

They just slowly shook their heads as if it was a foolish question.

He was inexperienced, had no family background to draw upon and knew nobody of any influence. With the Depression still biting, an applicant almost had to know a director of the company or the principal *Sun* owner, Sir Hugh Denison, to get a start.

Tom soon realised that if he could get on to the copy desk, it was a stepping stone to a cadetship as a reporter. So he kept asking if there were any jobs for copyboys.

Sometimes he bumped into other lads asking for jobs and they would go for a milkshake. "None of us will ever get a job on *The Sun*" said one youth. "It's *who* you know. You have to be someone's son."

Early one afternoon Tom went to *The Sun* front desk and seeing the copyboy supervisor sitting behind it, said to him: "Any jobs for me today, Mr Allen?"

A gruff, red-faced man with a withered hand and white hair, Barney Allen looked like a misfit, but he ran the copyboys with military efficiency. Vigorously beckoning Tom inside the newsroom, he demanded: "How old are you?"

"Sixteen."

"Sit down over there!" Barney brusquely indicated the end of a long bench where the boys were seated, gradually moving along until one of the reporters hammering a typewriter called "boy!" The one in front hurried to the reporter and took his copy to another desk where two other boys pulled out the carbon paper, put the remaining sheets together and took them to a wire basket in a room where a sign said "sub editors." Several earnest men were seated here, some wearing tennis eye shades.

Tom watched this going on. When it came to his turn, he ran to the reporter and took the "copy" over to the other desk and sat down again at the end of the copyboy line.

"You!" Barney called him over. "Are you a casual?"

Now Tom was sure - Mr Allen *was* pissed. He answered yes, and Barney said: "Well, now you're permanent. Give us your name and address." That done, he said: "You start tomorrow. Eight o'clock. Be on time."

That was how Tom entered the portals of the Fourth Estate. He'd hawked for more than a year, walking everywhere.

Leaving *The Sun* building he bumped into Tom Ellis, who had a school leaving certificate and had been trying unsuccessfully to get into newspapers for two years - later he too would become a reporter, telling everyone how gut-wrenching it was to live through the Depression.

But at the time they met outside *The Sun* he was in awe of Tom for pulling off a coup, even as a lowly copyboy. "Jesus," he said to him, "I'd give my eye teeth to get a break like you. How'd you do it?"

This writer can probably tell him. A similar situation occurred in the early 1960s when, as Chief of Staff of News Limited's Sydney Daily Mirror, I received an enormous number of applications for cadetships, which became available only occasionally. Every week a slender young woman named Anna Torv came to the inquiry counter and asked if there were any cadetships. Unfortunately, I had to say no.

She eventually got a routine clerical job somewhere else in the building, but Anna still came around every week and asked about journalism. One day when a cadet vacancy cropped up, I remembered her earnest face and her keenness, pulled out her application and put her name through for the vacancy. Anna later married News Limited's proprietor, Rupert Murdoch.

Barney Allen, too, even after a liquid lunch, noticed the earnest desire of a young person in Tom Jacobs trying to get started and gave him a go. I knew Barney in the 1950s and he still helped the kids who tried.

Tom Ellis later said of his friend of those days: "Tom Jacobs had an enthusiasm about him I've rarely seen in other people. His eyes shone when he talked. I worked in Canberra as a journalist for many years and met all the big shots, Ministers, a couple of Prime Ministers, the Queen's uncle the Duke of Gloucester when he was Governor-General, and they all had dead eyes compared to Tom.

"With his humble background he should have considered himself lucky to end up after the Depression as a taxi driver or tram conductor or even a cleaner, maybe in a factory, but not as a journalist.

"What else do I recall? He was polite and conservative although he had the gift of the gab and at 16 he seemed already grown up and nicely dressed. Oh, and he kept his pants under the mattress at night to stay pressed."

Colin Davis, who became a copyboy at *The Sun* before Tom and went on to be a journalist elsewhere, said the Tom Jacobs of those days was a young man in a hurry. "I don't think he knew where he was going, but he was going somewhere," he said. "Keen and ambitious. Wanted to travel. A real eager beaver."

Peter Finch the actor was a copyboy there just before Tom. Also on the paper then was Len Smith, who became an international footballer and boss of trotting in NSW, Paul Brickhill of later *Dambusters* book fame, and Bill Hudson, the well-known aviator.

Tom was the keenest kid on the benches but even so he sometimes sat there dreaming - *all this news coming in from around the world...* One day he didn't react to the call of "boy!" and an empty milk bottle whistled past his head and smashed into a cupboard.

"Get this into the subs" ordered a red haired second year cadet named Alan Reid, later famous as a political writer and dubbed The Red Fox.

Reid took a liking to him and they became friends. On a rainy day Alan would come into the office wearing a hat and long raincoat pulled up around his ears, and Tom would look up to him and fancy himself as being just like this hotshot young reporter.

Apart from running copy he was a dogsbody at everyone's beck and call, making tea, getting sandwiches, cigarettes. But he made the most of it, watching the reporters at work, listening to them on the phone, reading the copy before handing it in until at times the disgruntled chief sub yelled "give me that bloody copy, son."

He was always running, always pushing, but all the same he could see a cadetship might be a long way off. Anyone who had a job held on to it and there were no vacancies.

Opportunity knocked when the old *Labor Daily* which had gone bust, rejuvenated itself as the *Daily News*. Tom heard there was a job going as an assistant in the police rounds section. Not as a journalist, but a helper to the roundsman. A sort of upmarket dogsbody. He applied and was hired.

The *Daily News*, run by the Labor Party, was a real sweat shop, short of money and staff. The offices were in a seedy part of town just off Oxford Street. His role was to answer the phones, take messages and ring up sources like the police and fire brigade and pass details on to the police roundsman.

The roundsman usually had other stories on politics or industrial relations to do as well and was under pressure. Tom pounded the phone and with drive, talent and enthusiasm created a journalist's role for himself.

Instead of just passing on details, Tom began typing the stories in finished form with two fingers and handing them to the roundsman. Soon when Tom mentioned a story the roundsman would say "type it up and let me see it."

Outside his normal task of ringing hospitals to check on the condition of people in the news, he'd ask what else was doing, establishing contacts, staying back late and coming up with all sorts of human interest stories on hole-in-the-heart babies, celebrities, unusual medical cases and the like.

He wrote and handed them in and lo - they appeared in print.

He bamboozled the *Daily News* staff to some extent because they came to look on him as a cadet reporter due to his keenness and professional output. Zeal, energy and smartness made the difference between success and being an also-ran.

ABOVE: Tom Jacobs, as he was known when famous as a Sydney newspaperman and radio celebrity. Had a certain star quality about him. (Later when he became a property developer, he changed his name to Tom Hayson, an Anglicised version of his Lebanese family name.)

ABOVE: A formal affair: The marriage of Tom Jacobs' parents Frederick Thomas Jacobs and Mary Lavina Jacobs (nee Nader), at St. Paul's Catholic Church, Moss Vale, in 1917. From left: Beth Alam, Victoria Mansour, best man Alex Alam, groom and bride, bridesmaid Ada Nader (bride's sister) and Mary Alam.

LEFT: Frederick Jacobs, Tom's father at 21.

ABOVE LEFT: Always musical, Tom at 13 blows a tune on a brass band's tenor horn at Cobbadah, a small bush hamlet near his home town of Barraba in northern NSW. His father and Uncle Paul, owner of the old jalopy, look on. Circa 1933.

ABOVE RIGHT: Tom at 19, a rising young reporter on Frank Packer's Daily Telegraph, a few months before WWII.

ABOVE: Tom at 10, playing the violin at Barraba while sister Pauline banjos on. Even as a lad, music would move him to tears.

ABOVE: The loving, hard-working parents of Tom Jacobs, first generation Australians, Lavina and Frederick Jacobs, pictured in 1965. Both knew racial discrimination. To overcome it in a predominately Anglo-Saxon society, Lavina encouraged her family to put their Lebanese heritage behind them.

LEFT: Joe Alam, a cousin of Tom Jacobs, sets out on his first day as a hawker after losing his job in the 1890's when miners at Wallsend in NSW downed tools and "refused to work with a dago." He later became a prominent businessman. Tom too had to resort to hawking to survive at one stage.

ABOVE: The first motor garage in Barraba in 1912, just before it became a general store owned by Tom's grandfather, old Tannous Jacob, who emigrated from Lebanon in 1886 and saved his pennies from hawking.

BELOW: Tom's parents took over the general store, losing it in the Depression. Behind on the banks of the Manilla River, young Tom dreamed of travel.

ABOVE: The site of the former Albury home of Lebanese migrants Kanin and Amelia Nader, Tom Jacobs' grandparents.

ABOVE: Hume Street in Albury where Tom's hawker grandparents lived after moving from the poor end of town down by the Murray which locals called Cowshit Flat.

RIGHT: The lovingly tended grave of Tom's grandparents in Albury.

PRAY FOR THE SOUL OF
KANIN NADER
DIED 5 JUNE 1915,
AMELIA NADER
DIED 15 JULY 1930

R·I·P

ABOVE: Handsome newsman Tom when he married Ngaire.

LEFT: Young lovers Ngarie de Nett, 22 and Tom Jacobs, 21, in 1942 shortly before their marrige.

ABOVE: The beautiful young Ngaire when Tom fell in love with her.

LEFT: Nursing sister Ngaire de Nett at the time of her marriage.

ABOVE: The Jacobs children, Ian, Rosemary and Paul in 1952.

RIGHT: Rosemary and one of her many champion dachshunds exhibited at shows.

Below: Proud father Tom with his boys before leaving on a long news assignment abroad.

It opened up a new world for him and he loved it. For the first time in his life he found fulfilment. Nobody gave a damn about the colour of his skin or what he looked like. And nobody name-called him or passed anything remotely like racist remarks.

All was directed at gathering the news and creating the best possible paper. Nothing else mattered except producing copy to deadline and printing the paper on time. Suddenly he had found an outlet for his creative energies.

Tom couldn't believe his luck when he heard Frank Packer's *Daily Telegraph* was looking for a cadet. He applied, showed the scrapbook of stories he'd written at the *Daily News* over the previous year, and they put him on as a second year cadet.

Tom was 19. It was mid-1939, just before the outbreak of World War 11 on September 3 of that year, a momentous time in history to become a newspaperman. Robert Gordon Menzies had just become Australia's Prime Minister.

He was hospital roundsman but with the paper suddenly short of staff as the war gathered pace, he was thrown into all types of assignments. Sink or swim. The *Telegraph* was a tightly-written, professionally edited newspaper and Tom honed his developing skills in this atmosphere.

He was a quick learner and some rough edges were smoothed out by the paper's experienced sub editors.

The legendary journalist Brian Penton was editor, insisting the reporters use short staccato sentences and active voice in their stories. Other outstanding journos were there, King Watson the news editor, Ray Walker of the Falstaffian figure as chief sub editor, Otto Beeby and Alan Green among the subs. David McNicoll would soon join as a war correspondent.

In this period Tom often pondered on his status as a member of the Fourth Estate, which he'd heard about and studied in the office library. Edmund Burke, the 18th century statesman, had given the press this standing after the three Estates of the Realm in Great Britain.

"Gee," Tom said proudly to his parents, "only the government, judges and the church are more important than journalism."

Colin Davis, who had moved on from running copy at *The Sun* and was now a reporter on the *Daily News*, later credited Tom with making a prophetic comment at this time.

He and Tom found themselves as rivals one day interviewing an executive at radio station 2CH on the 14th storey of a York Street city building. From the window Tom admired the bird's eye view of Darling Harbour railway goods yard, but the executive dismissed it as an eyesore.

"No sir, said Tom, "the main Harbour is just around the corner and Darling Harbour could be a showplace for Sydney one day." That was in 1940.

Just as Tom was beginning to make a name for himself as a good young reporter on the *Telegraph*, he suffered his worst moment, showing that the ruling passion of his life, journalism, could also be a fragile and ephemeral mistress.

On August 13, 1940, disaster struck the Australian Government, already racked by internal fighting as it tried to crank up its lagging industrial war effort. A plane crash in Canberra killed three Cabinet Ministers.

One was Sir Henry Gullet, Vice-President of the Executive Council and a distinguished former journalist who happened to have been a war correspondent for the *Daily Telegraph* in earlier days, a war historian, director of the Australian War Museum and a politician of illustrious standing. He also happened to be a friend of Frank Packer.

Covering some aspects of this major story, Tom found himself at Sydney's Central Station to report on Lady Gullett's departure by train to attend the funeral in Melbourne. The Melbourne Express had a record of always leaving on time, but this day it was 15 minutes late. Tom wrote the story, saying the train was late waiting for Lady Gullet to arrive.

When he turned up at the office on Friday afternoon after the story appeared that morning, the Chief of Staff said: "The big fella wants to see you."

Wondering why, Tom went to the managing director's office. A secretary ushered him into the commanding presence, saying: "Mr Jacobs to see you, Mr Packer."

Without looking up from the paperwork in front of him, Packer growled: "You're fired Jacobs. Now get out of here."

Stunned, Tom stammered a little as he asked: "W-what's this about, Mr Packer?"

"You know what it's about, Jacobs. You said the Melbourne Express was held up because Lady Gullett was late getting there. I'm informed she wasn't late and it wasn't her fault the train was late. I won't have false reports going in my paper. Now, get out of here and go and collect your money." The Boss had spoken.

Shaken, his shoulders drooping, he went to the Chief of Staff and told him what had happened. "The story is right," he said. "I saw her arrive late with my own eyes."

He told chief sub editor Ray Walker the same thing. Ray, a decent human being, said: "I don't know if I can do anything..."

There was nothing left but to walk slowly out, leaving behind the exciting, thrilling, hectic scene he dearly loved being part of every day.

He went home and told his parents the grim news. They looked ashen. Next day he looked in the jobs vacant columns of the *Sydney Morning Herald*. Nothing of interest there. He agonised over the weekend, wondering what to do now. Work on some small paper in the bush?

Late on the following Monday morning Tom answered the phone at home. The rasping voice of Packer was unmistakable. "That you Jacobs? What are you doing at home?"

"You fired me, Mr Packer."

"Well, you're hired again. Get in here and report for work."

Tom never got to the bottom of it and it was quickly forgotten with so many things moving along quickly in the newspaper office, where nothing was as stale as yesterday's news. But he heard that Ray Walker had taken up the cudgels for him after his story was checked and found to be right. He also heard that Lady Gullett was a friend of Mrs Packer and had complained to her about his report.

It shook his confidence and commitment for a while to think that a person's career could be ruined by a phoney complaint made behind the scenes. But unfortunately newspapers were like that, as they still are today, along with television - careers are often decided over a good lunch and an intense oak shiraz rather than on a person's ability. But Tom admired Packer for making the call himself and putting things right.

A cheeky new player was about to join that most exclusive of institutions, the newspaper proprietors' club.

Basically the Fairfax, Packer and Denison families had the Sydney newspaper game by the throat. They all published daily broadsheets. Ezra Norton's *Truth* was the infidel tabloid, but came out only weekly.

Ezra was the son of John Norton, a rogue politician and boozy but talented journalist, orator, editor, wife-beater and whoremonger who wrested control of *Truth* from the man who founded it in 1890.

Old John Norton, the father of yellow journalism in Australia, scuffled with opponents in the NSW Parliament, was embroiled in sensational defamation cases and as a fire-eating editor was known, bottle in hand, to bawl out hymns above the roar of the presses and blast off a few revolver shots in the news room when the mood called for it.

An enigma to the end, Norton disinherited his wife and son when he died in 1916, leaving his estate to his daughter and a niece. But Mrs Norton fought it in the courts and Parliament, enabling Ezra at 25 to own *Truth*, which also published *Sportsman*.

The paper continued to feature divorce and sex scandals, but it crusaded against injustice too and stood up for the battlers against authority and the establishment.

Ezra once told famous English journalist Hugh Cudlipp, boss of the London *Daily Mirror*, how old Johnny had indoctrinated him in the mysteries and responsibilities of fearless publishing.

While sitting with the boyish Ezra on the balcony of their Sydney city home in Pitt Street one day, old John observed the good burghers of Sydney town on their way to church. "Look at them in their Sunday best, the bloody hypocrites," said John.

"Never forget this, son, when you carry on my great work in *Truth*. Keep up its traditions without fear or favour. Then you'll be in the same position of trust as me, always able to pour a bucket of shit over the lot of them."

Tom, always on the lookout to better himself, applied for a job when he heard early in 1941 that Ezra Norton was planning to start an afternoon daily tabloid to build up his empire.

He was hired as a D Grade reporter - the lowest grading then for a qualified journalist, but a big lift in wages and standing from fourth year cadet status. By ambitiously moving around, he'd completed his four-year apprenticeship in two years.

Tom had recently seen the Hitchcock movie *Foreign Correspondent* in which Joel McCrea played an intrepid but laid-back reporter caught up in a nest of spies. He noted the hero's stereotyped dress, trench coat and wide brimmed hat.

Next thing he went out and bought a hat and trench coat that due to his short stature, almost touched the ground. At home he turned the collar up around his ears like McCrea, praying for rain so he could wear it quickly, hoping that by moving to the Norton paper he would have a better chance of becoming a foreign correspondent. Indeed, he set his heart on it.

It could not have been a worse time to start a newspaper. The war was looking grim for Britain in what were dark and desperate days, with the fortunes of the free world at their lowest point in history.

Hitler was rampaging through Europe with Mussolini's support as Britain braced itself for the Nazi bombing onslaught. Australian troops, after being savagely defeated in Greece and Crete, were locked into a fierce Western desert campaign.

The strictest censorship ever introduced had been clamped on the press and manpower controls made it difficult to recruit suitable staff. Most of the men were marking time until they signed enlistment papers.

Tom was called up for military service but was ruled out several times on medical grounds because of a severe skin disorder caused by active sebaceous neck glands. He desperately wanted to go to the war.

Materials were in short supply, particularly rolls of paper for printing the newspapers and merchant seamen risked their lives to bring the newsprint to Sydney. It was rationed and so was petrol, affecting newspaper delivery trucks. And the established newspapers, not about to make it easy for Norton to start up in opposition, tried to squeeze his newsprint supplies.

Then they persuaded the Federal Government to cancel his licence for the new paper, but after a hard fight he had it reissued.

Even the supply of cable service news was bedevilled by censorship and enemy action. Norton set up his own news service in London to get an edge on the big war news. If he had not already owned a printing press and premises for *Truth*, was tough and resilient and knew the ropes, it would have been mission impossible.

Gradually Norton lured key staff from the other newspapers and for four months while some worked out their resignation times Tom and the others did dummy runs of the new paper, going through the motions each day as if they were actually competing with their afternoon rival, *The Sun*. Tom was the police and hospital roundsman.

Finally on Monday May 12, 1941, the *Daily Mirror* was born, a difficult wartime baby entering a world of death, drama and disaster with great armies on the move. When it hit the streets, the first edition sold out within an hour, its bold front page informing readers of the Luftwaffe's worst night bombing raid on London so far.

The *Mirror* quickly proved itself to be a lusty brat, thrusting, assertive, competitive, finding immediate acceptance with Sydney readers. Within three weeks, the paper's flamboyant London and European editor F.E. (Eric) Baume achieved one of the greatest scoops of World War 11.

Baume got the tip from Lady Osford, widow of the Earl of Asquith, a former Prime Minister of Britain, while living it up at the Savoy. A shrewd mover and shaker, Baume had shifted his office into the Savoy where he entertained lavishly.

He was having an affair with Lady Margaret Stewart and had put her on staff. She introduced him to top level VIPs, including Lady Osford. Baume plied important military and establishment figures with French champagne, pretending to join them but drinking only lolly water while he sucked their brains.

Colourful stories came out of London about Eric, surrounded by important visitors as he paced up and down his Savoy suite smoking a cigar and dictating his stories as the bombs fell, describing the "glorious sights" of Nazi bombers falling out of the sky.

Early one morning in June, 1941, Lady Osford called Baume to her suite, also in the Savoy and said: "Winston's just left. The Nazis are going to invade Russia." Knowing the story had to be right coming from Churchill himself, he hastily added background material, cabled it and the *Mirror* boldly ran it front page.

Soundly scooped and unable to confirm it, other papers in the West could only quote the fledgling *Mirror's* report.

Three weeks later at 4 am on Sunday June 22, in spite of a non-aggression and friendship pact, German troops, tanks and planes attacked Russia - Hitler's first big mistake of the war.

That and other incisive stories of the war and the local scene gave the paper a sharp edge and fuelled a fierce circulation battle with *The Sun*. Tom mostly kept the *Mirror* in the front line on local news with murders, other crime, accidents, and hospital stories.

Conditions for newspapers were primitive compared to later. Those days were before mobile or digital phones and lap tops, before two-way radios and walkie-talkies, or even teleprinter machines. But car radios were tuned to the police network frequency. The only technical aid reporters had to file their stories back to the office was the standard old-style telephone. They needed to write shorthand and punch typewriters.

Reporters had to chase down stories and follow through to the end, getting out into the streets and interviewing people. The later lazy habit of "telephone journalism" when reporters sat on their backsides and merely rang up, was not tolerated.

In the news room Tom felt hot-blooded passion at work. Reporters were so keen they would argue and fight with one another to get a scoop even on workmates. Yet they helped colleagues when it came to a team effort.

The *Mirror* news room in the *Truth* building in Kippax Street, Surry Hills, was a cauldron, a mixture of razor sharp competitive keenness and co-operation where necessary - a daily co-operative effort on a scale that probably did not exist in any other commercial sphere in the world.

A few months after the world exclusive on Germany's invasion of Russia, the paper again showed its grasp of teamwork. Guarded cable reports indicated war was likely to erupt between the US and Japan, but nobody knew when or how.

In early December of 1941 Tom and other staff remained on duty even in the weekend. When Japan attacked Pearl Harbour on the morning of Sunday, December 7 - early Monday morning in Sydney - they were ready to rush the story into type and hit the streets early while Sydneysiders were still on their way to work.

The big war stories affecting Australia continued to make the *Mirror* headlines: Singapore fell, General MacArthur set up his south-west Pacific headquarters in Australia at the request of Prime Minister John Curtin, Japanese midget submarines caused havoc in Sydney Harbour and the cruiser HMAS Canberra was sunk in the Solomon Islands.

A tradition was growing in the paper to get the news first and worry about the circumstances later. Excuses for missing a story were not acceptable. If *The Sun* had a story that Tom didn't have from his rounds, the only result was a metaphorical kick and a tongue lashing.

The staff was small, putting pressure on the reporters to perform. Every day was a challenge. After finishing each day, Tom then hurled himself into the fray again next day as the pressure was on all over again. But he was so keen he could hardly wait to get to the office each morning.

Gathering and printing the news was a daily dog-eat-dog business. Competition was everything and getting the story first before the opposition was the most important thing in the world.

At the end of each day he was so churned up and excited he needed to unwind. He went to an unpretentious little knockabouts' cafe near Central Railway called the Hole in the Wall, a great social leveller. They called you "mate" and treated all types equally.

When asked "what are you having today mate?" Tom always had "the works" - pie, peas, potatoes and gravy, costing sixpence.

He then graduated to Harry's mobile Cafe de Wheels at Woolloomooloo when the original owner had it. Tom was so locked into the afternoon newspaper culture that he gave Harry a solid ear bashing every night on what was happening, talked to taxi drivers and anyone else who came along and then wandered around the city and Kings Cross for two or three hours soaking up the atmosphere before going home to bed.

But he was not into the pub culture, a nerve centre second in intensity only to the news room. Tom didn't drink or smoke, although he smoked later. Not that he was a wowser, but when confirmed in the Catholic Church at 14 he'd made a vow to the bishop never to drink because an uncle of his was an alcoholic and he didn't want to grow up like him.

He tried going to the pub and drinking ginger beer but it didn't work out. When his colleagues began talking aggressively and "monstering" one another while in the grip of the grape, he felt an odd man out and left. His dislike of pubs was heightened one night when someone spiked his soft drink with a gin mickey finn.

Tom's abstemiousness was a drawback in his police rounds work. The cops from the Criminal Investigation Branch drank like thirst-crazed miners after a long shift, and he sometimes missed stories because his rival Noel Bailey had boozed with the cops.

He dreaded it each morning when the first edition *Sun* came in, riffling open the pages to see if he'd been scooped before the news editor came dashing around to harangue him. But he gradually made up for this by being a terrier, gaining some valuable contacts at the top level.

Later the new Police Commissioner Colin John Delaney and CIB Chief Joe Ramus, of Italian background, came to trust him and gave him hot stories off the record. He could always go back to them because he never breached faith.

Although they could be ruthless when chasing the news, the early *Mirror* executives were all professionals and Tom got on well with them - chief sub editor Ian Smith, news editor Len Richards and editor Mark Gallard, also Fatty McGuinness who came in as editor when Gallard went to editor-in-chief.

Tom showed early flair by having an eye for the unusual with human interest stories. He was young, only 22, when he saw something special in the death of a Sydney Greek fisherman who'd been called up for military service in Greece. To avoid going back he just walked into the surf at Bondi and suicided.

Racism was strongly evident in the community then and normally nobody would have given a damn about a Greek ending it all. Lucky to have rated one paragraph. But Tom, through his own ethnic background, saw the human side of the Greek's turmoil and gave expression to his feelings.

He wrote a beautifully sensitive story in a dozen paragraphs headed "He sings no more to the wind" telling how the Greek sang songs when fishing and was reminded of his native Ithaca by the smell of iodine in the Sydney surf.

It touched people's emotions. They wrote in and telephoned, even a reporter from the opposition *Sun*, who rang Tom after taking the trouble of finding out the writer's name. Reporters didn't get bylines then because Norton thought they would be poached by another paper and offered more money. Two *Mirror* executives, including Ian Smith, congratulated him.

Smith dubbed him "More to Come" because he always typed "mtc" at the end of each story, hitting the phone and intending to add more until told in times of tight space to "stop writing this bloody stuff." Tom was also called Jake for Jacobs and Clement's Tonic because of his second Christian name of Clement.

Nearly everyone had a nickname, among them Germs, the Mexican Parrot, The Afghan and the Chinless Wonder. Baume would be called The Black Bastard.

Contemporaries among the reporters were George "The Stutterer" Richardson, a humorous wisecracking stereotype of a character who almost drank the pub dry every day, Hugh Mountjoy, Basil Sweeney, George Hawkes, Alan McClure and two sisters, Betty and Elizabeth Lambert.

The women were rugged types. Isabel Grace kept a bottle of whisky on her desk, taking regular libations, and most other women reporters displayed grog on their desks too, while the men coyly stowed it in their desk drawers.

It was wartime, staff were hard to get and nobody took much notice as long as they did their job.

One reporter, perpetually boozed, was called Zig Zag. Early one morning he zigged into the police rounds section which was open to everybody passing by because the toilets were situated just behind it, and said to Tom: "You know, I woke up last night to see a huge snake crawling over my ceiling.

"I keep a double-barrelled shotgun for such purposes. I reached for my gun and blew the snake right through the roof. It left a bit of a hole but I got him." And he zagged off. The story was true, at least as far as the ragged hole blasted in the ceiling was concerned.

Newspaper offices have always been vibrant places for affairs of the heart, and behind the professional facade of the *Mirror* there was action aplenty, not always of the *social* intercourse variety. Everyone knew what was going on but pretended not to see.

"The Stutterer" was a noted man of letters, French style. In the photographic section a comfortable casting couch rested in the centre of the large darkroom, where it was said many a negative girl was developed.

Photographers kept a scrapbook of pornographic content. Over at the *Daily Telegraph*, a favourite late-night trysting spot for romantic insomniacs was the files of the *Sydney Morning Herald* in the library, which were just the right height and where the centre spread in newspaper terms did not mean the main feature page.

Tom was not left forlorn in this palpably amorous atmosphere.

While waiting on after ringing in for a copytaker to become available, he used to chat to a switchgirl, a divorced blonde beauty. One thing led to another and Tom soon found there were other pleasures in life than reporting for work at 5.30 am every day.

But no matter how bleary-eyed he might be from the athletic pursuits of the night before, he always turned up on time, never tiring of the challenge, eagerly meeting new people and seeing life in the raw.

The murders were always written up as fascinating, never mundane, and among the people he came to know well in writing about the razor gang days were underworld queens Kate Leigh and Tilly Devine.

He also knew the Shakespeare-quoting Sydney eccentric Bea Miles who used to jump into taxis, police and press cars and refuse to get out. Sometimes when Tom needed to get back to the office and she refused to budge from the *Mirror* car, he did the only thing he knew would work.

He told his driver to pull into Central Police yard where some of the cops knew how to move her without using strongarm. A cop would sit in the back with her and say, with lustful emphasis: "Bea, I'm going to ---- you." A prudish Bea would call him a filthy beast and jump out, slamming the door amid coarse laughter.

Some of Tom's colleagues were highly strung and just as difficult to get on with as the people they chased for news. Photographers were strong and resourceful characters who worked in with reporters to steal pictures from inside homes or offices or take sneak shots on the run.

Irwin Luke was Tom's favourite whom he always tried to take on jobs. A former mechanic and racing car driver, Luke had a hotted-up Studebaker illegally fitted with a police siren which he sounded while driving in a blur to get to scenes before the cops.

But if some other lensman got under his neck on a job, he was likely to go ballistic. One morning he missed a planned picture after Tom, unable to locate him, took another photographer. Later, as Tom hammered out the story in the police rounds section, Luke confronted him but Tom was dismissive, telling him he'd turned up late for work.

Luke sailed into him with his fists and they fought for two or three minutes, with most of the staff standing around watching. Tom got the worst of it with a bleeding nose. Back to work! No executive spoke to them about it, regarding it in the scheme of things in getting the paper out as a minor event.

But one of the most intriguing characters Tom met and often bumped into was Ezra himself.

A quip off the old block, he was usually in drink and loved to tear strips off his executives, being alternately polite, insulting or cuttingly humorous. To keep them sharp he would ring and ask about some aspect he thought was missing from a story in the paper, such as the name of an accident victim, and if they didn't know he would give a free character reading. Some said Ezra could even make "Merry Christmas" sound menacing.

Sometimes he paraded his executives outside their offices and berated them just loudly enough for the staff in the general room to hear: "You're not an editor's bootlace, are you?" "No, Mr Norton..."

Or he held a "boning and gutting" session in the editor-in-chief's office, speaking deferentially to the most junior person present and calling him "Mr" while insulting the rest, referring to them scornfully by surname, often mispronouncing the names for extra effect.

He would ring the company accountant, a studious Englishman named Parrott, and say: "Get off your perch Parrott and come to my office."

On one such occasion Ezra was stripping his executives to the bone on what was wrong with the paper. Jack Finch, a fat jolly chap whom Ezra called "Beetroot Puss" because of his reddish face - another reporter was "Whisky Joe" - thought he would try to ease the tension a little on behalf of the assembled suffering group by acting as a court jester.

Every time Norton laid down a direction, Finch said amiably "she's apples, Mr Norton, she's apples" to indicate it was as good as done.

He said this several times and finally Ezra said "you may go, Flinch."

Jack just got to the door, pleased to be out of the firing line at last and leaving it to the others to get it in the neck when Norton called out engagingly, "oh Finch, do me a favour, will you?'

Jack bustled back to where Norton was seated, smiling warmly, rubbing his hands in anticipation. "Yes, Mr Norton?"

"Shove those apples in your arse!"

"Yes, Mr Norton."

There could be only one reply, because of Ezra's unpredictability.

One editor, Charlie Buttrose, father of Ita, later of women's magazine fame, made several complaints to Ezra one day ending with the fact that the paper was also short of sub-editors. Ezra said: "Is that so, Buttrose? Well, you give them a hand."

He was demoted on the spot from his exalted position and put on the subs' desk next day.

Ezra was a master of the instant insult. To show his clout to committeemen of the Australian Jockey Club, he used to run columns and columns of copy verbatim on inquiries by the AJC stewards, being a thoroughbred owner himself.

Dale Mummery, a young reporter and good shorthand man, was usually called in to write up these inquiries. One day he made an error by mishearing "laying a bet" for "paying a bet" and some of Ezra's acquaintances at the Randwick track had ribbed him on it.

A boning and gutting session was summoned.

Mummery, a polite private school boy, went to the editor-in-chief's office to face Ezra, flanked by various executives. After outlining the facts, Ezra looked at young Mummery for a second or two and said quietly: "Son, don't go out into Elizabeth Street - there are trams out there!"

I had a few encounters myself with Ezra as a young reporter on the Mirror. *As film critic, I used to fearlessly express an opinion which apparently upset the movie company advertisers and the news editor conveyed to me two or three times that Mr Norton wished me to be less critical of the films.*

Being young, brash and idealistic, I took no notice. One day the news editor rushed up to me in the news room and said: "quick, put your coat on and come in. Mr Norton wants to see you."

I went in. A full complement of ashen-faced executives was sitting stiffly on chairs, Mr Norton seated casually to one side.

"So you're the film critic?" he inquired in a soft, almost apologetic voice. "Have you been getting my messages.?"

"Yes, Mr Norton."

*"Oh you have, eh? Well, what's the po-**zish**-on." The word 'position' was drawn out as a form of emphasis.*

"Well, Mr Norton," I said, deciding quickly that attack was the best form of defence in this prickly situation, "I don't feel I can praise all these gimcrack shows. It would be dishonest and unfair to our readers. There are some very crook shows on at the moment and I couldn't in all conscience praise them to the sky when I don't think they deserve it."

*"So that's the po-**zish**-on is it?". Then, "very well Mr Perkins, you may go."*

I walked out, convinced attack was the best way to handle Ezra.

A few minutes later the news editor leaned over my desk and said quietly: "As of now, you're no longer the film critic."

The camaraderie that developed in the *Mirror* was largely due to the staff combining with a kind of herd instinct to protect itself from Ezra's rampages. Anyone who broke the unwritten rule and dobbed someone in was treated as an outcast.

Whenever he left his Hosking House city business office to visit the newsroom at the other end of town, a friendly phone call would be made to the newspaper and an executive would tell Tom and other staff members: "Look busy. Ezra's coming. Pick those papers up off the floor."

But Tom appreciated the air of independence that existed on the paper because of Ezra's attitude. Norton was afraid of nobody, would attack politicians or anybody at all to keep them honest in the public interest. He ran some campaigns based on personal preferences but mostly they supported the readers' interests.

Norton and his new fighting paper were both feared and courted by politicians and other power people like judges, even his fellow newspaper proprietors.

He had a fixation about Sydney's Taronga Park Zoo, believing animals should not be caged. Once when Tom had knocked off and was leaving the building, Ezra stopped him in the lift and said: "I want you to get over to the Zoo right away and write about those elephants being cooped up."

Tom returned to the newsroom and relayed Ezra's instructions to the news editor. But he was told: "Oh forget that. He's always on about it. Go home." He did, hoping to God he didn't bump into Ezra again quickly.

Stories of Ezra's personality traits circulated almost daily. One evening a patron who strolled a little too close to Ezra's table in Sydney's exclusive *Princes* restaurant was told: "Get your arse out of my soup."

But for all his withering ways, Norton was loyal to his staff and provided they did their job properly he'd back them to the hilt. Tom had a lot of respect for him but often said to himself: "Gee, he owns these two great newspapers but is always boozed."

Norton repeatedly ran campaigns against police commissioner W.J. McKay. If a murder was unsolved, Tom on police rounds would be told Ezra had instructed him to get on to it.

Every day the police would be reminded of the situation: "It's now 15 days since this crime and the police are still bumbling on..."

By taking a close personal interest he kept everybody on their toes. A sub-editor trying to excuse a mistake on "a moment of aberration" was sent a personal letter by Ezra: "If you suffer from blackouts, see the company doctor."

After the jarring phrase "cunt lunches" appeared on the front page of the paper one day instead of cut lunches, a post mortem went on for weeks.

Finally Ezra himself questioned the linotype operator responsible, getting right down to the nitty gritty of asking him if, when his fingers hit the keys to produce the type in hot metal, he had sex on his mind.

If an errant reporter or sub-editor owned up and told the truth rather than trying to finesse Ezra, he could be quite reasonable, although still likely to show his biting wit. He hated hedging.

Ezra Norton was the original hands-on proprietor whose small but zealous staff and harassed executives performed frantically under the gun. It was no joke that they called the paper the *Daily Miracle*.

One story that had a big influence on Tom Jacobs' life was The Boy in the Iron Lung.

Young Johnny McMahon suffered from infantile paralysis, later called polio, and came from the country to be admitted to the Royal Alexandra Hospital for Children. His lungs had to be monitored and treated so he could breathe, and to save his life he was placed in a large iron lung with only his head protruding.

As hospital roundsman, Tom wrote several stories about him but only from a distance, quoting spokesmen on his condition. To protect his delicate health, the press was kept out.

Then Tom was ordered to interview him and get a picture. So he took a photographer and walked boldly into the hospital ward, to be confronted by the junior sister in charge, Ngaire de Nett. He sweet-talked her, saying he would write a lovely story.

Reluctantly she agreed, Tom interviewed the seriously ill boy and they took an exclusive shot of him in the lung which appeared on the front page of the *Mirror* next day.

Matron Kircaldie was furious. She carpeted Ngaire for breaching the rules by letting a pressman in and threatened to dismiss her.

Ngaire rang Tom and told him she was in trouble and reproached him for printing her name. Tom rang the medical superintendent, apologised and took the blame.

That afternoon he fronted up at the hospital to apologise personally to Sister de Nett. To make up for it he invited her out to dinner that night.

In case he thought his charm was winning her over, she told him over dinner she'd agreed to go out only because he was the first man to spell her name correctly.

He asked her out again and they continued seeing each other. Ngaire was a pretty young woman with a fair Anglo-Saxon skin which Tom thought was a nice contrast against his olive complexion. He'd always wanted to marry someone who was fairer than himself and knew his mother wanted him to marry an Anglo-Saxon.

On the first date he didn't even try to kiss her but soon realised there was a mutual feeling between them. In those disciplined days the doors of the nurses' quarters were locked at 11 o'clock at night. Tom sneaked in before the curfew and stayed until the early hours.

They spent their time in the physiology lecture room making love. There was life among the rattling skeletons! Then Ngaire would let Tom out through a window to beat the system.

Tom was proud to introduce Ngaire to his mother, knowing she would approve of his distancing himself from their ethnic past in his choice of a girlfriend.

To please his mother Tom had told her he would prefer to marry an Anglo-Saxon rather than an Italian or Greek girl.

Tom didn't discuss his ethnicity with Ngaire but she happily described how her mother's parents had migrated from Scotland to New Zealand, coming out by sailing ship as a family of five. Her father, William Dennet, of English descent, was born an Australian in Tasmania and had met her mother, Margaret Drummond Christie, in New Zealand when he worked in Wellington as a builder. They were married there and had five childen, Ngaire being the youngest with her twin brother, Trevor.

Ngaire's parents had come to Sydney in 1920 when she was one year old. After moving to Brisbane for a while, they returned to Sydney where her father built the family's Federation home at Bellevue Hill in the eastern suburbs. Ngaire trained as a nurse at the Children's Hospital.

She proudly told Tom that her brother Trevor, attached to the RAF early in the war as a pilot, was one of the famous Few who had recently fought in the Battle of Britain, flying a Spitfire.

The relationship boosted Tom's confidence in himself. Here was a beautiful young woman with blonde hair, a milky white skin and as Anglo-Saxon as could possibly be, and yet she was attracted to him despite his "inferior" olive skin.

After a few months they planned to marry. But religion was a serious problem. Tom was a devout Catholic, Ngaire a staunch Presbyterian.

Her mother was adamant she should not marry in the Catholic Church. Indeed, her mother didn't think she should marry Tom at all because in her view journalists drank too much.

Tom's parents although strongly pro-Catholic, understood and were not too fussed by it. By now his father was Anglicised in almost everything except food. Too old for active war duty but wanting to do something for his country, Fred Jacobs had enlisted and joined an Army band, playing violin and double bass.

He was in Darwin just before the Japanese bombed it. Later he would join the RSL, enjoying a few beers with his mates and playing bowls. He even "looked Australian" and no longer mentioned Lebanon.

But religion then was something that stirred strong passions, and Tom was a keen churchgoer. On the side of Ngaire's family the union was not given any hope for future happiness because of the conflict. Her mother tried to persuade her to break off the relationship and declared the family would not attend the wedding.

Tom hoped Ngaire might relent at the last minute and marry in his church. He even took her to a priest for instruction but it made no difference. Ngaire and some of her relatives were so implacable that she told Tom she didn't want to see him any more and ended the relationship.

Thinking she'd been in love with him, he dropped his bundle. Life didn't seem worth living any longer. In every girl he passed, he saw Ngaire's face and figure.

He began ringing her at the hospital but she either hung up or left a message saying she was busy. One morning after six weeks she stayed on the phone and he asked what she was doing that night. To his surprise she said nothing and knowing she adored the dancing of Fred Astaire and Ginger Rogers, he asked her to a film of theirs that evening, saying he would take her straight home later.

She accepted and by the time they returned to the hospital the romance was reignited, the skeletons rattling once again this night.

In the end he compromised, agreeing to marry Ngaire outside his church in the Anglican faith, which was seen as middle ground. Oh well, he thought, she might have a change of heart *after* they married - a misjudgment that would cause much pain and heartache until finally he was able to accept the inevitable.

While this family drama was being played out, a Japanese submarine in one of the war's worst crimes, torpedoed and sank without warning the Australian hospital ship, Centaur, off Brisbane with the loss of 300 lives. In Europe, the RAF Dambusters blasted the Mohne and Eder dams in Germany's industrial heartland.

A month later, in June 1943, Tom and Ngaire married in St George's Church of England in Hurstville, Sydney. Tom's parents were there, so too were Ngaire's mother and a few of her relatives, if somewhat reluctantly.

Tom had just £28 in the bank.

The biggest police rounds story Tom ever covered for the *Mirror* was the Pyjama Girl murder. War news took second place to it except for the D-Day landing. It yielded a personal insight into Tom's past, too.

For years, ever since September 1, 1934, when a young woman's partially burned body clad in distinctive yellow and green pyjamas was found in a culvert near Albury, the case had proved the most baffling in Australian criminal history.

The mystery of the woman's identity was so bizarre it gripped the whole of Australia with morbid fascination. The police investigation did not cease for 10 years, extending to more than 80 countries before the killer was brought to justice. In that time speculation, rumour, theories and pseudo scientific sleuthing abounded while the body with severe head wounds reposed in a bath of formalin at Sydney University. The case had more twists and turns than any fictional thriller.

Tom was on hand early in 1944 when the breakthrough came in finally identifying the victim as former theatre usherette Linda Agostini. He was one of the few called to the office of police commissioner W.J. McKay who announced they had picked up Linda's husband, Antonio, and charged him with murder. In writing his stories, Tom was given inside help by his good friend and contact, Supt Joe Ramus, who briefed him off the record.

The case had a special meaning for Tom. It took him to Albury where his grandparents had lived and his mother grew up. And for the first time he learned how tough things had been for them.

For his news reports he pieced together a picture of life in Albury when the Pyjama girl mystery began in 1934. The Depression was still on, men tramped the roads seeking jobs or handouts, living alfresco under bridges or in rough shelters on the banks of the Murray.

On the area known as the Common there were humpies and tin lean-tos, hardly anyone among the townspeople owned cars or telephones and farm land was selling for about £7 an acre. A weatherboard house could be bought for £350.

Tom had followed the mystery from the time he was a kid of 14. Within weeks of the murder, after Pyjama Girl exhibits of photos, pyjamas, the towel and the sack found with her plus the bullet from her brain, police found 350 girls who had gone missing. This figure would eventually reach several thousand.

Missing Melbourne woman Mrs Linda Agostini was an early suspect victim but was ruled out by conflicting dental evidence. Her former dentist in Sydney said she had eight fillings but a government medical officer, who had examined the body initially, said the pyjama-clad girl had only six fillings. An inquest returned an open verdict on her death.

Inquiries were complicated by an amateur Sherlock Holmes, Sydney physician Dr T. Benbow, who was convinced the Pyjama Girl was Anna Philomena Morgan, an illegitimate daughter of a NSW woman, Mrs Jeanette Routledge. With his "scientific evidence" she fought a number of abortive court cases trying to prove it.

The final clue came when Commissioner McKay assigned fresh detectives who discovered on rechecking the dental records and lifting the preserved body from its formalin bath for inspection, that two porcelain fillings had fallen out and this had gone unnoticed by the government medical officer.

McKay called Antonio Agostini to his office. He'd known Agostini early in the war when the Italian worked at the swank Romanos restaurant as a waiter. Agostini confessed but claimed his hard-drinking wife had put a gun to his head and in a struggle it had gone off, killing her accidentally. And the head injuries? These he claimed happened when he fell while carrying her body downstairs.

After an extraordinary trial, he was found not guilty of murder but guilty of manslaughter and sentenced to six years, and later deported to Italy.

Tom's lasting memories from all the running around he did on the story had little to do with the case itself.

From his inquiries and observations in Albury he learned for the first time something of the poverty his grandparents faced and the struggle they obviously had. And he knew now instinctively why his mother had always wanted to put her ethnic past to one side and look to the future, trying to erase the memories of hardship and the racial taunts she was subjected to in her early life.

He learned how his mother had grown up and what she did and now he knew why she had steered him away from things Lebanese. Until then it had been a mystery to him.

For the first time he realised and appreciated the honesty, hard work and striving his forebears had demonstrated in their lives after they came to Cowshit Flat. The way they toiled without respite, asking no favours but sticking to their daily task, filled him with admiration. He could wish for nothing more than to earn that same respect and admiration in his own life.

From the pictures he formed he would from that time carry a spectre of his grandfather, Kanin Nader, a tiny stooped figure, pushing a heavy cart around Albury in order to survive. That would be part of Tom's consciousness, along with his ethnicity and religious faith. He marvelled that the gentle old man could have had the strength to do it.

But maybe, Tom mused, something good might have emerged from it. Maybe the strength of those genes had come through to him.

With the war over the *Mirror* became a bigger paper with more staff, but still not enough, and life revolved around a daily knock-down-drag-out circulation battle with the rival *Sun*, now a tabloid and owned not by Associated Newspapers but the Fairfax group.

A reporter was not only as good as his last story but the last edition - and there were five a day. In both newspaper offices each edition of the rival paper was rushed to the news desk and hastily scanned to see if anything had been missed. The competition was so fierce that if one side could knock a story in the opposition paper, they did so with glee - another reason for the need of accuracy.

Tom had made hospital rounds his own domain. Most hospitals then were fairly aloof and unhelpful to newspapers but he opened them up with his friendly, sincere approach, winning them over by writing constructive medical and human interest stories.

He was so successful it became part of journalistic folklore that he sometimes audaciously donned the doctors' white coat and stethoscope to get some of his bedside interviews. He never denied it but it wasn't true.

He won over the nursing staffs with flowers, chocolates and by keeping confidences. But another shrewd *Mirror* reporter, Tony White, was later known to don the white coat.

The larger-than-life Eric Baume was now with the *Mirror* in Sydney, having had his wings clipped by Ezra Norton in London. Ezra had repeatedly complained to Baume from afar during the war about his hair-raising expenses at the Savoy, but Baume ignored Norton's directions and blustered his way through.

He felt justifiably on firm ground, producing the goods, arguing that he was actually saving the company money. While Fleet Street papers were spending thousands of pounds keeping their war correspondents at battle fronts, Baume was slinging people in Fleet Street for copies of the correspondents' reports, obtaining valuable background information for peanuts and rewriting it.

But Ezra had the last say. Able to travel at war's end, he turned up secretly in London and headed for the Savoy. The story went that as Norton was about to enter the hotel, Baume swept imperiously out the front door, dapper in Savile Row pinstripe, spats, gloves and homburg, and settled comfortably into a chauffeured Rolls without spotting the bespectacled little man from Sydney.

Baume was quickly sent to Sydney, following what was said to be an interesting "boning and gutting" session.

Baume did little to increase harmony in the office. He rowed with everyone. But he was a terrific newspaperman, one of the most articulate men Tom had ever met. Colourful, egocentric, he defied most of what was expected of a senior newspaper executive.

Sometimes he would stand in the newsroom and boast of his London sexual exploits. "I used to ----'em as quickly as they could pull 'em from under me," he would brag.

At other times he would give sound advice to young reporters as he passed them on the fly in a corridor: "Keep up and widen your contacts, my boy. I'm a Jew, but I also don the masons' regalia and I go to the Catholic Church." Later he would become a star of radio and television.

One newcomer in the office whom Tom was glad to see was the knockabout comedian Barney Allen, who gave him his start at *The Sun*. Barney was now in charge of *Mirror* copyboys.

As the pressure and competition increased, Tom's enjoyment in his work lessened. Whereas it had all been part of a wonderful learning curve, he now felt some aspects to be distasteful.

He hated having to do "death knocks" when a family was hit by tragedy through an accident or murder, and being told: "Don't bother coming back to the office unless you've got the story and pictures." The executives were hard men and meant it.

In those cases he had to connive with a photographer to either take pictures on the sly if it was a difficult job, or once inside, steal them from a room when nobody was looking. When this happened he would feel embarrassed, return the photo later and try to explain it away.

Once when shot late to the scene after two ships collided under the Harbour Bridge, he was instructed by the news editor: "Don't come back unless you have eyewitness accounts." It was impossible to find any witnesses, so under the pressure of tight deadlines he did what some other reporters resorted to with their backs to the wall - he made it up, based on his own observations or whatever details he had.

In the style of the day, reporters had to be objective and could not comment personally as they do today. Tom sometimes got around the problem by picking a long street and using a mythical common name - quoting Bill Smith of Parramatta Road, Leichhardt, or Bill Green of Victoria Road, Ryde.

To get the facts out, without commenting, he also relied on quoting the usual geometry - reliable quarters, well-informed circles. And to protect his sources he learned to do this skilfully without getting anyone into trouble. He had to be careful, too, using this technique because the opposition, not having the story, would want to knock it.

Tom had a problem which does not afflict many modern journalists in that he had a conscience. If they were crooks, he would serve them up but if he felt something would harm someone unnecessarily, he would leave it out. He sometimes remonstrated with "The Stutterer" over his stories.

"Why didn't you leave that paragraph out, George," he might say, "imagine what this poor fellow felt like when he had to face his wife."

As if these matters were not enough to trouble a sensitive soul, the office logistics of getting his stories written were proving more difficult.

Although Ezra was generous with expenses on away jobs, he was incredibly mean in supplying office facilities. There were never enough chairs or typewriters. One reporter tackled the problem head on, chaining his chair to the desk with lock and key.

Tom was sometimes frightened to go to the toilet because when he came back, his chair would be gone. By the time he'd retrieved his chair or was quick enough to spot another one momentarily left unguarded, his typewriter would be missing.

No use ringing the copytakers to phone his "outside" copy from inside the office - a banned practice, anyway - because the typists were busy with other reporters already doing the same thing. All of this induced an atmosphere of creative tension, otherwise known as stress.

As for obtaining a rise, that was more elusive than finding a virgin in a Hong Kong massage parlour. The paper's front page columnist Murray Sayle summed it up one day when he remarked dryly: "I'm expected to have the wisdom of Solomon, the prose of Bacon, the wit of Danny Kaye and be paid only as a D grade."

But in this tough game Tom learned the sound qualities by which he could base his whole future life and career. He learned about discipline and the need to keep his nose clean and remain out of trouble, to recognise temptation and vice and resist them, becoming a Justice of the Peace like his father to help him walk a narrow line.

He saw how temptation could drag people down and he came to see life from all angles, knowing the weaknesses of many prominent people who were outwardly respectable but inwardly corrupt and dishonest.

The newspaper experience gave reign to Tom's natural curiosity, enabling him to ferret things out. A good reporter had to be a good ferret. By working hard he gained enormous satisfaction and knew how far he could push himself.

Newspapers also taught him the essence of accuracy, how to check and recheck everything and take nothing for granted, no matter who told him what. The facts were what mattered and no longer did he hold anyone in awe.

Newspapers had opened up the world at large to him, and as he watched the new chattering teleprinters he realised how quickly information could flow to and from the other side of the earth.

He saw how the essence of time was so important, how split seconds and attention to detail could make all the difference between success and failure.

Nothing was more thrilling, instructive or satisfying than to pick up a last minute story right on edition time and, as the presses were stilled with the whole newspaper operation and even the building itself appearing to wait expectantly on him, see his copy ripped out of the typewriter paragraph by paragraph for rapid editing and type setting.

A few minutes later he felt the presses rumbling underfoot and the walls vibrating slightly. Then this latest edition would lob on his desk still smelling of familiar wet ink, the creation of many like minds combining their efforts in ultra quick time. If anything else in the world was more exciting or personally rewarding than this, Tom did not know about it.

As he gained in experience and confidence, he learned to stand on equal footing with the Premier, Cabinet Ministers, police chiefs and other important people, even the Prime Minister.

It also gave him a sense of power, but he knew this must be used carefully. It helped him realise his own ability, potential and self worth and proved to him that he had a talent for creativity.

Above all, he felt equal with others in an environment where the only criterion was ability.

Tom knew he would always feel the newsprint in his veins.

But right now it was time to move on.

7

THE WORLD'S MOST
ADVENTUROUS BROADCASTER

THE call came out of the blue. Father Meany, founder and chairman of Sydney radio station 2SM, wanted Tom Jacobs to start and run an independent news service.

The time was 1946 just after the war, which had given commercial radio its greatest boost ever with advertisers turning to radio to sell their wartime products due to newsprint shortages.

Radio's golden days were just beginning. Independent production companies were springing up to churn out serials and plays, national networks were being formed and big Australian variety shows were replacing the foreign imports or American-influenced shows of earlier years.

Radio dominated Australia's daily life to an enormous degree as the main source of entertainment, laughter, news and information. Vaudeville was still strong, comedians like Jack Davey, Roy "Mo" Rene, Willie Fennell and George Wallace were kings and serials such as *Mrs 'Obbs, Blue Hills* and *Dad and Dave* all the go. Grace Gibson Productions had *Dr Paul* and AWA Productions *When a Girl Marries.*

Among the top-rating suspense shows were *Night Beat, Dick Tracy* and *Larry Kent.* Nearly 70 per cent of listeners sat around their sets on Sunday nights with ears glued to great dramas presented by Lux Radio and Caltex Theatres, performed by young Australians like June Salter, Gwen Plumb, Queenie Ashton, Alistair Duncan and Leonard Teale.

The star system made radio personalities the big new celebrities, some rivalling even movie stars.

One of the biggest changes was in news and information. An isolated Australia had heard voice reports from its own wartime correspondents like Chester Wilmot for the first time, giving background and comment to the straight radio news bulletins. On-the-spot interviews and current affairs were just around the corner. But television was still 10 years off.

Among the first to air pre-recorded interviews with witnesses to big news events was the 2GB Macquarie Network in 1946. In that year the ABC produced its own independent news, and Sydney stations 2GB, 2UE and 2UW also formed their own news services.

That background prompted the Catholic station, 2SM, to approach Jacobs. He took the job as news editor of the station. To help organise a news service, he hired his young police rounds assistant at the *Mirror*, Ted Simmons. Tom's salary rose from £8 a week to £11 and 10 shillings and he thought he was rich.

Only 26, he felt radio would give him more freedom of expression and a better outlet for his creative urges than the ruthless daily cut and thrust of afternoon newspapers, also it would be less intrusive into people's lives.

He thought he could be a personality in his own right whereas in newspapers without bylines you could work your guts out and nobody outside the organisation noticed. Your best was often not good enough due to time constraints. Many newspapermen died early or became alcoholics because of the tension. But he still intended to be a journalist first, out to beat the other man to the story.

He and Ngaire lived in a flat at Bondi, life was fairly simple and they didn't expect a lot in creature comforts.

Calling out "rabbit-oh," a bushie came around selling cleaned rabbits once a week, others sold clothes door to door and the iceman came with big ice blocks which most people wrapped in newspapers to last longer in their ice chests. The big outing was once a week to the movies. Life was family oriented, although Ngaire's family were only just talking freely to her again after the shock of her marrying a Catholic three years earlier.

To produce his daily news bulletins, Tom was mainly a one-man band.

He'd take what he needed from the morning newspapers, cut and paste it up·or rewrite it to sound different and hand it to the news reader. He also listened to other radio bulletins to pinch what he needed, pounding the phone to get the latest information from police and other sources.

He installed a radio system tuned to the official police network and although technically illegal, it enabled him to listen in and pick up quickly on any robbery or police activity, giving a lead on breaking stories.

He hardly began the service when the news reader had a coughing fit early one morning and frantically motioned to him through the on-air studio glass partition. Tom ran in and the announcer, unable to continue, signalled him to take over. So he picked up the bulletin he'd prepared and began reading. It was a shocker as he stumbled over words. Listeners wrote or phoned asking if this bloke came from the bush?

But from the moment he sat before the microphone he liked it. Why write it for someone else to read? He secretly took voice lessons from former ABC chief announcer Bryson Taylor who thought he had a good baritone voice but was delivering it wrongly.

Taylor taught him to speak from the diaphragm instead of the throat, knocked off the rough Ockerish edges and the "er's" and "ah's" and after practising in private Tom was raring to go.

After filling in for the duty man one day, he soon became the regular daily news reader, dynamically reading his own copy. The first time he came off air after being rostered on as the official reader, he had the overwhelming feeling he'd been talking to the world.

The station offered him an announcer's job, but he declined, not wishing to become just a talking head. Indeed, he wanted to *make* the news as well as write it. No use sitting in the office letting others do it.

To show his innovative talent for being first with the news, he arranged for a Swiss migrant friend, Helimut Hendon, to stand by with his three wheeler Hamil car. On the back over the two wheels Tom tied down a heavy big 33 1/3 rpm recording disc working off batteries, the forerunner of wire and tape recorders. The full equipment was too heavy for one person to lift. When a call came over the police radio saying fire, accident, shooting or suicide, Tom would phone Helimut to say "on your way," and by about the time he reached the front of the radio station in Carrington Street, City, Helimut would speed up in his three-wheeler.

With Tom clinging fearfully to the back of the vehicle, Helimut drove to the scene like a madman, often arriving before the cops or ambulancemen.

Tom interviewed every eyewitness in sight, did his own description and comments standing alongside the strange looking vehicle where he plugged in the mike, and hurtled back to the studio. Confounding the technicians who said it couldn't be done, he played back the disc on a kind of big turntable or gramophone to produce his recording, editing as he went, usually changing the diamond needle to improve the sound, which wasn't excellent but clear enough to broadcast for up to 15 minutes.

While he was doing this the announcer would be whipping up interest: "Tom Jacobs will be on air in a moment to bring you a dramatic eyewitness account of this incident..." A few minutes later Tom's report was first to reach the public, even before the *Mirror* hit the streets.

He was the first roving reporter in radio, pioneering on-the-spot broadcasts in Australia, often with a time lag of only 15 or 20 minutes - quicker than television was doing it 50 years later. Previously radio eyewitnesses had to come to the studio. At other times he brought immediacy to radio by telephoning someone near or at a news happening and putting his own voice report to air right away.

Helimut, an aspiring actor, could hardly speak English but he knew how to make a quid, advising Tom to "get into business." He persuaded Tom to put up half the money to buy a dozen surplus Army huts for £5 each, reselling them for £10. It proved money could be made but Tom was too interested in his radio career at the time to think much of it.

A first-up interview with Father Dunlea, founder of the newly-formed Alcoholics Anonymous, came across so sincerely that drunks rang teetotaller Tom in the middle of the night asking "how did *you* get off the grog, mate?"

Then, lugging his heavy new wire recorder, he came up with another first, an actuality broadcast from atop the Harbour Bridge. It doesn't sound exciting today but it was different then and also hard to organise, insuring himself out of his own pocket before being allowed to clamber to the top of the arch. To make matters worse it was a windy day and when he reached the top it was almost at gale force, causing him to hang on with one hand while holding the mike in the other.

He described the scene all around the Harbour and to the Blue Mountains so vividly that he made it come alive for listeners. Hundreds wrote in and phoned saying they could hear the wind howling and felt they were on the bridge with him. Give us more, they said. It stamped him as a natural broadcaster who could describe anything and make it interesting. His ability to articulate and ad lib came from his newspaper background.

When a small fleet of yachts sailed out of Sydney for Hobart on Boxing Day 1945 to celebrate the end of World War 11, it was just a humble competition between friends including the Australian Earl family and English ocean racing enthusiast Captain John Illingworth in *Rani*. It probably would have remained a leisurely family cruise if half the yachts had not become "lost" for weeks after a southerly gale battered them.

The drama made the front pages and a classic was born. It also gave Tom Jacobs an idea for the next year's race, although 2SM's general manager said it couldn't be done, forget it. Bullshit, Tom told himself.

None of the yachts in the first race had carried radio equipment. Before the second race in 1946 Tom approached the Cruising Yacht Club organisers and offered to set up a communications system combining Morse code and voice reports through tiny two-way radios to pinpoint the yachts' positions. He co-ordinated those reports back at 2SM after they were picked up by Sydney's South Head signals station.

The technology was crude and restricted by distance and weather conditions but it worked. At certain times the few yachts that had equipment would pass on their positions and sightings of other yachts and when these finally reached Tom, he would update a big map in the studio.

Apart from being first on air with the news, Tom officially fed this information to the rest of the Australian media, a service he provided for the next decade or so. It was the first yacht race communications system in the world and publicity helped make the race an annual household affair, attracting more than 3,000 blue water sailors from around the world and a fleet worth almost $100 million in its 50th year.

As he sat in the studio nearly all day and night while the race was on, straining to hear faint voices, he thought he'd have a little joke on one of the numerous journalists who popped into the studio for details.

He simulated an SOS voice report spelling disaster for the yacht race favourite and the *Daily Telegraph's* Mike Ramsden, after scribbling furiously, rushed to the phone. Only then did Tom stop him. After that Ramsden always greeted him with "you bastard!"

To improve his system Tom thought he'd better get some technical experience. So after *Kurrewa 11* finished the next Sydney to Hobart race, Tom flew to Hobart to board the ketch as it sailed on to Auckland to take part in the first Trans-Tasman race back to Sydney. He'd never even been in a row boat before.

The crew was amused to learn that Tom had brought along pyjamas, green ones at that. The sailing master told him he'd have to take his four-hour turn strapped to the helm. No worries!

But they filled him up with fruit cake, one of the worst things for anyone who suffers from sea sickness. And as the Antarctic weather pattern known as The Roaring Forties hit, the boat pitched and tossed in the wind and heavy swell. Tom turned the colour of his unworn pyjamas and the fruit cake went overboard with a muffled scream.

Sleep was impossible, not only because of his uncomfortable fitted-out wet weather gear and sea boots but his bunk tilted at nearly 160 degrees, moving violently up and down as the ketch sailed off the back of one wave and into space and way down on the other side before crunching to a stop with a stomach-wrenching crash. Tired and hungry he actually looked forward to going up on deck, although water repeatedly crashed over it, because the air below was putrid with every ventilation point closed to stop water from entering the main cabin.

The next problem was how long before he relieved himself? - a tricky thing for a seasick man in heavy seas.

Then a violent storm struck, forcing them to batten down with furled sails and the big ketch was tossed about like a small speed boat. For the next 12 hours he was either harnessed to the rail up on deck or locked in the tiny galley after the door jammed shut.

As the wind screamed through the rigging and the hull creaked in protest, Tom prayed as never before. When the storm blew itself out the yacht was almost 100 miles off course. A ribald cheer went up as Tom finally pointed Percy at the porpoises after several days. His pyjamas had turned mildew and were ceremoniously thrown overboard.

Tom flew back to Sydney from Auckland and quickly made further improvements to the radio system to cover a longer ocean distance for the Trans-Tasman race a few days later, enabling him to track *Kurrewa 11* throughout. Later, after talks with the Cruising Yacht Club, a mother radio vessel with engines became a permanent part of future Sydney-Hobart races and the system which Tom introduced became near perfect.

It showed that Jacobs was the type who would tackle anything. The more challenging, especially if it hadn't been done before, the better he liked it. But he always knew what he was doing.

Always impulsive to get things done quickly, he decided to buy a car.

But first he asked his friend, Colin Davis, to teach him to drive. In his old Dodge sports Colin gave him about an hour's driving lesson at Mrs Macquarie's Chair in the city, then down he went to the registry office in Woolloomooloo to get his licence.

Somehow he passed the practical test but when they mentioned questions, Tom said "what questions?" He didn't know the rules and they wrote "failed" across his permit. He made such an indignant fuss about them defacing his permit that they rubbed it off. Then after another hour swotting the rules, he went back and got his licence.

Buying an early edition of the *Herald* one Friday night at midnight he spotted an ad for a 1927 flap-top Studebaker coupe at Drummoyne for £20 or near offer. Cars were hard to come by at the time, he could afford only £15 but couldn't wait to get his hands on a form of transport.

Incredibly, to beat others to it he was on the doorstep at 3.30am with his mechanically-minded brother-in-law, Jack Saldern, to check it over. The owner came out in his dressing gown, grumbling and calling out "who's that?" through the door. When Tom said he was there to buy the car, the man's wife was heard to say from inside: "They've got to be so desperate coming here at this hour, why don't you just give 'em the bloody thing?"

It was a bit of a bomb, although the engine sounded all right. The owner mentioned one problem, the wheels were seized to the axles and could not be removed. It also had a sudden death clutch and leap frogged on takeoff.

After some glib talking Tom bought it for £10. Jack managed to drive the bucking beauty out of the yard in the dark without cleaning up the fence, tinkered with it at home and got it working reasonably well.

Proudly taking Ngaire for a spin, Tom was crossing over George Street at the Sydney Town Hall early one evening and as he let out the clutch, the Studebaker bucked asthmatically into motion. The sergeant directing traffic jumped theatrically out of the way and called out in Hollywood Lone Ranger style, "hi ho Silver!"

Another time while he drove Ngaire down the steep winding Bulli Pass to Wollongong, an even older jalopy went past and the driver, with kids aboard, shouted that his brakes had failed. Tom speeded up and got in front, letting the runaway car nudge him behind, braking and bringing it to a halt. His enthusiasm knew no bounds.

By this time Tom had passed a private, all-important milestone in his life. His first of three children had been born - and his worst fears allayed.

He would never forget the moment Ngaire was rushed to the Royal Hospital for Women at Paddington to give birth to their first child. He had not expressed his fears to her but as he hailed a taxi to the hospital he said to himself: "Pray God, he or she is not dark."

He told himself that some Lebanese were quite dark and with his olive skin he didn't want his children to suffer the same way he had. When first glimpsing the baby, a boy, his eyes moistened and he offered a silent prayer of relief - the innocent newborn looked the same as any ordinary Anglo-Saxon child.

"That's wonderful," he said to Ngaire, not explaining the real reason for his joy. Tom was still at the *Mirror* and named the baby Ian after his old newspaper mentor Ian Smith. He went through the same churning emotions and overwhelming relief soon after joining 2SM when his next born arrived, Paul, and later Rosemary.

He still didn't tell Ngaire his innermost thoughts but after Ian was born he felt "well, here's a Lebanese who is good enough to marry into an Anglo-Saxon family. The baby isn't pure Anglo-Saxon but a true Australian, a union of two cultures and a forerunner of the Australian of the future coming from different races and cultures."

It was rather forward thinking for the time, just after the war, but his perception as a journalist told him how the future pattern would develop, that with so much land here and so many displaced persons in war-ravaged Europe, Australia would soon have an explosion of immigration.

By pre-wedding agreement, the children were to be christened in both the Church of England and the Catholic Church. That was a sacrifice by Ngaire because of the attitude of her mother and family, and a sacrifice too by Tom, who had committed a sin in the eyes of his church because he had married outside it. But only Ian would be christened in both churches.

Tom would realise later he erred in his attitude by clinging to the false hope that Ngaire would change her faith to co-incide with his, and would one day remarry him in the Catholic faith. Also, he changed their original understanding and insisted the children be educated in Catholic schools. Being male, he tried to assert his dominance.

LEFT: Tom Jacobs talks eccentric philanthropist Sir Edward Hallstrom into a contra deal sponsoring him as the world's first roving news reporter.

BELOW: At the 2SM mike presenting some of Australia's finest classical music programmes, such as "Masters of Music."

ABOVE: Interviewing famous London fight promoter Jack Solomons as one of the world celebrities for his programmes broadcast around Australia.

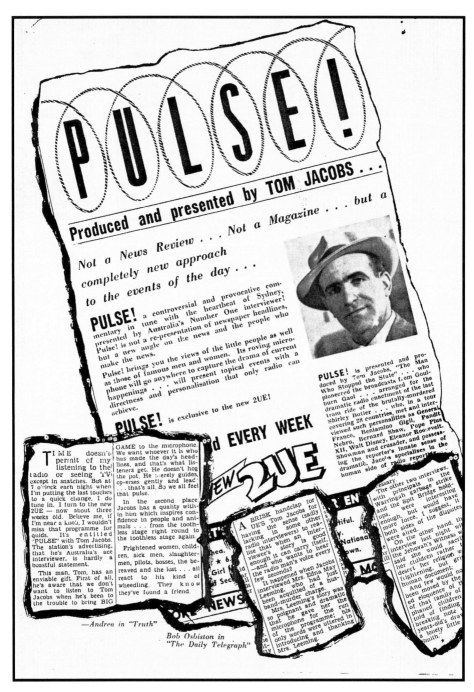

ABOVE: Tom Jacobs, the leading broadcaster of his day in Australia, made headlines around the world with some of his innovative news and documentary programmes. He was ahead of his time in on-the-spot news and actuality broadcasting. At 2UE, apart from topical programmes like *Pulse*, his job was to get out early and present the news.

ABOVE: At the Savoy with Walt Disney, one of hundreds of celebrities on his *World Today show.* Disney inspired Jacobs, telling him; "Fashion your dream and make it come true."

BELOW: Another first, broadcasting from the top of Sydney Harbour Bridge in the late 1940's on a windy day.

ABOVE: A proud Tom and Ngaire look on with Lady Joy Taylor and Sir Charles Kingsford-Smith's widow (dark glasses) at the historic opening of Tom's first big property development - as a memorial to *Smithy*.

LEFT: Greeting old friend Maggie Thatcher at Darling Harbour.

Below: Owning *Boomerang*.

TOP LEFT: Architect Bob Perry, co-designer of Darling Harbour's Harbourside.

TOP CENTRE: The forgotten man of Darling Harbour, American architect Professor Mort Hoppenfeld.

TOP RIGHT: Co-designer of Harbourside, architect Bob Blackmore.

LEFT: Tom Hayson, "Mr Darling Harbour" himself.

ABOVE: The Girl in the Red Bikini (well, pink dress here), with husband Ian and Tom and Ngaire at the Haysons' *Golden Gate* opening.

ABOVE: Pushing ahead with his dream for Darling Harbour, Tom Hayson arranged for this civic reception for Baltimore's Inner Harbour chief executive Martin Millspaugh and wife Meredith (right) with Sydney's Lord and Lady Mayoress, Doug Sutherland and Patricia Feodusio.

ABOVE: Tom Hayson and Darling Harbour (as it was).

RIGHT: The edge of a barren Darling Harbour before Tom Hayson persuaded the Wran Government in NSW to do something radical.

ABOVE: The two minds behind Darling Harbour, Tom Hayson and James Rouse, looking down from the Hayson office.

LEFT: Darling Harbour movers and shakers, construction chief Bob Penecost, left and Minister in charge, Laurie Brereton.

RIGHT: The floating Aquashell stage, one of many "firsts" by Tom Hayson to boost Darling Harbour.

BELOW: Tom and Jerry - Gleeson, that is, the powerful public servant who got behind Darling Harbour.

ABOVE: Charismatic Premier Neville Wran - gave the green light to Darling Harbour against a firestorm of opposition.

Ngaire never personally made an issue of religion as long as she retained hers and she allowed the children to go to Catholic schools, although harbouring resentment over it. That would remain a bone of contention between them for some years until Tom came to the conclusion that it was wrong of him to try to have his way.

Eventually he was able to take a worldly, ecumenical view, believing that in a mixed marriage it was best for one partner to give in completely to the other, unless one walked away in the beginning.

When he accepted that in the long term it was unimportant and didn't really matter anyway, the new understanding between them tended if anything to strengthen their relationship and have the effect of making the children more ecumenical. Religious tolerance, Tom decided, should be the same as ethnic tolerance.

Above all, Ngaire never raised any question on Tom's ethnicity, accepting him for what he was. And secretly he felt thankful for her attitude and support.

In the circumstances he reasoned there was no point in going to church.

He regretted no longer going to confession or Holy Communion, but believed he was a better person for it because he was able to stand on his own without the church to help him.

Being his own priest he often said short prayers during the day when he thought he'd sinned, even in having carnal thoughts about a pretty girl walking by - a temptation he had in common with every other man on two legs.

But if troubled by a personal problem, he would sometimes pull over in his car when passing a church, even a Protestant church, go inside and sit for a few minutes to make his peace with God. If he went to a Catholic church, perhaps to a funeral, he felt a pang in not being able to take communion because he'd been brought up to believe in it.

But generally he kept his resolve in deciding not to go to church in order to be true to himself and to Ngaire.

Inspired by Wendell Wilkie, who challenged Franklin D. Roosevelt for the Presidency and offered to send an American journalist around the world to promote his concept of One World, Tom decided it was time to realise his childhood dream to travel the world.

He was also motivated to do something exceptional by the deeds of the great American broadcaster Edward R. Murrow, who roamed the burning streets of wartime London describing The Blitz to the world, his booming voice beginning each broadcast with "This is London."

Murrow's voice alone announced the D-Day landing. He and American journalist-producer Fred Friendly after the war had set the standard by which quality news programs would be measured.

But how would Tom do this and who would pay for it?

He was friendly with Edward Hallstrom, already wealthy from selling his early Silent Knight refrigerators and an eccentric animal lover who ran Sydney's Taronga Park Zoo. Hallstrom's office chair was topped by a stuffed lion's head, and when he drove across the Harbour Bridge a chimp reached out and paid the toll.

"I've got this idea for a trip around the world," Tom said to him one day, "and it would be wonderful for Silent Knight refrigerators if you paid my expenses. You'd sell a lot of them..." After chewing it over Hallstrom (later Sir Edward) agreed to sponsor him.

Next stop, Qantas. Chairman Hudson Fysh (later knighted), tried to fob him off for an appointment. But he persisted through the public relations man and chatted up Fysh's female secretary. Fysh was sceptical of the idea: "What have you got to offer in return?"

A top salesman even then, Jacobs said: "I'm going to interview famous people of destiny around the world and send the interviews back as I travel. Qantas will get all the benefits of this..."

That was 1949, when Qantas flew only the Kangaroo route to London. To get to Europe and America Tom needed the co-operation of the then British Empire Airways and British Overseas Airways Corporation. Then he said he needed to get to cities not covered by those airlines. Hudson Fysh was a bit irritated: "I've arranged BOAC and BEA, now you want me to fix it with SAS, KLM and Lufthansa. Where's this going to end?"

The 2SM management, although doubtful, went along with it, but then sold the programmes to an unprecedented 70 stations around Australia and made money out of it. Lugging a wire recorder weighing more than a big Underwood typewriter, Jacobs would put together 80 shows called *The World Today*, the first journalist to go around the world editing, packaging and sending his discs back for airing as he went.

It was the first big media contra deal in an era long before the jetset days when Australians were just emerging from isolation and insularity and people were hungry for travel and international knowledge. The Lockheed Constellation had come in only a year before and now took a miraculous four days flying the long hop to London, replacing the old flying boats which had taken up to 14 days and as many as 43 stops on the way.

Jacobs would be away six months. When he returned he would be a celebrity.

Working seven days a week he interviewed a bewildering array of famous people and world figures in England, all over Europe including the Scandinavian countries, the US and Canada, people like Pandit Nehru in India, the Pope, King Farouk in Egypt, Winston Churchill, Clement Atlee, Sir Stafford Cripps, Sir Alexander Flemming, Norman Hartnell, Herbert Hoover, Beniamino Gigli, dictators General Franco in Spain and Dr Salazar in Portugal as well as movie stars such as Bing Crosby and his wife Dixie Lee. Wherever he sniffed a good human interest story like the famous Dionne Quintuplets, Blue Baby surgeon Dr Blalock or Mrs Eleanor Roosevelt, he interviewed them.

Jacobs had a cheekiness about him but also a sincerity enabling him to ask direct and penetrating questions that got people talking and drew them out. In New York he asked conductor Andre Kostelanetz about his divorce from famous soprano Lili Pons. After Franco kept him waiting in a Basque city for three days, he asked the old dictator about the need for democracy without being thrown out.

Over afternoon tea he found Richard Rogers a nervous man with such an inferiority complex that he could hardly speak. Rogers and Oscar Hammerstein created their famous *South Pacific* and other music while living on opposite sides of the US and writing "Dear Mr" letters to each other. After Hammerstein posted off the lyrics, Rogers sat down at the piano and wrote the music. Rogers urged Tom to come and live in America and offered to write the music for an Australian national anthem, an offer Tom regretted not taking up before the renowned composer died.

In Paris Jacobs got a gem of an interview with General de Gaulle, persuading the aloof old president, speaking in English, to relax and open up on his wartime experiences and days with the Free French.

Then, right at the end, his wire recorder suddenly malfunctioned and broken wire poured out everywhere. An embarrassing disaster. He spent the next six hours in an adjoining office in the Elysee Palace trying to rewind nearly a mile of wire. But the interview was lost.

Tom put his head in his hands and wept. He did the fastest talking of his life to see de Gaulle again, this time for only 10 minutes. Repeat interviews are never as good and he would always regret it.

The great playwright George Bernard Shaw, white beard flowing, gave this advice to young people from his home just outside London: "Don't aspire to be great because you will never have a happy life. Marry the baker, butcher or candlestick maker. Then you can enjoy great music and books. But don't aspire to greatness yourself because from that moment your life will be hell, lived in a narrow channel. If you put yourself on a pedestal, there is only one way to go - down."

Prolific writer J.B. Priestley was philosophical in his apartment near Piccadilly: "You got here in four days. In the future you'll get here in an hour and go around the world on an express pass. Who will want war when we're so close together? By then other living things will be discovered in the universe and we'll have to prepare for that. We'll have to band together as one race. There won't be black, white or brindle. Just one nation. It will happen."

But it was Walt Disney who inspired him. Still in his 30s, Disney was a dreamer and visionary who spoke of how he could change the world through entertainment. They talked heart to heart, finding common ground.

Disney said to him: "Most people can dream but don't have the ability to make it come true. You have it in your demeanour to achieve. You can do it. Fashion your dream and make it come true."

From that point the maxim "fashion your dream and make it come true" would always adorn Tom's office wall. However, he added the rider "but you have to work at it."

Yehudi Menuhin said some harsh things about his Jewish countrymen in Israel, Trevor Howard turned up plastered and poured himself a few noggins while recording and the only person who didn't front for an arranged interview was singer Ethel Merman who was rude about it when Tom rang her. The only other person whom he would find as rude was evangelist Billy Graham, warm and pleasant while recording but cold and obnoxious afterwards. Regarding him as a phoney, Tom decided never to mention his name again after that broadcast.

He wrote articles on his travels too for Australian magazines and newspapers, ranging from the rich cultural diversity of India to the dazzling "White Way" of New York's theatreland.

Back in Sydney people stopped him in the street or spoke to him in trains about his shows. He felt a bit humble after his brush with the great and powerful, and uncomfortable with his new star status at home. Were people acknowledging him for his achievements, or just being chatty?

His trip had given him a lust for travel. He'd loved looking at other races, especially those of mixed origin, watching faces in the street trying to imagine their character and background.

For the first time in his life he had mixed with people of many different nationalities and observed how proud they were of their ethnic backgrounds. That was an eye opener. In the 40-odd countries visited, he was recognised as an Australian, with Australian values, speech and looks. The swarthy colour of his skin was never raised, only his Australianness.

He had been thrilled on returning home to receive a letter from a priest he interviewed at an orphanage in Osaka where the Japanese had banished children deserted by their Australian servicemen fathers in the occupation forces. The Japanese didn't want the spectre of white children with oriental eyes in their community. The priest, who saw Tom on to the plane when he left, wrote to him: "I can still see you at the top of the gangway. I saw the map of Australia carved on your face."

Tom wept. For the first time he realised he was indeed Australian.

It seemed that only in his own country was he regarded by many as some kind of foreigner. Ever since childhood the hurt and confusion had made him want to achieve to overcome his feelings. Now he was being seen as an achiever and he would need to come to grips with it.

But he still felt confused over his ethnicity. All he wanted was to be known and accepted as a good Australian in his own country.

At that time 2SM had some of the best voices in radio, among them John Dunne, John Sherwood, Tommy Jay, Robert Ainsley and Dom Harnett.

Reg Grundy, who would later become mega wealthy through his TV game shows, was then a struggling sports director at 2SM and Garry O'Callaghan a junior who doubled as a voluntary lift driver.

But it was Tom Jacobs who, with his mellifluent tones and sincere delivery, became known as the golden voice of radio - God's gift to the human ear as one over-zealous fan called him.

He became the station's program director and graduated to his own shows. In between producing shows of a distinctive nature, he took every trip abroad that came along, anything that took him to foreign parts like airline inaugural flights. Some of his colleagues became jealous and moaned about him getting all the trips but if he didn't organise them, sponsors asked for him anyway because he delivered the goods.

When in front of the microphone he was oblivious of the surroundings and concentrated entirely on his listeners, often closing his eyes to "see" his audience and project the right feeling. After the station closed at 11 pm with Peter McCormack singing "When you come to the end of a perfect day," others would go home but he often sat in the lifeless studio, dreaming a little of the thousands of listeners now cut off, thinking how the station could still be broadcasting through the night, remaining partly entranced by the power of great music he'd just presented.

He presented several popular classical-style music programmes of 90-minute duration, among them *Masters of Strings* and *Masters of Music*, usually beginning with concertos and ending with symphonies. As he played Beethoven, Mozart, Brahms and other great composers, he thought of their lives as well as their music. He researched and chose all his own music, increasing his work load. He hated the commercialism of commercial radio and reduced advertising in his shows to a minimum.

The music affected him emotionally, aiding his creativity. He felt the power of it working on him as he listened in solitude.

He believed problems could be solved with courage and persistence but felt that music helped the process. He always turned to the solace of music in difficult personal times. A violin concerto could bring tears.

He took over John Dunne's *In Town Tonight* live interview show, moving it along and injecting reality with the city's sounds. You might hear the paper boy shouting "paper, paper," the trams rumbling and Tom suddenly calling "stop!" After a few bars of John Charles Thomas's *Open Road,* he'd interview someone in town, say Maureen O'Hara.

He chewed up material so fast he'd sometimes be short of a finish and would send out a runner to rush in Harry the chatty paper boy from nearby, asking him what was new on the street.

Always looking for something completely different, he next came up with three programme ideas in the early 1950s that were so adventurous for the time they were written up or copied in several other countries.

He convinced the authorities it would be therapeutic for inmates of mental asylums and prisons to form themselves into an orchestra or concert group and broadcast their talents to the world.

Journalists were just as mistrusted then as today but he always kept faith. The Director-General of Public Health in NSW, Dr E. Sydney Morris, said at the time: "The reason I've let Tom Jacobs into mental hospitals and kept others out is I can trust him to do what he promises and to not look for negative angles."

Tom spent three months with a pianist inside various mental hospitals auditioning inmates for an unusual talent quest. He ignored the Jeremiahs in radio who made carping comments along the lines of "why waste your time going into a looney bin to do a programme with nutters? It will be bloody morbid."

He recorded three hours of the best singers and instrumentalists, waiting for the right moment to record one lovely soprano when she was not in a strait jacket, refining it all into a one-hour concert for broadcasting.

The finale of *"The Callan Park Hour"* which he produced and compered was a choir of 20 mental patients in a moving rendition of *The Nuns' Chorus.*

It was a stunning success. At the end of the show, in a forerunner of later big TV telethon appeals, Tom organised 20 open 2SM lines, raising £10,000 from listeners for a male after-care hostel.

Doctors and nurses appreciated the unique broadcast as helping to lessen the stigma attaching then to mental patients and reduce public apathy towards mental institutions.

With those artists Tom then produced a live concert for NSW Education Minister Clive Evatt and his wife and all patients at the Callan Park mental hospital in Sydney. He had a few worrying moments when the inmate audience became unduly excited over Wilbur Kentwell's rhythmical work at the electric organ.

He did a similar thing touring NSW prisons to find talent and formed an orchestra, broadcasting a live concert every three months for years from Goulburn Jail to stations all around Australia, the first in the world from behind prison walls. The 26 orchestral members were long-term prisoners, lifers, murderers, rapists, holdup men.

The conductor, a birdlike figure nicknamed Sparrow who was a talented composer and musician, had poisoned his wife. Tom and Ngaire sneaked cigarettes, chocolates and tobacco to them at prison rehearsals.

The one-hour broadcasts from the prison chapel were sponsored by Aeroplane Jelly, making famous its *"I Like Aeroplane Jelly"* song.

Not missing a trick Tom had one lifer, a rich baritone, sing *"Don't Fence Me In."* As each show ended with the orchestra playing and singing *"Beyond the Blue Horizon,"* the chapel clock chimed boing! boing! right on eight o'clock. And as the compere-producer said "This is Tom Jacobs, good night and bless you all from Goulburn," the warders came in and marched the prisoners back to their cells - artists one minute, jail birds the next.

The Minister of Justice, Reg Downing, attended each concert and everything had to be scripted and approved beforehand by him. Going to air live with a bunch of crims, Tom was never sure what might happen.

But one night he let his sentiment take over and allowed the conductor to do an unscripted voiceover for a special song he'd written and arranged for the orchestra called *The Jessamon Waltz*.

As the music went low this fellow, who had not seen the stars or night sky from his cell for 15 years, reached for the mike and in a moving soliloquy dedicated to his daughter, told listeners all around the nation:

> What is it that makes for hope in a prison cell?
> It is no mystic ology or ism,
> 'Tis one word my dearest...'tis love.

And the music swelled.

Over the next week piles of letters arrived at 2SM saying "This sensitive man should not be in jail, the Minister should be." Minister Downing was furious. He carpeted Jacobs and warned: "Break the rules again and you're out." But Tom's broadcast concept, regarded as good therapy for prisoners, was followed in the US.

Another broadcast he did recreating the last tram ride by a murdered Sydney girl on Christmas Eve in 1952 made headlines and history too.

Shirley Butler, an attractive auburn-haired 21-year-old wearing a red blouse, caught the 11.55 pm Lane Cove tram from Wynyard Station in the city and alighted a few minutes later at Waverton on the North Shore. Her battered body was found next day on a vacant lot near her home.

Working with CIB detectives, actors and a script writer, Jacobs dramatised the last minutes of the young woman's life and tram ride, including the characters on board right down to a boozed reveller singing *Auf Wiederseh'n*. By next day detectives had the names of everyone on that ride as fresh information came in. As a result they eventually believed they knew the murderer but could not pin it on him. But he went to jail for other crimes including rape anyway.

It may not sound too dramatic in today's world of global communications and TV cop series but at the time it was ground-breaking stuff to use radio dramatisation to hunt criminals, and it was widely publicised abroad.

Not every Jacobs broadcast created good vibes, though. His confusion over religion and ethnicity landed him in trouble as he compered the closing of the National Eucharistic Congress from Sydney's St Marys Cathedral in 1952. With tens of thousands clustered around the packed Cathedral in Hyde Park listening to loudspeakers, Jacobs played a message from Pope Pius, sent privately to him from Rome, then Father (later Cardinal) Freeman ended the liturgical part of the service before handing the microphone over to him to say goodbye to everyone.

Jacobs stunned listeners with: "Father, all I can say is God bless everyone - *and thank God I was born a Catholic.*"

The 2SM switch lit up with enraged callers, letters poured in and the papers had a field day claiming his gaffe caused division between Catholics and Protestants. In a public statement the State Minister Clive Evatt said: "Jacobs and 2SM should be ashamed of themselves. Why shouldn't anyone also thank God for being born a *Protestant?* Or something else?"

It took Jacobs a long time to live it down. He had simply been carried away emotionally trying to over-compensate for not going to church. Also he wanted to let everyone know he was a Catholic, that with the name Jacobs he wasn't really a Jew working on a Catholic radio station.

It taught him a lesson and had the effect of making him more ecumenical, causing him to insist on sending his two sons to Riverview College in Sydney hoping the Jesuits would give them a broader education. Ngaire's comment was "we must be the poorest parents sending our kids to this private school."

But in one good thing to come out of the Eucharistic Congress Tom met former footballer and boxer Frank Hyde singing in the Congress choir and, despite his gravelly speaking voice sounding like tearing calico and the reluctance by other 2SM management people to use him, coached him and gave him a start as sports caller for Stadium fights and Rugby League. Frank became a legend, never beaten in football ratings over 40 years.

Always looking out for that new experience, Tom took his microphone into hospitals to describe and record operations and in a major coup was first, in his *Salute to Life* programme, to interview Dr Harry Bailey and describe his infamous deep sleep therapy. Later Bailey suicided before a Royal Commission found that his Chelmsford Private Hospital "therapy" had caused the deaths of 26 patients and the suicides of 22.

Restless, on the move, breeding dachshunds for an extra interest and exhibiting them at shows, often changing the family home to live in different suburbs ("just one step ahead of the police" he joked), he began turning his mind to business, dabbling in real estate with a limited purse.

Then living in a Burley Griffin house at Castlecrag, he bought two blocks of land there for £1,000 each and sold them for £1,300. His friend L.J. Hooker had recommended five blocks but he didn't have the cash.

Recovering from serious head injuries after crashing his new Holden car on loose gravel while returning from Taree on the NSW North Coast, he threw his spare-time energies into organising and establishing a much-needed commercial radio station in the Taree district - the first licence allowed in NSW for 20 years. He talked Postmaster-General Larry Anthony into it then built it, employed the staff and sold the programmes, retaining only five per cent of the shares.

But not wishing to live locally he sold his interest after his good friend the chairman, Ron Butterworth, dropped dead at the microphone as Tom introduced him at an on-air charity fund raiser.

Oddly enough soon afterwards the chairman of 2SM, Father Meany, the man who gave him his start in radio, died in his arms after suddenly taking ill at the station one morning. The lights began going out for him after that.

Things had been falling apart at the station for a while due to a feud between the general manager Bernie Stapleton and sales director Kevin Byrne, a good operator who wanted to take over Stapleton's job.

The station, surviving but not booming, was owned by the Church with the big decisions made by Cardinal Gilroy. Finally Byrne said he would resign unless Stapleton went, and the staff was forced to take sides. Tom sided with Byrne.

After Father Meany's death, Monsignor Tom Muldoon took over but little changed. Late night boozing took place at the station as some members of the factions passionately discussed the problem. Monsignor Muldoon left to soon become a bishop, and the Church moved a young parish priest, Father Prendergast, into the chairman's job. But he proved to be a disaster. All he wanted to do was play more Strauss music. After Kevin Byrne rebelled against his bumbling interference, Cardinal Gilroy declared "the priest stays, and anyone who doesn't like it can go."

Tom and about seven others resigned en masse as a matter of principle, and it became a hot press topic. Reg Grundy was one who elected to stay.

With nothing to do, seeking spiritual comfort in the restful gardens of a monastery on Sydney's North Shore, Tom thought about a family recently wiped out in a road accident. And it gave him an idea to create road safety awareness.

He persuaded the then NSW Premier, Joe Cahill, to let him Stop the State, bringing all trams, buses and other vehicles momentarily to a halt. It was to be Stop the Nation but Liberal Prime Minister Menzies would not co-operate with a Labor Government. Cahill gave Tom an office and staff, and for the next three months he threw himself into gaining the support of the media and other organisations to halt all traffic for one minute at 8 o'clock on the night before Good Friday.

Nearly all traffic stopped, the theatres, cinemas and even ring events at the Royal Easter Show. The *Mirror* put out a poster after the Easter weekend: "Stop the State Works!"

Needing to earn a living and pay off his Castlecrag house, Tom approached Chief Secretary Gus Kelly for a job in tourism. Typically Gus promised the world but delivered only Woolloomooloo.

He offered him the post of Director of Tourism, but instead made him a PR man in the Chief Secretary's Department. Tom hated being a bureaucrat and grew tired of Gus kissing babies and being told no, don't worry about that story, no, we don't want the press asking questions...

Tom got out of there to go back to radio.

After all, he still hadn't sported that trademark trench coat.

8

FOREIGN CORRESPONDENT

BILLED as a newsman, showman, crusader and "one of Sydney's most colourful personalities," Tom Jacobs joined 2UE in Sydney early in 1957 as the station's early morning news interviewer.

His job was to get out on the road early and bring the newsmakers to people on their way to work, although technology still didn't provide for instant outside voices to go to air. He had to lump his big tape recorder to the source and return to the studio to play it, or bring the subject in. People like Bob Askin, even after becoming Premier of NSW, would talk to him in his pyjamas as he brought in the dustbin.

The timing was right for a new lease of life at 2UE, Sydney's first commercial station. To meet the challenge of television, 2UE had just expanded its news coverage and gone to 24-hour broadcasting, promoting its personalities. A gangling young bloke named John Laws came from the bush to join the team.

Apart from his daily news spots, Tom also ran a nightly interview show, *Pulse*, quickly acclaimed as *the* programme for listeners wanting to know what was going on in the public interest. As the only journalist-broadcaster who had come up in the rough and tumble of print journalism, he had a natural advantage over others, knowing where to go and who to talk to on any issue. Few can successfully change from newspapers to radio but he became a voice of authority as politicians, judges, criminals, doctors, scientists, anybody in the public eye, came on his nightly show.

The big thing he had going for him was that people trusted him. He had a manner that gave confidence to people and "even animals" as they say in the best of cliche terms, and he didn't hog the limelight. They all thought they'd found a friend. But he could put up the tough lines too. And he had an eye for the unusual and light-hearted.

He had a crack at television interviews but decided it wasn't his forte. He was then a mature man nearing 40 and realised TV was a young man's game. Beside, horror of horrors, he was nearly bald.

He bought a wig, wore it once or twice and thought he looked ridiculous. And he knew he would never recover from the embarrassment if it slipped off and people realised he had a hairpiece. So he said to hell with that, threw it aside and gave no further thought to a small-screen career. His talent was in painting word pictures.

Never one to stand still, Tom was responsible next for introducing Andrea, one of radio's future institutions. He admired the gossipy, hard-hitting columnist from *Truth* and the *Mirror*. Andrea, real name Dorothy Jenner, was a genuine character from the Australian bush who was polished at a posh girls' school before leading a life of high adventure - acted in silent movies with W.C. Fields, a stuntswoman for Cecil B. de Mille, had an affair with Rudolph Valentino, married a few times, had a fling with the King of Greece, starred in early Australian films, war correspondent in Asia and spent four years in a POW camp.

Talking to Tom one day from the *Mirror*, Andrea said to him: "I've had these shits up here."

"Do you think you can talk and create a word picture as good as you can write?" he asked her.

"Of course I can. No trouble."

He gave her an audition. She was awful, insisting on reading from a script. It sounded stilted and unnatural. Get rid of her, said the general manager. No, said Tom, there's more to her than that, let me try her without a script.

Management wasn't interested but he brought her back again and instead of her being a single commentator, he became part of the discussion, simply picking up the paper and feeding her bits of information. Andrea pitched in, airing her knowledge and making biting comments on people. He concentrated on public figures or personalities, and as he recorded it, her colourful phrases flowed out naturally.

When Tom played the stuff back to management, they couldn't believe it, authorising him to put her on salary right away. And so began *Andrea and Tom*, in which Andrea insulted everyone including Tom.

He was the nice guy feeding this bitch who fancied herself as a society belle! Every time they broadcast, the phones ran hot and the programme was a top rater. She was uninhibited, claiming she was so frightened of her husband she slept with a pistol under her pillow.

The show was responsible for radio's first dump button, or three second pause. First, the station was sued for defamation by socialite Nola Dekyvere after Tom pointed out how much money Nola had raised for charity. "Yes, but she sure knows how to get charity to work for her," said Andrea, among other acid things. It helped make her famous.

Then Andrea referred to Riverview College. "I know your boys go to the snobbish GPS school St Ignatius College at Riverview," she told Tom, "but I can tell you a few stories about boys there who should be expelled for drinking grog." The president of the old boys' union wrote in and complained and Tom read the letter on air.

Andrea's comment to the president : "Up yours for the rent."

The phones buzzed and Tom saw a face peering at him through the glass. General manager Alan Faulkner gesticulated wildly. Tom put a record on and they went out. Faulkner blew up and after that they couldn't go to air without Tom having a dump button. Andrea refused to talk to Faulkner again, although doing the programme for two more years, going on to greater things with her own show. Those were more innocent days but Andrea was outrageous by any standard.

The *Andrea and Tom* show was really the harbinger of Australian talkback radio in the sense that listeners rang in with questions while they were on air and these were passed through in writing and answered by Andrea on the spot.

Tom was indirectly responsible also for Eric Baume becoming famous in radio. He'd interviewed him earlier in London several times when Baume represented the *Mirror* and told him how good he was. When Baume's newspaper days ran out he took Tom's advice and went to radio and later TV, including *Beauty and the Beast*.

In this period Tom did one of those rare, classical broadcasts that demonstrated the art of the gifted interviewer. Strolling through Sydney's Botanic Gardens early on the first morning of spring looking for a story, he stopped to chat to a six-year-old boy named Raymond, the son of the curator, idly tossing pebbles into a pond.

As the birds sang he tapped into the lad's purity of mind, chatting to him about life and freedom and his parents and how God was probably looking down on him and the birds and all the other wildlife that came into the gardens. In this sensitive, philosophical exchange the boy quoted his father's wisdom: "Dad says it's later than you think."

Played at the end, Matt Monro's *Born Free* gave special meaning to the words "as free as the wind blows, as free as the grass grows..."

At 2UE John Laws and some other station announcers replayed it for the next 20 years on the first day of spring.

Meanwhile, the old Australia of prejudice and discrimination that Tom Jacobs had known was beginning to change - gradually.

In 1945 Arthur Calwell, the Labor Immigration Minister, had greatly expanded immigration from non-British European countries. That was due to the Government's "populate or perish" policy for defence, the need for post-war economic development, and out of humanitarian concerns for the millions of displaced persons in Europe.

Mr Calwell, the man who made the crack "two Wongs don't make a white," excluded displaced persons of Asian background. Australian officials in Europe's refugee camps screened out Asians and those of non-European appearance.

The White Australia policy was still entrenched and non-negotiable.

But racism wasn't a one-way street. The Japanese in their wartime propaganda had presented their invasion plans as an "unselfish crusade" to rid Asia of "Anglo-Saxon tyrants" and American and European imperialists, all under the uniting cry of "Asia for Asians."

Many non-white refugees had entered Australia during World War 11 and most left voluntarily at the end of the war. Some had married Australians and wanted to stay. Mr Calwell aroused strong resentment when he sought to deport them.

The new conservative Menzies Coalition Government in 1949 continued to encourage European migration in the 1950s and would do so into the 1960s, especially migrants from Southern Europe like Greeks and Italians.

But the Government went a little further in 1949, taking the first tentative steps towards a non-discriminatory immigration policy, tilting at wartime Labor Prime Minister John Curtin's statement that "this country shall remain forever the home of the descendants of those people who came here in peace in order to establish in the South Seas an outpost of the British race." Harold Holt, the Immigration Minister, decided to allow 800 non-European refugees to stay and also admitted Japanese war brides.

In 1951 the Colombo Plan saw the beginning of thousands of Asian students attending Australian universities.

Then in 1957 the Menzies Government allowed non-Europeans with 15 years residence to become Australian citizens. A year later a revised Immigration Act introduced a simpler entry permit system and abolished the controversial dictation test in a language unknown to the aspiring immigrant.

However, Tom Jacobs knew the Menzies Government had no intention of letting in large numbers of non-Europeans and that a big percentage of the Australian population was still prejudiced against the foreign born, especially those with coloured skin.

The new waves of migrants were now generally tagged "reffos" as well as "wogs" like his parents and brothers and sisters had years before.

He felt deeply sorry for them, knowing from his own experience it would take at least a generation before things changed for them. At the same time he was elated that the politicians were beginning to recognise Australia as a place for all migrants. Even the Anglo-Saxons had been migrants at some point. He personally did not mind where they came from as long as they were healthy and of good character.

As millions migrated to Australia from all over Europe, Tom could see this was the greatest experiment in racial mingling since vast numbers of Europeans flooded into America last century. Australia could be a young America, even better, hopefully able to learn from America's mistakes.

He could see the change occurring even on the surface as foreign names cropped up in sporting teams. In spite of the name calling and other outward displays of prejudice, he observed the benefits already taking place - the mixing and acceptance of other cultures, a greater degree of tolerance, a wider and more varied range of food as Australians were introduced to the best of European and Continental cuisine.

But he hoped and prayed the delicate experiment would succeed in the long term with people of all nationalities living together peacefully and with understanding.

On the racism front, history repeated itself with only one of Tom's children. Ian often came home crying from school after being taunted as a wog. Paul was fair and nuggetty and sometimes taken to be Jewish but

Rosemary had long straight hair and was accepted as any other young Aussie girl, although slightly Italianate in appearance.

They were better able to handle it than in Tom's youth and were half Anglo-Saxon anyway because of their mother's background. Attitudes had changed and the colour chasm was being bridged by time and evolution as large ethnic groups settled in. But the typical Aussie greeting to anyone of non-Anglo appearance was still "where'd you come from?"

Ian, who looked most like his father, was the only one with a slightly olive skin, which was not obvious as a child. He spent a lot of time in the sun or at the beach and his suntan accentuated his colouring. It used to hurt him at Sydney's Homebush primary school in the mid-1950s when the other kids called him a bloody wog.

That's when he came home crying. Ngaire would say to him: "Don't take any notice of them, son." And she would tell him about her own Scottish and English background, saying "you're an older Australian than 90 per cent of them." Tom, too, helped soothe the pain.

The youths at Daceyville police boys' club would say to Ian "you bloody wog" just for the hell of it. Anyone then with a name like Jacobs who had a Lebanese background or who had an olive skin was automatically a bloody wog. Any migrant who worked hard or who had a better car or home than the older Aussies was a bloody wog.

As Ian grew older he tended not to take any notice, putting it down to jealousy or ignorance. But as a kid he defensively kept his father's ethnic background bottled up and talked about it only inside his family.

When the family later moved to the more upmarket North Shore suburb of Castlecrag, it was all right for Ian to gather oysters from the rocks of inner Sydney Harbour, but if an Italian collected a bucket of mussels there, he had to be a bloody wog. Fancy eating mussels!

In his early teens Ian noticed a remarkable thing. He was mostly called a wog only at night. He had clear blue eyes, which confused most Aussies in the daytime. But he still copped it in school football matches, even at Riverview College, no doubt because he was a good Rugby player.

Ngaire reacted to this racism one day just after Ian left school and was playing Rugby in a junior team for salubrious St Ives on the leafy North Shore against Hornsby.

Whenever Ian made a break a woman spectator screeched "Jew" and "Jew boy." As he dashed down a sideline she screamed "get the bloody wog, get the bloody wog." Ngaire took him out of the club at once.

Tom knew of others from different ethnic backgrounds who'd had similar experiences in that early post-war transition period, but had settled in to be accepted as good Australians.

Anthoula Yappas, 12, from Egypt and Chrysostomos Agathocleous Constantinou, 11, a Greek from Cyprus, arrived in Sydney in 1955 with members of their families on the same Italian ship, Caste Fellecia, out of Port Said. Their fathers had migrated earlier.

In Egypt Anthoula was looked after by nannies and her mother never worked, but in Sydney she had to go out to work and Anthoula took responsibility for cooking the meals and looking after her younger brothers. They did it hard settling in.

On Anthoula's first day at Tempe primary school the headmistress said "you're Anne," and she was ever after. Nobody could pronounce the name of Chrysostomos Agathocleous Constantinou and he became Chris Costa, after his father's first name.

Anne was not name-called at the school but one of her brothers was regularly beaten up for being a wog. And when Anne and her mother travelled to the city to buy olive oil, cheeses and olives, they had to whisper in trains and buses if talking in their own language to avoid unfriendly glances and occasional wog comments.

Chris weathered the racial interplay without much trouble at school, always fondly remembering his teacher, Miss Long, for taking pains to teach him English. His memory of the late 1950s and early 1960s was that any adult Greek or Italian and just about any non-Anglo was a dago, especially if working overtime in factories to get ahead and keep their jobs, causing Australians to fear losing theirs.

Anne and Chris married in 1965, Anglicising their name to Constantine. Oddly, one of their two daughters aged five would get the wog treatment at school in 1971, although she was fair and had hazel eyes. But she didn't speak English very well, and unusually wore earrings in pierced ears.

The Constantines worked hard, started their own clothing factories and established lots of Aussie friends.

In another example, Bohumila Oksana Plawajko was born in Sydney in 1949 to Ukrainian parents who had migrated a year earlier. Like Tom she craved to be an Australian, but had a painful emotional journey through childhood.

Unlike Tom, her problem was not one of colour but ethnicity.

Right from her first day at Marsfield Primary School she was acutely embarrassed at being "different." She was blonde and had a fair skin, but that woggy name! Nobody could pronounce Bohumila and she told everyone she wanted to be called Oksana (later changing the spelling to Oxana to make it less woggy).

The kids promptly called her Roxana or Rexona, after the deodorant. To stop them calling her a wog, she told them her name was Shirley. Her older sister, Bohdanka, who had an olive skin, changed her name to Anna.

Her parents had difficulty settling into a new cultural environment, but they worked hard, eventually moving into Eastwood in Sydney where theirs was the only privately owned house in a Housing Commission street - and they were called wogs because of it.

Oxana just wanted to blend in and be the same as other Australian youngsters, but her parents wanted the family to cling to their Ukranian heritage. They spoke Ukranian in the house, but she deliberately answered in English. The discipline was so strict she was not allowed to play with Australian children out of school hours because they were considered "too free and easy."

She had to introduce herself by saying "hello, I'm Ukranian," attend a Ukranian school and church once a week and accept her father's opinion that the Ukraine was the best place on earth.

Another embarrassment was her "woggy" lunches at Ryde High School, beginning in 1961.

They called her a smelly wog and poked fun at her thick slices of black bread, sour cream, gherkin, salami, sauerkraut and strong cheeses.

Oxana envied the ordinary neatly-cut white bread sandwiches of other kids. But an Aussie classmate named Jill helped her out by exchanging her Peck's paste and vegemite sandwiches for Oxana's Ukranian tucker.

Learning to speak up for herself, Oxana always replied when someone at school cattily asked her why she didn't go back to her own country: "This *is* my country. I'm an Australian just like you."

She felt so strongly about being accepted as "normal" that she was even glad her parents were working and unable to attend school functions because they looked so unmistakably European.

But her story ended happily. Oxana met and married Sydney businessman and property developer Morrie Muller, of German and

Danish background, and they had three well adjusted children - all as Aussie as meat pies.

Karam Ramrakha, a Fiji Indian who came to Sydney in 1950 to study law, had a different concept of what Australia was like in the early postwar period when Tom's children were growing up.

Isolated, with no borders, the country to him was a white oasis.

He felt a very strong black and white divide. Most Australians made no apology for the White Australia policy but for him it stopped at the gates of Sydney University. Inside the privileged environment there was no racism. Once a black man qualified at university, the chances of a professional person being discriminated against was low.

He was joined by his two younger brothers who would later study medicine as fee-paying students after being withdrawn from a public school and enrolled at private fee-paying schools because they weren't citizens. But he was impressed at the concern shown by an immigration official for the welfare of his brothers in having to change school. As a colonial, Karam and his family were used to being told what to do and they abided by the rules - that was the lesson of empire.

Soon after arriving in Sydney Karam remembered being made welcome at a workers' picnic. The ladies gave him food and a glass of milk and he had the feeling that although the white man had a more privileged society, he didn't take it out on the black man as a result.

Karam's own sense of the black/white divide was played out on the sporting field. The West Indies had beaten England and were now coming to Sydney to play Australia.

Karam waited for the clash with the three Ws - Walcott the big hitter, Weekes the consummate cricketer and Worrall the classic craftsman. Toss in Sonny Ramadhin and Lance Valentine and my goodness thought Karam, they're going to give the Australians a darned good thrashing.

A friend of Karam's was a displaced Ceylonese named Eric George Vaughn Weinmann, a Dutch burgher who fled Sri Lanka when independence came. The burghers, meeting the criteria of being 51 per cent white, were made welcome in Australia. But Eric felt like a fish out of water because he was neither black nor white, resented the fact and could not cope with it. He took to drinking wine heavily, visiting Karam at home for solace. Eric used to sit in the trams inebriated, shouting "one black man against eight million bloody whites."

Anyway, the Windies didn't win, depressing both Eric and Karam. Eric, who saw the match, told Karam that as Australian Sid Barnes came in to bat the cry rose from a section of the Sydney Cricket Ground Hill: "Come on Siddie Barnes, blast these niggers to hell!"

Karam's desire to see a black team beat a white team was purely racial.

Nothing personal, it was just the situation at the time and a thread that ran through society then. If a black man proved himself in sport against a white man, he could at least say he was equal. And as the West Indian team had Indians playing in it, he wanted to see fellow colonials succeed - in his colonial background the British powers ruling over Indians had made it clear the white man was superior and should rule the black.

After graduating, Karam returned to Fiji where he ran a tabloid newspaper, became a member of Parliament and Opposition Whip and was president and secretary of the Fiji Law Society. After a colourful career he returned to Australia, an eclipsed politician.

He finally saw the West Indians play Australia in Sydney in the 1980s. His wife warned him against barracking. "Don't worry," he said, "I'm cheering for Australia this time."

After the Windies won a thrilling game, an Aussie with a big beer gut called out on The Hill next to him: "Who taught these bloody wogs to play cricket?" But as the West Indians left the ground, Beer Gut was one of the first to stand and clap enthusiastically.

The incident proved to Karam what he already felt about Australia.

Racism was only superficial and not carried to the point where the Australians wanted to harm anyone. It was not nearly as overt as the caste system in India where people were actively suppressed, or in other eastern countries where open racist hostility and divisions were standard.

A respected city lawyer, Karam Ramrakha felt grateful the second time around that Australia had given him a new life.

He was impressed by the views of a Sydney Greek solicitor who said: "There's a basic honesty about the Anglo-Saxons. Where else in the world would you have the dole system across the board like here? To make things equitable to everybody, and the rich sharing with the poor. Although some Anglo-Saxons have aggressive views, there's a basic honesty about them."

Tom could relate to the truth of that, also the views Karam would express later about the Australia of the 1980s through and beyond 2000.- it was still an oasis in the world, although no longer overwhelmingly white.

But fervently Karam hoped the problems he could see creeping into God's country through the incompatibility of some racial groups would not end up destroying a wonderful experiment in multi-racial harmony.

One day while doing a story on migration for 2UE, Tom interviewed a young part-time Lebanese interpreter for the Australian Government. They became friends, causing Tom to think profoundly about his ethnic past and to finally confront the shame he felt.

The interpreter, an accountant, liked to talk about Lebanese history and over coffee said to Tom: "You know, your name can't be Jacobs."

"Why is that?"

"It couldn't possibly be. Probably it's one of your Christian names because you're a Christian. In the Old Country the surname was never used except for filling out official papers. And if they were Christians their second name was invariably taken from the Bible, something like Jacob, Isaac or Moses.

"So if their first name was Tom, they would be called Tom Jacob, Tom Isaac or Tom Moses. In the early days of migration, there were no interpreters here in Australia for migrants who spoke Arabic, and their second Christian name usually became their surname."

"That's strange," said Tom, "because my grandfather and his brother came out here last century and my cousin, who is the son of my grandfather's brother, goes by a different name. He calls himself Hayson."

"He's probably Anglicised it. Why don't you go to the Lebanese Consulate and ask about your name?"

"No," said Tom, "I wouldn't like to do that."

"Would you like me to do it for you?"

"Yes, if you wish."

The next time they met his new friend produced a copy of old grandfather Tannous's 1892 naturalisation certificate in the name of Tannous Sacomb Elhessen, the "Sacombe" being something of a mystery. It was supposed to be Yacoub.

"Your cousin has obviously decided to Anglicise his name from Elhessen to Hayson," he said. "You're entitled to do the same."

"Gee," said Tom, "I'll have to think about that."

"You should feel proud of your background. Your race goes back thousands of years to the Phoenicians. I'll get you some material on them."

Tom thought here I am running around calling myself Jacobs when other members of our family are calling themselves something else based on our real Lebanese name of Elhessen. Some people think I'm Jewish and others take me for a Greek or an Italian. I'd better do something about it.

He began reading about Lebanon and the more he learned the more important he realised this transition would be in his life.

He found out that Elhessen meant beauty in Lebanese, from Our Lady of Hessen. And he wondered why he could not feel the same pride in his background as his younger Lebanese-born friend.

He now knew why he still felt inferior, stemming from the way his grandparents were treated in earlier days, the way they battled to survive and the insults they had to endure, the struggle of his parents and the way they had to suppress their background, the way he felt as a boy and how his brothers and sisters had felt too because of their skin colour.

Then he was embarrassed over the way he felt about himself.

Suddenly he had renewed sympathy for other minority ethnic groups, especially Chinese. And he was sorry for the way he'd treated the Chinese market gardener in Barraba, looking down on him as the lowest of the low, holding his nose and saying "hello Pong:"

He told himself he'd surely only done this to gain acceptance from other kids, not from any personal prejudice.

Why did I do that? he asked himself. Now here I am striving to become an Anglo-Saxon in Australia and I never can be. I'm what I am.

As he read about the Phoenicians and the land of his forebears, he began to understand that his was a great heritage. He thought: "I'm actually purer than the Anglo-Saxons who are a very mixed bag, because I go back to Christ and beyond. I come from a land of great culture thousands of years older than any other, where the trappings of civilisation began before anywhere else. I'm not a Bedouin, not an Arab, but even they contain white Caucasians among their many different races..."

His confusion over the black/white issue, of being neither black nor white, was still pressed into his psyche.

Tom knew the Registrar-General and approached him to change his name. He could have done it by deed poll but wanted to be more definite about it, waiting a year before he could formally change Jacob to Hayson on his birth certificate. As always, it was all or nothing with him in everything he did.

He spoke to his parents. They didn't wish to change, and weren't interested in Lebanon. They said Old Tannous's brother Josef had influenced his son Diab to change his name to relate to their past.

Tom's parents were living in a Housing Commission flat in Greenway Towers near the Harbour Bridge, and although he wanted them to move into better accommodation, they were happy to stay put.

Ngaire changed her name but the children would have to wait until leaving school or transferring to another for the changeover. And although Tom was now officially Hayson, he would continue to use Jacobs in radio.

Tom never had much money and in this respect nothing had changed.

He had a small amount set aside but struggled to keep his boys at their private school and give his daughter a good education. With a bit of time on his hands while starting so early each day, he looked around to see what he could do. A little more dabbling in property seemed the only way.

Casting about, he found a small rundown block of flats for private sale on Sydney's lower North Shore. It needs a coat of paint, he observed, wonder who owns it? And how can I raise the money? At a time of tight financial control on loans, journalism came to his rescue.

He rang Roy McKerihan, head of the NSW Rural Bank whom he'd interviewed, saying he could buy a block of flats for about £220 and wondered if he could borrow the funds, receiving a favourable reply.

Two of the four flats were empty and two occupied. He negotiated with the tenants to leave so he could renovate the block. He couldn't do the work himself but spoke to a carpenter. No, the job was too big for him but perhaps if he spoke to this small firm...He worked out on paper how much the job would cost and had it done.

Tom then sold the flats and made 100 per cent profit. They came in off the street to buy and he could have made 150 per cent profit if smarter. "Gee whizz," he told Ngaire, "I've made enough in two months to cover my wages for the rest of the year in broadcasting."

Being a reporter had opened the doors for him but they opened even more due to his broadcasting. After that he either rang McKerihan or would say at the end of an interview: "Oh by the way, I've got this thing going...any chance of getting a loan from your bank or another bank?"

It made him realise the importance of always working from the top, not having to produce all the references and documents required by staff down the line. Tom unabashedly took advantage of these opportunities but to avoid embarrassment, always asked if it was all right to mention it, and he always paid back on time.

In this way using other people's money he continued to buy up small properties, refurbishing them for sale or renting, fiddling around the edge of the property market. Ngaire managed the flats, arranged servicing and collected any rents. Tom did not want to manage people but Ngaire sorted out the roughies and was known to change the locks if a cheating renter was determined not to pay.

In one incident at Neutral Bay, Ngaire showed her determined Scottish trait with a schoolteacher and her daughter who had blatantly not paid the rent in their flat for several months. It would have taken at least six months going to court to evict them and Ngaire decided to take direct action. Tom, chickening out, said: "Don't tell me about this, I don't want to know."

Ngaire waited until the tenants went out, changed the locks, called a removalist and carried all their belongings out to the van. The teacher returned to find herself trumped. Ngaire last saw her sitting in the van waving a fist at her, screaming "I'll bloody take you to court over this..."

To cash in on the early days of squash Tom built courts at Parramatta where the family went to live. Andrea the radio terror was an investor. He also converted a building at Harbord into squash courts. Ngaire looked after them, even running a mothers' club, teaching them to play squash.

Ngaire was the backstop who did the family chores and looked after the children, running everything to a tight nurse's routine and leaving Tom free for his radio work and property interests. He was the budding entrepreneur who found something, set it up and moved on, leaving the detailed work to Ngaire to get it going quickly. She was highly practical, not interested like Tom in colour patterns, frills and obscure touches.

Without her strong support he would not have been able to do his radio work at all hours, go on trips and play around with property as if he were still a single man. But when Ngaire thought he was spending too much time on business and not enough on his home and family, she told him so and it caused arguments, although not serious ones.

They were interested in helping each other and although his time was limited, he was a good family man within the hours available to him. He had no time for extra marital activities even if inclined that way, - indeed, if having an affair, he would have had to conduct it standing up in a crowded bus on the way to the radio station.

Tom didn't play golf or any other sport but loved to watch it, being a loud one-eyed barracker at his sons' school football games. Ngaire and Rosemary were so embarrassed they would often go to the other end of the field.

They never had any time left over for the cocktail circuit or entertaining which was just as well because they were private people. On Sundays if they had any spare time they took their children or Tom's parents for a drive. Ngaire was especially kind and friendly towards Tom's mother, learning from her how to cook traditional Lebanese dishes such as tabbouleh, kibbi, stuffed marrows and cabbage rolls.

Juggling small property deals in between broadcasting made Tom feel something of a split personality. But he wasn't about to give up his day job.

In the period of Indonesia's confrontation with Australia, when it was feared Indonesia had territorial designs on Australia, Tom pulled off one of his most remarkable radio efforts, scoring a world scoop but nearly getting shot for his initiative.

At the time, 1962, the Australian Government feared President Soekarno might invade Australia. Indonesia had been supplied with arms and jet fighters from Russia, Soekarno controlled a huge army and Australia was no match for his big defence forces.

A dynamic, unpredictable character, he was sabre rattling against the Dutch and others and relations between Indonesia and Australia were extremely strained. Clashes occurred on the Australian-New Guinea border with Indonesia. Soekarno was world news because of his aggressive international rabble rousing.

Tom told 2UE: "I can get an interview with Soekarno."

Of course he didn't know he could, but *thought* he could, never taking no for an answer. Management was cool on the idea but reluctantly agreed.

He flew to Jakarta and joined a string of other journalists from the UK, other parts of Europe, America and Australia - all wanting to interview Soekarno.

He was there almost two weeks hanging around with other correspondents, but all his efforts to break through failed. Soekarno had only recently survived an assassination attempt and was surrounded at all times by vigilant guards toting Tommy guns.

Then about 20 journalists were invited to the Presidential palace, not to interview him but to hear him make another speech, obviously a new rabble rousing tirade designed to impress his captive home audience and put the wind up the Western world.

Inside a large hall in the palace the correspondents were directed by guards to stand in a restricted area at one side. Minutes later Soekarno, resplendent in braided white military uniform, strode in and began making his way to the dais and a forest of microphones. As he did so, Tom broke ranks and walked towards him, microphone in hand.

Suddenly guns were trained on him. He raised his arms in a gesture of compliance and to show his radio gear. "I've only got a microphone, a microphone and recording equipment," he said.

Before the guards could intervene, Tom had reached Soekarno's side. In that tense moment, fingers on triggers, the guards wondering what to do, Soekarno held up his right hand to call them off.

Jacobs, in the best traditions of foot-in-the-door journalism, switched on his machine and came right to the point. "Mr President, do you have any designs on Australia? I'm an Australian, just come from there, and I thought I'd ask you."

President Soekarno, caught on the hop, decided to co-operate. "No," he said, "why would I have designs on Australia? It's a wonderful place. I've got islands everywhere, hundreds of them. Why would I want another one. Our slogan is unity in diversity."

Other correspondents were muttering "cheeky bastard," wishing they had been game enough to do something similar.

Jacobs followed up: "It's been suggested that your population is now over one hundred million and you need more space, like in Australia."

Soekarno: "I've got all the space I need in the world. No, I repeat, I haven't got any designs on Australia at all."

Jacobs: "But they say in America that you do, and they think in Australia that you do."

Soekarno: "Well, I'm telling you I don't."

Tom kept popping the questions. What was it like since the Dutch left? Soekarno attacked the Dutch, saying they had left the people illiterate and plundered Java, forcing a war with them before they would go.

It developed into a long intense interview. All the other correspondents were anxious to talk to Tom but he left the palace as soon as possible and headed for the Government-owned Radio Jakarta to file his story by radio telephone. The equipment was old and inefficient and the first technician simply walked off, replaced after a while by another.

It took more than an hour to get the story through to 2UE in fits and starts, playing the tape in front of a microphone linked to a landline.

His exclusive broadcast, relayed all over Australia, was also played in the US and caused a stir in Washington and The Hague.

American radio stations then aired other interviews of his with Indonesian Foreign Minister Dr. Subandrio and General Nasution. In these he described Jakarta and many other cities as being like vast military camps with men and women, even boys and girls, undergoing military training in parks, sports ovals and on vacant allotments.

The Australian Minister for Foreign Affairs, Sir Garfield Barwick, asked for a copy of the Soekarno interview and later Tom personally handed him a tape.

When the adrenalin stopped pumping Tom realised the risk he'd taken. The guards were trigger happy and correspondents had been warned by Indonesian officials to follow directions as the situation was dangerous.

Looking back he conceded it was probably a foolhardy thing to do.

He knew at the time he was taking a calculated risk. *But Jesus, he wanted the story.* And through him Soekarno made a statement to the world, picked up and commented on in capitals where the big world political decisions were made. But apart from one or two brief mentions, he didn't get any credit from the rest of the media for it.

That wasn't the first time he'd risked his neck to get a story. On his first world tour in 1949 he talked his way in London onto a DC3 cargo plane loaded with coal bound for Berlin to help break the tense Russian blockade of the city.

Freezing and perched on top of coal, he braced himself and watched anxiously as his plane was buzzed by Russian Yak fighters when it came in to land at Berlin's Tempelhof airport. The RAF had pulled out a window in case he had to parachute out. The aggressive buzzing was repeated as he left for Wiesbaden on a tiny aircraft - just to interview Australian Air Force personnel assisting West Berlin survive the Cold War.

After further trips and several more years in radio, Tom thought it was time to give his foreign correspondent's trench coat a good workout.

In 1968 he planned another world trip, even more extensive than in 1949, again sending back material as he went. This time he concentrated on war zones. And for the first time, he would take Ngaire with him.

His father had just died of a heart attack, aged 71. The passing caused Tom to relive the struggle his father had gone through to raise the family, and his cultural battle to be accepted as an Australian. Tom was pleased that as his financial position had gradually improved through property speculation, he'd been able to make sure his parents were comfortable.

And he gained pleasure out of the pride his father had felt in his achievements. When he heard Tom's interview with Churchill or some other dignitary on the radio, he would say: "That's our son." He was buried in the name of Jacobs.

Tom planned a flexible itinerary to hit the trouble spots as they hotted up, filing on-the-spot reports for 2UE and the Major Broadcasting Network, interviewing celebrities in between.

In all he would be away almost 10 months, his travels as a roving correspondent giving him a few close calls and taking him to 58 countries, from a rocket-blasted shell of a house in Saigon to the humble home of an Arab shepherd in occupied Jordan, from soldiers who spat at one another across the 38th Parallel in Korea, to the Defiant Ones of Czechoslovakia as Russian tanks rolled in to put down an anti-Communist uprising.

First call was Vietnam. Suddenly Tom and Ngaire unexpectedly found themselves in the middle of the Tet offensive, the final Vietcong assault on what was still called Saigon. They were holed up in the Continental Hotel for two weeks as mortars fell all around.

A six o'clock curfew each night meant that anyone going out into the street could be shot on sight or bombed. Tom stood on the hotel roof at night with other correspondents as American gunships flew over and Vietcong shells blasted off only blocks away. They thought him crazy when he introduced "Ngaire, my wife."

One day he hurried through some interviews in a building at the Saigon military airport because Ngaire, not allowed to enter, was waiting impatiently about 100 metres away. As he reached her side a rocket blew to pieces the building he'd just left, killing six of the occupants including two of the airmen he'd been talking to and wounding all the others.

Pan Am was the only airline flying out and they went to the airport six times trying to board a flight. Each time the airport was mortared. Once they narrowly escaped death when a mortar landed in the main lounge area and 40 American soldiers standing nearby were killed. When they finally boarded a plane the airfield was mortared as they took off.

As they headed for Singapore the co-pilot came down the aisle and said: "It's OK - we've now passed the point of no return." Tom sighed with relief but Ngaire said: "I really enjoyed that. It was a real thrill."

In London he set about interviewing the first of a long list of endearing personalities, including Lord Louis Mountbatten, Dr Ramsay the Archbishop of Canterbury, Len Deighton, Richard Attenborough, Anna Neagle, Mantovani, Sir Alec Guinness, Lord Hunt who led the first successful assault on Mt Everest and Sir Bernard Lovell, explaining on tape at Jodrell Bank Observatory that you could hear a signal coming from outer space that was thousands of light years away.

Ngaire collected autographs for Rosemary, telling Tom he had the hide of a rhino to ask personal questions of Mountbatten.

Cities visited rolled off a long list as in a junkie traveller's dream, among them Frankfurt, Salzburg, Vienna, Berlin, Bratislava, Copenhagen, Moscow, New York, Montreal, Ottawa, Toronto, Banff, Calgary, Vancouver, Bermuda, Los Angeles, San Francisco, New Orleans, Las Vegas, Geneva, Amsterdam, Rome, Paris, Cairo, Nicosia, Tel Aviv, Jerusalem, New Delhi, Seoul...

While strolling in Rome with a priest from The Vatican, Tom bumped into Sydney newspaper columnist Jim Macdougall at the Trevi fountain. Each threw in three coins.

The once confused, impoverished and curious kid who lay on a bank of the Manilla River at Barraba gazing into the sky and wondering what was out there beyond the horizon, was having a ball.

In Mexico City, as political-based violence flared in a leadup to the Olympic Games, he had a close shave as soldiers sub-machine gunned protesters in the Square of the Three Cultures.

He and his driver lay flat in their taxi as bullets ripped all around them. When the shooting stopped, 30 students lay dead. He saw their bodies dragged into a hotel foyer like sacks of coal. He felt sickened at the violent deaths he'd seen in a dozen or so places.

After covering the Mexico Olympics and the US Presidential elections for 2UE, Tom was just about ready to come home. But first he had to visit the most important place of all.

The road up the mountains from Beirut was winding, narrow and dangerous. Cars from the opposite direction seemed to come straight at him as drivers madly honked their horns.

"They're just saying hello," said his driver unconvincingly, as cars hurtled by. It would take nearly an hour, the driver said.

With Ngaire beside him, Tom did not know what to expect as he prepared to turn the clock back on his past.

But he knew a lot had happened in the Middle East recently and tensions in Lebanon were high. After Nasser declared he would annihilate the Jewish State of Israel and formed military alliances with Syria and Jordan for that purpose, building up troops along the Israel border, Israel launched a surprise all-out attack on Egypt in June 1967. The six-day war that followed ended with Israeli troops occupying Egypt's Sinai Peninsula, Syria's Golan Heights and Jordan's West Bank.

In the wake of that Arab defeat, revolutionary passion swept through the Arab world. One effect was the rise of the Palestine Liberation Organisation (PLO), under the obscure guerrilla Yasir Arafat.

Using economic and political support from Arab states, the guerrilla groups took control of Palestinian refugee camps bordering on Israel, particularly in Lebanon and Jordan, from where they continued their war against Israel. Retaliating against these raids, Israel caused tensions between Palestinians, Lebanese and Jordanians. Internal factions in Lebanon added fuel to the fire.

Religious differences were the immediate cause of friction inside Lebanon. Back in 1920 France under the League of Nations had formed the republic of Greater Lebanon. Then in 1943 Lebanon's Christian and Muslim leaders had agreed on a so-called National Pact to share power and to balance Lebanon's Western and Arab orientations. This allowed the republic to become independent of France.

In this pact the Muslims, mainly the Sunnis and Shiites, agreed to abandon their demands for unity with Syria in return for the Christian Maronites cutting their links with France and accepting the notion that Lebanon would be an "Arab" country.

The unwritten agreement also stipulated that to preserve Christian dominance a Maronite would always be the Lebanese President, and the parliament would always have a six/five ratio of Christians to Muslims.

But to ensure the country's Muslim-Arab essence, it was agreed the Prime Minister would always be a Sunni Muslim and the Speaker a Shiite.

That was fine while the Maronites and other Christians made up about half the population.

But by the time of Tom's 1968 visit, Lebanon's religious balance was turned on its head. The Christians had shrunk to about a third of the population with the Muslims and Druze making up the majority.

The Christian Maronites refused Muslim demands for political reforms to strengthen the role of the Muslim Prime Minister, insisting they stick to the original balance of power agreed upon.

The Maronites formed private armies to maintain their position, mainly the Phalangist militia and the Tigers militia. The Lebanese Muslims and the Druze also organised private armies to enforce change.

At the same time the conflict between the Palestinian Arabs and the Jews was hotting up and with Lebanese factions ready to take sides, Lebanon was on the brink of civil war.

In this agitated atmosphere, far from the calm and relative tranquillity of Australia, Tom continued driving up into the mountains of North Lebanon to try to trace his humble beginnings.

He carried two passports in the name of Jacobs, arranged with the Australian Government. The first had enabled him to visit Israel without showing a visa to indicate he would visit an Arab country, and the second allowed him to enter Lebanon without them knowing he'd been to Israel.

Tom talked volubly to the driver, an Australian Lebanese who had returned to Beirut to live, telling him how his family had come from here. Suddenly the driver said "this is it."

Aitou. A small village with just a few shops, a church at the end of the street elevated on a narrow flat rocky strip surrounded by gorges. Glorious views on all sides, to the mountains further up or the valleys below. He looked down on this clear day from about 5,000 feet up and could see the blue of the distant Mediterranean washing against Tripoli.

Tom felt the emotion welling up. Then he said aloud but to himself: "I might have been born an Australian but for the first time I feel as if I'm really home."

They stopped the car and looked about. The driver began describing the hamlet's features. Pointing to a Christian church with its landmark spire, he said: "That's where your grandfather would have been christened, in there."

"I want to see that. As soon as I can." Tom was excited, his words tumbling out.

"What's he doing there?"

"Harvesting figs."

"And there?"

"He's just milking his goat. Basically it hasn't changed since your grandfather left. That building up on the hill is a little St Maroun monastery. Beside it is a convent for the nuns."

Here they are back in Australia, Tom thought, saying how primitive and culturally inferior the Arabs are and yet I can climb this mountain and step into a cultural and ethnic history that goes back so far.

He said to the driver: "Here we are standing in the country itself where the ancestors of the Lebanese, my ancestors the Phoenicians, were the first recognised ethnic group in the world, a place full of history and tradition."

Looking up the street in the distance he could see people moving about. "They might be living in poverty and their dress simple," he told Ngaire, "but their bearing gives them a certain dignity."

Even after all his years of vividly dreaming about this place, he had not known what to expect, whether it would be full of Arabs in flowing garb. But now, before his eyes for the first time, it was as his grandfather had described it, even better than he imagined. He didn't want to change a thing.

They drove on a short distance and stopped beside some houses so Tom could ask about the location of his grandfather's house.

They knew enough English to converse with him. He mentioned he was of the Elhessen family. An elderly woman said: "Oh yes, we've heard all about you, we know about your family. The house is just down there, turn right and go along the lane..."

As he talked, word of a stranger who had come home spread quickly.

They came out of their houses with little decanters of coffee. A woman appeared with a man beside her, speaking to him in Arabic which he could not understand. He suddenly regretted his mother had never taught him Arabic. The woman handed Tom a bunch of fresh green grapes, the man black grapes.

Few people normally stopped in Aitou. Most drove straight through to the resort of Ehden further up the mountains. Not only were they pleased that a stranger had stopped in the village but this was a homecoming.

Surrounded by a small happy group now, he wanted to be alone, finding it hard to keep his emotions in check. The tears ran down his cheeks on to his shirt. For the first time in his life he felt completely accepted, without having to explain. These people were beautiful, kind, compassionate.

He knew where this hospitality came from. The Lebanese were the great compromisers of life who had learned to live with others. They understood what it was to suffer and be humiliated, relying on their wits to survive.

All the conquerors had passed through here, yet the Lebanese had retained their identity. Nobody in this little village had the thrusting personality and antagonism of many he'd met in the Western world.

He suddenly felt divided between two lands, one ethnic, the other his home and birthplace. He knew now more than ever he'd been driven by the lack of acceptance at home.

Someone pointed up the hill. "See that water tank up there? Your relative put that up there. To supply the town."

Ah yes, nodded Tom. That must have been Diab, the child who left here on a donkey in 1886. He became quite wealthy buying animal skins in the New England district of NSW, selling to dealers in New York.

Diab had been back to Aitou twice. He was the one who first changed his name, to Ted Hayson. Tom had known from his grandfather how poor this village was, and he felt ashamed he'd not done something for it.

Eventually he was able to move on and find the plot of land where his ancestors had lived. The house was a crumbling ruin. Only parts of the stone walls still stood. One old villager said it was at least 600 years old.

He thought about old Tannous on whose knees he sat as a boy to hear tales of Lebanon, the Phoenicians, this house. He picked up a piece of stone and wrapped it in his handkerchief, a keepsake for his office desk.

Then he kneeled and kissed the earth. He had found his roots.

In the time left there remained only the church on the hillside. He found a Lebanese lady, her face lined, a shawl over her head, wearing baggy but clean clothes and she opened the door for him. He gazed around, taking in the simple elegance of the little church, and fell on his knees and prayed.

The feeling of belonging was so strong as he contemplated the past that the tears ran freely. He didn't want to leave.

After three hours in the village the feeling of elation stayed with him as he drove up the mountain to Ehden, a snow-covered resort contrasting so much with Aitou that he thought he was stepping into the French or Italian Riviera. Now he could understand why Lebanon was often called the Switzerland of the Middle East.

He headed straight for the Cedars.

He found a grove of them, dark green against the snow, reminding him of the Psalms verse: "The just man will flourish like a palm tree, like a Cedar of Lebanon shall he grow."

Only about 400 patriarchs remained, fully protected, from the once great forests that covered the upper reaches of the mountains. He approached one cedar that looked to be 20 or 30 years old, its limbs bowed down with snow, but was told it was several thousand years old.

He flung his outstretched arms against the huge knarled trunk and said quietly: "Gee, it's beautiful to feel a mind that is free, that doesn't have to battle against the odds to have its place in the world accepted."

Ngaire, standing a short distance away, was quite used to this eccentricity. She had seen him wrap his arms around the pines at Sydney's Manly beach.

When feeling downcast Tom would slap his palms against a tree and say "you don't have to worry about anything, you survive fires and storms and remain strong." He believed he could feel the tree's strength running through his body. Then he would tell himself: "Why should I worry? I'm breathing, I'm like this tree."

To him a tree was a friend, strong and undemanding. That's why on radio he once interviewed famous tenor Donald Novis, who sang the song *Trees* based on American poet Joyce Kilmer's famous poem about a tree growing on a highway under the Californian sky, containing the line "for only God can make a tree."

But this was different. By touching the ancient cedar he was stepping back into almost 7,000 years of history.

Everything he'd learned and read about Lebanon was defined in this moment. The cedar was at the very heart of the country's history.

He knew archaeological diggings had shown that the first people in this land were Stone Age farmers and fishermen in about 5,000 BC at the sea port later known as Byblos, making it probably the oldest permanently inhabited city in the world. Then about 3,200 BC came a Semitic tribe known as the Giblites who introduced the Bronze Age, cutting the sought-after cedars from Mount Lebanon behind Byblos and trading with the Pharaohs of Egypt who used cedar as a sacred wood to honour the dead.

Caravans from the east brought riches to Byblos in the form of spices, wool, grain and precious stones and this drew conquerors and destruction.

Around 2,300 BC the fierce Amorites and Canaanites invaded Byblos. From here they gradually improved their primitive coastal navigation methods. The history of the Phoenicians began in the next phase of change with the arrival of the mysterious "Sea Peoples" in about 1,200 BC. Historians knew little about them except that they were originally a nomadic Semite people from the Sinai desert.

After ravaging part of Lebanon, they joined the two most important ethnic groups there, the Amorites and Canaanites, to found the Phoenician nation. Through fusion they became a mixture of the melting-pot of races in Lebanon and a people on their own, forming their own identity.

For the next thousand years or so until toppled by Alexander the Great, the Phoenicians pioneered trade through long voyages and colonies as far afield as Spain, revolutionising the lives of everyone they made contact with in a more positive way than any invading army. They came to be regarded, with the Greeks and Romans, as the builders of the world.

From a series of trading posts along the Lebanese coast, their new round-style ships brought fresh ideas such as dyes and glass blowing, ingenious wares and an alphabet of 22 letters on which the world's modern version of 26 letters is based.

The Phoenician city of Byblos gained its name from the Bible because it traded in papyrus rolls for paper from Egypt in exchange for the valued cedar. *Byblos* was also the Greek word for papyrus and when the writings of the Hebrew prophets were translated into Greek, they were given the city's name - the Bible.

Tom learned that the use of papyrus probably explained why no writings survived of the history of the Phoenicians, the people who taught us to write. Papyrus mouldered and rotted in the damp air in cities by the sea.

The Phoenicians daringly sailed their advanced ships to the ends of the known world, extending its limits. Many historians believe they carried their trade to India and Cornwall in England, circled Africa and even reached America 2,000 years before Columbus sailed the ocean blue.

They also sailed the sleekest of fighting galleys, like those of the later Vikings. Their exploits gained for them the name sea lords of antiquity.

Their empire was built not so much on fortress-cities by the sea and land masses but on fleets of ships. They arrived, offered their wares, bartered and departed. The land bases they built in coastal Lebanon served only as launching pads for these nomads of the sea in the same way they once roamed the desert.

By all accounts the Phoenicians were no saints, resorting to a bit of piracy or force when necessary to facilitate their trade. In Greece they had a reputation for kidnapping young girls.

In the annals of history the Phoenicians were regarded as clever, bold, diplomatic, intrepid, energetic, ingenious, inventive, untroubled by scruples and not only venturing into places where none had gone before but also possessing the qualities that could make a nation commercially strong and wealthy.

And they had survived, through to the modern Lebanese. As in their thriving port of Beirut.

Tom decided right on the spot that in future a symbolic green cedar would be the logo on his business cards and letterheads.

He knew he had only scratched the surface, that there was so much more he wanted to know about his forebears and the country, such as seeing the excavations of ancient cities. But time was up and he vowed to return.

On the flight back to Australia he wrestled with all the images crowding his mind. He felt so proud to have learned at first hand that the Christians of Lebanon had withstood the invaders and somehow kept their ethnicity intact, absorbing different cultures and characteristics.

What pleased him most was to know that among the Christian Lebanese were those with blue and hazel eyes. He had seen it himself as he walked around, the redheads and blondes with blue eyes. Probably, he mused, some were among his own forebears, among the first Lebanese to arrive in Australia.

It meant that instead of being ashamed, he should feel pride in his ancestry, just as he believed Australians of convict stock should feel proud of their forebears. They were the adventurous people who would take a chance. The colour of a child's skin from circumstances beyond one's control should not come into it.

He thought of the early Lebanese Christians who migrated to Australia.

They had gone out into the bush and the country towns, worked hard and integrated with Australians, and were among the best migrants the country had known. Unlike the Greeks and Italians then, many had married into Anglo-Saxon families and their children, instead of having pinky white skins, had olive white skins, blue eyes and dark hair or dark brown eyes and blonde hair, some even with freckles.

The racist thoughts that had long exercised the minds of Anglo-Saxons were now beginning to die out.

The second and third generation children of those Lebanese Australians, together with the children of Greeks and Italians and the future offspring of Germans and other Europeans, would be the real Australian of the future, merging with the children of early Anglo-Saxons, who were really transplanted Europeans.

The Australian was in transition.

He wished he could be reborn in 100 years' time to see the change. If the Lebanese could preserve their identity and their qualities against tyrants in tumultuous times, Australians had an even better chance now.

As they landed in Sydney after nearly 10 months away, he said to Ngaire: "I'm glad to be home. And I don't want to see another war zone."

But he had a private war of his own to face.

9

"I AM REAL ESTATE..."

THE headlines said it all: "Tom Jacobs to quit job with 2UE."

While he'd been away on his latest trip abroad, a friend at the station onpassed letters from listeners complaining about the way his interviews were being presented. He checked and found that in a hunt for ratings the station had changed its policy and not told him- everything was now short and sharp. No interviews more than 90 seconds long.

He was sending back in-depth interviews of 10 minutes and they were being butchered. Nothing personal, just new policy. From London he wrote to general manager Alan Faulkner, the man Andrea said had ice in his veins, voicing his disappointment and was told bluntly: "It's your function to get the material and what we do with it is our business."

That abrupt stuff was a bit rich to a man slogging his heart out around the world but he abided by his contract and finished the job.

On his return he rang Faulkner and quit, although he would maintain good relations with 2UE. The *Mirror's* radio writer Heather Chapman made a big story of it.

Two other radio stations wanted him but it wasn't what he had in mind. To consider his future he took a break at the calm and friendly home of an uncle at Gosford on the NSW Central Coast where he'd sometimes gone to unwind.

Nothing was heard of him publicly for months. It was almost as if he'd vanished. Then nine months later on the first day of spring in 1969 radioman Bob Rogers replayed his interview with the boy in the Botanic Gardens, and at the end said: "I wonder what happened to Tom Jacobs?"

123

In seeking a new direction to his life, Tom hadn't been spending his time smelling roses. As he faced his career crisis, he was exploring an idea to start a new radio station and thinking about becoming a serious property man.

Disenchantment with radio had been growing for some time. He knew that in the media he would always be subservient to one person, the boss, or a board. And he'd never found one he could sit down with, reasonably confident of being allowed to do what he wanted. His ideas were original and he always had to fight for them.

Others may have thought he was different because of his ethnicity but he believed it was something else as well - he thought he had a special feeling inside him to do something new and radical and he was always trying to give expression to it.

The media was a confining industry because things had to be done a certain strict way. He blessed the day he'd gone into journalism and broadcasting but now he wanted to go beyond their limitations.

As a kid he'd watched the swallows building their mud nests, industrious, always on the wing. They flitted freely at all times. He yearned to fly free like them in everything he did.

While in London on his recent trip he'd been encouraged to focus on his predicament. A friend, a property developer, asked him one day: "Do you make any money out of these radio programmes you put together?"

"No," said Tom, "I'm only on wages, the dollar equivalent of your fifteen pounds a week. The station makes the money."

"Well, you should think about this. You are a man of ideas with vision. You have this innovative, very creative brain. But you're not building up anything solid, nothing permanent or tangible you can hang on to. You do your broadcasting and it goes out into the ether and disappears.

"Why can't you apply your mind to property with the same concentration? You'll make a lot more money and it's substantial, you're putting something worthwhile in the ground. If I were you I would seriously think about doing full-time what you're now doing on the side."

Tom listened thoughtfully and his friend then said: "Get fully into property. You'll get a lot of satisfaction out of putting one brick on top of another, a hundred on a hundred, a thousand on top of a thousand..."

The friend was right. Broadcasting was too transient an occupation. He was 49, had been in radio 22 years and his future was probably behind him. Analysing it, he'd scooped the pool but really all he'd gained was the intense satisfaction of being creative. But that had begun to wear thin.

He was too old to embrace TV, felt inadequate now with just a mike and a word description without the picture, and wondered what to do.

John Laws, the king of Australian radio, later said of Tom Jacobs: "That transient mentality didn't suit him. He wanted something more permanent and lasting, a monument perhaps. That feeling developed in me later, too.

"That's why I built a beautiful garden on my Cloud Valley farm so that when I die they will say well, at least he left that.

"Jacobs was ahead of his time in radio. Imagine what he'd have done with today's satellite facilities and modern technology? His radio work was different, exploratory, pioneering stuff. Nobody else did it."

Out of a job, Tom finally decided to take two courses.

He believed the NSW Central Coast needed its own radio station as a parochial, independent voice. Whenever he stayed at his uncle's house, he could rarely pick up stations from Newcastle, the nearby city. But how to persuade the Government and cut through the bureaucratic jungle?

Tom had been present at a secret meeting at the home of Federal MP Billy Wentworth to give advice on plans for John Gorton to run as Prime Minister and oust Billy McMahon. As a result he had a pipeline to Gorton. When he put his idea to him, the new PM said he needed justification before the Broadcasting Control Board would consider it.

So he gathered evidence including support from Police Commissioner Norman "The Foreman" Allen, saying it was difficult to get police radio messages through to Central Coast people needing help, and sent the brief to the Prime Minister who referred it to the Board.

They agreed to hold an inquiry but decided he would have to compete for the licence with other contenders - a favourite stultifying Government ploy after someone else has found the idea and done all the hard work.

A dynamic organiser, Tom fired up a lot of local people to get behind his plan, the leading orchardist, newsagent, garageman, solicitors, some joining his Central Coast Broadcasting Committee.

Among those competing for the licence was not only media magnate Sir Frank Packer but also Tom's newly-departed employer, 2UE. That spurred him on to become, on one columnist's description at the time, a bulldog with his teeth into the pants of the Broadcasting Control Board.

The Board held an open inquiry over several days, Tom and four other groups made their submissions - and a year after he started work on it he was awarded the licence. His group won the day because, apart from a strong proposal, he wasn't greedy - he had wide local representation and capital and kept only five per cent of the shares himself.

He named the Gosford station 2GO, arranged the staff and premises and set it up, becoming the first managing director. But it was the same story as with Taree - they wanted him to live there. He relegated himself to the role of director, only attending board meetings. But soon he sold his interest to Packer and moved on.

He then jumped full-time into property, concentrating around Sydney's lower North Shore. Now he had a double challenge, to be successful *and* make money.

At that stage an old real estate man with an office at Castlecrag gave him some friendly advice. "Slow down," he said, "slow down. You're always on edge, always wanting to face a challenge. It will take a great toll on your health if you don't watch it. While you work late, I get away early to tend the fruit trees in my orchard. Money isn't so important. The most important thing is to live a tranquil life."

Tom smiled wryly, saying yes he would pace himself. But of course he didn't. If involved in something it was his nature to be enthusiastic and committed almost to the point of obsession. He was so restless that since his marriage 28 years before, he'd moved home about 20 times.

But he had some reservations about becoming a total property man. Still only buying for investment and selling for profit, he was aware that some of the big operators in the game, the property developers, were regarded as a bunch of legal crooks, greedy rapacious people who wanted to destroy perfectly good buildings and put up rubbish for a quick quid. That was their image.

He believed that to grow bigger, he would probably have to become embroiled in a world of greed, trickery, treachery, dishonesty and power.

The people who succeeded had the reputation of being often those who believed property was where the opportunities for corruption and dishonesty presented themselves for exploitation.

It troubled him because he already sensed that if a businessman wanted to succeed financially at the top level, there was no room for conscience.

That didn't mean a man had to be a crook but if a businessman wanted to climb to the top, morality had to go by the board. Otherwise he could not succeed. He did not see himself in that mould.

His conscience was such that an early business associate once suggested to him he should become a priest. Something might be legally right but morally wrong, but his sense of right and wrong was almost suffocating at times. If in doubt he leaned towards it being wrong.

The property game was not for soft people. That didn't mean it was a game for dishonest people, but it was so full of risk in terms of money borrowed, uncertainties and grappling with councils that nothing was certain until the day you had it all wrapped up. To succeed you had to be a tough personality.

He knew he didn't have the ruthlessness to win through in the big league.

All the same he had an uncanny eye for a bargain. Already he'd demonstrated astuteness as a property trader who was quick to spot a bargain. Those who knew him in his early days marvelled at the way he could skilfully search out a property and negotiate its purchase. He had the ability to see ahead and pick a bargain before it was apparent to others.

But even then he was a visionary rather than a hardnosed businessman.

He also considered himself a pioneer in the field, just as those early Lebanese migrants went out into the backblocks and pioneered assimilation in the Australian community.

The satisfaction he gained from his early success in knowing what to buy and sell, gave him the urge to make property his future life. It promised him the freedom he'd always wanted. That was the lure.

He remembered flying into Hong Kong on his way home from London after his friend gave him the sound advice, looking down over The Peak and saying to Ngaire: "Look at that smorgasbord of property below."

He said the same flying into Sydney.

He found a certain addiction in property dealing. And by the time he'd established the Gosford radio station he was already hooked on property, gaining added inspiration from a plaque he discovered on the office wall

127

of a friend, property developer Sid Londish. It contained the wisdom of an unknown author.

After reading it he thought: "This is what property and development are all about. If taken seriously, here lies the secret of fortune."

"I am the basis of all wealth, the heritage of the wise, the thrifty and prudent. I am the poor man's joy and comfort, the rich man's prize, the right hand of capital, the silent partner of many thousands of successful men. I am the solace of the widow, the comfort of old age, the cornerstone of security against misfortune and want. I am handed down to children through generations as a thing of greatest worth, the choicest fruit of toil.

"Credit respects me yet I am humble; I stand before every man bidding him know me for what I am and possess me. I grow and increase in value through countless days. Though I seem dormant, my worth increases, never failing, never ceasing, time is my aid and population heaps up my gain. Fire and the elements I defy, for they cannot destroy me. My possessors learn to believe in me; invariably they become envied.

"While all things wither and decay, I survive. The centuries find me younger, increasing in strength, sound, unfailing. The thriftless speak ill of me, the charlatans of finance attack me.

"I am trustworthy, I am sound. Unfailingly I triumph and detractors are disproved. Minerals and oils come from me. I am the producer of food, the basis for ships and factories, the foundation of banks, yet I am so common that thousands, unthinking and unknowingly, pass me by.

"I am real estate."

Tom Hayson made a humble start as a property developer, with no hint of what the future would unveil.

Once out of the public spotlight, he'd already changed his name to Hayson when dealing in property. Ngaire had changed over too and so had the children Ian, Paul and Rosemary after leaving school.

A strange thing occurred with Ian. He became Hayson the day he'd left school and as soon as he did, Aussies stopped calling him a wog. Obviously they associated Jacobs with being Jewish.

Even in his last couple of years at Riverview, they'd name-called him if having an argument. He was either a boong, a black bastard or a fuzzy-wuzzy from New Guinea. But Ian always gave as good as he received.

After studying law for a couple of years at Sydney University, where his brother Paul would also do law, Ian worked in Eric White's city public relations firm for a while as a junior consultant and took his first trip abroad. He returned with a Dutch bride, Ietsje, while Tom was still sorting out his own future. Ian thought he would try real estate and took a salesman's job selling blocks of land for Yaramba Estates on the NSW Central Coast, advertised on 2UE. The only trouble was the land was prone to flooding, but he hadn't been told that.

His job as a junior salesman was to roam Sydney in a radio car and call on potential clients to deliver a brochure and sales pitch as soon as a response came in from the ads. Another sales team took clients to the estate to close the deal.

A woman buyer from Bondi recognised him as the youngster who sold her a watery block and in full cry angrily chased him down Wynyard Station ramp in Sydney brandishing a furled umbrella and hurling abuse. He left that job pronto.

The drainage problem at the estate was solved and when he bumped into the same woman three or four years later, ready to duck for cover again, she thanked him - the value of her land had increased fivefold.

He tried selling encyclopaedias but lasted two days before tossing that in. Exploring food franchising didn't last long, either. Searching the newspaper ads, Ian found one seeking a salesman who had the ambition to "earn $25,000 a year."

It turned out to be with Stuart Upton, a real estate firm where Tom knew the marketing manager, Ray Learmont. Ray gave Ian a month's trial and hired him, declaring him to be one of his best salesmen. He set a record with the company for selling houses and blocks of land.

After a year Ian decided to start his own real estate business, telling Tom: "I'm making a lot of money for other people but little for myself."

At that stage Tom was operating out of an office he owned at 320 Military Road, Cremorne with just a loyal secretary, Andreé O'Toole. He knew a real estate agent named Don Skinner whose agency, D.J.Skinner Pty Ltd, was just down the way at 523 Military Road, Mosman.

Tom, who had bought some land from Skinner, was aware that he rented his office space at 523 Military Road but his lease had expired.

Wanting to help his son, Tom said to him: "I think I might be able to do a deal and buy half Don Skinner's agency. If I can, why don't you set up with him?"

He did the deal and they established a small agency with Don Skinner to sell real estate - half owned by Skinner, the other by Ian and Tom. By doing that Tom thought he could keep an eye on Ian and help him make the grade in real estate.

To give Ian security Tom then took out mortgages and bought the building at 523 Military Road, although he stayed in his own office nearby.

They called the agency Skinner Hayson and Associates, but that looked crook. *Skinner* flogging real estate? Hayson Skinner seemed likely to frighten off customers too. It ended up Hayson Associates (Sales) Pty Ltd.

"At least," Tom said to his son, "I won't have to pay agency commission fees on my deals any more."

Later when Ian obtained his own real estate licence Tom bought out Don Skinner who would continue to work for the Haysons as a highly valued executive for the next 30-odd years.

From this small beginning would grow the Hayson Group of Companies, a property empire set to change the face of Sydney and make developers around the world sit up and take notice.

10

HERO SMITHY AND HARD LESSONS

FROM their small real estate agency in suburban Mosman, Tom and Ian Hayson began to expand.

As equal partners they jointly made decisions. But Tom continued to wheel and deal in properties on his own behalf while Ian sold real estate all around Sydney's Lower North Shore and Mosman areas.

The family had moved to a new home in Undercliffe Street, Neutral Bay, when Ian was still at university and Paul and Rosemary were finishing high school. A mansion of a property on about half an acre, it had large gardens and a big house with several flats upstairs. Ngaire still collected the rents from Tom's various flats and kept the tenants in order.

They expanded the agency partly by creative marketing, taking ads at the bottom of page 3 of the *Sydney Morning Herald*, graduating to full page ads on page 6, going from classifieds into the news pages. The Haysons started a trend here, and others soon followed. They also hired good salesmen and trained them to become salesmen of the year.

To give the agency a bigger frontage so more people would notice, they bought and converted a Chinese restaurant next door at 525 Military Road, Mosman. Later, satisfied Ian had been well and truly "blooded" as a real estate man, Tom sold both properties to buy a new corner building at 515 Military Road, and moved all his operations into this office, including a newly-acquired construction arm through a merger with the building firm, A and R Constructions. He also sold his old office in Cremorne.

From here the Haysons really spread their wings.

Tom's modus operandi was to buy a property, then quietly acquire others all around it, amalgamating sites for the future.

He had bought several properties around his Neutral Bay home over a period of several years, mostly old blocks of flats, ostensibly as investments. Ngaire collected those rents, too, while Tom mostly walked around looking at his properties and thinking.

Don Skinner, a director of the Hayson real estate agency, had drawn Tom's attention to a large vacant area of land in Spruson Street, Neutral Bay, overlooking Kirribilli and the Harbour Bridge. A less favourable building site would be hard to imagine. On the side of a steep hill, it was a bushland rubbish dump, rocky and landlocked by the fences of surrounding properties. An eyesore. Venturing on to the land to check it out, he was stung by a bee from a hive someone kept there in a box.

He was also stung by the vision he had when gazing down from the roadway above the land, recognising Anderson Park below.

From his knowledge of history he knew at once this was the spot from which his boyhood hero Smithy, aka Sir Charles Kingsford Smith, had made a daring flight. As a boy in Barraba, he'd listened to a little crystal radio set which his father helped him make, trying to catch news of Smithy's exploits as he pioneered world air routes that would later be flown by millions in big jets.

He had dreamed of travel and flying free like Smithy.

Over the next year Tom bought up the entire three acres and a couple of access properties from eight owners without anyone having a clue to his intentions. Even his accountant, John Leece, wasn't awake to what he was doing, thinking he was just buying good houses for investment through a different company. Only flats or houses, not home units, could be built on sites then, in 1973. He now held two of the largest single landholdings on the Lower North Shore.

Ian, selling hundreds of properties in the area, was Johnny-on-the-spot and kept himself well informed on what was happening in the local councils. One day he went to Tom and said: "Listen, that land of yours with your home on it is worth a lot of money now. The council is about to change the zoning in your area to allow for a lot of home units."

"I know it's valuable, that's why I bought it" said Tom. "How much do you think?"

"You'll get X amount of dollars dad, but if we develop it ourselves, you'll get a lot more. Why give the development profit away?"

The idea of home unit strata titles had been invented in South Australia but was still a major problem in Sydney because councils had not yet related it to their own land zoning regulations. A few high rise buildings appeared on an ad hoc or willy nilly basis on the Lower North Shore, upsetting residents because they stuck up like huge stalacmites and there was no proper plan. Councils decided to stop those developments until a proper plan was prepared for their areas.

Within a year or two, several councils including North Sydney decided to allow residential high rise. Willoughby Council zoned a part of Artarmon for home unit use where previously only houses had been allowed. The zoning was later changed in the area of Tom's properties in Aubin and Undercliffe Streets, Neutral Bay, where he lived.

Previously any flats Tom sold to individual buyers had to be done under company titles with owners holding shares in a company. These were not popular and difficult to finance.

Joining forces as developers, Tom and Ian watched councils closely to observe their zoning changes then talked to property owners to take options over six or seven properties to put a home unit site together, either to build on it themselves or to sell to other developers. Under one ownership, the value increased.

They decided to develop Tom's own landholdings themselves.

Ian was the nuts and bolts man who did most of the energetic running around, the marketing, spotting, day-to-day organising, learning about and watching the role of engineers and architects. Tom was the wise head who sorted out major problems, the communicator who did the high level contacting and arranged financing, waiting for what Ian called "a big one" so Tom could throw all his creative efforts in. When it came to financing, Tom gave credibility to Ian's pitch by just walking into a bank with him.

Only about 26 at the time, Ian often sat in the office with Tom when they had development problems, trying to sort it out. After an hour Ian tired due to the intensity of it all but Tom's mind would be working methodically until he solved the problem, setting it out on a piece of paper. Ian wondered if he'd ever be as good.

The "big one" which Tom decided to develop was the rat-infested rubbish dump overlooking Anderson Park.

That was the first of his two main sites freed up by council for unit development. His associates knew nothing of his plans until one day he told them of the vision he had for quality apartments there when first gazing down on the land from a rocky cliff at the street level above. He saw the whole development in his mind's eye at that time.

"Do you know," he said to accountant John Leece, surprising him at the apparent reason for the project, "the park below is where Smithy took off from in 1934 in the Lady Southern Cross?"

He called the site *Southern Cross Gardens* after Smithy's famous Fokker monoplane in which the pioneer aviator made the first crossing of the Pacific from the US to Brisbane in 1928. Tom always believed not enough had been done to acknowledge Smithy's remarkable deeds, including his record solo flight from England to Australia in 1930.

Apart from Mascot airport named after him, his famous Southern Cross being housed in a glass hangar at Brisbane Airport and Smithy's face on $20 notes, that was about it.

Tom remembered the story as soon as he looked down on Anderson Park. Smithy and P.G. Taylor had taken off from here in July, 1934 in one of the most daredevil takeoffs ever attempted. The great aviator, wanting to compete in that year's Mildenhall (UK) to Melbourne air race, had shipped the plane in from the US. It was an American Lockheed Altair, which he would name Lady Southern Cross.

The Sydney City Council refused to allow him to take off from Macquarie Street in the city to fly to Mascot, so he barged it across the Harbour and arranged to fly from Anderson Park. They took down the power lines but the grass mini-runway was less than 150 metres long.

Going right to the end of the "runway," Smithy and Taylor jumped in and opened the throttle to full against the brakes, with a tug-o-war team of strong men holding the wings and tail back for extra braking power. When Smithy gave the signal the helpers jumped clear and the plane leapt forward. It cleared the seawall with only inches to spare.

Red tape and a damaged engine cowling after a hawk flew into it in Queensland on the way to England prevented Smithy entering the race in the end, but that didn't matter. The Anderson Park flight was one of Smithy's last - he disappeared without trace soon after in the Bay of Bengal. To Tom it was historic stuff and he wanted to do something for his city by building a permanent memorial to Smithy.

He meticulously planned the project, embellishing the luxury apartments with historic memorabilia, bronze artefacts and walkways bounded by beautiful gardens with ferns, wattle and other native shrubs.

This was to be a top quality development to make even the most exclusive suburb proud.

As soon as he announced the project it ran into trouble. Local residents opposed it, wanting to preserve the bush, although it was a cliff-side rubbish tip and private land with no public access. Some aldermen on North Sydney Council then made disgruntled noises, determined to knock it at all costs. He told everyone it would be a memorial but that made no difference. Having taken an attitude, the aldermen didn't want to back off.

Persistence was one of Tom Hayson's strongest qualities. He dug his toes in, saying "I'm going to win this" and the fight was on. He'd fashioned his dream and intended making it come true by working at it.

Before it was over he would know it was almost impossible to be a visionary and a successful businessman at the same time. If he'd looked at it purely as a business proposition, he'd have walked away. But the desire to achieve and the challenge of doing something worthwhile drove him on.

He kept putting the plan into the council and they kept knocking it back. Some aldermen wanted only houses there, others suggested it should be resumed for parkland.

At that stage he thought it dishonest to lobby a council, simply conferring with his designers, architects and builders to make sure everything conformed with council's codes and believing it would go through on merit when presented, while spending all the money he could borrow and afford to put the plan together. How naive!

Although he spoke to several aldermen, his only serious form of lobbying was to try to win support from a Miss King, who lived above the site and happened to be a member of the council. She objected to the plan, thinking it would block views of residents like herself. Tom took her over the site and patiently explained his intentions.

"Look, he said, "I can understand you wanting to preserve your view and the tranquillity. But this rubbish dump will be transformed into a showplace with beautiful gardens. It's going to cost me a fortune to do it. We'll have to gouge out rock and burrow into the side of the hill so the units won't annoy anyone above. The tops are only three storeys tall and won't obstruct anyone. This place will remain a garbage tip unless I do this..."

While that was being played out the Haysons were pressing on with other developments with A and R Constructions to joint-venture new buildings.

With A and R the Haysons began a hectic six or seven year period in which they would build high rise blocks in and around Neutral Bay, Artarmon and Mosman. The strata conversion of flats - the division of air space titles allowing individual ownership - had been made possible for the first time in the world by the South Australian legislation and the Haysons were in on the ground floor, among the first in Australia to do it.

They quickly became the largest developer of home units on Sydney's Lower North Shore by taking advantage of the rezoning of land on which houses or flats previously stood, putting up new residential blocks.

One of these would be *L'Hirondelle,* the site where Tom lived in Neutral Bay. He named it from the French word for the swallow after seeing a French restaurant of that name in London.

He had a figure of the bird embossed in the "o" of the name on his building. On the top floor of his new block of units he built a penthouse for his family - their first luxury home.

Tom was putting one brick on top of another, a hundred on a hundred and a thousand on top of a thousand...and like the swallow, he felt free.

Importantly for him, he was doing it without being hard and tough.

In a block he bought for renovating at Neutral Bay, one elderly lady remained and he was told she didn't want to shift. Someone suggested: "Oh, just go and put pressure on her and she'll go." He couldn't do that.

Instead, he went to see her and said: "Look, we've bought this block and I just want to sit down and talk to you."

She made him a cup of tea, they chatted and he told her she needn't worry and could stay there for the rest of her life if she wished. She put her arms around him and said "thank you" and he left her there.

His essential humanity made him not want to hurt people. He was soft in dealing with personalities and lived by the creed that he should let people associated with him realise their full potential. That caused him to sometimes rely on the wrong people and they tended to take advantage of him. But when it came to dealing with another businessman, he could drive as hard a bargain as anyone. He was simply not a ruthless person who wanted to walk over others, without regard for anyone but himself.

Tom used to say to Ian in those early years: "Son, there are two ways of getting to the top. One is walking over people. The other way is to go around them like greased lightning. That's the way the Hayson family does things."

Whenever there was a setback, Ian saw Tom suffer every blow, every knock because of his soft nature. He saw him many times with the stuffing knocked out of him as a development went wrong or a financial crisis hit, or when he almost made it but the prize was taken from his grasp at the last minute. Others could see the writing on the wall but not Tom - he had an amazing capacity to keep going and usually get there.

Ngaire saw him as a workaholic, fastidious with detail who delegated but still liked to check things himself, although he had excellent people working for him. He expected others to play the game fairly but if they hurt him he didn't hit back or seek revenge, he just simply turned away.

Tom regretted not having an accountant's mind or a background of business management training. In the big time the need for accuracy in figures was critical. He even tried a correspondence course in accountancy but gave it up. He was simply no good at figures but could look at a situation and say it would work because of some innate ability to get close to working out a deal without relying on some accountant watching the bottom line as if his life depended on it.

Wealth was not his motive but he knew if a deal worked, the money would look after itself. He had people around him who could work out the accountancy aspects, considering it more important to keep his mind free to plan and create.

An old-fashioned man, he could not use calculators or computers and still looked at things in the old imperial terms of inches, feet, yards, acres and miles.

Tom Hayson learned some hard lessons from *Southern Cross Gardens* and other early projects.

He learned about the rottenness of the development game, the viciousness and uncertainty of market and financial cycles, the illogical and unreasonable behaviour of some council bureaucrats, the intransigence of unions and a whole range of other things.

He had an early chance of avoiding the trauma that *Southern Cross Gardens* would become, but didn't take it.

After spending $300,000 to buy the site, he was offered $900,000 by Sir Paul Strasser of Parkes Development for the right to develop it. But instead of taking the $600,000 profit, he wanted to develop it himself.

In another long-running battle he bought a large house site in Harrison Street, Neutral Bay where he sought to build an eight-storey block of units. Already eight and 12 storey blocks had gone up in the street.

His plan conformed to all council's regulations and guidelines and, being on an elevated area with views of the city, the building could not have blocked anyone else's views. But some of the local residents didn't want another block in the street - and if residents who vote the aldermen into power can raise enough stink, councils will go to water. In this case his proposal was knocked back after two years of effort.

Tom went to the Land and Environment Court. On the day of hearing the council sent its own bus around to Harrison Street, picking up all the malcontents who packed the court in a show of strength. The Court rejected his application.

Some time later he was walking in Harrison Street past units near where he had intended building his block. A woman watering her lawn asked if she could have a word with him. He stopped, recognising her as one of the leading protesters.

"Mr Hayson, I want to apologise to you," she said. "We did a terrible thing to you. I'm sorry we complained to the council and had your project knocked back. I now realise it wasn't justified. I feel we wronged you and it has been playing on my conscience."

He looked at her and said softly: "I thank you for what you've said. I'm glad you've finally owned up. You did me an awful lot of damage. But thank you for saying what you did. I appreciate it." And he walked on, hoping it would stay on her conscience a long time.

That exercise in the first instance had cost him a quarter of a million dollars in cash, which he could ill afford at the time. He'd bought a property at the back of the site from the owner, a Chinese, for $350,000 to give his proposed block two entrances. When the unit deal was rejected, he was forced to sell this property cheaply, after the same Chinese owner approached him and, knowing he was caught, knocked the purchase price down to $100,000.

Five years later he heard the same man made $1.25 million by selling the site for townhouses - a profit of $1.5 million at Tom's expense.

That taught Tom to have great respect for the Chinese in business.

The *Southern Cross Gardens* took more than a year from the time he bought the site to get the plan through the council by a narrow margin, including Miss King's vote. A minority of aldermen then stirred up trouble.

Rumours abounded and stories appeared in the papers suggesting there had been wrongdoing in the Haysons obtaining approval, that some improper influence had been at work.

"We must have an inquiry," said the stirrers.

The council appointed a rising young barrister and later QC, Murray Tobias, to investigate, holding in abeyance the approval that had been properly given. That went on for months before the barrister found there was no case to answer, exonerating the Haysons from any suggestion of impropriety and making the council look silly.

The delay had the effect of wounding the Haysons financially because interest rates suddenly went up, adding substantially to their costs and holding charges for the idle site. But the sawdust Caesars of the council couldn't give a rat's functional orifice for the problem they had unfairly caused.

The adverse publicity attracted further unwelcome attention which gravely embarrassed the Haysons.

Tom had borrowed several hundred thousand dollars from the NSW Permanent Building Society through his friend the chairman, Angus Moir, brother of Bishop Hulme Moir, the Anglican Bishop of Sydney. The loan was for projects other than *Southern Cross Gardens* which was backed by finance from the then Bank of NSW. The building society would later become a bank too.

The society had two tiers of loans, one at ordinary interest rate for housing and another at higher interest for commercial projects. The loan was at the higher rate, made legitimately to Tom through a company which he and Moir had formed for another purpose.

That company played no part in the *Southern Cross* development. But somebody leaked it and the press had a field day imputing all sorts of offences from fraud to immorality and robbing intending home buyers of scarce funds.

The ABC's *This Day Tonight* TV programme mercilessly attacked Moir and Hayson. When the story broke, Tom was made to look like a scoundrel and Moir his partner in crime.

As it hit the papers Tom went into a newsagent's at Neutral Bay and, seeing people stare at him, felt like a leper.

He rode through it because he knew he'd done nothing wrong but the unfair allegations had such a devastating effect on Moir that he later went to live in New Zealand.

The next problem was union building lurks and on-site guerilla warfare.

That was in the period of early green bans and the rise of Jack Mundey as boss of the Builders Labourers' Federation and other militant union leaders. Building workers played merry hell with the construction of the *Southern Cross Gardens* units, designed to blend in with the surrounding environment.

Most of the workers knocked off early, around 3 pm and went to the pub. Some would come back after 6 pm when the site was deserted and deliberately destroy or damage the work that had been done.

This applied particularly to plaster work and even brickwork. Next morning it would be sliced through or knocked over. Sometimes as much as half the work done the previous day would have to be done again.

The damage was usually done inside the building where the culprits could not be seen, simply to make the job last longer and get more money out of it.

That wasn't the only rorting. If any special work was needed such as gouging deeply into rock to provide underground parking for 150 cars, workers' leaders would have to be slung special payments.

At one stage a crane driver was needed but the man the building company wanted to employ was not in the union and unacceptable. An inexperienced union man was put on but he was so hopeless damage was caused and the job delayed. Eventually a capable crane driver was hired but a union boss had to be paid on the side.

The Haysons had nothing to do with these arrangements, made by the building company. Tom fumed later at the thought of it but that's what went on in the building industry and the builder decided it was either cop it or have further trouble, maybe even bringing the job to a halt.

Naturally costs blew out. Half way through the project Tom was certain he would not make any money out of it. A developer friend who looked over the site said to Tom: "You've spent too much money on this. The rooms are too big. The excavation work is too costly. It's going to be a white elephant. You'll go broke on this."

The economy tightened under the Whitlam Government and at one stage of construction the group's interest rates climbed to 21 per cent. Tom had suspected when a quarter of the way through he was unlikely to show a profit and he could have pulled back at that stage, sold it off in pieces and still made a profit.

He realised later he should have made that commercial decision but he'd told everyone this was to be a memorial. He didn't like defeat, and pride and the desire to have a public success on his hands carried him through, even if in his heart of hearts he doubted it was worth all the trouble.

It took nearly three years to plan, gain approvals on and build - a long haul that can destroy any developer as circumstances change. Instead of $6 million, it cost $12 million. The gardens alone cost $2 million.

He lost about $500,000 on the deal, but could have saved himself all the troubles associated with building it and walked away with a profit of $600,000 by selling the plans on to Parkes Development. All up, it amounted to a total loss of $1.1 million.

In spite of the financial problems, he spared no expense in making the opening, on April 23, 1976, a smash hit affair.

For the ceremony he flew in Smithy's widow, Mrs Mary Tully, first class from Canada, landing her by helicopter on Anderson Park so she could have a bird's eye view of the memorial to her famous late husband and get a thrill stepping out on Smithy's pocket handkerchief takeoff spot.

Other guests included Lady Joy Taylor, widow of Smithy's old co-pilot Sir Gordon Taylor, John Ulm, son of Charles Ulm who flew with Smithy and Smithy's old engineer, Harry Purvis.

The three luxury blocks of 52 units, reached by Smithy Drive, connected by Charles Ulm Walk and decorated by the leafy Sir Gordon Taylor Sanctuary Garden, each had an aviation theme name - *Altair* after Smithy's Anderson Park plane in which he soon after lost his life, *Avian* after the plane in which he made his record England-Australia flight and *Aries* after an RAF Lancaster which made a record flight on the same route in 1946.

Mrs Tully, who had married Smithy after a whirlwind shipboard romance on her first sea voyage, unveiled a stone-mounted propeller identical to the one on his Lockheed Altair as a focal point of the memorial.

Opening the complex, Premier Sir Eric Willis applauded Tom Hayson's spirit to invest millions of dollars while others were offloading their commitments and said more than being just a new apartment block, this was a dream fulfilled.

Seated among the dignitaries with the sun sparkling on Sydney Harbour below them, Tom looked into the blue sky, nudged Ngaire and said: "Get a load of this, Smithy."

Tom couldn't believe his ears one day in this period on hearing the comment of an Italian friend, indicating how much Australia had changed.

The Italian, whom they called Roy, did carpentry work for the Haysons. He and his family were interned here during the war because they had not been born in Australia and were regarded as aliens.

Roy wanted to buy a property near Chatswood railway station and asked Tom to look at it for him. He did so, saying he thought it could go to $250,000 at auction but advised Roy not to pay more than about $200,000.

A few days later a beaming Roy announced he'd succeeded and described his battle at the auction.

"Mr Tom, I boughta that house, I do justa as you tella me. I did not starta my bid until it went to $190,000. Then a bloke said $191,000. I said $200,000 quick smart. This other bloke he said $201,000 and it went up by thousands until I get it fora $230,000.

"But Mr Tom, do you knowa who the other fellow was? You wonta believe it, but he was a bloody dago!"

Tom laughed, thinking how things had changed. Migrants were now feeling they belonged so much in this country they were taking over from the Anglo-Saxons and knocking other migrants.

He had observed with satisfaction too how race was gradually being removed as a factor in Australia's immigration policies.

In 1966 the Liberal Government's Immigration Minister Hubert Opperman had announced changes in migrant applications - now "well-qualified" people could apply if they were suitable as settlers, could integrate readily and had qualifications useful to Australia.

The Government also decided to allow "temporary residents," who were not required to leave Australia, to become residents and citizens after five years instead of 15 as previously required.

Restrictions on non-European migrants were also eased. The term "well qualified" replaced the criteria "distinguished and highly qualified" and the number of non-Europeans allowed to migrate would be "somewhat greater than previously."

The White Australia policy had been quietly shelved. The number of non-European settlers had risen from 746 in 1966 to 2,696 in 1971 and part-Europeans in those years from 1,498 to 6,054.

The Whitlam Labor Government, having removed race discrimination from its own party policies while in opposition, had gone further in office in 1973, legislating to make all migrants, regardless of origin, eligible for citizenship after three years of permanent residence.

It also issued instructions to overseas posts to disregard race as a factor in selecting migrants. But the number of non-European migrants did not increase substantially until after the Fraser Liberal Government was elected in 1975. Large-scale Asian migration had just begun in 1976 and the new policy of multiculturalism was just around the corner.

Australia was now an irreversible immigrant society, having peacefully absorbed nearly five million migrants from 100 countries. Many stories of impoverished migrants succeeding were showing out.

Tom fervently hoped that although his homeland was now a poly-ethnic society, the Anglo-Saxon culture and traditions on which the European majority was based, would prevail as the principal culture to absorb and reflect the minority ethnic groups now making Australia culturally rich and diverse.

He had gradually changed his attitude towards the Anglo-Saxons.

That was due to his wife who, after 35 years of marriage, had never once cast a slur on his ethnic background, and to his greater understanding of the Anglo-Saxons in their own country. He'd studied them on several visits to England with Ngaire and had come to respect their long history and the traditions they had passed on to the rest of the world.

In this way the Anglo-Saxons in Australia, now forming the nucleus of the future Australian, had inherited their tolerance and understanding even in this distant part of the world to the extent that they could handle the changes now taking place through the mix of races. He sincerely believed that. He knew the Australians could still be abrasive and hurtful but thought that deep down they didn't really mean to be racist.

When an Australian asked "where do you come from?" it wasn't intended to be offensive. It was a directness born out of living in a vast and often inhospitable land, a curiosity, if somewhat curt, arising from being isolated for so long from the world at large.

Looking at the situation then as a middle-aged person, he could not think of any other race in the world apart from an Anglo-Saxon society who would have welcomed so many people into their midst with so little trouble. The final proof, though, was still to be seen as new racial groups came in.

Privately he still felt inferior from the racial taunts of his schooldays. And the feeling that he needed to achieve to prove himself was still as strong as ever.

To learn more about his background he returned to Lebanon with Ngaire shortly before the 1975 civil war erupted but decided not to stay too long after a bomb blast at Beirut Airport. His racial inquiries encouraged Ngaire to ferret out her own ethnic past in England and he accompanied her to numerous places in England and Scotland to search records.

Their son Paul added to the family's multi-racial mix by marrying an Australian bride of Italian origin. A solicitor by profession, Paul was handling most of the legal work for Tom and Ian's developments.

From the *Southern Cross Gardens* experience, Tom Hayson formed a poor view of councils which would not be erased over the years.

How could it be otherwise when an alderman who had spent all his life as a cleaner on trains set himself up as an authority on town planning, or an aldermen who as a hairdresser tried to shove down his throat what to build or how to carry it out?

He had been the victim of council factions, of people who didn't have the vision to see even a WC built on the site when what he wanted to do was build something of beauty and lasting value. If an apartment block could mean that, he had achieved it against the odds.

But from now on he would try to steer clear of the press who had only wanted to give space to controversy, putting him on the receiving end.

In future he would go about his business with as little fuss as possible until he reached a stage on developments where he had the ammunition to answer any critics.

And he would fight. No longer would he sit back and make a clay pigeon of himself. He would lobby. All councils were bureaucratic, usually fairly evenly divided into those who favoured development and those who didn't.

In future he would find out all he could about the aldermen and, envisaging the whole council in front of him, work out a war plan.

Starting with the mayor, he would work down the list to form pluses and minuses - Bill is a doubtful quantity, I'll investigate Dick's background to see where he's coming from, Harry will be honest in his judgment, you can forget Bert...

Perhaps there were things in the plan he could alter, maybe the height or width, or a little more garden space. Even if they didn't knock his plan outright, he knew someone would oppose some aspect and he'd have a better chance if he could find out those objections and address them.

Then Tom would draw up another list to assess the council staff, the planner, engineer, even the social workers. Making his own inquiries so nothing was second hand, he would find out about these people and if possible get to know them. Then he would phone the mayor and ask him about his development and seek a meeting with him with his expert officer present to ask their opinions.

If the mayor or planning officer indicated some aldermen were against something, he would take heed of that and make amendments. By the time he submitted a plan he would have a good idea of winning over the numbers for approval.

He would impress on council officers the merits of his scheme and outline why it should be accepted, watching every minor detail. He would fight hard and if necessary see every alderman to neutralise opponents. He knew he would not succeed unless he did.

But the one thing he would not do was pay a bribe.

He knew any hint of that could ruin his reputation and integrity for life and retaining his good name meant more than any amount of money or getting a project through. He was always careful what he said when in the presence of any council person whom he suspected of, or had been told, was open to corruption, so that nothing could be misconstrued.

Everything he'd done with *Southern Cross Gardens* had been right except for one thing - the market went down and interest rates went up.

No matter how brilliant you made a project, it could go wrong. Tom realised he should decide whether to be a visionary or a developer.

A developer friend who started with nothing was then worth $200 million. He did it by measuring every cent, squeezing every carpenter, electrician and contractor to the last drop after lining them up to get the best deal.

His friend would have taken the $600,000 *Southern Cross Gardens* profit without building it, bought existing properties, improved and rented them out rather than building something new. These would sustain him through a bad cycle. In the commercial premises he rented out, he even used recycled soap and reduced the water flow in the taps - that's how he succeeded.

This man was honoured and respected for his success. But to Tom, he was miserable and represented the walking dead.

That was a sure way to make money. Tom knew all the business tenets of sound property development. Essentially they were summed up in an old Lebanese saying - don't be greedy, if there's a profit in it, take it and leave something for the next man. By not squeezing the lemon dry, a prudent developer was usually safe from cycles or other troubles.

He also knew he should not try to weather the storm and develop a project to its ultimate stage unless he had enough substance behind him to carry on if it failed for some reason. Just like buying shares - you never bought shares unless you could afford the money you were spending on them because the share market was more volatile than real estate.

But against those truisms he tried to balance his urge to build something decent, lasting and permanent which people could admire.

After the *Southern Cross Gardens* loss Tom said to Ian: "Well, we gained great experience out of that. We've still got our lives ahead of us.

"Let's learn from this because honestly, it gives you the freedom to do what you want."

It merely whetted his appetite to do better next time.

H

THE GOLDEN GATE

TOM Hayson could hardly wait for the dawn to break each day.

Lying awake, he'd be ready to bounce up and get dressed, eager to get on with it and meet whatever challenge the day might have in store for him. Often as the sun came up, he'd be dressed and ready to go.

He was so keen that at times he emerged from the bathroom trailing a stream of toilet paper on which he'd written notes for himself while sitting on the loo.

He firmly believed in the principle that you cannot achieve anything worthwhile except by the sweat of your brow. No quick solutions, only constant hard work.

That had been made plain to him as a boy by old grandfather Tannous when he visited him on school holidays. "Look at an oak tree," said Tannous, "it cannot grow overnight. An acorn must go into the ground first and develop over a long time before you get the oak tree. People can be lucky but there are no short cuts. You can't succeed by cheating or taking someone down. Success only comes through hard work."

The property development industry was just beginning in Australia with Sydney its centre and the Haysons were in the forefront of those who called themselves developers. Most people thought developers were just builders, misunderstanding their role. But if a builder went bust, they thought he was a developer, not realising a developer could be the victim of a builder like anyone else. Later they would look upon most developers as shysters, even when unjustified, whereas in America the property developer is on a pedestal because he is seen as a creator.

The Haysons were traditional developers who drew together all the expertise and money to complete a project from the ideas stage up.

They brought in under one roof all the disciplines needed from acquiring the land, providing the builder and the finance to pay everybody, the designers, planners and architects, the people to sell and market the finished product and deliver it on time and hopefully within budget.

They motivated everyone to act in unison, borrowed the money and took the big risk. In short, as developers they were entrepreneurs like movie producers who made it all happen.

As entrepreneurs the Haysons were hands-on people who liked to be in control as far as possible. And busy as they were, they were always ready for new opportunities.

They were in the early stages of building *Southern Cross Gardens* when the next major venture came up.

A cousin of Tom's named Frank Jacobs rang to say he'd found a terrific site on the booming Gold Coast...Ian flew in and checked it out. Indeed it more than fulfilled the fail-safe real estate test of *location location location.*

One block from the beach at Surfers Paradise, right at the intersection of the main north and south highways. And the site could be amalgamated.

Tom fashioned his dream. This was a standout site in Australia's premier tourist and resort area, worthy of something new and spectacular that would not only excite the rest of Australia but cement the reputation of the Haysons as property innovators.

At the time the Hayson Group was doing well, having built up a good asset base on Sydney's Lower North Shore by acquiring properties and building highrise blocks. The group had built two 15-storey towers in Neutral Bay and made good profits, with 8-storey residential blocks under construction at Artarmon with their joint venture partners.

They weren't builders *per se* but were skilful at putting sites together, relying on the expertise and co-operation of their partners, A and R Constructions, for the building skills to deliver the project on time and on budget.

Tom and Ian planned the tallest and largest residential block in Australia for the Surfers Paradise site, 35 storeys of luxury apartments offering the latest in leisure living. The highest building on the Gold Coast near it was 12 storeys. So it would be a landmark, the tallest residential block then in the southern hemisphere.

To provide the quality and international standard of accommodation they envisaged, Tom studied the latest luxury features in Honolulu and Miami.

Every one of the 177 apartments would face north-east with similar ocean beach and mountain views. From about the eighth floor up, the beach vista would stretch for 60 kilometres and on a clear day even the skyscrapers of Brisbane would be seen beyond the glistening sands. Surely one of the most superb views in the world.

The building would be fully air-conditioned with its own power supply plant, four high-speed lifts including one of see-through glass on the outside, two acres of Polynesian-style gardens with swimming pools, picnic and play areas, a running brook, a waterfall and a three-hole putting green, with underground parking for 200 cars.

On the top would be four magnificent two-level penthouses, each with its own sea-water swimming pool, spa and sauna, 360-degree views, framed by a natural garden. To justify that, you would think they were situated in Honolulu in one of the world's richest money belts.

Inside with their chandeliers and gold-plated fittings, the penthouses would represent the last word in luxury living.

Add to that restaurants, cafes, bars, shops and other facilities and you had a complete resort lifestyle at a level Australians had not previously enjoyed.

The Hayson Group borrowed some millions of dollars for the first stage of this massive building and set to work. On the strength of *location location location* it was a reasonable risk. Their figures showed that even on a 50 per cent devaluation of their units in the market, they would still make money. That's how good the site was on all factors considered.

Tom decided to call it *The Gateway* because it was at the gateway to the Gold Coast. Out of the blue he received a curt legal letter from Sir Reg Ansett, one of Australia's most aggressive businessmen, saying if he used the name he'd sue him. Ansett had three or four Gateway Inns at various airports.

Tom didn't want a legal brawl to hold up development, so he wrote back saying he intended only calling his building *Gateway*. That seemed to go further up Sir Reg's nostrils. Do it and I'll sue, he said. A solicitor told Tom he'd win but it would take time through the courts.

When in San Francisco Tom had always made sure he crossed the Golden Gate Bridge to take in the Bay scenery and decided to call his building by that name.

He then noticed a small motel just outside Surfers named Golden Gate Motel. He checked and the name was registered. Jeez! And not far from it were the Golden Gate Apartments.

The initiative from his old newshound days came to the fore. Looking in the dictionary he saw the French words for Golden Gate were La Porte D'Or. So he registered La Porte D'Or and underneath in brackets put *The Golden Gate*. Naturally everyone called it *The Golden Gate*.

Special techniques had to be used in construction. Some of the walls in Gold Coast apartment blocks were so thin you could hear the ecstatic cries of lovers bonking in the next unit. To overcome this irritation and ensure privacy, concrete walls more than 20 centimetres thick were used, requiring the builders to have their own cement works on site.

Local protest groups then tried to stop the work proceeding. One problem, blown out of proportion, was that wind caused water from the penthouse pools to spray down below. At great expense, the Hayson Group had large models built and tested in a wind tunnel at Sydney University, modifying the pool areas to prevent spray in the highest winds. In a world first, the rooftop water fed the building's sprinkler system.

Then the protesters claimed that as the builders dug down for foundations, the sea would gush in. After more experiments, giant concrete foundation slabs were developed to prevent the slightest risk of that occurring. As one complaint was overcome, another broke out - sand was being blown by the wind...

The locals had never seen anything on this scale before. The Haysons invited various community groups to inspect the site but they never did.

That was mere skirmishing. The real trouble began when interest rates rocketed under the Whitlam Government. It gave the Haysons their first experience of being completely in the hands of a bank as with *Southern Cross Gardens*, or in the case of *The Golden Gate*, an insurance company.

They had borrowed from QBE Insurance at 7 per cent and based all their feasibility on that figure. By the time the Whitlam Government was sacked in November, 1975, interest rates had risen to 21 per cent. And within two years in the credit squeeze that followed under the Liberal Government, interest rates for development money went even higher.

The sudden rise to 21 per cent was right in the construction period of both *The Golden Gate* and *Southern Cross Gardens*. The extra 14 per cent killed the developer's profit. Worse, it made it extremely difficult for people to buy the units because they couldn't get finance.

It became a vicious circle. People in that period didn't expect interest rates to go through the roof. Australia had been on the sheep's back in earlier years, you borrowed money at around 7 per cent and it stayed near that level. Nobody had any experience of such a radical credit squeeze, the worst since the Great Depression.

Just as people generally weren't used to dealing with a serious credit squeeze, neither were the banks. They simply panicked and pulled in their loans. They were able to do that so easily because in those days a lot of their money was lent on a monthly or 90-day basis - a foolish notion these days but then it was the norm.

The whole scenario changed right through for the next 20 years. No longer could you rely on your banker. Prior to that period the banks traditionally stood by their customers. They lent big money to people in the bush, the farmers and graziers and stood by them in droughts and periods of lower wool prices, knowing they would recover. But in the period from the last Whitlam years to around 1977-78, ethics and morality went out the window because the banks panicked and dropped their bundle. No longer could you depend on your banker in times of need.

The tightness came on quickly. Banks even pulled back from loan agreements in writing if they hadn't physically lent the money. Or at best they said you can have the money but it will cost you twice as much.

Suddenly the Haysons had to use more of their cash than anticipated, money earmarked for other purposes. They had to pull it from somewhere to fill the gap. It limited their ability to do anything else except concentrate on the projects in hand. Their asset base was squeezed as they sold off units at reduced prices, doing anything they could to bring in cash.

They were unlucky too because they were building super quality projects, which took more time for approval and was more costly to build.

They were really unsuited for that sleight-of-hand development world where the general attitude was make a quick quid and get out as soon as possible, building as cheaply as you could. They weren't interested like some others in putting up boxes around the place.

They were motivated to create something different for which they would be recognised, and in preserving their reputation, integrity and principles.

They could not lose anything by doing that - except money.

At one stage Tom was so strapped for cash he could not see how he could pay for the building and other running costs on *The Golden Gate* beyond the next fortnight. He couldn't borrow in Australia and unless he raised money in a hurry, there was a risk that work on the building would stop. Also, he was staring bankruptcy in the face.

As in other times of desperation in his life, he turned to music for courage and inspiration. Sitting alone he listened to the soaring and soulful works of some of the great masters, violin concertos, symphonies and it stirred his creativity. Although he couldn't really afford it, he flew to London to try to get a loan.

He tried a few sources there but the English financiers only wanted to know Australians in the good times. When things were bad, as they were then in the Whitlam years, all they wanted to do was wriggle out of any deals they had with Australia.

As a last resort in London he spoke to a dear architect friend, Dr Walter Marmorek, who rang a contact of his, the head of the Belgian Bank in Hong Kong, and said: "This friend of mine will call and see you on his way back to Sydney. You can trust him with your life. Help him if you can."

As a precaution before leaving Sydney, Tom had told his main bank manager at North Sydney that someone abroad might try to get a line on him and, knowing how distrustful bankers were, he asked him to mention his good record if contacted.

Sure enough when he got to Hong Kong the astute Belgian, after getting his banker's name from Tom's London friend, had checked on him.

Tom and the Belgian, Pierre Mardulyn, had dinner at ultra expensive *Gaddi's* in the Peninsula Hotel and after chatting generally Pierre said: "The bank won't lend you a cent."

Tom's heart dropped. Pierre went on: "But I will. I've had a good look at it. We'll do it through a group of friends. Now, you need half a million to keep going? Mind you, we'll want a good interest rate, twenty per cent..."

He borrowed the money in American dollars and it kept them going until they were able to do a deal with the building's financiers, QBE Insurance, to finish the job.

They thanked their lucky stars they weren't dealing with a bank as financier of that project because banks were selling out property from under the people to whom they'd lent money. And they would continue to cut and run in this fashion every time there was a downturn.

They went to QBE and laid it on the line. "We simply can't pay this 21 per cent," Tom said. "What's more, the units will be very difficult to sell because we won't be able to get the finance for them. I know we'll be able to do it if you lend us the funds to finish the building. But we need you to stand by us."

The insurance company came back with an arrangement by which interest would be frozen at 10 per cent, and anything above that would be equally shared. "But," they said, "you Haysons have got to do all the work. You have to go and sell the units without further input from us. Now it's up to you." A fair deal, said Tom.

The QBE group then kept advancing the money to finish the building.

But before all that fell into place, the Haysons took a hallmark decision to break up their partnership with A and R Constructions by buying them out and gaining full control. The partners were proving to be incompatible and the big projects were not being delivered on time.

As managing director, Tom Hayson needed to demonstrate to QBE and to the banks in their other projects that they could be certain the Haysons controlled what was going on and could remove the problems of delays and finish the projects.

When it reached the stage where the roof went on, Tom and Ian flew to Surfers to inspect it. Treating it as a big deal the builders sent a limo to Coolangatta airport to meet them. Standing at the foot of the towering edifice and gazing up, Tom showed a nice touch of the ridiculous by saying to Ian: "Did we build this bloody thing?"

Before it opened they were selling the units. People who rang to inquire were surprised to find themselves talking to either Tom or Ian. To make it happen in a credit squeeze, they personally did the selling, taking newspaper ads mainly in Sydney and Melbourne. Potential buyers were invited to their office in suburban Mosman, shown a slide presentation and if serious, were flown to Surfers in a Lear jet at the Haysons' expense.

The final cost ran out at $28 million. The champagne opening ceremony, in May, 1977, was delayed while 200 guests waited for VIPs from southern States to be flown in by private jet owing to commercial airline congestion in the wake of a long air controllers' strike.

In his address Tom Hayson lashed "ratbags, conservationists, knockers and so-called friends of the earth" whose protests he said had cost his group an extra $4 million. And he bucketed air controllers and others for causing a national malaise of disruption.

Warming to his subject he said: "In building, there are still people left with pioneering spirit and sheer Australian guts and they are not afraid of work. We built this structure because we knew that Queensland is the last bastion of free enterprise."

That was the right stuff for feisty Queensland Premier Joh Bjelke-Petersen, who officially opened *The Golden Gate*. Flanked by Federal Treasurer Phillip Lynch and Queensland Minister Big Russ Hinze, he also gave disruptive elements a good pasting, commending the Hayson Group and their financiers for showing spirit in overcoming obstacles.

The Golden Gate generated enormous publicity.

Not the least of this was when Phillip Lynch bought a unit there as a holiday hideaway for his family. He was pilloried in Parliament and the newspapers, the suggestion being that either he had been given favoured treatment for a loan, or corruption and skulduggery were afoot.

Disastrous for the Federal Treasurer, it was a boon for sales because it attracted numerous well-to-do people to the *Gate*. But it was unfair to Lynch who was probably the least wealthy of the top Liberals then in Government.

The loan, arranged by Ian Hayson, was done in the normal way.

Ian had done a three-week course with a building society to enable him to fill out loan forms and send them to the society for approval and a second signature. They had what was called special loans, for $100,000 or more. Lynch could muster only $25,000 as a deposit and went through the normal procedures, supplying income statements.

But when it was leaked to the press that he'd received a "special loan," his political opponents and the press made a Roman feast of it. Still, he survived well enough to be knighted later.

The publicity opened the floodgates for Tom and Ian, who became the first in Australia to develop a highrise fully-serviced apartment complex.

Within a few weeks they had sold dozens of units. And it gave them the clue to use testimonials in their advertising with the permission of the more celebrated people who bought units to live in or for investment. In about 18 months they had sold every one of the 177 units and three of the penthouses.

The Golden Gate became famous. Commercial aircraft used it as a beacon, television as a logo. At least 30 millionaires bought in, most of them living there among Qantas pilots, doctors, lawyers, actors and the new rich like vegetable distributors and used car dealers.

Investors rented their units to holidaying outsiders and among those who stayed there in its early days were Marlon Brando, pop group Sherbet, Julie Anthony, Paul Hogan, Kamahl and the cast of the TV's *Naked Vicar* Show. The burghers of Toorak and Vaucluse, too, had somewhere to go on the garish Gold Coast that was world class.

It gave the Gold Coast its greatest promotional and investment kick since sugar grower J.H.C. Meyer built the first hotel there, the Main Beach, in 1888. Just as world-weary American and European jetsetters were drawn to the playgrounds of the rich and famous at Monte Carlo, Acapulco, St Tropez, the Seychelles and Aspen in Colorado, the rich and not-so-rich Australian tourists flocked more than ever to Surfers, joined later by the Americans and Japanese.

Gold Coast Mayor Sir Bruce Small showed his appreciation one night when he rang Tom in Sydney and said: "We've got another blackout up here. The only lights are in your wonderful building. It's lit up like a firefly."

For the second time in a short period Tom and Ian learned the lesson: Don't build a costly project without the substance to survive a severe credit squeeze and market slump.

They didn't make any money out of it but kept a penthouse for themselves which they would later sell for $1 million. So on that score they finished in front. Ian worked it out that they would have done better if they'd put the money they originally invested in the project in a bank at 3 per cent and left it there.

To survive a gut-wrenching credit squeeze and make a profit was a notable achievement. They were the only company putting up a major building on the Gold Coast at that time which didn't go into receivership.

The Haysons may not have made any real profit out of their super effort, but it gave them credibility as serious developers.

Suddenly people in the industry like Sir Keith Campbell, head of the Hooker Corporation, were taking them seriously.

Ever the innovators, they were already moving in a new direction.

12

BOOMERANG

THE first big recession in which the Haysons were caught made one thing crystal clear: Nobody could be sure any more when the bubble in Australia would burst.

Any developer who tackled a big venture had to be prepared for mega risk. But if he made money out of it, he was likely to be tagged a "dirty developer" who had somehow rorted the system. His risks were ignored.

Tom Hayson knew people generally did not appreciate that Australia, with its small population, was vulnerable in the world market.

The trouble was we played follow the leader to the US and UK and as a nation were too subservient to those influences. If they were having a bad time, you could bet your bottom dollar Australia would too - often, Tom believed, for artificial reasons.

Australians, too, were generally knockers who seemed to resent anyone making money instead of striving to do the same as did the early migrants, most of whom arrived dirt poor. Until that attitude changed, the country could not become great.

An example was when Ian talked Tom into reluctantly buying a new Mercedes. Ian had a Mercedes first but Tom happily held on to his old Holden. Soon after buying his gleaming Mercedes he parked it in Mosman on a hot day and opened the sun roof.

A man leaned over the opening and growled "capitalist bastard." A week later someone cut a deep scratch along one window. Tom left it there as a reminder that *he* should never envy anyone.

Later he took to lunch a town planner who was giving him a hard time over a development. They reached a compromise for the council and

Tom drove the planner to where he'd parked. "Here's my car," said the planner, "it's nothing like your Merc. Just an old Holden."

As he closed the door he said: "You know, we win the battle but you bastards win the war." Everything favourable Tom had said about his development was forgotten in that one bitter comment.

In property the cycle will surely come. In the more established US and Europe markets, cycles gradually reach a plateau, dipping but not going right down before hitting bottom. In Australia a cycle not only hits with a bang but it also goes down more quickly and stays down longer. That dip can last as long as five years. In the US it might last only two years.

Tom knew Australia was on the winds of change of the rest of the world.

What they dictated was what happened to us. Although possessing great natural wealth, we were small in the distribution of wealth around the world. And it would never change while our politicians thought in global terms for trade and currencies.

Tom blamed the media to some extent for that situation. It didn't help newspaper sales and TV ratings if things went along smoothly for too long. So financial downturns were beaten up, and the banks reacted to the gloomy headlines.

The banks were fair weather partners. When it rained, when things were bad, they pulled the rug out from under you. Just when you needed a financial umbrella, they exposed you to the rough weather.

You didn't just get wet, you were drenched. You knew the sun would shine again some time but it could take years. One minute you could start a venture on 90 per cent funds from a bank, the next when things suddenly tightened they pulled the plug and left you holding the bag.

That's why businessmen and hardnosed developers learned the lesson: *If there was a chance of that cycle going down and there was a profit in it now, take it and bolt.* Those people made the magazine wealth lists.

Property is the great catalyst that drives everything. When it goes down, so does the economy. When it goes up, the economy follows. It feeds the sales of millions of refrigerators, washing machines and square metres of carpet and keeps engineers, carpenters and others in work.

Tom Hayson realised there was no real place in property for gamblers. Risk-takers, yes. But straight gamblers could finish on their uppers because the cycles would surely catch up with them. Greed clouded judgment but he didn't think he was gambling, although it always involved an element of risk. You just had to know when to stop.

The Hayson Group weathered the Whitlam years storm and the subsequent credit squeeze with a bit of luck and good management. They could have saved themselves a lot of trouble and heartburn by opting out of *Southern Cross Gardens* and *The Golden Gate* in those hard times and finishing up with at least some profit. But they were committed to quality building, hanging on and proving themselves first-class builders.

They also finished a number of highrise unit developments on the Lower North Shore, relinquishing one big project on which they began work in Ourimbah Road, Neutral Bay. They dropped it and lost almost $2 million, but if they'd kept on and finished it, they could have lost much more.

They led the way in Artarmon, a dormant suburb when they first assembled sites there for highrise unit developments. After they developed some of those sites and sold others to the fledgling Meriton development group owned by Harry Triguboff, Artarmon became a major multi-unit area.

Tom's philosophy was if you took on something and made it better than it was, the bottom line looked after itself. Unfortunately in a dog-eat-dog world, that was often wrong. In trying to do that, he sometimes got stripped somewhere along the line.

He knew the score, including the most basic tenet in property: *Buy as cheaply as you can, sell for as much as you can make out of it.* If you didn't live by that credo, you'd get done.

He would like to have made money out of every deal, but he wasn't trained to do that, nor was it his philosophy. He saw his work in terms of benefits to individuals or the community and if possible, of lasting benefit. That made him the visionary, not a normal developer interested only in the profit motive.

Tom was also aware of the old rule that business is business, in the sense that business meant making or losing money, although he never lived strictly by that rule.

But the Haysons were quick learners. From seven years of building blocks of units they learned a few things that would put them at the cutting edge of property development. And that's where they would stay indefinitely - right up with, or one jump ahead of the field.

Among the North Shore units of up to 15 storeys they built with A and R Constructions were the *Aragon*, the *Barclay*, the *Covington*, the *Montrose* and the *Peidmont.*

In doing so they realised a simple truth: By pulling down perfectly good real estate, they were digging a great big hole in the ground, which meant no income until the new building was finished. For the next two or two-and-a-half years they had to put up with all the problems connected with that, the main difficulty being unions.

While trying to finish a building over such a long lead time, things could happen outside their control - the government could change, interest rates rise, council policies change - and it affected profitability.

Union worries were the worst. The union problems they had on the *Southern Cross Gardens* work and to some extent on *The Golden Gate*, sickened them. Comparing notes with their friend, developer Sid Londish, they found he had to endure similar problems on his sites.

Bomb scares were the big go. On one major site Sid could look down on the job from his office and literally see a worker go to a phone box and make a call. Sid would then be informed by one of his staff that a bomb had been planted on the site. The bomb would turn out to be a brick wrapped in paper with "bomb" written on it.

The workers would stand out in the park until told to go home - and they'd have to be paid for the day. A real bomb was never found.

Sid and his team were a bit clever one day, expecting another "bomb" after three clear days. Amazingly, after going out in the park, the workers would walk into the building where the bomb supposedly was and get their cars out. Sid ordered the place locked so they could not get their cars out, and when the alert came, they were stuck. After that, whenever they went to get their cars out first, Sid knew a "bomb" was coming.

Another trick concerned wet weather. If it was wet they would down tools and walk in the rain to the railway station, but they could not walk on to the site. They also wouldn't walk across concrete unless duck boards were laid. Umbrellas had to be provided, then wet weather gear, even when they weren't working outside. All to delay the job and get paid for doing nothing.

Safety issue was a good lurk. These fit, strong workers couldn't walk up or through anything and timber steps had to be built-up one side and down the other - so they could walk over scaffolding. Until this was done, they'd stop work on everything. And they went through the whole site, erecting steps and taking them down. One man was permanently employed shifting the steps.

Asbestos was a beauty. How the hell can you have asbestos on a new building site? Easily. Conveniently on top of every rubbish heap would be found a piece of fibro cement containing asbestos.

This required an investigation for two or three days by outside experts to find out what other asbestos was on site. They stayed around, not working, but being paid.

A priceless piece of tomfoolery occurred over sand allegedly in meat pies. First Sid had to supply meat pie warmers and rooms with air conditioning where they could sit to eat their pies. Unbelievable as it may seem, the workers had to have their feet and finger nails cleaned before going in there. A bunch of pansies, no less.

Anyway, on this day they went on strike. What's this all about, Sid asked the union reps. Sand on the building site. But said Sid, gritting his teeth, there's always sand on the building site. Ah yes, but these workers bought some meat pies and took them to the 11th floor to eat and a westerly blew up and they got sand in their pies.

Warren, the *Daily Telegraph* cartoonist, lampooned the hilarious setup with two blokes eating pies and one saying: "There's a grain of sand in my pie - shift everyone out until we all get one!"

That wasn't all. Furniture moved into the building in daytime was taken out at night and security guards were too intimidated to stop it, fearing they would be bashed. The police came but nothing would be done. The $24 million job cost Sid Londish about $100 million in the end.

The Hayson workers did not get sand in their pies, lucky chaps, but Tom and Ian had most of the other problems. The last straw for Ian was when building the highrise *Aragon* in Neutral Bay, they were forced by the union to erect a covered walk-way from the work shed to the building 20 metres away - just in case it rained.

It came to a head one day when Tom and Ian looked at an old building they'd bought, intending to pull it down to put up a new unit block. The credit squeeze was still on and no bank would lend them the money. They sat down and looked at the figures and took a closer look at the building.

Then they realised they didn't need the bank money - they could make more by renovating the old flats, stratifying them and selling them off.

The Haysons were fortunate in this new approach by having a detailed knowledge of values. Ian guaranteed he could look at any house or property in an area where he'd worked and give a true value within five per cent either way. Tom would give what he jocularly termed "the finger test" - he'd moisten his right forefinger when going into a deal, hold it up and give his opinion and he was rarely wrong.

They set up a complete operating machine within the Hayson Group, a marketing arm through their real estate agency, a renovation and financing team so they could do all the buying and selling and renovations themselves. That was the first time in Australia a fully-integrated developing company had all these facets under one roof.

Most importantly, it enabled them to sell the flats after separating and stratifying them for half the price of the new units they'd sold before.

It meant that all those people who couldn't previously afford to buy a home unit in Neutral Bay or Cremorne, suddenly found a market there for themselves. They had been pushed out to the outlying western suburbs of Penrith and Parramatta by high prices. Now they could buy on the Lower North Shore.

The Haysons in one single stroke opened up a whole new market that hadn't existed for 10 years, and demand quadrupled. In one weekend they would literally sell out a block of 12 units.

All they had to do was buy old blocks of admittedly run down flats under one Torrens title, renovate them with new kitchens, bathrooms, paint and carpet, new plumbing if necessary, stratify them and buyers had a perfectly good and cheap older property with individual title.

By renovating they turned many slum buildings into respectable habitable places for people to live in, uplifting their lifestyles.

It had the big advantage to the Haysons of not making them a union target at a time when the unions were at their most militant.

They quickly became the biggest developer of existing real estate in Sydney, renovating 2,000 and more units a year. They pioneered the concept. Bob Hamilton, who later founded the giant building company Mirvac, was also early in the field.

Even when putting up new buildings the Haysons were never called "dirty developers" who razed a property just to make money at any cost.

Tom believed in preserving something that was worthwhile, but not to the extent of keeping a building that ought to be knocked over. He knew bureaucrats and politicians who would preserve anything, even an outside dunny.

After moving into renovations, their good name continued. If a tenant was elderly or a pensioner and wanted to stay on, or was rent controlled, they allowed them to remain, unmolested.

Most developers had ethics and a code of honour among them then. If Tom was interested in a building and found that Bob Hamilton was also looking at it for stratifying, he would say "OK, that's yours Bob," and Hamilton would do the same. To outdo each other only raised the price of a building and caused extra costs to buyers.

By seeing the opportunity and seizing it, the Haysons cornered the market. They did it on such a mass scale they ran out of old flats to buy on the North Shore and had to expand their horizons by crossing the Harbour Bridge into inner eastern suburbs areas like Elizabeth Bay, Darlinghurst, Potts Point and Kings Cross.

They were smart enough to realise that people wanted to live in the city or near to it and they started that post-war movement in Sydney.

At first they concentrated on Elizabeth Bay, which had an image problem. In those days, the mid to late 1970s, Neutral Bay was considered a better area. Elizabeth Bay had been a salubrious suburb in the 1920s and 30s but it was then run down and property there was even cheaper than in Neutral Bay.

But Elizabeth Bay was similar in that it had solid, older-style buildings and was even closer to the city. The Haysons bought block after block of flats there that nobody wanted, renovating and strata titling them and again creating a market that had not existed.

While flat out doing these "slap and tickle" jobs, a chance remark one day sent the Haysons out on the trail of buying Australia's best and most prestigious mansion.

A young engineer, Roger Kohler, had begun working in the Hayson real estate agency in 1977 and became a partner in the residential side of their business. One of his functions was to search out councils all over Sydney for blocks of flats and ask the owners if they wanted to sell.

After doing a search on a block of flats at Elizabeth Bay he rang a contact for the owners, the publicity-shy Albert family, who said: "I don't think we want to sell the flats but we might sell the house."

When Roger repeated that to Ian, he was told: "Give me the bloke's number. I'll handle this."

The first job Ian Hayson had as a self-employed person had been selling 182 apartments in Onslow Avenue, Elizabeth Bay, for Stocks and

Holdings. Nobody else could sell them after they were on the market nine months but Ian did, standing there day in and day out for 18 months. As he stood in the street, he looked down on *Boomerang* in Billyard Avenue.

Gazing on the big wall around the mansion which told the whole world to go to buggery, Ian said: "Gee, that would be a good place to own one day."

The "good place" was a unique Spanish-style waterfront mansion that had been built in 1925 by Californian architect Neville Hampson in the style known as Spanish mission, also called Hollywood fantasy. It was Australia's version of the San Simeon extravaganza of newspaper baron William Randolph Hearst outside Los Angeles, portrayed in *Citizen Kane*.

One of the few untouched houses of its type left in the world, *Boomerang* was created for the late Frank Albert, publisher of the *Boomerang* song books and a media mogul who was one of the pioneers and founders of Australia's radio industry.

With the song book proceeds, the Albert family bought the Australian copyright to hundreds of songs by Tin Pan Alley pop writers such as Cole Porter and Irving Berlin and that goldmine along with investments in city buildings and radio formed the basis of the family fortune.

Frank Albert had died in 1962 and the dynasty was carried on by his son Sir Alexis, one of Australia's most reclusive millionaires. Nobody could ever remember him speaking publicly about his company since 1934 when he wrongly predicted the decline of "Tennessee type" music.

But everyone knew of *Boomerang*, the opulent Art Deco house set in spacious grounds and 100 metres of Harbour frontage in which only the finest of materials were used - Travertine marble-lined halls, a marble and bronze staircase suitable for a Hollywood set, mahogany, lacy wrought iron, magnificent parquetry floors and a splendid series of stained glass and bronze-framed windows revealing glorious Harbour views.

The house had 25 rooms, an indoor swimming pool, a theatrette and a grand ballroom - but nobody to dance. Maintained by a caretaker and gardener, the house had been mysteriously closed for 16 years since Frank Albert's death. The big iron gates were locked.

All sorts of speculation circulated as to why nobody lived there. Was it haunted or hiding some dark unspeakable secret?

The mystery only heightened its allure. Many millionaires had sought to buy *Boomerang* over the years but had not reached first base.

Ian conferred with Tom who had also admired it many times. Tom walked casually passed the house, stepping out distances and noting what was on the estate. He and Ian did their sums and Tom said: "Go."

Ian finally made contact with Sir Alexis Albert, an intensely private man virtually unknown outside the media world and topdrawer Sydney society. He had no need of publicity, shunned the press and why not? The family fortune remained intact more than a century after the dynasty began.

But he was proud of his family's achievements. His flamboyant grandfather, a 34-year-old Swiss migrant named Jacques Albert, arrived in Australia in the late 1880s with his family. An inventor, watch repairer and vegetarian, he started a violin importing business in the Sydney suburb of Newtown. But it wasn't until his son, Michael Francois, joined the business in 1894 that the family name became well-known.

Michael Albert looked like a Swiss psychoanalyst but he was driven by an immigrant ambition and aged 22, anglicised his name to Frank and soon had things humming with his *Boomerang* song books. After his death Sir Alexis imposed reclusive measures on the business and kept out of the limelight.

Tom gave Ian the job of negotiating with Sir Alexis and it went on for months. Sir Alexis, who lived in a mansion of his own in Coolong Road, Vaucluse, was in no hurry to sell and indeed, was indifferent to the sale. His main concern was he didn't want *Boomerang* pulled down or redeveloped.

In their talks he confirmed the rumours that *Boomerang* had been empty for 16 years, just as old Frank had left it. And he laid the many myths to rest. "The fact that it is still empty has nothing to do with spooks," he said.

"None of my family killed themselves in the garden, nobody hanged themselves there as everybody says. I have maintained it as dad left it because of one thing - dad told me, and used to drill it into the family, that waterfront property would never do anything other than appreciate. And because of what dad taught me, I've never sold it."

Then he indicated why he had recently thought of selling: "My second wife hated *Boomerang* and wouldn't live in it, so I've just kept it knowing it would appreciate, waiting for one of my sons, any one of the children, to live in it. The reason we're sitting here talking about it is my last son to marry has now decided he doesn't want to live there. So that's why I'm thinking of selling."

On the day they struck a deal, Ian sat with Sir Alexis for hours in a park near the house, trying to convince him he wasn't like the other developers who had approached him, all intending to redevelop the site. Ian and Tom had found a way around the stumbling block.

"Nominate any lawyers you like in town and I'll agree to a covenant going on the property that will not allow it to be pulled down for a minimum of 10 years - that's the only way I can show my bona fides," Ian said.

Nobody else had thought of that. The house was classified by the National Trust which didn't have teeth. But the covenant, which could only be effective for 10 years, would preserve the house until the more powerful Heritage Council came into play. To Alexis, preserving his father's house was more important than price.

The deal was done to buy not only *Boomerang*, the best house in Australia, for more than $1 million but also the whole estate - nearly two hectares on the waterfront containing another opulent house, *Berthong* three blocks of flats, a piece of land with tennis courts and *Boomerang*'s six-car garage and workshop.

That was in 1978, right in the middle of the credit squeeze, when $1 million was a pot of money. All the Hayson money was tied up and they had to borrow to do it. But Tom had worked out they could probably pay for it all by selling off the extraneous parts of the estate and paying for *Boomerang* that way.

The Haysons were experts at cutting up and stratifying and that's exactly what happened. They sub-divided and sold off *Berthong* which was later bought by News Limited chief Lachlan Murdoch, stratified the blocks of flats into units, all with Harbour views and sold the tennis courts to the Mirvac company who tried to build a block of flats there, but it became a park on the insistence of Woollahra Council.

They paid back the money they borrowed from the bank and owned *Boomerang* for nothing. It was part of the growing Hayson success story to keep turning their real estate over and by selling parts of it, continue to own the balance at no cost.

When Tom and Ngaire first walked into Australia's most coveted waterfront home, they could see at once it was an architectural and decorative masterpiece of a bygone era. As a mansion empty for 16 years, it had a slightly eerie, even ghostly feel about it.

Through the graceful wrought-iron gates, a curved drive led past sunken gardens, meticulously tended. Only splashing fountains broke the silence in the gardens, in the courtyards and in the magnificent vast entrance hall with its archways and pillars.

The marble reception hall opened through superb glass sliding doors to the drawing room, dining room and smoking room and into a huge conservatory with sunny Harbour views.

Also on the ground floor were the large kitchen and pantries, staff room, guest bathroom and butler's pantry.

The grand staircase with its ornate bronze handrail was illuminated by sunlight streaming through colourful Cathedral-like stained glass and leaded windows.

They walked to the upper storey and looked in the four bedroom suites each with bathroom, dressing room and balcony terraces. The bedrooms boasted enough space to house a royal wardrobe. One cupboard had a revolving hat stand that the lady of the house could twirl so easily to select her headgear.

The bathrooms with sunken baths and 10-jet showers, were decorated with Wedgwood motifs for "her" and brown leather for "him."

One bathroom had a secret stairway and a door that led down to one of the courtyards.

It set the imagination racing. Did old Frank perhaps have a secret lover who needed to make a discreet exit after a bit of frivolity without the knowledge of the lady of the manor?

It took some time before they inspected the lower ground floor with its private cinema, huge wine cellar, storerooms, workshops, plant and boiler rooms.

Standing on the parquetry floor of the conservatory gazing out on the rear gardens sweeping down to the private jetty on the Harbour at Elizabeth Bay, Tom said to Ngaire: "Would you like to live here, love?"

"No. It's a bit too grandiose for me."

"I feel the same way. It would take half an hour to lock up this place before going out. Maybe Ian would like to live here."

Tom wished his father was still alive to see it. He knew his aged mother would be proud of him when she saw it.

He thought of his grandparents and the struggle they went through to survive as poor migrants, and he contrasted their situation with his.

The Haysons had come a long way since the days of Cowshit Flat down by the river in Albury.

13

SEX SHOPS AND LADIES OF THE NIGHT

JUST as Tom Hayson had an uncanny knack of ferreting out major opportunities, Ian was an active spotter in the marketplace sniffing out good real estate sites.

Their business of buying, renovating and selling old blocks of flats under strata titles had grown so much they needed 17 different entities to handle it, eventually operating through 112 companies.

While working the inner eastern suburbs they often glanced at a huge site at Kings Cross called *The Pallisades*, bounded by William and Liverpool Streets and Darlinghurst Road. They knew it as "the developers' graveyard" because many developers had gone broke there.

Towards the end of the 1970s boom period the big finance companies had lent truckloads of money to people buying large areas of real estate. When the withering 1978 credit squeeze hit on top of several bad years, owners couldn't sustain payments and the financiers moved in and took over the properties, inheriting the financial burden of seeing their values slide downhill.

Billions were lost in Australia and some of the financial organisations themselves, including Industrial Acceptance Corporation (IAC) and CAGA, were tottering.

A firm that went bust at *The Pallisades* after borrowing millions from IAC was Home Units of Australia, one of the nation's biggest builders. IAC took over *The Pallisades* site but looked like going under itself and had to be bailed out by its 50 per cent partner, Citibank America. The Federal Government did a deal with foreign-owned Citibank America, granting them an Australian banker's licence in return for saving IAC.

Previously developers wanted to put up huge 50-storey towers at The *Pallisades* but the green movement and Jack Mundey's aggressive Builders Labourers' Federation demanded nothing higher than two or three storeys. The story went that some people had paid substantial bribes trying to get the project going - but in the face of the green movement's noise, the City Council would not allow the towers.

Many Hayson "slap and tickle" developments were being financed by IAC and Tom and Ian knew the Citibank people well. The bank had tried to sell the troubled site for 18 months but nobody would take it on.

One day in late 1978, a Citibank executive approached the Haysons and said: "We've got all this land at *The Pallisades*. Everyone has different ideas. You're the experts. Will you tell us what we should do with it?"

They looked at it and without even more than a cursory stroll around the site knew what could be done. And after some quick arithmetic they had a good idea of its worth. They advised Citibank it would be too risky to try to put up tall buildings.

"That's what we think too," said the executive. "We think we'll sell it."

"We'll buy it," said Tom, "depending on the price." They wanted $6.5 million for the lot, the whole 3½ hectares.

When it came to the art of the deal, Tom Hayson was right up there with the best.

"Look," he said, "we can't afford to pay you six and a half million in cash, but what we'll do is take the properties off your hands, all of them, and we'll put a million dollars down. We'll cut them up, sell them off and pay you the rest as we go."

The bank wanted to know how long it would take and, told a year, they accepted the offer. Somehow the Haysons had to quickly find $1 million, a fortune in that tough financial climate.

Realising their finances were stretched to the limit, Tom and Ian could see no quick solution except disposing of *Boomerang*, which they had owned for only eight months. They had hoped to let it appreciate and were considering restoring the house to its former glory.

After staying in *Boomerang* one night and recovering from his original fears that it might be inhabited by a ghost, Ian intended living there. Numerous people had wanted to buy it including John Singleton and Kerry Packer. Kerry had invited Tom to breakfast one morning to ask advice on some property interests and wanted *Boomerang* as a potential legal casino.

They sold *Boomerang* in January 1979 for $1.05 million - the first house in Australia to fetch $1 million.

Later as demand for waterfront mansions soared, the landmark residence would be owned by a range of well-known people including bookmaker Mark Read, film entrepreneur Peter Fox and developer Warren Anderson, ultimately reaching $19.2 million.

Only the Haysons had the guts and vision to see what could be done with "the developer's graveyard." The bank, happy to get rid of a nagging problem, offered to lend the balance of $5.5 million which Haysons would have to pay back out of sales. The bank did not have a clue the properties could be developed piece by piece until the Haysons outlined it.

The deal came at the right time for Citibank, wanting to clear its books after obtaining the first Australian bank licence for many years. In its books the bank had already written down to zero the $6.5 million owed to it from the site, and when the money came in from the Hayson Group, they would be making a $6.5 million profit. Such are the wonders of finance!

For their $1 million deposit and the borrowed $5.5 million, the Haysons bought a massive amount of *Pallisades* real estate, 60 properties in all, blocks of derelict flats, boarding or "flop houses," vacant land, even a vacated Marist Bros school and one mansion which had seen better days.

The place looked like a wasteland but they knew it was worth three times what they paid for it if they cut up the buildings into 300 stratified units, renovated and sold them off in parts.

As mortgagee in possession, the bank had not wanted to spend any money on the problem site. The flats and flop houses were in a disgusting state of deterioration, inside and out. Most were uninhabitable and as rent tenants moved out, squatters had moved in.

But the site contained some beautiful old two and three-storey heritage buildings which others had wanted to pull down. The Haysons planned to refurbish those. The only new building they planned from the ground up was *Rosebank*, a luxury development in the old style of Kings Cross on the William Street frontage, costing several millions. They quickly sold off some of the vacant land to developer Harry Triguboff who built several blocks there.

Squatters were the biggest problem. They infested the empty blocks of flats, would not move when asked and prevented work going ahead. A war of attrition was imminent.

They were living like pigs, sleeping on filthy old mattresses, throwing rubbish including syringes out the windows. All attempts to remove them failed. When the construction workers moved their belongings outside, the squatters were not only back in the building overnight but they also formed action groups.

The law was quite clear they were there illegally, but court action could take months and the developers didn't know any names to serve papers on anyway. What was the use? - "John Smith" would disappear and someone else would take his place.

The squatters managed to get the green movement and the newspapers on side by orchestrating a claim that the Haysons were throwing elderly and underprivileged tenants out into the street. Jack Mundey jumped on the bandwagon, threatening to clamp a black ban on the site.

Nothing could be further from the truth. Tom Hayson, from his own poor start in life and because he knew what it meant to feel inferior, had a strong sympathy for the elderly, infirm or underprivileged.

He and Ian had reassured a dozen or so elderly folk still living on the estate that they were safe, offering to rehouse them from grimy surrounds to renovated flats there at the same low rent.

But knocking stories appeared in the papers. A Mike Willesee TV current affairs team arrived to expose the situation but after Ian showed them around and introduced them to the elderly people who were being rehoused, they went away satisfied the allegations were a beatup.

Ian invited Sydney Lord Mayor Doug Sutherland to see for himself. After Doug talked to squatters in numerous properties and was repeatedly told to f--- off, he appreciated the problem. He summoned a top-level council meeting attended by council community service officers, Jack Mundey for the unions and Ian as the developer.

As a result, a committee was formed including unions to visit every property in *The Pallisades* to see who was underprivileged. Out of about 600 people, only seven were found to be poor, the rest freeloaders who could afford to pay normal rents.

Had it not been for the Haysons taking an official stand and being open handed, the whole development could have been halted on false grounds.

That still left the squatters.

Mostly young people who could afford to live elsewhere, they were just taking advantage of the situation to avoid paying rent. Many were university students, others were from well-to-do families who just liked the thought of communal living.

Tom saw his main function in all of this as playing the general, sending Ian and Roger Kohler in as the foot soldiers while he kept a low public profile but a high private profile with the banks to borrow money for his projects. Without it the Haysons could do nothing.

In the squatter war the Hayson construction team bolted the doors and secured them with big locks and chains while the squatters were absent during the day, but next morning the doors would be open again - squatters simply snapped the chains with bolt cutters.

Then they barricaded the flat entrances with steel doors and placed iron bars on the windows, but just as quickly the doors were knocked down, the bars removed and the squatters were in again.

Security guards were posted at the gates, at great cost, to stop the squatters entering the site.

It was against the law to strongarm them and guards were instructed not to touch anyone, just to look fierce and try to bar their path. But the intruders posted lookouts and still got in. At one stage the Haysons had 20 guards on a 24-hour roster, but the cost proved too great.

Eventually Ian said to hell with it, we have to renovate the places anyway so we might as well pull out everything, the kitchens, bathrooms and cut off the water supply. But even that didn't beat them.

The squatters used buckets for their toilet needs, somehow obtained fresh water and cooked by fires lit on the wooden floors. The match of wits continued, with squatters' belongings piled up in hallways and doors locked up, only to be cut open again.

Ian usually didn't lock his car when parking on the site and one day he returned to find someone had tipped a bucket full of excreta and another of urine on the plush back seat of his Mercedes. They did the same thing to his foreman's vehicle, parked alongside. The smell was so nauseating that no amount of cleaning could remove it and Ian had to sell the car at a loss.

Even after the underprivileged were rehoused in decent renovated accommodation elsewhere on the site, squatters were still preventing the construction team starting on the other flats. Costs were mounting and the problem had reached a serious stage.

Sitting in his office wondering what the heck he could do about it, Ian was chatting to his construction foreman about one of the buildings.

"All the floors have had it and we'll have to replace them," said the foreman. "In fact, we'll probably have to replace the floors in about 90 per cent of these blocks."

Suddenly Ian sat forward, excited. "I've got it, I've got it," he said.

"What a good idea. OK, start taking all the floors out now. That should fix 'em."

While the squatters were absent the constructors went through the flats systematically taking out the floors and most of the ceilings.

In one single stroke the squatters were stopped in their tracks. How could they live in space?

They screamed abuse at the development team and Tom, whose office policy was to take calls from anyone who rang for him, was threatened and abused on the phone. He advised Ian to wear disguise when going on the site.

As the floors were ripped out of each block, steel doors were fitted. One morning it was reported that screams were heard in the night after a door was smashed down and concern was felt that a squatter might have plunged to the floor below. Tom and Ian nervously inspected the building, expecting to find a body.

But none was found. Did the fellow step inside in the gloom and fall down, yelling and limping away into the night?

Nobody knew but the squatters were defeated and gradually moved out.

The Haysons were the only ones in Sydney to effectively deal with the problem. Other developers had to sell their real estate cheaply or wait long periods to clear their buildings, suffering financial loss.

One developer who went broke was Frank Theeman. Squatters in his Victoria Street, Kings Cross, buildings caused such a row that green bans were placed on them so they could not be pulled down. It took 10 years before the site was developed. In that dispute the anti-development campaigner, Kings Cross editor Juanita Nielsen, was murdered.

The Haysons showed the importance of going to the core of the problem by persuading various officials to physically inspect the problem at its source. Squatting was a world-wide phenomenon in that period. The Haysons could have made a packet as consultants helping civic officials solve the problem in London, Berlin, San Francisco, New York and other capitals.

From their *Pallisades* renovations and sales, the Hayson Group paid back borrowings from Citibank in six months - half the time. After that, the bank had a healthy respect for them. They had developed only a quarter of *The Pallisades*, with the rest going for them for nothing.

A few months later, the Haysons spotted another opportunity.

They learned that the finance company CAGA was in trouble over a big site they'd taken possession of in Kellett Street, Kings Cross, and wanted to clear their books like Citibank. Tom and Ian negotiated and, seeking a similar deal, offered to put down $75,000 deposit.

The CAGA people finished up saying "give us a deposit, exchange contracts so we can say in our books that by June 30 it's sold and you can pay us the rest of the money by selling off bits of the property." They wanted $3.5 million.

Only after exchanging contracts did they have a good look at what they'd bought. Literally just up the road from *The Pallisades*, it was nearly 2½ hectares right in the heart of The Cross, all the buildings on both sides of Kellett Street, from Bayswater Road through to Roslyn Street and into part of Darlinghurst Road, with blocks of flats all over.

To the Haysons it was a steal. But nobody else wanted it. They were the only buyers, the only people at that time who had the experience, expertise and the operation to tackle the mammoth job of improving the properties and marketing them.

But they nearly freaked when they found their properties contained 28 brothels and six sex shops.

While coming to grips with that culture shock, opportunity knocked once more. It arose because TNT and its boss, Sir Peter Abeles, were having a rough time over a one hectare development site TNT had bought in Royston Street, Kings Cross.

Same story - rundown buildings which TNT intended developing were full of squatters and when TNT tried to empty them out, the squatters conned the unions and press on side and TNT received bad publicity.

A strong action group had painted graffiti all over The Cross: "TNT Sucks" and "Abeles Sucks." Every day when Sir Peter drove past to and from his office, the signs glared scornfully down at him.

At that stage TNT was in the throes of trying to take over Ansett Airlines and Peter Abeles was obviously hurting from the bad press.

Out of the blue he rang and spoke to Ian, asking him if he'd come and see him. "We'd like to sell this site," said Sir Peter. "You're the people with all the experience, you know how to deal with squatters. Can you help us out?"

Ian said: "The price would have to be right."

Tom and Ian discussed it, and a further meeting was arranged between Ian and Sir Peter. After some tough horse trading, Ian negotiated a purchase price of $2.9 million on a $200,000 deposit.

But Sir Peter said: "If you're going to buy these places on terms, that means we'll still get all this bad publicity."

"Yes," said Ian, "we've seen it. 'TNT and Abeles Sucks.' Disgraceful."

The deal was done, the Haysons raking up the deposit by selling some property of theirs from around the place. They got over the point raised by Sir Peter by holding a press conference and announcing they were taking over the Royston Street properties.

Within a week, all the graffiti against TNT was sprayed over with new signs: "Haysons Sucks!"

But they soon got rid of the squatters.

The Haysons were the biggest property owners in the area, 7½ hectares in the most densely populated spot in Australia, mostly containing dilapidated buildings. But they had the confidence and ability to move quickly, selling parts off in a hurry to pay for the purchase.

More than that, selling quickly showed they had strong vision to go for their objectives, sacrificing some profits so they could make bigger profits elsewhere, not holding out for the top dollar but going to other developers and saying here's an opportunity with some profit for you.

It indicated they weren't driven by greed but had the ability to see the bigger picture. Ian had obviously inherited this quality from his father.

John Leece, their long-term accountant who became a partner in Burrough and Partners, one of the nation's biggest accountancy practices, often saw them ignore profits to seek better opportunities.

At other times they traded on quickly to repay money they owed to the banks arising from the tough construction programme they went through from 1974 to 1977. Describing their operations, Leece said they went for a bigger goal like *The Pallisades* to clear problems from the past so they could maintain the integrity to move ahead with confidence.

Buying *The Pallisades* and the other Kings Cross sites was not just a simple matter of acquiring a street and selling it off.

The sites had vacant land, interesting buildings, presenting many different opportunities to test their creativity. Developing it was not cold hard business but a challenge to make their plans work. That gave Tom and Ian a buzz. The more complex and difficult a situation in turning a derelict site into something worthwhile, the more satisfaction they gained.

John Leece became a wealthy property investor by watching what the Haysons did and in particular, by taking Ian's advice over Kellett Street.

The street had old flats on one side and wide three and four-storey terraces, once stately homes, on the other. Within one week of buying Kellett Street, they had wholesaled all one side to smaller developers for up to four times what they'd paid for them.

Cleverly, this technique eliminated their risk by giving them an initial profit and enabled them to complete their purchase.

Then they developed other blocks on their own. In buying stock and selling off parts quickly, they were able to gain equity and pay for the rest. The Haysons always bought well.

Ian offered a ragged old block to Leece for $280,000 after paying $100,000 for it. Leece thought it too much to make $180,000 out of him in one week. "John," said Ian, "if you don't buy this, you'll never buy anything."

He bought, the market moved and every time it did the 18 flats he'd bought also moved and each flat he expected to sell for $20,000 went for $50,000.

The brothels posed a difficult problem. Tom took delight in telling his clients he owned 28 brothels and six sex shops, and when they looked surprised he grinned and said he was only the landlord.

But Ian found as he began selling off empty buildings that many buyers shied away. They didn't want to be next to a brothel, worried about the type of people there. Something had to be done about it and Ian went to the girlie premises to negotiate their moving.

He walked into one large apartment block they owned in Ward Avenue, which cost $1.765 million, to find the entire ground floor filled with prostitutes. After telling the girls he now owned the premises and wanted to take possession, they said: "We can pay you in kind."

When he explained that wasn't really what he had in mind, they said: "You'd better see the madam."

He came back and saw her. She showed him around and said: "You'll have to see *him*."

Ian told Tom: "The whole floor is wall-to-wall girls. And gee, dad, you ought to see what they've got there. Never seen anything like it. Chains, steel mattresses, big steel balls, whips. You've got no idea what this bondage room is like."

"I hope you didn't deal too closely with them," said Tom, sounding a caution from his newspaper days of knowing how seedy was The Cross. But Ian could look after himself.

Tom always sent in Ian, who usually went with Roger Kohler. They liked doing business concerning The Cross, finding it different, exciting and diverting. Tom didn't want to get too close to the action. But he didn't mind owning property there.

He was wary about sending salesmen there to check on what was in the buildings. They all said the girls wanted to talk business.

One young salesmen came back and said the head girl had told him she would move out of the premises if he moved into her flat with her. "OK, don't go anywhere near the place again," said Tom.

Ian then arranged to meet a real estate figure who was said to represent the interests who owned the brothels. The man said bluntly: "If they don't want to move, there's no way you'll get them out."

Ian took that seriously and negotiated with the madams to meet the person referred to as "him."

A meeting was arranged in a coffee shop. The mystery figure turned out to be a colourful Sydney identity whose name was as well known as the Prime Minister's, and often referred to in newspaper headlines, sometimes as Mr Sin. Ian found him charming to meet. The colourful identity said he might be able to help by speaking to "the people concerned."

But he stressed: "With these people, business is business.

"I can understand that," said Ian. "But we own these premises and the girlie houses are scattered all over the place. We can't sell the properties because of it."

The man said: "I'm sure these people will not move from the area but I think I might be able to persuade them to relocate." Ian thanked him and suggested another meeting after he'd had time to think about it.

At a further meeting Ian proposed that all the scattered brothels be relocated in Kellett Street. That was agreed to, and there was even talk of turning it literally into a red light district like Amsterdam where the girls sat naked in luridly-lit windows like so much displayed meat as prurient chaps strolled by, hands in pockets, gawking or making a choice. But nothing came of that.

With the brothels moved to a specific area, the rest of their real estate was freed up for sale. Properties furthest from the red light area were renovated and sold as units and those nearest to it became restaurants and offices.

In one aside, the Haysons bought famous Italian restaurant *Natalinos* as one of the many properties in the Kellett Street deal.

Natalino wanted to buy his place and offered $50,000. Another restaurateur offered $25,000 more but Ian learned that he intended kicking Natalino out and starting a new restaurant. Ian, who often ate there, sold the restaurant building to Natalino for the original price.

When Natalino heard about it from a real estate agent, he said to Ian next time he came in: "You never pay for your meals here again."

Ian would not accept free meals, but Natalino always sent over a liqueur on the house to show his gratitude.

Then Ian had a dream. He thought that by generally upgrading the buildings and turning lowbrow seedy spots into upmarket addresses, he could change the degenerate nature of The Cross and give it a new image.

But he was a little bewitched by the exotic, cosmopolitan atmosphere. He eventually realised nothing would ever change the nature of the place.

The Haysons gradually sold off all the buildings they owned around Kings Cross, renovating and marketing them through their own group. They made $15 million profit out of *The Pallisades* alone.

But if they'd kept the three quarters of the nine hectares they owned and had going for nothing after selling the rest as renovated premises, those remaining properties would have been worth at least $1 billion by the year 2000.

They went to all the trouble of obtaining the building approvals, but then passed the sites on to other developers.

They didn't want to be constructors themselves, believing a good constructor had to be a qualified engineer but they could have become developer-investors, selling off just enough to get their outlay back and renovating the rest, sitting back and living handsomely off the income from their properties. And as Sydney grew, the properties galloped ahead in value.

But that was too slow. They had skills and wanted to do things quickly, moving into bigger things.

Tom Hayson was not accumulating money. He had other visions and was accumulating achievements, a philosophy dictated by that ethnic past.

Through the Hayson Group "master planning" the run-down *Pallisides* site, it became an uplifting mixture of luxury and low-cost mostly strata-titled housing, shops, offices and restaurants accommodating more than 2,000 residents and business people.

They continued buying solid old blocks of flats, moving into the Woollahra area of Sydney's eastern suburbs, then Bondi and Coogee, wherever there were suitable buildings for strata titling.

By the time they ended that phase of their operations, they had restored and sold nearly 15,000 units, establishing themselves by far as the biggest provider of home units in Australia.

Even billionaire Harry Triguboff's giant Meriton machine of later years could not top their annual volume.

They kept ahead of the field but as copiers moved in, suitable stock was soon in short supply.

By then Tom Hayson had already moved on to new pastures.

14

DOING A HAYSON

THE newspapers had a phrase for it.

"Doing a Hayson" meant taking an old building or existing situation, breathing new life into it, pocketing a quick profit and moving on to the next challenge.

But it also meant being innovative and staying ahead of the pack. The phrase became popular jargon in newspapers and the building game for being at the cutting edge.

The Haysons had literally changed the face of inner Sydney by recycling not hundreds but thousands of blocks of flats and providing attractive units that people could afford. They used the best quality materials and employed the best people, the standard of their refurbishment work being respected through the industry.

But as others jumped on the bandwagon they went looking for new opportunities. Both Tom and Ian thought those would be found among Sydney's commercial buildings in the central business district.

The opportunity insinuated itself when least expected.

One day in 1980 Ian Hayson sat chatting with surveyor John Higgins, who did strata title work for them. Studying a residential building plan, Ian wanted to make the flats bigger. Would the strata law enable him to add a studio unit to a one-bedroom unit?

"Yes," said Higgins. "Amendments to the legislation mean you can now actually draw lines where there are no walls. "

"What do you mean?" asked Ian.

"It's usual to follow the walls around but theoretically you can take a space in a building and say there's going to be a strata there and, as long as you build the walls there one day, it's capable of being strataed."

Strata titling was new and nobody had thought of creating separate titles except in flats or apartments. Suddenly Ian saw this could be done with offices in commercial blocks or even car spaces in a building. If it worked, the opportunities were enormous.

He could hardly wait to get back to the office to discuss it with Tom.

"We'll have a field day with this if it works, dad," he said. "If I go and buy an office building in the city occupied by a whole tenant and they move out, I'll be able to draw lines and break up those floors into small pieces and sell the office space to various people. Small companies can then own their own offices within a building.

"The point I'm making is that we should be able to do it, although those offices don't physically exist at the moment."

Tom agreed. He saw the need for professional tenants in commercial buildings like doctors and lawyers to own their own piece of a building instead of having to worry about regular rent increases and other changes.

The legislation, introduced in 1973, was a little unclear and they weren't sure they could do it. But they decided the risk was worth taking, giving them a 50/50 chance at least of not losing money.

Tom thought Macquarie Street was a good place to start, somewhat neglected but historic, containing many of Sydney's earliest buildings, a wide boulevard blessed with lots of sunshine because it wasn't part of the city's concrete canyons, and adjoining the Botanic Gardens with Harbour and ocean views from the upper floors of its commercial buildings. You could even see a liner entering the Harbour through The Heads.

They read in the papers that the insurance companies Legal and General and Prudential were looking at their properties 20 or 30 years old with a view to buying something newer.

The Haysons picked out *Park House* at 187 Macquarie Street opposite Parliament House. Legal and General might be wanting to update but to the Haysons, the building was like brand new stock to start off an experiment. It had about 180 tenants, nearly all specialist doctors.

Standing on the roof as they checked over the 12-storey building, Tom said to Ian: "This was built 25 years ago, but just look at the position and the views. It's the right one to start with. Wouldn't mind a penthouse myself on the top floor."

They began negotiating with Legal and General, an English-born company, naturally without saying what they had in mind. Tom made a verbal offer of $7.25 million.

Negotiations were going smoothly when suddenly a spanner hit the works. A developer who had closely followed and copied their residential developments had got wind of their offer and jumped in, offering $1 million more to the head of the company. They were being gazumped.

Tom was worried because no contract had been exchanged yet.

The Haysons had always kept their word and held to any agreed price, and even if they found they'd sold early units in a block too cheaply, they never penalised those who had agreed to buy. They hoped Legal and General were honourable, too.

But as it turned out the Haysons didn't even have to speak to the company chairman. The executive he'd dealt with said to Tom: "Mr Hayson, we did a deal, verbal though it was, but it stands."

It gave Tom a different perception of insurance companies. He'd always thought they were parasites. But here was a big insurer turning down $1 million in favour of a deal made without even a handshake.

After that he was always a strong ambassador for Legal and General, feeling they had inherited their integrity from the Old Country. By that he didn't mean Lebanon any more, but Great Britain.

Each time he visited England with Ngaire - and he always seemed to find the need for a regular "fact-finding tour" there - he came back with more respect and admiration for their traditions.

He understood the English had carefully honed their skills in property deals and would take your shirt, but regarded the Chinese as far worse - they'd take your singlet too and your pants. Hard and sharp, the Chinese were the ultimate horse traders and difficult to beat.

However, the English in their own country, unless the deal had been made, would give you a chance to meet the other person's price if someone tried to gazump you. But the Americans would always take the best price up to the time a contract was signed and if they could get you into an all-in Dutch auction to jack up the price, so much the better.

Tom had learned that unfortunately the word of most Australians in property dealing was not binding. He found the Scots honourable in that they wouldn't deal with anyone else until you dropped out, so would the Welsh, and both were like the Irish in that they were not sharp in business.

He didn't like dealing with the Japanese whom he found changed their minds even after a contract was signed.

After buying *Park House,* the Haysons brought in surveyor John Higgins to draw lines around all the doctors' surgeries - 180 of them - strata titled them and sold them to the doctors for about four times what they paid for the building. What's more, even with the difficult renovation work that had to be done, they completed it in six months.

That was the first time strata conversion of commercial offices was done anywhere in the world.

But a few things needed to fall into place before it was achieved.

First, that little bit of luck in talking to the surveyor. Next, Tom and Ian realised they would need a big city name to sell the converted offices - they were still only a residential name based in the suburbs, upmarket though Mosman was.

Ian went to see agents and valuers Jones Lang Wootton, but they weren't keen. "I want you to do it because I've been buying property through you people for a long time," he insisted. As a favour, they put two of their salesmen on the job for three weeks. But not one sale was made.

So Ian mustered his own salesmen, keen young fellows who had been selling the Hayson residential units, and geed them up.

"We're going to sell these little offices to the doctors," he said. "And we're going to open the building for inspection just like we normally do for a residential building. We'll put flags all over it to make it the hottest building in the city, flags and bunting all over it to attract attention, and put up a big For Sale sign."

No office building for sale in the city had ever been opened for inspection before. Conservative city real estate agents selling to the big institutions considered it beneath their dignity. They couldn't come to grips with the Hayson concept of a big building that would normally be bought by someone like AMP, to be broken down into component bits and opened for the ordinary public to see. Little people buying part of Sydney for the first time and owning a small slice of the CBD? Not on.

But 90 per cent of those strata-titled office spaces were sold to the doctors who said hang on, we're not going to let investors buy our surgeries, they'll boot us out at the end of our leases and put up the rent, and the goodwill for all our years as Macquarie Street specialists will go down the gurgler. So they jumped in quickly.

As soon as Tom and Ian saw the sales beginning to go they knew it wouldn't be long before the Jones Lang Woottons of the property world put out the message to their clients to buy. So Ian went around and quickly took options on five other big city buildings on the market.

When agents who earlier couldn't see the potential, or had no confidence in his idea, went to the owners to tell them they could now get bigger prices for their buildings, they would be reduced to saying Jesus, too late!

One young investor from South Africa bought a whole floor and became a millionaire from his rents. The Haysons owned the busy car park below *Park House* and sold that off too.

Over the next few years they strata-titled a stack of big office buildings in the city. One was *Mena House* at 225 Macquarie Street, filled with barristers, which they bought for $10 million.

They renamed it *Windeyer Chambers*, after a famous judge. They sold the restaurant in there along with the one in *Park House*. They could have become wealthy from those eateries alone.

They bought *Beanbah Chambers,* an historic eight-storey building opposite The Mint in Macquarie Street, for $500,000 and turned that into strata titles. Other single-ownership buildings to get the renowned Hayson "slap and tickle" treatment and become individually-owned surgeries, offices and legal chambers included 142 Elizabeth Street (bought for $4.5 million) and 181 Elizabeth Street ($1.6 million).

As Tom envisaged, Macquarie Street became Sydney's most attractive street where professional people and their clients sat outside on footpaths Monday to Friday dining Continental style.

The mass strata conversion of office blocks, one of the many "firsts" by the Haysons, would soon become a routine part of the property industry, just like their other innovations.

The Haysons sold off all those offices, whereas in hindsight they should have sold only enough to return their outlay. Tom's original intention when they went into office blocks was to keep the surplus and build up a portfolio of assets against which they could borrow for other projects. But poor legal advice turned him off that idea.

A lawyer advised them they would have to pay too much capital gains tax that way and the better course was to sell all the offices and use the money to buy something bigger which they could turn into taxation benefits. He went along with that but it proved to be a fallacy.

If they had kept some of those offices and residential units, they would have retained ownership of scores of valuable properties all over Sydney.

From that experience Tom repeatedly gave this advice to property investors:

If you want to be a developer and remain safe and not grow into a huge entity where you are vulnerable to all the vagaries of economic climates, downturns, cycles and taxation problems, sell only enough to get your money back and keep the rest. You have that going for nothing.

You have something better than money - bricks and mortar. Put one brick on top of another, a thousand on a thousand and soon you'll have a hundred thousand and eventually a million. They won't go away, they'll stay. They'll take you through all the recessions and they are recession proof because you will still be getting rent.

Tom Hayson at the time had a good excuse not to practise what he preached. He had dreams and visions and wanted to move ahead.

The Haysons were "pure" developers in that they always had original ideas and had the ability to come up with whole new areas of opportunity.

When other developers were playing catch-up on commercial strata titles and suitable office buildings began to dry up, Tom and Ian were already pioneering something else new to the Sydney skyline.

They began buying up old warehouses for "other use" development.

That introduced the trend of New York-style loft apartments to Sydney and the rest of Australia, years ahead of other developers. A few people like Jamie Packer were doing it nearly two decades later in the late 1990s.

One of their first ventures in this field was to pay $3 million for the old Bryson warehouse building and former Jaguar car dealership in Woolloomooloo, spending $1 million to convert it into 63 residential loft apartments. To refurbish it just from bare standing walls, they stepped back into the role of builders, which turned out to be a doubtful financial exercise with that project - they didn't make any money out of it.

Costs blew out and were difficult to control. Their executives didn't keep a tight enough rein on supply and use of materials for one thing, and unknown people took advantage of the situation through theft.

That was one undesirable aspect of the development industry which had caused Tom to avoid his earlier practice of building from the ground up.

He preferred to take an existing building and renovate it rather than run the construction risk with a new building, which left him more vulnerable to the vagaries of the economy over a longer period and to other risk factors.

One of those other factors that can affect any property developer in a tough, highly-competitive industry is corruption.

Most developers play it hard and tough but honest, trying to survive by staying within the rules. But a few resort to skulduggery to get their projects up and running and gain an edge over others. Although in the minority, their actions give all developers an undeserved bad reputation.

Corruption in the development game is no worse than in any other industry or business - it exists everywhere in one form or another, in every industry, profession and human occupation, even ironically in the realm of the administration of justice, as this writer has observed.

It should be said though that the overwhelming majority of council members are dedicated, conscientious people genuinely interested in local government and in trying to do the right thing.

But bribery can take many forms, depending on who you talk to and what or how much it costs. It can be an alderman looking for a favour to obtain architectural work for a friend, or somebody's brother who happens to be in the legal profession and would like to pick up some contracts. Let the mind be imaginative and it can cover the field.

The reality is that anybody in a position of power who can hand out favours can also receive favours. Most of it from all accounts is for trivial amounts but it's inherent in human nature and can never be stamped out.

When an approval is given and developers in the industry know it has not been possible to obtain that approval, you may well ask why. How can a rezoning take place when nobody else can obtain that rezoning, yet the deal is suddenly done without it going to public tender?

Many big jobs in Australia have created suspicion by being carved up among very few people on the basis of friends in the right places.

A large developer once told this writer he understood that when he was operating in the big time, $1 million had to be set aside for some politicians if a developer wanted to win the contract for a really big building project in Sydney.

It happens all over the world. And what happens in Australia is child's play to what goes on in many other countries.

Tom Hayson was among the majority of developers who preferred to battle their projects through the hard way without paying bribes.

It took him years to get some projects through and somewhat naively he wondered why others could get theirs through in a matter of months. Often he believed his plans were better than other people's, yet theirs were accepted, and quickly.

On one project he battled for 3½ years before finally getting a knockback, spending money all the time to amend it. A developer he knew laughed and said: "The fellow who could have helped you is a sugar bag - you should have slung if you wanted it through."

Tom's training as a newspaperman was probably his saviour.

Knocking around the courts and dealing with black and white situations of right and wrong showed him the trouble that could dog people for the rest of their lives by giving in to temptation.

Apart from his own conscience, he had a fear of doing anything wrong and having it come back to haunt him. Fear and conscience motivated him to avoid trouble - do it once and it could resurface.

If the temptation arose to take a short cut to gain some temporary advantage, he consciously held back from taking that step.

Short cuts could probably have saved him millions over the years but he never wanted to compromise his freedom, never wanted to hear that knock on his door that he couldn't face. He liked to go home at night, put his head down and sleep. In his view, no amount of money could buy that.

If he suspected anyone in his organisation was open to bribes or guilty of dishonest practices, he'd flush them out. He suspected that some things went on in his organisation that were questionable, but he didn't know about it. Sometimes one of his executives would come to him and say they thought they could get something through a council for $5,000 or $10,000 but he would say: "Don't do it - just keep badgering away." As patriarch of the Hayson family, he was confident his family took their cue from him.

Mostly his executives kept anything of a dubious nature from him. But sometimes he found out months after a project finished that skulduggery had been afoot, probably after someone had been given the heave-ho.

One of his project managers had been on the take from various sub-contractors, doing cash deals in the pub in return for giving them jobs. To get the job an electrical contractor would have to say OK, here's $2,000 in your pocket. On a big job it would be $10,000.

One foreman, he learned later, built his house from slings while working for the Hayson Group. The bricks he used were pinched from Tom's building sites.

187

Nobody ever asked Tom for a bribe straight out. But sometimes early in his career subtle hints were made by aldermen and others saying: "it's going to be hard but we *might* be able to do something about it..."

One developer explained to him the significance of such a remark.

"That is the first step," he said. "When that happens, I then take that person to lunch and over a few drinks offer him something.

"Your trouble is you don't drink or take anyone to lunch, yet that's how most business is done. Public servants, aldermen, politicians all love lunches. I try to meet them in their favourite restaurants or watering holes."

The only time Tom went into a pub was to have a piss!

Anyone who worked for Tom Hayson knew he was generous. Meanness was not a factor. He simply considered it no achievement to pay someone to get a development approved, preferring to climb over obstacles to see it accepted according to its own worth.

Tom never complained about suspected bribery because he wasn't involved and neither were the developers with whom he did business. Win some, lose some, he took the view there was always another good deal around the corner.

But he was concerned about the level of expertise on councils. Instead of hairdressers, cleaners and other unskilled people making arbitrary council decisions, he believed they should be assisted by a representative panel of experts drawn mostly from the Government - architects, town planners and also developers - to be present when applications were considered.

If that happened, he believed the cost of housing would come down.

The time wasted by council people who didn't know what they were doing resulted in a costs blowout. Developers had to return to councils time and again and the extra costs like accumulated interest and holding charges had to be paid by the developer who passed it on to the consumer.

In his experience he found that those delays could increase the estimated price of a unit from $100,000 to $150,000.

Not only the public suffered. The developer was often also seriously affected, limited in the maximum price he could ask by the real estate market and the state of the economy.

The norm for any developer was to build into his costs an over-run of six months on every development, allowing a contingency of 10 per cent for delays. But in Tom's experience the frustrating, unnecessary delays by councils stretched this to nine months or a year.

Even on a house it was a foolish developer who allowed only a 10 per cent costs contingency for delays caused by councils.

He believed only a small percentage of developers were in for the quick quid, ignoring the regulations. The system usually stalled due to unqualified council people making judgments such as claiming plans were not economically feasible.

Months later a stalemate ended in the Land and Valuation Court after much time was wasted. It would be more sensible if developers could sit down with councillors in a spirit of compromise rather than confronting a group with axes to grind.

When facing a major council setback, Tom usually found inspiration and relaxation by taking in nature. While living on the beachfront at Manly, he'd wrap his arms around the Norfolk pines, slapping his hands against them as he walked along the promenade from Queenscliff to Shelley Beach and back. Then he'd sit and watch the waves wash on the rocks, listening to the sounds and reading meanings into the movement.

He could live comfortably in his own thoughts, another reason why he never wanted to feel ashamed of anything he did.

While other developers were looking to the eastern side of the city for opportunities, thinking the city should be moving east to Woolloomooloo, the Haysons had different ideas.

They had started the redevelopment move there, had just refurbished the old Bryson warehouse building in Woolloomooloo and were fresh from starting a shift in the business district of the city.

By encouraging small businessmen like accountants and lawyers to own their strata-titled offices, the Haysons were responsible for a shift in the narrow business district from Martin Place down towards Circular Quay upwards to Elizabeth, Phillip and Macquarie Streets.

To bring that about they had spent $28 to $30 million to buy seven major buildings on which they had spent about $10 million in renovations, for a profit of between $6 to $8 million.

As a result of the shift to the east, people were looking down from the Macquarie Street ridge to Woolloomooloo and the Finger Wharf area with the idea of building office blocks near the Sydney Eye Hospital.

The Haysons were looking in the opposite direction, to the western side of the city. That was the dirty backside of Sydney. Old buildings were dotted through Kent, Clarence and Sussex Streets but were of little value because the city's business centre had not moved that far.

Beyond that stretched the derelict areas of Pyrmont and Ultimo, separated from the city by the expanse of water known as Darling Harbour.

Pyrmont and Ultimo were once thriving areas with a population of about 50,000. At that time wool was transported into the Darling Harbour goods yards from all over Australia and ships entered Darling Harbour and loaded the wool in bales to be processed in places like Manchester and Birmingham.

Now the wool handling was being done elsewhere, the goods yards were hardly used and only about 2,000 people lived in the area. The Pyrmont-Ultimo areas behind Darling Harbour to the west were downtrodden and decaying - the sink of Sydney.

The Haysons saw it as an area just waiting, crying out for development.

Tom said to Ian: "One day we might be able to change that area. One day it's going to be developed, with Darling Harbour as the centre..."

Emboldened by their success in transforming the old Bryson warehouse, they went looking for other warehouse-style buildings they could convert to residential. That's when they realised the potential of the huge woolstores, then little used, on the western side of Darling Harbour.

Ian negotiated with the Elders company to buy two of the woolstores, the AML & F building and the adjoining Goldsbrough Mort and Pitt Son and Badgery buildings. Flying to the company's headquarters in Adelaide, he noticed early paintings on the walls worth a fortune and on meeting the chairman and board members he thought how elderly they looked.

The old-world atmosphere caused him to study the Elders share price and his knowledge of real estate convinced him they were worth taking over in what would be an ambitious move.

He began quietly buying Elders shares through the Macquarie Bank and, on returning from a holiday, saw that the shares had gone through the roof.

Someone else was buying. That person turned out to be John Elliott from Melbourne, who had also decided to take over Elders, combining with IXL to win the day. Ian sold the Hayson Group's Elders shares to him after Elliott agreed to sell the stores. Elliott, who also took over

Carlton and United Breweries, would only deal if all the group's stores were sold.

Tom and Ian finished up buying the woolstores known as Elders No 1 and No 2 and all the other woolstores rimming Darling Harbour, including the Pitt Son & Badgery and Farmers and Graziers' stores - six in all, covering two and a half blocks and a massive 5½ hectares spread over eight streets. The stores, some so big they had privately-owned roads running through them, totalled eight million square feet of building space.

The purchases, begun in 1979 and completed in early 1982, cost $10 million. To help raise the funds, Tom and Ian formed a consortium as joint partners with Pierre Mardulyn from Hong Kong, who brought in various investors including a big Belgian company, Tractionel. But Tom had to go to Belgium to win over the whole board. Another investor was Han Suyin, author of *Love is a Many Splendoured Thing* which became a hit movie.

The Haysons had proved their bona fides to the Hong Kong banker after borrowing for *The Golden Gate*. Soon after Gough Whitlam was sacked, the Australian Government had revalued the dollar and an anxious Pierre Mardulyn phoned Tom from a golf course after hearing the news in Hong Kong , saying "our profits are going to be wiped out now."

Instead of saying bad luck, Tom assured him he would make up the difference based on the original currency, and he did.

Soon after the woolstore negotiations Tom walked into Ian's office one day, put his arm around one shoulder and said: "I've just thought of something, son. You don't do it the same way as I do, but the result is the same."

It didn't change anything between them, but to Ian it was a turning point that would carry them forward together for the challenges ahead.

Ian had often wondered if he would ever be as good as his father and this casual but sincere acknowledgment meant everything to him.

Once more the Haysons were ahead of their time in focusing on new opportunities in property.

They would soon be at the centre of a development as imaginative and well-known as the Opera House and the Harbour Bridge.

15

DARLING HARBOUR DRAMA BEGINS

THE huge mostly empty woolstores dominating the western skyline behind Darling Harbour were called The Great Wall of Pyrmont.

Planners and architects saw the obsolete six and seven storey monoliths as an impenetrable barrier between the city and the seedy residential areas of Ultimo and Pyrmont, both in need of rejuvenation.

But what to do with them? Nobody seemed to know.

The Sydney City Council left the century-old woolstores out of its 1980 strategic plan for revitalising the area. However, due to National Trust interest in their architecture, the State Government included them later in its study area.

But one man knew their value. Tom Hayson called the ridge on which they sat the Golden Mile, realising the woolstores were vital to the rejuvenation of both Darling Harbour between them and the city to the east and Ultimo/Pyrmont behind them to the west.

When buying them he carefully pointed out to his joint venture partners that their real values would definitely increase but it would take some time.

As wool handling began transferring to nearby Enfield in 1973 and then Yennora on the outskirts of Sydney and the rail yards servicing Darling Harbour ran down, it was no secret that this historic area - once Australia's gateway to world trade - would one day be a major redevelopment opportunity.

When buying the last of the stores, Tom had the extra incentive of knowing then there was a good chance of World Expo going into Darling Harbour.

As a young reporter in the early 1940s he'd foreseen the potential of Darling Harbour when looking down on the scene from 14 floors up in radio station 2CH . And later in the early 1970s he took a visitor from the Isle of Man, Bryan Stott, to Darling Harbour and impressed on him how one day soon this would become part of the city proper.

Banker Murray Sime told this writer that when buying the first woolstore in 1979 Hayson had taken him to Darling Harbour and for two hours passionately imparted his vision for the future.

He could see it in his mind's eye, a dream to redevelop the whole area.

He envisaged the bare contours of the land with the city near at hand, and a great residential hub behind Darling Harbour whose waters would be lapping new entertainment areas.

Tom believed it could be more important to Sydney than the twin city development of North Sydney, separated by the main Harbour.

He saw the commercial possibilities of the empty space around Darling Harbour long before any plan was mooted for it.

Often when in the city he drove there and moved slowly around the streets of Pyrmont where it reached Darling Harbour, enjoying the quietness, studying the quaint little decrepit houses and thinking if he bought any of them, which were then very cheap, he wouldn't want to move the elderly residents. Many were rent-controlled, but they'd lived their lives here and he wouldn't want to push them out.

Tom looked at the little old pubs, the factories, the sugar refinery and walked to the water's edge where he could see North Sydney and almost around to Balmain. And he said to Ian: "Gee. Everybody is developing five miles out of the city, yet here are hundreds, thousands of near-city acres just waiting to be developed.

"And right in the middle of the whole thing are the upper waters of Darling Harbour, going up to where the trains stop."

The State Government owned the goods yard and nearly all the land surrounding Darling Harbour, but the Haysons in their view had next best - the woolstores, standing like giant sentinels just behind on the western Darling Harbour periphery facing the city.

But few agreed with their commercial judgment. Various developers, architects and planners thought they were crazy to go in there as they did.

They said to Tom and Ian: "You won't get anywhere with those downtrodden areas. It will be many years before anything is done there because it's too far gone."

Some actually laughed and joked to their faces, tossing in the words "white elephant."

While planners and the Government dithered, the Haysons tried to seize the initiative by recycling at least some of the woolstores to fulfil modern residential needs. They were ideal for inexpensive loft-style apartments and the concept fitted in perfectly with long-term plans to rejuvenate the Haymarket, Pyrmont and Ultimo areas.

But the City Council stalled and refused their applications to change the woolstores' zoning from industrial to residential and commercial. Getting a major decision from the faction-ridden council was like cracking the lottery.

Then the council proposed that the phased-out Darling Harbour goods yard be converted into a giant park to mark the 1988 bicentennial year.

They also wanted to put public housing into this unique area, the only major unplanned site left adjacent to the city. Some aldermen even wanted to preserve the rundown train sheds - an elephantine eyesore.

Meanwhile, the Hayson woolstores were eating their heads off in bank interest and holding charges. And suddenly in late 1981 interest rates began shooting up as a new cycle hit. Rates soon went to around 18 per cent and 21 per cent in some cases.

The City Council continued to stall on the woolstore rezoning as the market began drying up. It meant people were generally not buying residential property in the inner city and because of that and the council's indifference to change, the Haysons missed the market there with their initial plans for loft apartments.

Tom realised the only way to make the woolstores more valuable and to get things moving was to find some way of having the old goods yard land between them and the city upgraded to some new usage. It would lift the whole area.

In an atmosphere of frustration and growing financial anxiety he went to see Neville Wran. The meeting of these two minds would be crucial to the future.

Wran, the efficient, tough-minded Labor Premier of NSW, had his own views on the rat-infested, broken down Darling Harbour area fringed by decaying wharves and rotting tin sheds.

His view was born out of anger and a bit of vision too for the future - yes, even a politician can have vision at times.

Initially, in 1978, he thought he would bid for the 1988 Olympics and in the back of his mind considered that the untapped Government-owned Darling Harbour goods yards might be a likely site. Later a Government committee reported on the costs and facilities that would be needed for the Games, mostly at Homebush Bay.

Darling Harbour did *not* get a mention, the committee suggesting indoor sports be held in an upgraded Showground at Moore Park. But Wran decided the Games were too risky and costly a venture for Sydney then, and the idea lapsed.

Then in late 1980 he decided to put NSW forward against Victoria to win World Expo 88, to coincide with Australia's bicentennial celebrations for 1988. He asked his departmental head Gerry Gleeson to find a site and they came up with Darling Harbour. Plans were drawn up for Sydney Expo to turn the area into an exhibition centre.

Wran met Liberal Party Prime Minister Malcolm Fraser early in 1981 to negotiate Expo arrangements, the idea being that NSW and the Commonwealth would each pay half. The full cost was $2 billion - and customarily after Expo the buildings were to be pulled down.

He told Fraser the cost was too high and suggested a scaled-down version for $1 billion to be shared equally. But the *Bureau de Nationale Exposition de Paris* held out for the full works.

Next, a double cross occurred and Expo went to non-Labor Premier Bjelke Petersen of Queensland - for a modified version costing less than the figure acceptable to Wran.

Naturally Wran was annoyed, stunned that Expo could be stolen from under his nose and stung by criticism for missing out on the opportunity.

The Haysons were disappointed too, knowing they would now have to rely on something else to boost the woolstores.

Not called "Nifty Nev" for nothing, Wran said to hell with it, we'll have our bicentennial celebrations on the proposed Expo site at Darling Harbour and we'll go one better because what we build there will be a permanent fixture. He put his planners to the wheel.

The problem was how and what to develop as something of suitable magnitude by 1988?

Nifty partly skated over that issue when he announced the Government's sketchy draft plan for the Darling Harbour-Haymarket area on April 14, 1982, shrewdly not setting a definite timetable but saying he *hoped* it would be finished in time for the bicentenary celebrations.

The draft plan included public and private housing for 4,000 people - partly provided by the Housing Commission - a hotel and convention centre, a few restaurants and food stores and probably a national maritime museum.

Not very imaginative for such a prime site, but a slight advance on just a convention centre, which had been talked about almost since the days when Bennelong was a boy. And anything at all was an improvement on the City Council's ideas. But public housing still?

Privately Tom was unimpressed and disappointed with the proposal. He believed the Government's insensitivity had already ruined the superb potential of Woolloomooloo on the other side of the city with the wrong mix, too much ugly public housing and fortress-like concrete parking stations. And at night it was a dangerous place.

Wran and Tom Hayson met for the first time on October 12, 1982. They didn't know each other and were on "Mr Premier" and "Mr Hayson" terms, with Tom having to go through third parties to get the appointment.

Basically Tom wanted to get a fair go and have the zoning for the Darling Harbour area changed from industrial to a mixed use of residential and commercial - so he could develop his primitive woolstores.

Wran was co-operative, knew what Hayson was talking about and said he'd try to assist.

Hayson took the opportunity of selling the Premier on the idea of dropping the Government's unimaginative, bureaucratic ideas and producing something special in Darling Harbour for the bicentenary, pointing out that for 1888 the city had gained superb Centennial Park and the Sydney Town Hall.

Nothing happened and Tom waited for a while, knowing that things moved slowly with Government planners. Impatiently he met Wran again, on March 17, 1983 seeking an update and giving him another enthusiastic burst on the potential of Darling Harbour.

Wran said to him: "Look, I really want to do something there."

The Government appeared to have only a hazy idea of what should go in there, but Wran listened with genuine interest.

What, indeed, would be suitable for this magnificent 50 or so hectares of land on the inner harbour right beside the city's CBD?

In this slow frustrating period of Tom's life, his mother worried about him. A tender, loving woman then in her early 80s, Lavina said to him: "Tommy, I'm concerned because I won't be here to look after you."

She had never lost that wonderful mother's reassuring quality of worrying over his welfare. When he courted Ngaire and just beat the milkman to his front door, she would lie awake, unable to sleep until she knew he was safely home. She'd stood by him all her life and never made any demands on him.

Lavina had suffered from cancer two years earlier and it had recurred. He would never forgive the prominent surgeon to whom he took his mother on the North Shore. Not the kind and humane type but rather the grossly vulgar who was oblivious to people's pain and suffering, the surgeon said brusquely to Tom: "Why are you bringing her to me? Nothing can be done for her." And he turned away callously.

In the last few months of her life he placed her in a nursing home one minute's walk from his Mosman office and every day sat beside her and talked, sometimes for hours. As fragile as she was, Lavina helped the nurses look after other ladies and sang to some of them.

One day after she began lapsing into unconsciousness, someone said he was urgently wanted on his office phone. Leaving one of his brothers and his sister-in-law to maintain a vigil, he hurried to the phone and told the caller: "I'm sorry, I can't talk to you, my mother is dying," and rushed back to her bedside.

His brother Claude, holding Lavina's hand, said quietly: "Mum has just slipped away."

He had wanted to be there in that precious moment before she passed on, in the hope that she might know he was beside her.

But he'd lost that instant and would regret it for the rest of his life, sometimes crying at night when he thought about it. He buried Lavina alongside his father.

Still an omnivorous reader of newspapers from his old reporting days, Tom Hayson was riffling through the *Sydney Morning Herald* on October 10, 1983, when he spotted a feature story by reporter Jenni Hewitt on the rejuvenation of Baltimore's Inner Harbour in Maryland. As he read on, he nearly wet himself with excitement.

Baltimore's Inner Harbour looked similar to Darling Harbour in shape and had the same characteristics - it had been a sleazy, run-down, neglected waterfront area but after revitalisation was said to be now attracting something like 20 million visitors a year - more than Disneyland.

Studying a picture in the newspaper, he was able to superimpose it in his mind's eye on Darling Harbour. But whereas Baltimore's harbour development had its back to the city, Sydney's would face the city, separated from it by the waters of Darling Harbour and the Pyrmont Bridge.

"This looks good," he said to himself.

The article referred to the legendary American developer James Rouse and quoted the chief executive of the Inner Harbour Management Inc of Baltimore, Martin L. Millspaugh. He decided right away to go abroad to see what developments might suit Darling Harbour.

Trying to contact Millspaugh, he rang the Baltimore post office and chatted to the telephonist who said she'd put him through.

When the office switch operator asked who was calling, Tom put on his most authoritative voice: "Thomas C. Hayson, chairman of the Hayson Group of companies, calling from Sydney, Australia."

Millspaugh came on: "Oh Marty, my name is Tom Hayson from Sydney. I've just read in a newspaper over here about your wonderful development.

"We have an area over here in a place called Darling Harbour that is almost the exact size of your development and we're thinking of developing this for our bicentenary celebrations..."

It finished up with Millspaugh saying he would be glad to show Tom around when he arrived in six weeks or so, adding: "It will be the old American custom of our house is your house."

With Ngaire he did a whirlwind first-stage of their tour, calling first on Asian cities. After looking in on Singapore, Hong Kong and Tokyo and checking with other places, he decided there was nothing suitable in Asia.

Just before Christmas they flew to London where Tom met the chief executive of the huge docklands redevelopment scheme, Reginald Ward, but after seeing all seven miles of it he could find nothing there either that would suit Darling Harbour.

Before going on to New York he and Ngaire as usual were able to break the arduous nature of their "fact-finding mission" by popping into such places of serious study as the *Lido*, the *Folies Bergere* and *Moulin Rouge* in Paris and doing a bit of sight-seeing in Rome and Venice.

Back in London they rested in the Mayfair apartment they'd bought before seeing the Danny La Rue show that night.

He then looked over redevelopment work in New York Harbour, the Stock Exchange area and the Hudson River, but those skyscraper developments weren't suitable. He feared he might be out of luck.

When he mentioned to someone in New York he was going to Baltimore, he was told: "Nobody goes to Baltimore except to pass through the God-forsaken place."

He and Ngaire took the train to see the countryside. He'd been to Baltimore 30-odd years before as a broadcaster to interview Dr Helen Taussig, who arranged the world's first "blue baby" operation in the famous Johns Hopkins Hospital.

Pulling into Baltimore station he could see the Inner Harbour development and suddenly felt excited. Then as he checked into his room at the Hyatt Regency overlooking the Inner Harbour, he saw the full picture spread out below him.

Gazing out the window he asked the hotel attendant to point out the features. That beautiful building over there? The Aquarium. And over there? The convention centre. There? Oh, that's the heart of the whole place, Harbourplace. Both those two buildings? Yes, the northern and southern pavilions of Harbourplace...

The two pavilions were separated by a wide space and he quickly visualised placing these on the western side of Darling Harbour where most of the rubbish existed, right in front of his woolstores.

He imagined them not separated by space but joined together by a central dome. Right there on his first glimpse, he formed the idea of what would become the future Crystal Galleria for Darling Harbour.

He couldn't wait for his morning appointment in Millspaugh's office on top of the pentagonal World Trade Centre right on the water's edge of the Inner Harbour. He found he had much in common with Millspaugh, a tall distinguished man who spoke the same language. He acted nothing like a super bureaucrat, putting Tom and Ngaire at ease. He'd been an award-winning journalist before spending 20 years as the professional head of Baltimore's downtown redevelopment programme.

As chief executive he had administered the redevelopment of 300 acres of land and $2 billion of public and private investment.

He had so many awards for excellence it was unbelievable, including the American Institute of Architects honouring the Inner Harbour Development as "one of the supreme achievements of large-scale design and development in US history."

Walking Tom around the Inner Harbour, Millspaugh explained the background.

"It's taken us 20 years to do this," he said. "Five years to get the land and nearly 15 to execute the plan. People marched in the streets to stop us. For one thing, they didn't want to lose their casual food stands and the shops thought they'd lose business. We had to have a referendum.

"The city heart of Baltimore was dead. This place was as derelict as you could imagine. People feared to walk here. Now look at it. The middle of a harsh winter, yet people are thronging here, rugged up. Just look at them on the promenade."

Tom looked. It was indeed surprising.

"When we drew up the plan, we brought in Jim Rouse to set it up because he'd done Faneuil Hall Market Place near Boston's harbour front. The mayor there had called him in and said what can you do with these old closed-down warehouses in the middle of Boston? What he did was so radical they couldn't get anyone to lease any of the facilities in there.

"Opening day was nearly upon them and they had nobody in there. So they grabbed all the itinerants they could find who usually exhibited at craft shows and actually paid them to take space in the hall and display their wares. And on opening day 100,000 people turned up.

"Boston's development now attracts 15 million a year, triggering a chain reaction of activity and bringing new life to the centre of Boston. So we thought we could do the same with the Inner Harbour here in Baltimore."

Tom took in the scene around him, the blend of colours, people, restaurants, myriad shops, drink bars, the odour of freshly-brewed coffee, the aroma of freshly baked breads from a shop where you could see them mixing the dough and popping it into ovens, the fresh fruits displays, the jaunty sight of two young men tossing hot sweet liquid into the air and catching it before it turned into fudge...he knew he'd found what he was looking for on his journey around the world.

They talked on and compared well into the afternoon and Tom knew he just had to attract this man to Australia to help him, inviting him and his wife to have a holiday in Australia as his first-class guests.

Marty was eulogising the great man Rouse as a genius without whom the Inner Harbour wouldn't have happened.

Suddenly he said: "You can be another Rouse in Australia. You not only look like him, you talk like him. You're a visionary too. I can see it pouring out of you. You have the same enthusiasm and it shows in your eyes. You have the same love of your country as he has for America. You should meet him."

It was late afternoon. "Ring him now," said Tom, "I have to leave in a couple of days and there won't be time."

Millspaugh phoned Rouse in Columbia, the city Rouse designed and built about half an hour's drive away towards Washington DC, and said: "I want you to meet this man I have here from Australia today, you two would get on marvellously."

Sitting close, Tom could hear Rouse's voice: "Oh, I don't have time to see anyone. You'll have to deal with him yourself. Besides, I have to leave in the morning to address a real estate seminar in New York."

It was do or die. Tom signalled to take over the phone.

"Jim Rouse, it's Tom Hayson here. I've travelled all the way from Australia to see you. I have an area of land right on the famous Sydney Harbour. I don't want to tell the Premier of my State and the Prime Minister that I've failed.

"I just want to see you for a few minutes. Just give me five minutes. I just want to show you some pictures of this Darling Harbour area I've taken from the air. I'll walk in and walk out."

"Well, you're very persuasive," said Rouse. "One thing I will tell you. If it was any country other than Australia, in no circumstances would I see you. They come here to see me, pick our brains, steal all our ideas and we never hear another word from them again."

In 45 minutes Marty drove to Columbia, the model city on rolling farmland Rouse was supposed to have broadly designed on the back of an envelope, pulling up outside the four-storey stucco-and-glass headquarters of Rouse's famous Development Enterprise Corporation. They found him at his desk, a stocky little old man, bald, stooped, working in shirtsleeves.

"Hello Tarm," he said.

The office was festooned with plans, in vivid colours Tom had never seen used before. Colour was everywhere, in drapes, even coloured balloons were used as illustrations. In that single glance around he saw how colour could be used in the early stages of architectural planning.

They talked. Tom showed him the coloured aerial pictures of Darling Harbour and also of Sydney. "Do you mean to say this area you're talking about is in the heart of Sydney?" he asked, surprised.

Taking it all in, he asked: "Who owns these big buildings?"

The woolstores!

"Don't touch those," he said, "they'll make a lovely backdrop. And don't knock that bridge over..."

His enthusiasm bubbled over. They were still there more than an hour later. But when Tom asked him if he would come to Australia and plan the development for him he said: "I can't, unfortunately. I simply couldn't afford the time, especially to go all that distance."

He was one of the most sought-after men in America, in enormous demand for seminars, even asked to take part in conferences and committees by the US President. The most he would say was that he would seriously consider the invitation.

On the way back to Baltimore, Millspaugh said Rouse had been invited to visit and give advice to 120 cities outside the US but had not accepted once. He was the man responsible for revolutionising shopping malls, introducing fun and colour through festival marketplaces.

Rouse had designed Baltimore's Inner Harbour by forming a partnership with the city authorities through the enterprising Mayor, William Schaefer, and Millspaugh was the chief executive. Rouse's job was to bring in the private sector and take charge of the whole development.

Marty took Tom and Ngaire to his home that night to meet his wife, Meredith and wined and dined them, although Tom didn't touch the wine.

Snow was falling, adding softness and elation to the magical feeling of warmth and friendship. They had become good friends in a short time.

Soon after in Sydney, Ian Hayson's phone rang. "Son," said the voice, "you won't believe it, but I've got the answer."

"What do you mean?"

"I'm in a hotel room in Baltimore and I'm looking out at Darling Harbour."

"How the bloody hell can you be looking at Darling Harbour?" demanded Ian.

"I'm telling you, I'm looking at Darling Harbour. It's uncanny."

Back in Sydney after Christmas the first thing Tom did was to write to Marty Millspaugh officially inviting him and his wife to Sydney as his guests.

Millspaugh had laughed at the suggestion in Baltimore, thinking perhaps it was just an outburst of excitement from an impressed visitor and the enthusiasm would die after he left town.

Tom saw his first job as gingering up Premier Wran, hoping he would have something of the same vision as the successful people he'd just met in America.

The first shot in that campaign was a letter to Wran from Baltimore's Mayor Schaefer, which Tom had dictated in general terms to Marty before leaving Baltimore. A similar letter signed by the mayor (later Governor of Maryland), went to Sydney's Lord Mayor, Doug Sutherland.

The first letter Neville Wran received was from Millspaugh. It began: "We have been honoured by a visit from one of your leading citizens, Mr Thomas C. Hayson, chairman of the Hayson Group of Companies.

"It has been our pleasure to be his host and to make available to him detailed information about our Inner Harbour redevelopment, of which we are very proud..."

He mentioned the potential of Darling Harbour, the likelihood of him, the Mayor and James Rouse visiting Sydney and "reiterating how pleased we have been to have Mr Hayson with us, and to be able to assist him in his determination to aid in the future progress of your great city."

All good diplomatic, friendly stuff, aimed at stirring up a bit of interest for Tom.

The only problem was Rouse had made it clear to Millspaugh after Tom left that he had no intention of going to Australia.

Tom, too, wrote to Wran telling him about Baltimore, how Darling Harbour could be revitalised along similar lines and that he would be bringing out key people from Baltimore.

A breakthrough came soon after on February 20, 1984 when Tom received a letter from Premier Wran inviting him to a meeting in his office on February 27 to discuss the issues involved in redevelopment plans for Darling Harbour.

After waxing lyrical on the scale and challenge of "the most strategic redevelopment site in Australia," the Premier said he believed the private sector must have a dynamic role in the project.

He was seeking the views of key people like Tom and others in the business, construction and entertainment industries.

The ball was beginning to roll.

Behind the scenes the Government had been quite busy trying to work out what should go into Darling Harbour, following a directive from Wran that he wanted to clean up that site. Among those he called in was Bob Pentecost, the man in charge of the Government's capital works unit.

Wran said he thought the city needed good convention and exhibition facilities, he wanted "some green" and the waterfront to be available to the people.

"Now," he said, "go away and tell me what I can do to make this thing work."

Among others involved was Andrew Andersons, the then deputy Government architect. They either looked at or checked on reference projects in various parts of the world to see what they might do in Darling Harbour. Places considered were Battersea Park in New York, the docklands in London, some stuff being done in Japan and Tivoli Gardens in Copenhagen. Baltimore was in the compendium of thoughts too.

But that's all they were - thoughts. There was no plan.

Wran's reaction was that there were a lot of whatifs and maybes but no firm ideas.

He told his executives: "We don't know if a convention centre will work, how big it should be, all we know is there are a lot of ideas buzzing around. Let's see if we can get some assistance with all of this."

The Premier decided to call together the leading property developers in Australia, giving them a rough concept plan without saying what should be done in the hope of getting some positive feedback.

So a general zoning type of concept was drawn up using circles and dotted lines to show buildings on the edges and "green" in the middle.

Tom turned up at the meeting, one of 14. Looking around the Premier's Wing of the State Office Block, he found himself among the property industry heavyweights.

He sat at a long conference table amidst top executives from Lend Lease, Westfield, Leighton Holdings, AMP, Concrete Constructions, AIDC, Lloyds International, Wormald International, Pioneer Concrete,

Ansett/TNT and Yates Property Group. Also present was entertainment entrepreneur Kevin Jacobsen and Project Sunrise director, Luqman Keele.

Addressing the group, Neville Wran said the project to develop the goods yard was "a wonderful thing for the bicentenary and a wonderful opportunity for businessmen."

Then the presenters pointed out the various proposed features, the convention and exhibition centres, possibly a maritime museum. About half seemed to be parkland.

That over, the Premier said: "As you can see, it's an ambitious plan. Now, who among you wants to help me do it?"

Silence.

And it was a serious silence. In terms of body language, the reaction spoke volumes. There was much moving around in chairs and pushing back from the table, but no words.

Finally, Stuart Hornery, the most senior person present as chief executive of the giant Lend Lease Corporation, spoke up with an air of finality.

As far as anyone present could remember, his words were along the following lines.

"Mr Premier," he began, although they were on first-name terms, "it is a wonderful plan and as you say an ambitious one. You are to be congratulated for your foresight in having such a splendid vision for Sydney and especially for such an important event as our bicentenary celebrations.

"However, it is a very high risk project. We don't think the unions will let you build it in the short time frame of four years. And we don't believe the Government will have the nerve to commit large funds over that period and keep the project going.

"It's likely there would not be the commitment to keep it going for such a period and it would be watered down half way through. For that reason we could not recommend this project to our shareholders. I have to be honest and tell you also we would not put any money into a convention centre. But we'd be prepared to *build* it if you go ahead and pay for it."

Who wouldn't?

The Premier looked positively pale. "Anyone else?" he inquired.

Most of the others spoke but passed with just a few words, registering negative responses. All said they didn't think it could be done in four years anyway.

That left Tom at the end of the table, something of a mystery man to the Government officers and looking a little overshadowed by the heavy hitters.

But he spoke firmly and confidently. "I think it's an absolutely marvellous idea," he said. "And I believe it's possible to do it in time for the bicentenary. I've seen what's been done in Baltimore.

"The people over there have written to you and I've supplied you with details and I'm prepared to bring these people out.

"It's a magnificent thing and yes, it can be done. And I'm told by the experts overseas that it can be done, provided you have the vision Mr Premier and are able to push the buttons to make it happen. I am prepared to invest in it and do whatever I can to help you get it moving.

"However, I don't agree with this vague concept you've shown today. To succeed, it will have to be on the lines of what I've seen in Baltimore."

"Thank you Mr Hayson," said Wran, with undisguised relief.

Only one other person then gave a measure of support, developer Ian Yates, who had a parcel of land in the general Darling Harbour area.

Before they filed out Wran asked if he could have their ideas in writing within the next two weeks.

Wran was shocked.

He thought his pitch had been pretty good and he'd be knocked over in the rush by developers to get in on a great commercial opportunity. For sheer political reasons he needed a developer in there to put up his money and give it the hallmark of private sector endorsement to justify Government expenditure and gain public acceptance.

"I can't get over it," he told his staffers. "The only bloke to put his hand up was Hayson."

Gerry Gleeson, the Premier's right hand man, said he thought Tom was a lightweight. "Really, it's too big a bloody risk to take on the Haysons for a project like this. What's their track record? Mainly refurbishing buildings."

"Yes," said Bob Pentecost, "who the bloody hell is this guy?"

A determined-looking Wran said: "I don't care what they say, we've got to do it."

Turning to Pentecost he said: "I want you to draw me up a plan to make this work."

16

James Rouse, Master Planner

BY now, Tom Hayson had his dream.

His passion was not just to put up impressive new buildings on vacant land at rat-infested Darling Harbour but to turn it into the greatest place in Australia for people of all ages and descriptions, a place where everyone could intermingle and enjoy themselves, have fun and be uplifted.

Those three days in Baltimore had convinced him. The city had harsh, rigorous winters and naturally the crowds dropped off then.

Yet in near-blizzard conditions, he'd seen numerous people strolling about bent on pleasure.

At that point he realised the potential of Darling Harbour.

If Baltimore with its obvious ghetto race problems could draw 16 million visitors a year to its Harbourplace, Sydney could do at least as well operating in good weather for 365 days a year compared to about 200 days of reasonable Baltimore weather. But to achieve it, Darling Harbour would have to go the way of Baltimore.

Tom knew the NSW Government didn't have a clue on how to make it work. Neither did anyone else, judging from the reaction of those big operators at the Premier's meeting.

Millspaugh had explained that convention and exhibition centres attracted people inside only when they held functions. Few came to a park unless the weather was good and only about five million people a year would go through an aquarium.

Unless some other element was in place like Harbourplace with colour and life and excitement to attract visitors, the area would fail as a "people place."

He already felt that Government people were thinking the Haysons were not big enough to do a major development. And he wanted to show them he could do it.

He began planning to push hard, as if it was war.

Next, Tom received a letter from Wran on March 6, 1984 soon after the businessmen's meeting, thanking him for his interest. He wrote back at once - the only positive reply the Premier received.

Telling the Premier he could "do a Baltimore" at Darling Harbour, he sent coloured pictures of crowds at the Inner Harbour on Thanksgiving Day to focus his mind. But it would have to be Australianised through design and decoration. He also described how the legislation should work through a special act of Parliament. He even gave it the name - The New Darling Harbour Act.

Tom had closely studied how it was done in Baltimore and knew that Darling Harbour could never be completed on time if the Government had to put up with disruptive elements like faction-warring City Council aldermen and meddling Government departments.

Hayson also suggested it should be done on a partnership basis between the Government and private enterprise. Stoking it up, he said he would be bringing out the experts from Baltimore who knew what it was all about.

Neville Wran made a couple of quiet, significant decisions behind the scenes after that.

Less than a month after the businessmen's meeting, he went to the polls, on Saturday March 24. His Government was returned, but with a reduced majority.

The following Monday when chief adviser Gerry Gleeson walked into Wran's office, he expected to see him smiling. Instead, he looked serious.

"Come on, you've just won the bloody election," Gleeson chided.

"Mate, it's going to be bloody hard to win in '88, so let's start thinking ahead."

That was the killer instinct in Wran, already looking to the next election.

From that conversation, it was decided two things were to happen in Sydney - the bicentenary less than four years away was going to be a big event, and so was Darling Harbour. And they decided to run hard from there.

Soon after that, Laurie Brereton, the Minister for Public Works, Ports and Roads, was called in. "Here," said Wran, tossing down a file, "take this, Darling Harbour. I want you to get it together."

He considered Brereton, a can-do man with determination and a thick hide, the best executive he'd seen in Government.

Tom Hayson instinctively knew the nature of the mammoth battle ahead.

He was aware how stultifying bureaucrats were to new ideas, how they resisted change. They had comfortable jobs, liked their golf afternoons and didn't want their routine disturbed by radical ideas. Safe was best.

He also realised that not even the Premier understood what he had in mind for Darling Harbour, although Wran had reacted positively and had been cautiously impressed with his ideas. For that matter, neither did anyone else understand.

His ideas were so different to anything ever done in Australia before that he had difficulty crystallising his own thoughts.

No longer was it just developing the woolstores in which he had a vested interest. Certainly he wanted them to be actively part of the whole concept, the whole 2,000 or 3,000 hectares of derelict residential and industrial area forming the near western side of the city. But his passion was now concentrated on Darling Harbour itself.

As if to reassure himself, he walked up the stairs of three tall city buildings facing Darling Harbour and gazed out the windows. And when he saw the vista of decrepit Ultimo and Pyrmont stretching to the west behind Darling Harbour, he was convinced it was a visionary's dream.

To have a city as vibrant as Sydney sitting cheek-by-jowl with those thousands of hectares, with a stretch of water named Darling Harbour in the centre, adjacent to rusting railway tracks and other rubbish on one side and the main harbour on the other, was a remarkable opportunity just waiting to be seized. "Ripe for change," he murmured.

He was never more certain of anything in his life than knowing that this forgotten part of the city's CBD, this once commercial and industrial heart and cradle of Australian engineering where the Industrial Revolution came to Australia, was ready to be resuscitated.

He even took Ngaire into Darling Harbour and, as they strolled around the disused goods yard area in grass at times up to their waists looking at the city skyscrapers and across to the main Harbour, he outlined his ideas and hopes. But Ngaire said matter of factly: "Just make some wide promenades where mothers can wheel their prams."

The dream had now become a clear vision.

But how to beat the bureaucrats and Jeremiahs who would put their sticky fingers in the way?

He knew from experience that unless he could pull something out of the hat, produce some extraordinary support, he would be crushed by the conservatism of the bureaucrats and the platitudes and safety-first attitudes of the politicians.

The politicians promised the world but delivered little or nothing unless there were votes in it before an election. The only other way to motivate a politician was to corrupt him, but that wasn't an issue in this case.

Tom realised he needed outside help to bolster his ideas. He needed someone of the stature of James Rouse to say Tom Hayson's ideas were great. It was a sad reflection on the Australian character that Australians were reluctant to accept any home-grown idea unless a foreigner embraced it first.

To do something great in Australia, someone had to take a bloody big risk.

The country simply didn't have the depth of wealth or the risk-taking entrepreneurs of America where the likes of the Rockefellers and others had built superb art and charitable foundations entirely through the private sector. Australia just didn't have that same strong tradition of large private companies and entrepreneurs who took enormous personal risks, driven not only by money but also vision.

Unfortunately it was more a State system in Australia where entrepreneurs were killed off because not enough people considered the power of entrepreneurial freedom important enough.

In terms of European settlement we were a young country but instead of remaining young with creative new ideas, we had become an old country with increasingly conservative ideas, where small thinking dominated.

Being an entrepreneur naturally was about making a dollar but in a way that contributed to the country through new ideas.

Tom's fellow Australians had shown pride in war and sporting achievements like winning the America's Cup and Olympic gold medals, but that pride had to be extended to other areas to take in new ideas if the country was to become great.

Too much notice was taken of minority groups who opposed anything that was different, entrenching themselves in the past.

Tom knew instinctively the bureaucrats - the real governors of the country - were about to give trouble over Darling Harbour.

They were the ones in councils and Governments and on committees who killed off new ideas and concepts. They didn't reflect the common attitudes of the average Australian whom he believed still wanted to be motivated. He'd seen people give up on good ideas because it was just too hard to get things moving in a young country where ideas, instead of being applauded and given a go, were badgered and beaten to death.

He'd seen the bureaucratic tentacles of control from local grassroots government right through to the Federal Government, delaying, stalling, putting obstacles in the way.

It needed a political leader with balls to stand up to them. If the pessimists kept on ruling, Australia would not have any progressive future - the bureaucrats were not the ones who created wealth or ideas.

The entrepreneurs directly created the wealth. And by taking risks they also created the future.

Not that Tom wanted to see developers take over the town, but he believed that where a developer was genuinely trying to make a contribution, he should be given every opportunity to have his ideas accepted instead of being looked upon as some kind of money-grubbing enemy of the people.

In spite of his misgivings, Tom decided he would be the risk-taker to bring Darling Harbour alive.

Money, the bottom line, didn't really matter, although he believed if his development was as good as he imagined, he would not make a loss.

He knew that to build the kind of facilities that were needed to make Darling Harbour a successful "people place" and give it that imprimatur of style and class, he would have to go over the top to prevent the bureaucrats from imposing mediocrity and petty restrictions on his designers, planners, architects and builders.

211

He was aware that neither Wran, Brereton nor anyone else in power could be convinced to move along the right lines unless he encouraged them and presented them with evidence so overwhelming they could not reject it. To do so he had to plan as a perfectionist, using all and any means to achieve his goal. He could not allow knockers to put him down.

He knew that to pull this off he would have to put so much spirit and energy into it he'd have to risk running his whole organisation, business and health into the ground, forsaking everything around him in the unshakeable belief that what he was doing was right and worthwhile.

Already Tom had one of his three young architects from the firm of Clarke Perry Blackmore calling on him early each morning to form a strategy.

For the first time in many years he deliberately courted publicity, telling one radio audience "there's not gold in them thar hills of Pyrmont and Ultimo, there's platinum," meaning they were more valuable than gold.

He talked about how the prices for terrace houses there would skyrocket from the existing $15,000 or $20,000, how the whole area would boom. Some people thought him mad. Just a white elephant, they said.

To gee things up in an attempt to focus attention on the Haysons' place in the scheme of things, Tom announced on behalf of the Hayson Group a $120 million redevelopment of two of their vast woolstores into modern shops and commercial offices. Described as one of the biggest projects in the world, the restoration would cover two blocks, to provide accommodation for 6,000 people. Named Merino One and Merino Two, they would contain restaurants, waterfalls, trees and shrubs.

Glass atriums 160 metres long and up to seven storeys high were planned to cover the private roads between the woolstores, and work was expected to begin in about six months. The plans were seen in the press as part of the Government's Darling Harbour redevelopment, just as Tom envisaged. "Hayson Unveils Harbour Plan" said *The Australian's* heading.

At that stage Tom had no approval or even encouragement to do anything in Darling Harbour, but he was making the running.

He then staged Round One by bringing out Martin Millspaugh and his wife. Tom asked Chris Johnson, then President of the Royal Australian

Institute of Architects, if he could arrange the visit under the auspices of the Institute to give Millspaugh status, meeting all the expenses himself, and Chris kindly agreed.

Johnson understood the concept, would remain a supporter of Darling Harbour and was always helpful to the Hayson Group.

Millspaugh was presented to architects, planners and government officials at a swank function at Sydney's Regent Hotel, where he described how the Baltimore Inner Harbour development could relate to Darling Harbour. Tom introduced him to Laurie Brereton and other Government members and planners, arranged a civic reception for him at Sydney Town Hall and put him in the newspapers and on television.

Millspaugh's public message was that Darling Harbour could attract 20 million visitors in 1988, but the Government had to get cracking and set up an authority right away.

Among his press comments he gave a long interview on radio 2GB, setting out the uncanny similarities with Baltimore, saying that Sydney could bypass Baltimore's years of struggle to restore the Inner Harbour because the NSW Government already owned about 95 per cent of the Darling Harbour land.

Tom laid it on for the Millspaughs in every way.

Whenever they moved from their Regent Hotel, they were met by either Tom, Ian, Roger Kohler, executive Pat Gocher or architects Bob Perry, Bob Blackmore or Stewart Clarke. He arranged a Harbour cruise with VIPs and entertainers including Bobby Limb, slide shows and discussions with Brereton, meetings in the Premier's Department, Capital Works Unit, Department of Environment and Planning, City Council's planning department, not missing a beat.

To top it off, he treated his visitors to a holiday on the Gold Coast in the Hayson *Golden Gate* penthouse, also in New Zealand taking in Christchurch, Queenstown and Milford Sound and then on to perhaps the world's most beautiful island, Bora Bora in Tahiti.

Tom felt it was a start in getting the message through. But for Round Two he wanted Rouse.

Although Millspaugh had been well received, negative vibes were reaching the Haysons from some architects and planners.

They were being described as "just a small outfit," they had "a young team of unknown architects" and "anyway, what would Tom Hayson know about this?"

The Haysons may not have been one of the big boys but they had one major advantage over the giant corporations.

They had purchasing power like a public company but being run by a small group of individuals with Tom as the head, they had incredible flexibility. Instead of taking a month to crawl through committee stages, an important decision could be made on an intuitive basis in an hour, without faltering in that commitment afterwards.

Tom had written to Rouse urging him to visit, sending him coloured books on Sydney and aerial photos of Darling Harbour. By now he had learned more about this most celebrated American.

James Wilson Rouse, the developer and social architect who turned idealism into bricks, mortar and profit, was one of the most honoured of living Americans. The man who introduced festival marketplaces to the wastelands of despair in downtown American cities, he was probably the world's most self-effacing real estate developer.

His credits could have filled a book - but he wouldn't allow his Rouse Company to compile a list of the positions he'd held or the awards won because he didn't want to encourage personal publicity.

He was *Time* magazine's Man of the Year in 1981, installed in the same year in *Fortune* magazine's Hall of Fame for Business Leadership, on President Eisenhower's housing task force in 1953 and President Reagan's initiatives task force in 1982, to mention only two of numerous public interest posts.

Preaching his gospel of doing well by doing good, he was one of the most influential social engineers of his time.

Regarded as an urban visionary and referred to as the Great Rejuvenator, he transformed many decaying city waterfrontages in America as one of the world's most prolific builders of shopping malls, blending commerce and showmanship to have them meet people's needs and desires. He showed that man-made environments could be reshaped to enrich the quality of life.

He began building his shopping malls in the 1950s after anticipating the migration to the suburbs, in the 60s he created his model city of Columbia and in the 70s dreamed up the idea of festival marketplaces as fun places of immense, even chaotic variety to revitalise seedy city downtowns.

It was just a gut feeling, he said - people seemed to have a yearning for that sort of thing. In 1979 he retired as chief executive of his development company to form the philanthropic Enterprise Foundation, with profits from his developments going to house the poor in city slums.

In a frame on Rouse's office wall Tom had noticed the positive slogan by which he lived: "If someone hands you a lemon, make lemonade."

Rouse had told him one of his favourite dictums when they met: "Dream wildly," said Rouse, "because feasibility will compromise you soon enough."

Hayson already had one of Rouse's quotes in a framed and personally-signed illustrated address on his own Sydney office wall: "We must believe, because it is true, that people are affected by their environment, by space and scale, by colour and texture, by nature and beauty, that they can be uplifted, made comfortable, made important."

Although a multi-millionaire, Rouse considered people more important than money, declaring: "As people acquire position and wealth, they allow it to become a force in their lives. You have to resist it because it separates you from life."

Born into a comfortable life on the Eastern Shore of Maryland, Rouse did it tough at 16 when both his parents died within a few months of each other. The banks foreclosed on the family home. He did law at the University of Maryland at night, keeping himself by working as a car parker and poring over law books at lunchtime. He and a friend set up a mortgage banking business which later became the Rouse Company.

Looking like anyone's amiable uncle, Rouse dressed in mismatched clothes and loafers. He also looked like, and had been, an elder of the Presbyterian Church and although no Bible banger, seemed to have a sense of mission in everything he did. When the banks refused to lend his church money to buy and renovate two slum apartment buildings in Washington DC for the poor, Rouse lent the $750,000 needed.

American politicians elevated him almost to sainthood status. Typical was the comment of black US House of Representatives member Parren J. Mitchell: "I guess that every once in a while there comes along a rare kind of man. Rouse is that person."

But Tom knew that for all the Messianic accolades, Rouse didn't get there because he was a daydreamer. He made it because he hitched idealism to hardnosed realism. Tom admired him as one in a million who could be a visionary and a successful property developer at the same time.

The break-through came when Marty Millspaugh was half way through his Sydney visit.

Sunday night and Marty was enthusing on how good the Darling Harbour site was - better than Baltimore, so close to the city...Tom suggested he give Rouse a call in Columbia to inspire *him* a little.

Marty did and began telling Rouse: "You've just got to see this city, Jim."

From the conversation Rouse was obviously saying he would not be coming. "But this man is genuine and so earnest," Millspaugh went on, "he's not like the rest of them. He's just like you, Jim, What he's done for Meredith and me is unbelievable."

Finally Rouse said just a minute and began talking to his wife, Patty.

Then he told Marty he and Patty were going to Hawaii to celebrate his 70th birthday, and how far was Australia anyway? Just a few hours from there, direct flight. Tom seized the phone and said: "Jim, if you come out here we'll fete you like the President of the United States. Best hotels, first class fares for you and your wife, the best of everything."

"Well Tarm, we may come out and stay three or four days, no longer. I'd have to cut into my Hawaii time. But I won't get involved in any developments."

Tom said he would send the tickets and Marty took the phone again, saying excitedly "this is the most wonderful country, Jim. If we weren't so old, this is where we'd like to settle. Wonderful climate, and this Harbour!"

The deal done, the date of his visit was set for a couple of weeks ahead.

Tom set to with a will to arrange Rouse's visit so he could gain maximum benefit from it to ginger up the Government.

Thousands of contacts had to be made, hundreds of letters had to go out quickly with invitations to Government members, planners, architects and people of influence. Doing much of the organising himself, he spent long hours on the telephone, sometimes working three lines at a time, night and day, seven days a week.

More than ever he couldn't wait for morning to come, leaving home at 5 am, telling Ngaire he had "early conferences."

He either went to his office or walked around Darling Harbour as the sun came up, thinking, looking, planning.

Sometimes Ngaire had curbed him when she felt he was becoming too involved in a project, bringing him back to earth to spend more time with his family. Now she saw all the signs again.

But she knew he was obsessed this time and, as they were always interested in helping each other, decided there was little she could do except hang in there until it was over.

In the next episode on May 1, 1984, Premier Wran announced the Government's $200 million plans to redevelop Darling Harbour for the bicentenary, also its intention to introduce legislation to set up a Darling Harbour Authority to oversee the work.

The Premier precluded any interference by the Sydney City Council by removing them from the project so, he said, it could be finished on time. If they had objections, bad luck.

The plans covered convention and exhibition centres, a national maritime museum, harbourside park, a Chinese landscape garden, a "people mover" and "commercial developments." No details, of course.

That ruffled the feathers of most City Council aldermen who wanted public housing on the site. But it pleased Tom Hayson, especially when Parliamentary legislation soon afterwards revealed that the new Darling Harbour Authority (DHA), would also control the woolstore sites.

Tom was tired of the council messing him around over those sites and causing him to lose money.

He took some heart from the Premier's announcements. Wran had even used his suggested name - the New Darling Harbour Act. Things seemed to be going Baltimore's way, although nobody told him so, and Tom's timing for the appearances of his special guests was spot on.

Plans were well advanced for Rouse to address hundreds of influential people at Sydney's Regent Hotel on May 11.

But just as Tom Hayson's excitement reached a peak over the great man's imminent arrival, a last-minute hitch put enormous pressure on him and threatened to bomb Rouse's visit.

Tom had arranged through Qantas to deliver two first class return airline tickets to Rouse at his Columbia home, for his full trip to Hawaii and on to Sydney. They hadn't turned up and Rouse rang and gave Tom a deadline. "Look," he said, "if they don't arrive by 7 o'clock tonight, we can't come,"

His blood pressure rising, Tom called the Qantas boss in New York.

The tickets had somehow gone astray. "I don't care what it costs," he said," I don't care if you need a special delivery flight from New York, but those tickets must be there by 7 o'clock tonight, New York time."

A few minutes before the deadline, Rouse called to say they'd arrived.

The frustration and intensity of Tom's efforts over the past few months finally caught up with him.

That night he went to bed at 7.30, feeling unwell with pains in his chest.

Ngaire, as a former nursing sister, gave him pain killers overnight, thinking it was indigestion. But next day when the pain spread to his left arm and leg, she drove him at once to Royal North Shore Hospital.

After remaining in emergency for 24 hours, he was moved to a ward and kept under observation with monitoring equipment.

Two nights later at 8.20 the anticipated heart attack occurred. He was immediately wheeled into intensive care and doctors worked on him, giving him injections and oxygen. Soon after, a young man in the bed next to him died of heart failure and with clammy hands and perspiration oozing from his brow, he feared he also might not make it.

While he fought for life into the next day, the Rouses arrived in Sydney and Tom's daughter Rosemary Clifton was flown in by air ambulance from Parkes in the central west of the State, to give birth to her first and prematurely born baby. She too was in Royal North Shore Hospital.

Rouse, due to make his only public appearance in Sydney four days later on the morning of May 11, called at the hospital with his wife Patty to see him, propped in bed with tubes sticking out of him.

"Tarm, don't worry," he said.

Ian Hayson had taken over arrangements for the visit. Once again, Chris Johnson had kindly agreed that the Royal Australian Institute of Architects act as official host for Rouse's address. Tom had earlier written the words for the Institute's invitation, setting out Rouse's background and saying Rouse was consulting with the Hayson Group of Companies.

Nothing like writing your own publicity. And through Millspaugh, he'd made sure Rouse was kept up to date on things.

After looking around Sydney, Rouse talked long and passionately to 700 of the city's planners, architects, investors, developers and Government officials in the Regent Hotel. He held the crowd spellbound, also answering questions on his subject: "How Government and private enterprise worked together to achieve America's most successful harbourfront regenerations."

Architect Bob Perry showed slides of Rouse's redevelopments and right at the start Rouse said: "I came here because of Tom Hayson. He's got to be one of your greatest salesmen.

"I tell you, the picture he gave of Sydney and of this great dream he saw down there in Darling Harbour, was compelling."

He spoke of the deterioration of most American city centres, of the defeatist attitude towards his plans to rejuvenate Boston first and how financial institutions there would simply not touch it, not even the Boston banks after initial capital was raised in New York.

As a result they had to reduce the size of the Quincy Market project and were unable to lease much space for the opening. But refusing to cancel it they went out even to New England and brought in pushcart vendors and on opening day 100,000 people turned up.

Rouse described a similar situation in Baltimore, saying the waterfront area was a wretched, stinking place before his festival marketplace project attracted 14 million in the first year.

In New York's South Street area of Seaport, elegant, sophisticated people had said they didn't need it, they had everything. But then his waterfront development there was overwhelmed with crowds, all showing the same humanness and warmth as in other refurbished cities.

He said people came to a festival marketplace area just to see and be with other people, to sit, talk and experience the full life of a city. They walked more slowly, smiled, opened doors for one another, generating a spirit that led to vast changes in values and activities.

After saying Governments must go out and be the aggressor to get things moving rather than announcing a plan and standing back to see what was happening, he finished with a quote of Daniel Burnham, a great Chicago planner at the turn of the century: "Make no little plans, they have no magic to stir men's blood."

He even found an old friend in the audience, new City Council alderman and green bans exponent Jack Mundey, whom he'd met in Vancouver at a United Nations conference.

It was an inspiring, masterful address by a man with incredible runs on the board, and clearly his audience was moved and stimulated.

Tom wasn't the only one who missed the talk.

So did Laurie Brereton because of flu. But Andrew Andersons, the senior Government architect then in charge of the preliminary master plan for Darling Harbour, was apparently inspired enough by Rouse to take him to meet Brereton in Parliament House.

The message appeared to be getting through in a powerful way.

Bob Perry had been showing Rouse around Sydney and was surprised that he didn't take photos of scenic spots or landmarks like the Opera House. But when he visited the regional Chatswood shopping centre he whipped out his camera and took shots of displays in butchers' shops.

Shops like that didn't exist any more in the States. He believed, like the Chatswood butchers, in keeping in touch with his customers' needs, which was why his centres were so successful.

Rouse was struck by the lack of vacant land in Sydney shopping areas.

He worked out that Australians paid rates on the unimproved capital value of land, but in America owners were taxed only if their land was earning money - if you knocked down buildings and the land had no use, you left it vacant.

In those few days Rouse privately gave his views on architects. He'd built 75 regional malls and believed that in nearly every case architects were dominated by their egos, thinking every building was a vehicle for them to express themselves rather than to facilitate the well-being of others.

They didn't think of creating an environment where the merchant could get together with his customers in conducive circumstances. Money was wasted on architectural works with no real benefit to the customer.

Rouse returned home, greatly impressed. He wrote to Tom on May 15, saying "Wherever I go, including a speech in New York yesterday, I proclaim Sydney as the greatest city in the world and the people the warmest."

He told Tom he was right about Darling Harbour. It could be one of the most beautiful, humane and notable places in the world.

Rouse felt sure Tom had won over the Premier and the Minister of Public Works. But he sounded a worry and a warning.

"My only concern," he said, "is whether or not they have the capacity to conceptualise and detail the fullness of the Darling Harbour opportunity, and in that respect I do have concern about some of Brereton's associates.

"I left wondering whether or not they have the capacity, the will, the energy to discover and drive forward the development of Darling Harbour into the great place it ought to be."

Soon after recuperating, Tom went into Sydney's St Vincent's Hospital to have triple bypass surgery. He was worried because everyone then was conscious of HIV-infected blood and he didn't have time to donate his own for the transfusions.

He cracked hardy with his family the night before the operation but when they left in the night he was plagued by doubts.

He asked the nurse to put a "no visitors" sign on his door. Next morning the sister said: "Many people worry about their operations, but you're in the best hospital and the best man is doing the job. Have no doubts at all."

She gave him an injection, a warm feeling came over him and in seconds he was at peace with the world. They wheeled him into the theatre. He saw a friendly warm oriental face with big eyes partly covered by a mask lean over him.

"How are you Tom?" asked Dr Victor Chang. "We're going to put you to sleep, you won't know a thing until you wake up in 12 or 15 hours. Don't worry, you're in good hands and I'll see you straight after you wake up."

As they injected the anaesthetic they asked him to count to ten, but he was out to it after reaching one. The first he knew after that was a nurse saying gently, "are you awake, are you awake?"

"Yes," he said, surprised at his own loudness, "I'm awake and I'm alive!"

Dr Chang came along later to reassure him all was well. The doctor, already famous for his heart surgery and research, would become a close personal friend, discussing the most intimate things with him.

Darling Harbour had almost cost Tom his life.

If he had not been in hospital when his heart attack occurred, he believed he may not have survived. As it was, the right side of his heart was permanently damaged.

Tom wondered if at 64 *he* had the capacity to fulfil his dream.

17

THE GIRL IN THE RED BIKINI

PREMIER Neville Wran had set the scene announcing his Darling Harbour facelift when he said he intended "bulldozing" his plans through.

From that time, the project was bound to be enmeshed in controversy, suspense, intrigue and dark, passionate hints of favouritism and corruption.

It could hardly be otherwise.

As the politically shrewd Wran well knew, if a politician tried to do something, he'd be criticised. If he did nothing, he'd escape.

But this was something out of the ordinary - a big project on a huge slice of public land, with sharply diverging ideas on what should be done there, all powers now resting in a Government-appointed Authority, the whole thing exempt from planning and local government laws to make it impossible for anyone including City Council aldermen in whose area it was, to delay or challenge the work on legal grounds.

The Council wanted a big park and low-cost housing there. The NSW Government had a few different ideas, but nobody in Government was sure of the right mix that would bring it all together in a way that would succeed.

Obviously it would not be helped by militant unions, who would want every last drop of blood while building it. And with the bicentenary coming up in less than four years, they knew they could hang out to dry the Government and any entrepreneurs who might happen to be in there.

The Government could outfox the City Council but it could not legislate to prevent strikes and industrial problems.

222

The boots-and-all nature of Australian politics was another inflammatory issue. By saying he wanted this to be a bicentenary gift for the people of NSW, Wran had signalled he wanted kudos from it for himself and his Labor Government.

That meant the Opposition parties were bound to knock it - just for kicks, if nothing else. Any betting man would have put money on the proposition that there would be more knockers than supporters.

But at that stage things were fairly quiet. The newspapers were generally in favour of the scheme, at least in principle.

Something *needed* to be done there. But as the plans were in the embryo stage only, the critics were still in their cocoons.

Government planners were hard at it behind the scenes putting their draft plan together for presentation to State Cabinet later in 1984. They were also getting ready to prepare tenders for the various projects - the known buildings such as the convention and exhibition centres, and the "commercial developments," whatever they turned out to be.

Also some clearing of the site was being arranged, an exercise not without its problems. Although rotting wharves and sheds were nothing but rubbish, some people didn't want those "historic" or "heritage" buildings pulled down.

The Hayson Group, after stirring up all the interest it possibly could, was strangely now getting hardly any feedback from the Government. A lull had come in proceedings.

That was probably just as well for Tom and Ian Hayson.

Following his heart attack and operation, Tom had taken stock as he convalesced at "Toft Monks" in Elizabeth Bay where he and Ngaire lived at the time. He looked out of his unit at the magnificent Harbour views, the leisurely activity on the water and the gardener busying himself around the flower beds below.

He had learned a lesson, telling himself over and over that he must never let himself worry about anything again, that the most precious thing in the world was his health. Without doubt, health was wealth.

He remembered the days when he was running around frantically doing radio broadcasts abroad and a friend said to him: "Don't forget your family. Pull them around you because the world outside is walking around on hob-nailed boots and will tread on you at any time. Keep yourself and your family well because in the long run, that's all you've got."

He thought about all that and realised he would have to lessen the burden on himself if he was to continue enjoying his family and live long enough to see Darling Harbour through.

Tom had always been the chief executive of his group, taking the full responsibility and arranging financing while Ian did the energetic contacting and the nuts and bolts work, with Paul's legal firm doing the conveyancing work.

He considered that Ian in his genes had the flair for property development, had been well trained and was now experienced and capable enough to control the day-to-day affairs of the Hayson Group.

It was a difficult decision for a man who had always kept his hand on the pulse, but Tom felt he had no choice because of his health: He would hand over the chief executive and managing director's roles to his first son while he remained as chairman.

Tom convinced himself little would change. Ian would handle the daily running of the business but he would still be there as a backup and to help make important decisions and Paul would still do his thing.

But it would be a fateful decision for the Hayson Group, requiring Ian to jump from a hands-on role which was his forte, to corporate status more involved in strategy and planning.

For Ian the timing could not have been more critical either, for personal reasons.

Some time around midnight on Sunday, January 14, 1979, a slim young girl had donned her bikini, prised open the porthole in her cabin on the Russian cruise ship Leonid Sobinov and dived into the chilly waters of Sydney Harbour - and into the glare of world headlines.

The world was immediately captivated by the dramatic story of Lillian Gasinskaya, a beautiful 18-year-old who by escaping through the porthole, had defected from Soviet Russia for a chance of freedom in Australia.

The Cold War with the Soviet Union was still on and the girl's brave escapade was the best story to hit the West for years.

They couldn't get enough detail on her in the US where she became an instant celebrity. Lillian was their girl. Her story and pictures were splashed from coast to coast and Fleet Street went bananas over her too.

Lillian had swum around for nearly an hour to find a spot at Pyrmont wharf where she could climb up, dodging torchlight probes by the ship's crewmen who had heard her splash in the water. She was found by Australian security people, bruised and shivering, wandering around on a wharf wearing nothing but a worried frown and her oh-so-brief red bikini.

One of the security men contacted the press and a reporter and photographer were quickly on the scene. She spent the rest of the night incommunicado at the home of the photographer and his family.

He was from Tom Hayson's old paper, the *Daily Mirror*, newly owned by Rupert Murdoch. The paper took an early mortgage on her story, keeping her under wraps.

When the *Mirror* story and pictures hit the streets and the cable wires, she would be known to the world as the Girl in the Red Bikini.

Thousands of letters offering congratulations and support flooded in from around the world, and job offers poured in from Australians.

She was at once a controversial figure, an extraordinary personality, a celebrity of mega magnitude and many other things, all wrapped in one.

One of her qualities that stood out was raw sex appeal. Lillian had a dynamic effect on men. They fell over one another to be in her orbit.

Leaving her parents and young sister behind in Leningrad, she planned her defection from the Soviet system by doing a year-long stewardess course in the Black Sea port of Odessa where she joined the cruise ship. But her job was to clean the crews' lavatories and cabins and to help interpret for passengers who did not speak English.

Lillian was not allowed to get off the ship in England or Fremantle, Adelaide or Melbourne and crewmen under KGB orders patrolled regularly in ports. But in Sydney she waited until most crew were at a dance on board and, from her cabin, squeezed through the porthole.

The heat was quickly applied. The ship's captain, Constantin Nikitin, rubbished her, claiming she was a trouble maker and a lazy worker and would prove to be a "pain in the neck."

Lillian pleaded with the Federal Government through the newspapers to be allowed to stay and be given refugee status.

What else could Immigration Minister MacKellar do with a beautiful young woman in the circumstances?

While booting out others seeking refugee status and refusing amnesty to 60,000 illegal migrants, he gave her permanent residency.

Every word that dropped from her lips made the news. She wanted to be an actress, a model, took make-up and refresher English lessons and did a modelling course, thought she would do commercial ads and appeared in several forgettable TV soaps including *Young Doctors.*

Lillian worked in a boutique, as a disco dancer in a Gold Coast night spot, declaring she wanted a "big fast red sports car and lots of beautiful clothes."

Then she declared her undying love for the *Mirror* photographer who had rescued her, the father of three, at no less a gathering than a dinner attended by his wife and members of another family. When his wife reportedly said he already had a wife and three children to support, Lillian said: "I love him, I love him."

She broke up that family, going to live with him.

Lillian was her own person, and completely open.

Next came her *coup de grace.* She was paid $50,000 and given a car and a world trip to pose nude for the first Australian edition of *Penthouse.*

The publicity was intense for several months and men drooled over her bare curves. But ever the enigma, Lillian insisted on her genitalia being air-brushed out.

Lillian took her trip, dogged by further controversy. Statements in Parliament claimed she had returned to Russia to see her parents, partly fuelled by her own statements.

That set off a Government inquiry into her status, amid assertions that she was a KGB spy and her residency should be cancelled.

Although the Minister said she was "rather careless with the facts and the truth" and had made adverse comments on Australia, no action was taken after an inquiry that dragged on for months. She was saved because, although she had seen her mother in Europe, it had been outside the Soviet Union.

Lillian missed her parents, who sadly separated due to the pressure her defection caused in their lives. Her father lost his job as a music teacher in a State academy, and had to teach children for a living.

Surveys by the *Sydney Morning Herald* showed that she continued to receive more publicity than anyone else in Australia. As a defector she was as well-known in the world as ballet's Nureyev.

Ian Hayson was again enjoying the life of a single man, having been divorced from his first wife, retaining custody of his three children. He worked hard and played hard, with money jingling in his pocket.

He was probably worth several million dollars, had piercing blue eyes and women found his appeal irresistible. In between developments, he travelled the world to ski and have a good look around the place.

Ian had a quest for exotica, regularly turning over the pages of relationships and forming new ones, always with younger women. Tom noticed that his son was part of the modern trend of young men who preferred youthful material beauty rather than the inner qualities the older generation of his era had favoured when looking for an ideal partner.

One night a mate of Ian's at a *Penthouse* party rang him and said: "Listen, get over here. The place is full of girls."

He met Lillian there.

He asked her out to dinner, she said she didn't go to dinner with men she'd just met but would go to lunch. They set a date for three weeks away. But he worked out a strategy by saying at the last minute he couldn't go to lunch and she agreed to dinner. They hit it off and became an item.

Tom and Ngaire hoped and prayed the relationship would not last. Tom spoke to him about it and Ian said, "no dad, she's great fun to be with but I don't have any intention of marrying."

That satisfied them for a while. They had the clear feeling that with all the publicity and Lillian's escapades, a marriage would not succeed.

They hated it when gossip columnists wrote about Ian and Lillian at social functions, putting the family under a spotlight.

After each serious talk with his parents Ian assured them he would not marry Lillian. Then one day he came to them and said "look, Lillian and I are going to get married." They knew it was futile resisting any longer.

Ngaire had still not recovered from the nude pictures episode, not able to understand how a woman could expose her body for the world to see.

But to her credit she then accepted Lillian, even helping her with her wedding dress. She and Tom had suspected Lillian might be a gold digger but were prepared to give the marriage every chance, welcoming her to the family.

The wedding took place in secrecy with 40 guests at Sydney's Sebel Townhouse on July 20, 1984 - just after Tom's heart attack, just after Ian became chief executive - and as Darling Harbour was about to hot up.

From a life of economic difficulty under the rigid Communist system, Lillian found herself in a world of wealth and total personal freedom.

Ian and Lillian lived in a $2 million waterfront mansion in leafy Mosman, had a cruiser and runabout and a Citation jet which the Haysons partly owned for travel in Australia.

Lillian got her fast red Mercedes sports and had plenty of money to spend. Ian did everything he could to make her happy, even encouraging her to become a crack pistol shot when she showed interest in the sport.

He regarded her as one of the most beautiful women he'd ever met, highly intelligent, well read with a good general knowledge on many subjects. Also a bit fiery and flighty.

Lillian had met someone who enjoyed life as much as she did.

She had so much energy and spirit it was reflected in her normal everyday life, first showing out in the dramatic way she jumped ship. Her idea of a holiday was trekking in Nepal or skiing in France or Switzerland.

But as a friend said to him: "A bit hard to control, mate. Too much for you to handle with everything else on your plate."

18

BARBARIANS - *INSIDE* THE GATE

BEFORE Jim Rouse had left Sydney, Tom Hayson put a deal to him from his hospital bed to work together on Darling Harbour.

Rouse promised to think about it and they negotiated by telephone and letter. The legendary entrepreneur was reluctant but had genuinely fallen in love with Sydney and believed the site presented the best opportunity he'd ever seen for the Rouse "kiss of life."

He was reluctant because as responsive as Wran and Brereton seemed to be, he didn't think they had the iron in their souls to push it through against the technocrats, protesters and non-believers.

But he liked the Haysons and their young enthusiastic team.

On the last day before leaving Sydney he had said to Tom in the hospital: "You'll have to put steel into your politicians.

"From my talks here I'm worried that people have not grasped it. The potential of what can be done in Darling Harbour seems to have gone over the top of them. But you have time to put the main elements in place for the bicentenary. I'm just astounded that you can put this together in one basket. What a wonderful place this city will be if you can do it."

Three months after returning home, Rouse signed a contract with the Haysons for his Enterprise Development Company to act as consultant in the project. It was a tough contract - tough for the Haysons.

It required the payment of $75,000 a month and various other conditions, including a percentage interest if the project got off the ground.

That was just a retainer, anything extra had to be paid for. And they could not use his Harbourplace name for any festival marketplace.

That was big bucks then, especially as Tom had a cash flow problem while not developing anything and he couldn't really afford it at the time. It took courage to think big and bite the bullet.

When Tom told his accountant what he'd decided, John Leece's reaction was "hell!" The cash didn't worry Tom, it was *his* job to get Rouse committed and somebody else could solve the money problem. A temporary hiccup. If the deal was good enough, you could always find the money because there would be assets around to do it.

But it was a pain to his financial supporters, thinking a month ahead while Tom was looking several years ahead.

It showed his tenacity. Some years earlier, Dick Dusseldorp, who founded the giant Lend Lease Corporation, had been to see Rouse but Rouse concluded the interview without wanting to see him again.

Yet, from Hayson's first meeting with Rouse and Millspaugh, the idea of the Darling Harbour Authority was born. Tom saw the opportunity, gave the Government the grassroots information and Darling Harbour was taken out of the clutches of the City Council.

But now Tom and Ian began to worry that nothing positive was coming out from the Government.

After Neville Wran announced his Darling Harbour plans back in May, Tom had rung Wran before going into hospital to tell the Premier he was on the wrong track, that the ideas he was following were too sterile and would fail unless he introduced an Australian version of Baltimore to bring the place alive.

He and his team thought the message was understood after Rouse's visit and would be reflected in the Government's masterplan. But because there was no feedback, they suspected something else was going on.

People appeared to be listening but not reacting, which was intriguing. The process was supposed to be secret, but usually you could rely on a leak.

In fact, within the Government lots of plans on the project were being drawn up and redrawn, free from City Council interference.

A rare opportunity then presented itself.

Laurie Brereton rang the Hayson office and spoke to Ian - Tom had gone to England for a break after his heart problem and to see business friends on the Isle of Man, but he kept in daily contact, always looking for opportunities.

Brereton told Ian he was about to go to the US on a quick schedule to look at ideas for Darling Harbour. The Premier had told him to call in at Baltimore to "see what Tom Hayson has been going on about."

Could they help him meet the right people there?

Could they ever!

"Of course," said Ian, barely able to hide his delight.

As a result Tom and Rouse got their heads together on the best way to convince the Premier through Brereton that the Baltimore concept was the way to go.

From his office in Columbia, Rouse said on the phone to Hayson in his Mayfair flat just off Berkeley Square: "There's only one way to do it Tom, from our experience over here.

"We've got to produce our own plan and it's got to be so much better than theirs that they can see immediately it's superior."

They decided on the spot that at the Hayson expense, Rouse would send out his masterplanner, Professor Mort Hoppenfeld, to do a plan in the hope it might prove some kind of catalyst. The visit was to be secret.

By letter to Ian Hayson on September 11, 1984, Rouse said of Hoppenfeld : "You will find Mort to be a bright, talented, perceptive architect who understands urban design in its fullest meaning better than anyone I have ever known.

"He is fully experienced in all the work of the Rouse Company - was in charge of Planning and Design for Columbia and then of all Rouse Company projects before leaving to be Dean of the School of Architecture and Planning at the University of New Mexico."

Rouse had coaxed Hoppenfeld back to be Vice President of Planning and Design in his Enterprise Development Company. To some, Mort was a genius, to others he was at least a planner certainly attuned to Rouse's philosophies and objectives right down to understanding social matters, including the behaviour of people and retailing environments.

After saying he hoped they could make Darling Harbour one of the great urban places in the world, Rouse finished off his letter: "We look forward to Brereton's visit. Please let me know as soon as you can what dates he will be on the East Coast. I want to be sure we can reach out to him."

Full VIP treatment was arranged for Brereton with Rouse, Millspaugh and others for two weeks ahead.

The young Hayson architects at Clarke Perry Blackmore, who would soon rename themselves Architecture Oceania to give themselves a touch of class, set up a fully-stocked design room for him in their office.

For weeks Perry had been ringing the Government Architect's office asking when the Darling Harbour masterplan would be ready.

All they would say was "it will be out soon," not giving a clue what it might contain. Rouse's first advice to the Hayson architects had been: "Get the festival marketplace in the masterplan."

By an amazing co-incidence late on the day before Mort Hoppenfeld was due in Sydney, Bob Perry at Architecture Oceania received a call from Chris Johnson, then the assistant Government Architect, to say the masterplan was ready, inviting him to see it at the Darling Harbour Authority office.

Eagerly Perry made his way at once to the DHA office and was shown the plan. He was dismayed.

Nothing that Rouse, Millspaugh and Tom had talked about, on which so much time, energy and money had been spent, was in there.

Mort arrived next morning. On that same day, Brereton left Sydney on his study tour with a copy of the masterplan in his luggage.

Mort was met at Sydney Airport by Ian who invited Perry to lunch at Centrepoint Tower to welcome him. During lunch when the word "masterplan" was mentioned, Bob said: "I've seen it."

"You have?" said Mort, surprised.

"Yes. There's no festival marketplace in it. We've got a real problem."

"Do you think I can see it?" asked Mort.

Bob rang Johnson: "Chris, we've got a visitor here from America, do you think I could come around and have another look at the masterplan?"

Chris said he'd be out, but would tell his staff it was OK.

They looked at it in a semi-private office and Mort said quickly: "You're right. This is terrible. Hopeless."

He ran his eyes over the facilities, mainly cultural activities - convention and exhibition centres, a possible maritime museum, a few sites for unspecified commercial developments, a token international village, Chinese gardens, all the buildings linked by a carpark underneath one big podium.

Mort saw the podium as a major mistake. A low one-storey base occupying a large area of the site, it had the buildings on top of it, just as the Opera House sat on a huge pink podium. Mort explained that it committed all the construction activities to one big contract in order to tie them together, making it difficult for the private sector to have any flexibility for doing other things on the site.

It was, he said, a very bureaucratic thing to do, requiring huge Government funds to be committed to the one large venture. And it was obvious that the need for a festival marketplace, a people place, had not penetrated their thinking.

The result would be like a museum, passive, with no fun.

The facilities would draw crowds only when they held functions. It completely missed the genius of Baltimore's Harbourplace where there was something to attract everybody, then bring them back.

It seemed all the proven principles Rouse had spoken about publicly and privately to the Government and its planners, in spite of enthusiastic noises from them at the time, had deliberately been ignored.

A despondent Mort said: "They haven't listened to a thing we've said. There's nothing in this for us. I might as well go home. They're not listening."

Mort had a saying which he used now: "It's no use going into a city unless it's puckered up - ready for it. These things are a joint venture, after all. If the private sector isn't in it, it won't work."

But then a practical sense of reality took over. "We might not get another look at this," he said. "Let's try to memorise what's here."

He studied it again and said: "Sure, things like the convention and exhibition centres are needed, but they're just not arranged in the right way to exploit the critical mass of everything like in Baltimore."

Perry and his colleagues, Bob Blackmore and Stewart Clarke, were down in the dumps. Obviously what they were proposing through Tom as the career chance of a lifetime, wasn't going to happen.

Next afternoon, Hoppenfeld rang Perry from his hotel.

"Look," he said, sounding a bit less dejected, "I'm here now, and I think that in the next day or so we should rejig the plan as best we can remember, because if they put a festival marketplace there in the right kind of way, it might be made to work. Let's have a go at it."

He also told Perry: "It's not that their whole masterplan is wrong. It's just that they don't have the other ingredients that will make it magical. So let's not fight them, we'll rearrange their ideas and add to them."

He and Perry spent the next couple of days on the difficult task of drawing a reconfiguration of the Government's Darling Harbour plan based on their memories.

Then he wanted to look at the site. Bob Blackmore went to Darling Harbour with him to help articulate the alternative plan.

Blackmore found Mort a dry sort of person, very tense, not an enthusiast like Rouse but a pragmatist, fascinating in the way he could concentrate and suggest things that were not apparent to Bob.

Mort was dubious about anything actually happening and thought he was wasting his time. His attitude was, OK, let's just work on it and lay out the fundamentals and then it's up to the politicians and Jim and Tom to see what can be done with it. He thought it a great site, but too hard to pull off. In short, he thought he was being fed bullshit on the prospects.

"Even if they do understand, it will be a brave politician to steer this through and spend the funds," he said. "Don't forget, it took us 15 years in Baltimore."

At first they just walked around the place and looked, then stood in the middle of the railway tracks, taking in the scene of desolation, the rotting wharves, old sheds falling apart. Set in the shadow of the city's heart, it was as if the area had been forgotten by time.

An industrial desert, now disused and decrepit, it had no relevance any more, although right next to Sydney's western skyline, so close you could hear the hum of city traffic.

After walking all around they moved to the centre of the site again and Bob asked: "What do we do now?"

They just sat down, pulled out little scribbling pads, talked and drew lines. In a way they were creating history, because the piece of paper that would emerge from these observations and musings would be one of the most important in the whole Darling Harbour drama.

They varied that exercise for the next two days, Mort surfacing away from there only at night in a Thai restaurant at North Sydney where he chatted and theorised with Ian Hayson and Perry, telling them the feelings he was getting, how he'd make the gardens in Darling Harbour sweep up to where the exhibition buildings were on the Government plan so they would be less cold and isolated, why an entertainment zone like a Tivoli Gardens was needed in the eastern area...all of it to do with the concept.

Back on the site, Mort and Bob Blackmore were discussing where the Chinese gardens and the waterfront lines should be when Bob raised the problem of the ugly expressways cutting across the eastern edge of Darling Harbour.

Mort didn't see them as a problem. They weren't "expressways" but "bridges" which could be used as a canopy as if they formed a rain forest, with palms and vines growing up on the thick pylons to soften their starkness.

He went through the whole process, creating spaces with sight lines back to the water to make the place more open and friendly.

Mort's go word was *synergy*. He explained you couldn't just build one facility and leave grass. All the elements had to relate to one another and the plan would operate more effectively with a whole series of activities inter-related, rather than having one dominant thing such as a retail centre or a maritime museum.

He positioned a festival marketplace in there, knowing what would make the place function from his long, hard experience in implementing the creative philosophy and marketing insight of a genius in the field, Jim Rouse.

Then, instead of finishing off his plan in the design room prepared for him, he said to Perry and Blackmore: "Just give me some pens and pencils and stuff and I'll work in my room at the Regent Hotel."

That's where he stayed for the next three days until he came up with the final product, touching it up at the office by colouring in to show the new private sector components.

With no time to spare, he rolled up the drawing, eased it into a long round container, tucked it under one arm and jumped on a plane to return to Baltimore to give it a final touch-up.

Rouse and Tom had been fully briefed on progress and Tom had devised a careful plan. Hoppenfeld arrived home only the night before Brereton was due in town.

Laurie Brereton had a special mission from Premier Neville Wran, whom he regarded as the supreme big picture politician.

When Minister for Health in NSW, Brereton had pushed through some tough health reforms against strong opposition. That convinced Wran that Brereton was the right driver for his next mission impossible.

Brereton knew that Wran, stung by having been double-crossed over World Expo and losing it when Sydney was the obvious choice, genuinely wanted to see Darling Harbour developed as a legacy for Sydneysiders - and no doubt, privately, as a memorial to his own term in office.

That gave Brereton some extra zeal.

The problem was how to do it? He had the best efforts of his departmental planners with him in the plan he carried to the US, but although no expert, he had a few misgivings himself over the plan.

He didn't like the positioning of the proposed Maritime Museum, which was no certainty to be built anyway, or the idea that the Pyrmont Bridge was to be pulled down, leaving the site isolated from the city.

Arriving in the US he left Baltimore till last, looking first at New York's Seaport, a harbour development in Florida and Rouse's Faneuil Hall and Quincy Market restorations in Boston.

He'd previously looked at the London Docklands after Tom arranged for his friend Reginald Ward, the chief executive of the giant redevelopment, to fly Laurie around in a helicopter.

In Baltimore, Brereton and his barrister wife Trish were given VIP treatment. Marty Millspaugh had booked them into a new hotel, The Pier, jutting right out over the Inner Harbour, hoping a spa in their suite would not be too saucy for the Minister. It wasn't, they wallowed in it.

They met Jim Rouse and Millspaugh, chief executive of the Inner Harbour, and other key people, viewing the scene from Marty's office high above the harbour, with all the background explained in the way that Americans do so thoroughly.

Brereton took it all aboard, the political benefits to Mayor Schaefer who obtained a majority vote on the strength of the Inner Harbour, the revenue the city had gained from it, the refurbishment it brought to nearby areas of the city.

Even before inspecting it Brereton was impressed with the aquarium from Marty's office eyrie, deciding at once Sydney should have one. His wife was even more impressed, pointing out features and saying enthusiastically: "We'll have one of those, and one of those..."

Rouse left them and Laurie briefly produced his plan for Darling Harbour but Millspaugh had little to say about it.

Then they were shown all over the Inner Harbour, the entertainment areas, specialty shops, the multi-faceted features that helped make it an interesting, exciting place. They went to lunch there in the Pratt Pavilion, and Laurie was warming to his surroundings, saying "this is just wonderful, wonderful."

A special dinner was planned for that night with Rouse as the host, a relaxed, witty and urbane man for the rarefied social occasion.

But before that their secret weapon, held in reserve until the right moment, was to be casually introduced for Brereton's benefit.

Mort Hoppenfeld was deliberately kept out of the play until after Brereton had looked over the Inner Harbour, asked questions and formed an opinion. Tom and Rouse saw nothing remotely Machiavellian in their meticulous strategy. It was all a matter of timing.

The venue for this meeting was a bar on the top floor of the Hyatt Regency Hotel overlooking the Inner Harbour, specially chosen for its panoramic view. Rouse, Millspaugh, Brereton, Hoppenfeld and their wives met there for pre-dinner drinks.

From their seats they gazed out over the entire Inner Harbour, twinkling lights outlining its contours, yachts and cruisers riding jauntily at anchor.

Rouse gave Mort a boost as the planner who understood the structure and philosophy of this kind of development. And Laurie began talking to Mort in earnest.

"By the way," said Brereton, "we've finished our masterplan. I'd like to show it to you."

"I've already seen it. I'm just back from Sydney."

"Oh. Oh well, what do you think of it."

"It will fail. Badly."

Brereton was taken aback, even shaken, but not exactly rendered speechless in that elite company. He wanted to know what was wrong with it.

Hoppenfeld told him. In detail. He said the plan on one big podium made it look as if the whole place was Government funded, and it made no concessions in its architectural scale to the waterfront being a place for people to gather. And principally, it didn't have a festival marketplace which would be the glue that would hold it together and give people a reason to go there.

After a little more of the same, Laurie had heard enough to know he was in exalted company and out of his depth. Also, he was smart enough to work out for himself after having looked around that the main ingredient missing from his Government's plan was *commerciality*.

Mort's remarks, embellished by one or two deft observations from the Great Rejuvenator himself along the lines that he too thought the

Government plan a recipe for disaster, highlighted in bold headlines the impression that was beginning to form in Laurie's mind.

Eventually it got around to a deflated Laurie asking: "What do you think I should do about it?"

"I'll show you."

The timing was impeccable, as though this scenario had been specially scripted.

Mort rose, walked to the nearby umbrella stand, unfurled an umbrella and took out his rolled-up alternative plan which he'd refined only that day.

He returned to the table, spread it out in front of Laurie and said: "This is what I think you should do. This is how you could rearrange it."

It was really only a rudimentary drawing, prepared on the run and partly based on memory, but Laurie's eyes gleamed and were said to almost pop when he saw the way it put the various elements together, at the same time listening to Mort's reasons on why it would work.

Looking out over the Inner Harbour, he compared it with Mort's plan laid out before him and imagined what Darling Harbour could be like.

Clearly, Mort's plan relegated the Government's masterplan to an outpost further back than Wallah Wallah or the Black Stump.

As Neville Wran himself said later to this writer when asked what was the difference between the Government's plans and those by the men from Baltimore whom Tom Hayson brought in: "To our rather unimaginative minds, it was like a trip to the moon to see the scheme they had in mind."

Brereton and Wran were between a rock and a hard place.

They had committed themselves to doing something in Darling Harbour, but they needed a private developer to put his money in and give it credibility to get them off the hook and show they weren't wasting taxpayers' money on some politically-driven pipedream.

They were sceptical of the Haysons.

Doubts had been raised. People in Government were saying the Haysons hadn't done anything fantastic, even that their developments were "ordinary," writing them off as only small players. Then along came Tom like a "charging white knight with a bloody grand vision."

Wran, Brereton and co. loved Tom's enthusiasm but would have preferred one of the big boys like AMP or Lend Lease whom

Government was accustomed to dealing with - they thought it would have made them look a lot better in the eyes of the public.

Indeed, in the lull while the Government's masterplan was being drawn up, fresh contact had been made with some of the big developers, institutions and corporations, trying to get them involved, but none was prepared to even show an interest, let alone put up any money.

They simply would not invest in Darling Harbour because they could not see how they could make a quid out of it.

The Government was desperate but, like it or not, was stuck with the Haysons unless by some miracle a better offer turned up. Privately, that was the state of play within the Government, a situation they kept strictly to themselves.

Brereton quickly made up his mind as Mort was explaining what could be done. He came to the conclusion that Hoppenfeld was a clever fellow and these people knew what they were talking about.

He said to Mort: "Will you come back to Sydney and do a short-term consultancy, working with our new Authority? We'll pick your brains and lock ourselves into the initial plan."

Rouse spoke at that point. "I'm afraid he can't do that, Laurie. Mort's under contract to Tom Hayson. You'll have to ask Tom."

A number of things occurred in quick succession after that.

Wran happened to be in New York at that time opening a NSW Government office. Brereton contacted him there and told him what he had in mind. Wran agreed, saying Darling Harbour needed people like Rouse and Hoppenfeld to give it dimension.

Brereton's Sydney office rang the Hayson office and said: "We believe you have the Rouse Company under retainer as consultants."

Ian Hayson, playing a straight bat, said: "Yes, we do. Why?"

They wanted to know if the Haysons would release Mort Hoppenfeld from his consultancy contract so he could enter into a direct relationship with the Government as a consultant to do the masterplan for Darling Harbour.

Ian said he thought it would be "all right" but he'd have to confer with his father, the chairman.

Of course Tom, who was still in London, said certainly when the expected call came, but pointed out they would have to get Rouse's approval to give Mort the necessary time off.

Niceties had to be observed, even if the air was redolent of bullshit!

That was done. It all fell into place beautifully but had to be seen to go through the right channels to gloss over possible bruised egos and show everyone had clean hands.

In the circumstances it was a sobering experience to the top bureaucrats that they had to ask Tom Hayson's permission to get the man whom their political masters wanted to do their plan.

In Sydney, the Hayson architects were still wondering what was going on. They hadn't heard anything since Mort went back.

Tom rang from London: "Things are happening, I can't tell you what, but it's gone very well over there. You'll find out soon."

A couple of days passed and Bob Perry received a call from Chris Johnson in the Government Architect's office: "What was the name of that guy you brought in the other day to look at our plan?"

"Mort Hoppenfeld."

"I thought so."

A pause, then: "Do you know what?"

"What?"

"We've just had a call from Laurie Brereton in New York. He said freeze everything, put everything on hold - I've appointed Mort Hoppenfeld as the masterplanner of Darling Harbour!"

"Shit!" said Perry.

The Can-Do Man had struck.

So it is true to say that the plan for Darling Harbour was consummated in a bar on the top floor of the Hyatt Regency in Baltimore - give or take a fair bit of savvy activity here and there behind the scenes.

That piece of paper casually pulled out of a brolly at the last minute was the most important turning point in the incredible story of Darling Harbour.

Politics had moved with lightning speed to discard the official Government work, replacing it with a commercially-based alternative - and for all the right reasons and motivation.

Brereton was seen to have made a stunning executive decision. But in reality he'd had little choice if wanting a Darling Harbour that would work.

The news spread quickly among architects, a cliquey profession where egos and reputations are as important as the edifices they design and where pedigree, tradition and the right post-graduate studies are perceived by many as being everything.

These young upstarts, Clarke, Perry and Blackmore, who were not known to have done anything of note, had come in and pulled the rug from under the Government Architect's office in this monumentally important project. Toppled the Government Architect!

The traditionalists were no longer in control!

"Some Americans have talked the Government into building a bloody shopping centre on the waterfront," was one comment that rapidly went round.

Colonel Sanders had stormed the barricades and taken over. The Royal Institute of Architects was under siege!

The Barbarians were not only at the gate - they were *inside*.

Resentment began simmering against the young architects, and against Tom Hayson and his organisation - they obviously were to blame for this "outrageous insult" to local professionals.

A few weeks later Mort Hoppenfeld returned to Sydney, this time with his wife Jeanne.

He had drawn his plan in more definite terms, clarifying the concept with input from Garry King, one of Rouse's retail designers.

A lot of his efforts this time would be focused on the structure of the plan, discussing with the Public Works Department how he would implement it. Steeped in the mechanics of it all, he was an expert on servicing the buildings, knowing for instance where the roads and other essential facilities should go.

Another of his main tasks in Sydney, apart from intending to have the Government sign off on the plan, was to appoint some planners to work with him. His idea was to set these planners in motion, then leave them and come back later.

When he was no longer required to consult on the masterplan, he would return to the Hayson Group to work on the festival marketplace in Darling Harbour.

He was really enthused by the project now, seeing daylight in realising that Sydney did not have the same potential delaying problems Rouse had encountered in Baltimore. Here the Government owned nearly all the

land and could move, so different from Baltimore where they had to work
their way through dozens of private land owners.

All the essential elements could be planned at once, instead of some
coming later as happened in Baltimore. There the hotels and parking
facilities came late in the development, at a huge cost.

A friend of Mort's who owned a shop in Baltimore's Harbourplace
knew Neville Quarry, the Professor of Architecture at the Sydney
University of Technology. He was the only personal contact Mort had in
Sydney other than the Haysons and their architects, but under the ethics
of his profession he could no longer talk business to those architects while
he worked for the Government, and he played it straight.

Neville Quarry, as it became understood, introduced him to the
architect firm of McConnell Smith and Johnson; and their planning
division named MSJ Keys Young would become the masterplanners of
Darling Harbour.

Mort also arranged the formation of a Quality Review Committee to
review the designs in Darling Harbour. Nothing would be built without
the Committee ticking it off. Neville Quarry ended up as the chairman,
and Andrew Andersons, the senior Government architect who must have
been disappointed when Brereton dumped the first plan in which he'd
played a significant role, was also given a position on the Committee.

The review committee was generally regarded as a good idea. If the
normal public review process had operated with all its delays, there would
have been no chance of building Darling Harbour in time.

Mort was able to rejig the original Darling Harbour plan because he
understood all the things Rouse had made work in America by combining
his developer's skills with vision. Mort had helped pioneer those ideas.

Mort saw parallels between Darling Harbour and Baltimore and just
knew from personal experience how and why Baltimore had worked.

That gave him the background to arrange the elements in Darling
Harbour with such authority.

One of the things he did was walk the Premier around the site,
explaining how he'd make it "people friendly."

"You must give it a soul," he said.

Wran asked a lot of questions, including "what are you going to do
about these ugly freeways? People tell me they'll have to be pulled down."

"No," said Mort. "If we handle it right, they'll look like bridges when
you're in Darling Harbour. Good for shade on hot days, too."

[Wilf Cramp, an engineer who was in charge of the team from the then Department of Main Roads responsible for preparing the designs for those freeways - known as road traffic viaducts - later told me it never occurred to him or anyone else in the department at the time of building to run the freeways underground. They didn't anticipate Darling Harbour would be developed. Yet it was an expensive process building them above ground because the pylons had to go right down to bedrock.

It reminded me of another Sydney planning monstrosity referred to in a humorous story as told to me by Jack Beale, the Minister for Water and Conservation in the NSW Askin Government.

When a previous government was building the overhead Cahill Expressway on the waterfront at Circular Quay, a VIP from New York, seeing the half-constructed affair for the first time, said in all seriousness to an official showing him around: "I'm glad to see that you guys, like us, are pulling down these eyesores and opening up the beauty of the city to the public."]

A small group of officials gathered in Neville Wran's office when Mort presented his revised plan.

The Premier looked at it and said, "yes, that's what we want."

"Well, sign it, we'll never get another chance" said Mort, prophetically.

In what was a remarkable coup by Mort, the Premier picked up his pen on the spot and gave it his stamp of approval by signing off the document, adding the word "approved" after his signature.

Laurie Brereton signed it too, so did Mort, and so did Hank Laan representing the Darling Harbur Authority. It would be one of the most historic documents in the whole saga.

The Barbarians had won the day. But it wasn't over yet.

19

NOT SO TENDER PROCESS

THE public knockers were at it by the time Neville Wran officially launched his Darling Harbour scheme at the end of 1984.

At a boozy function in the glass and marble foyer of Sydney's Parliament House before a stellar business group, Wran took the opportunity to fire a broadside at the knockers who were already in albino pachyderm mode.

"We're going to hold competitions for sculptures in civic works," he said with cynical humour, "and it may well be appropriate that one subject be a white elephant surrounded by knockers rampant."

He identified some of the early detractors as Nick Greiner, Leader of the NSW State Opposition, Jack Mundey, chairman of the City Council planning committee and the *Business Review Weekly*.

A small army of whiners was yet to come forth. Nifty urged everyone to get behind the project, describing it as "one of the most important in Sydney this century." The cost was now mooted at $1 billion.

Then the guests tumbled outside and wandered back up the city streets to their offices bearing blue coloured sample bags with Mort Hoppenfeld's plan and other details inside, each carrying a little silver helium balloon proclaiming "Darling Harbour - a Place for People."

The message had got through at last.

Nothing was said publicly at that stage about what private interests were involved but clearly behind the scenes, the Government had been given the guts and confidence to go ahead by Tom Hayson's commitment to invest tens of millions of dollars in the project and introduce expert advice and experience.

ABOVE: The ancient village of Aitou high up in the mountains of North Lebanon, from where Tom Jacobs' grandfather emigrated to Australia in 1886 to escape poverty and religious persecution.
Here and further up the mountains, the Phoenicians cut the most famous trees in the world, the Cedars of Lebanon, for trade with the Pharaohs.

ABOVE: View of modern Aitou in its mountainous terrain. Visitors are surprised by its greenness.

LEFT: One of Aitou's four Christian (Maronite) Churches, looking towards the Mediterranean.

BELOW: Aitou seen from the ruins of the former home of Tom Jacobs' forebears.

ABOVE: Wartime wedding of Presbyterian Ngaire Margaret de Nett and Catholic Thomas Clement Jacobs at "neutral" St. George's Church of England at Hurstville (Sydney), on 26 June, 1943. It would last 57 years. Left to Right: Dianne Vout, press photographer Ernie Nutt, Thelma Vout, bride and groom, Ray de Nett, Ngairetta Vout, and journalist / groomsman Barry Young.

LEFT: The happy couple on their wedding day.

ABOVE: Tom Hayson proudly sports his Order of Australia gong for his Darling Harbour efforts, which won us the 2000 Games.

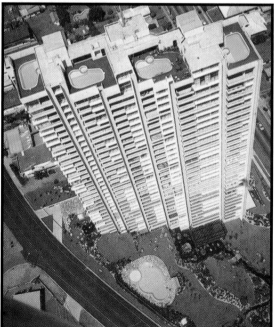

ABOVE: The Golden Gate, the Haysons' luxury Gold Coast apartments ahead of their time.

LEFT: Bird's eye view - note the penthouse pools.

ABOVE: Star-studded opening of Skygarden, the Sydney shopping complex which won international acclaim, embellishing the Haysons' reputation as developers and builders of excellence.

LEFT: Skygarden's award by the International Council of Shopping Centres for design and development.

ABOVE: The Duke and Duchess of Wellington with Tom and Ngaire Hayson at Skygarden's opening.

BELOW: John and Caroline Laws among the 700 heavy-weight Australian VIPs.

ABOVE: Baltimore's revolutionary Inner Harbour development, which provided the inspiration to Tom Hayson for Australia's Darling Harbour waterfront renaissance, replacing a rundown railway goods yard.

BELOW: Tom Hayson shown around Baltimore's development by American developer of genius, James Rouse and his wife Patty.

ABOVE: Work begins in what would become the great Darling Harbour complex. Shopping bag in hand, Tom Hayson had already anticpated events by buying up, with son Ian, all the woolstores behind Darling Harbour, including Goldsbrough Mort seen in the background.

BELOW: Legendary American developer James Rouse, whom Tom Hayson co-opted, stands before the Hayson artists' impression of what they had in store for the old derelict Darling Harbour goods yard.

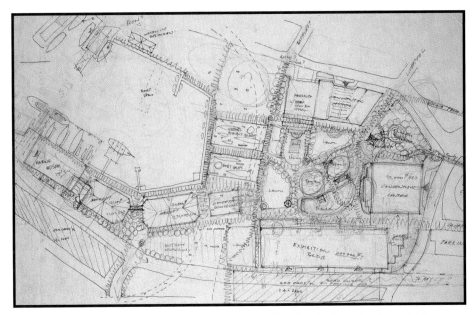

ABOVE: History was created with this rough sketch of what Darling Harbour should look like, by American architect Professor Mort Hoppenfeld, secretly employed by Tom Hayson. It was vastly different to the NSW Government's "masterplan."

BELOW: Touched up version of the above, presented in coup-like circumstances to NSW Public Works Minister Laurie Brereton - not in Australia but in a hotel bar in the US. It convinced the NSW Government to follow Tom Hayson's plans.

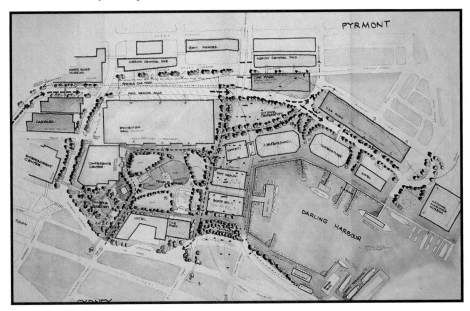

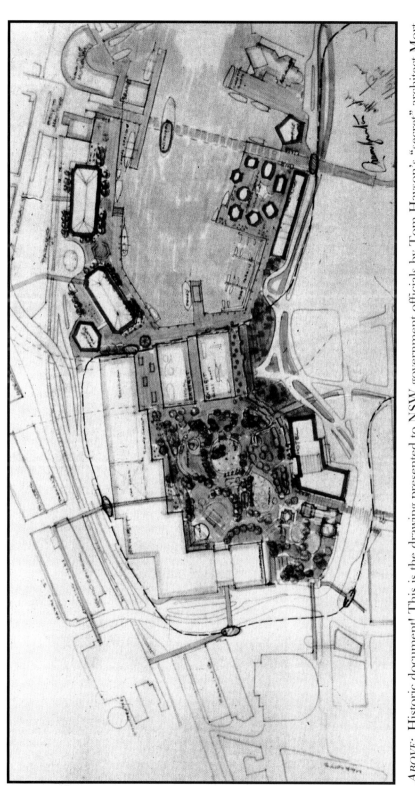

ABOVE: Historic document! This is the drawing presented to NSW government officials by Tom Hayson's "secret" architect Mort Hoppenfeld, and signed off by them as the basic plan for Darling Harbour to replace the Government's own "master plan." On seeing it, Premier Neville Wran said, "this is what we want." Hoppenfeld said, "well, sign it." And he did!

ABOVE: A partly finished Darling Harbour, showing its amazing close proximity to Sydney's central business district - amazing, because it lay undeveloped and an eyesore until Tom Hayson and son Ian saw the possibilities.

ABOVE: Darling Harbour railway goods yards. BEFORE . . .

BELOW: And AFTER Tom Hayson's group of companies and the NSW Government conbined to transform it into one of the world's premier 'People Places."

ABOVE: Father and son team, Tom and Ian Hayson, with their Harbourside development at Darling Harbour behind them. It brought fun, colour, excitement and new life to waterfront rejuvenation schemes in Australia, a trend widely copied by corporate rivals.

ABOVE: Tom and Ngaire Hayson say hi to the Queen at Darling Harbour's official opening. A beaming Premier Nick Greiner would not have bid for the 2000 Games in Sydney without Darling Harbour.

Left: Ian and daughter Melissa make the Queen's photo shoot.

ABOVE: "Psst! Now let me say this to you, Ma'am . . ." Tom has an intimate word in the Queen's shell pink while the Duke and Ngaire adopt a studious pose at the opening of Darling Harbour.

RIGHT: Crikey! How did Tom turn up on the balcony alone with the Queen, introduced as "His Royal Highness, the Duke of Edinburgh?"

ABOVE: Tom among the most famous trees in the world, the Cedars of Lebanon, near his ancestral village.

ABOVE: Tom and Ngaire outside his ancestral village in the mountains of North Lebanon.

LEFT: Ian and Lillian Gasinskaya - the Girl in the Red Bikini.

RIGHT: Tom and Ngaire's daughter, Rosemary and husband Grant Clifton.

But the young Hayson architects were still being denigrated, softened only by murmurings of "thank God it has come back into the fold," meaning the appointment of the local architects MSJ Keys Young to work with the Authority.

They were being written off in conversation as young Turks with no track record who should not be doing such important public ventures, although they were only designing the Marketplace, with help. Some snivellers said they were worried about the outcome.

The young architects felt strong animosity towards them. The establishment in the profession was still smarting over those in the Government Architect's office being sidelined.

Most Sydney architects worth their salt knew of the Boston Quincy markets project, a much-studied social phenomenon because it had worked. Some architects connected with Darling Harbour now had trained on that background and considered themselves admirably suited to do it.

What they had not fully appreciated was that it had needed the developer's role to succeed - in this case, the inspiration of Jim Rouse.

Rouse's pioneering concept of marketplaces would probably never have got off the ground without him first becoming wealthy by building his 75 shopping malls. His deep pockets then enabled him to take risks and hold out against the Doubting Thomases and entrenched conservatives.

Rouse had told Tom Hayson plainly that he was absolutely right in surrounding himself with young fresh minds, people who were not hung up on convention and in a rut. He believed it was essential to the success of the project. He didn't want to see the Marketplace buggered up by the staid habits of tired retail designers.

Hayson, too, was coming in for a good old shellacking through the rumour mill. Who was this bloke, what had he ever done to justify this "in" with the Government? He's too small to do something like this...

It only spurred him on. Instead of wasting time reacting, he was more concerned in building up his organisation by bringing in key people to face the coming challenge. One of his recent recruits was Pat Gocher, whom he stole from Lend Lease to become project controller.

He never told anybody that Darling Harbour occupied his mind not just in the waking hours but for almost 24 hours a day, seven days a week. He dreamed about it, sleeping fitfully, first on his mind every time he woke. He was sure he planned in his dreams, thinking how to generate things.

He could do that and live with it, but his detractors got under his skin when they resorted to racial slurs to undermine him.

The incidents were never confronting but came back to him through members of his staff who had ethnic backgrounds. "You shouldn't take any notice of what people are saying, Tom," they told him, subtly.

When pressed for details, they said some people were questioning his ethnic past, commenting on the fact that he was Lebanese and using it as a means of putting him down.

He shrugged it off to his staff members and tried to ignore it but it depressed him, causing him to go down to the Harbour foreshore where he could be calm and alone and think while gazing on the water. It brought back the hurtfulness, doubt and confusion of his childhood.

He imagined they were calling him a wog and a dago behind his back, although there was no evidence of that. He would never let anyone know, but for a while it tore him apart emotionally.

Gradually he was able to rationalise things. He recalled the priest in Osaka telling him he could see the map of Australia on his face. The Americans whom he admired and respected, Rouse and co, had accepted him for what he was - an Australian. They didn't worry about the colour of his skin or the source of his antecedents. They were interested in what he could do, and that helped his confidence return.

"I'm a second generation Australian," he told himself. "My father was born here. I have just as much right to be here as all the Anglo-Saxons."

It's remarkable how the vista changes when you get up off your knees.

He got up, and his determination returned. Once again he wanted to prove what a little Lebanese boy could do.

He liked to think there was a little bit of the Phoenician in him, that he came from a culture thousands of years old.

"I'll show the bastards," he said. Not *all* the Anglo-Saxons, just those who had hurt him in his life and who were trying to get at him racially.

It weighed heavily on Tom Hayson's heart to think that after putting so much effort and money into convincing the Government that a Rouse-type marketplace should be built in Darling Harbour, he could lose the lot.

Now he had to go out and compete with others for the right to build it. That was unfair, even indecent, but unfortunately the way of things in Australia.

You can go to a Government with an idea, put your heart and soul into it, even spend enormous amounts of money to prove it viable, then they put it out to tender and some carpetbagger can come along and knock you off and you can whistle for justice.

It has happened, will happen again and many fair-minded people live in hope that some uncaring or grasping Minister will be successfully sued for millions one day for squeezing a person who has had his good idea stolen by "the public process."

The policy of putting public land to tender, apart from unfairness to the person with the original idea, tends to end up with developments going towards the mediocre because concepts suffer as a result. It's a fact of life that growth is stymied when intellectual property has to be tendered for, because Government planners then do things not by nature but by constraint. The Government planning system basically builds on what is already there and is not looking at innovative things for the future.

The person who wins a tender may not have the same view of it as the originator. He might want to cut costs.

Public tendering may give the public the impression that the right thing is being done, but it can lead to corruption just as easily as giving a development to someone arbitrarily.

In the case of Darling Harbour the press was quickly on the trail sniffing for an alleged scandal. While tenders were still being considered early in 1985, the *Sydney Morning Herald* ran claims that "certain favoured companies had a lien on the plum private enterprise contracts long before tenders went out."

If that were so, nobody told Tom Hayson.

He thought he deserved to win the right to build his Marketplace, but was told bluntly by Minister Brereton that he'd have to compete for the tender. That was policy. End of story.

To people like Bob Pentecost in the Government's Capital Works Unit, the Marketplace lease was a serious one for 99 years. It was public land and the Government had to show responsibility and get the best financial deal, even if the Haysons had done a lot of leadup work.

As Brereton later told this writer: "This was a public bidding competition. If there was only one horse in the race, he would not be trying too hard. There's an old saying in contracting - if you don't have a bidding war, you don't have people with sharp pencils.

"The Haysons were trying to make a quid out of this and I encouraged people to go in there to protect the Government and taxpayers' interests."

It certainly worked because Tom Hayson spared no effort or expense.

To prepare his plan for the Marketplace, which he would call Harbourside, he sent architect Bob Perry to Baltimore to work with Rouse's Enterprise Development Company. Videos were produced comparing it with Baltimore, showing how Harbourside would relate to the rest of Darling Harbour.

Harbourside was drawn as two pavilions joined by a glass roof, and this plan was proof-read by Mort Hoppenfeld as the Darling Harbour masterplanner.

To gain backing and give himself more strength, Hayson persuaded the Custom Credit Corporation to join him in a joint venture. He convinced them by the zeal, energy and overpowering way he presented the opportunity. They were the first ones to put private money into Darling Harbour and without it, Tom may have had to pull out in the concept stage. Nobody was keen to go into Darling Harbour!

Custom Credit was fully owned by the National Bank, which also half-owned a group called Custom Resources International (CRI). The Haysons also brought them in, as a project management group.

After that, whenever the Government referred to the joint venture, it was always Custom Credit first and the Haysons last.

Before tenders closed for the Harbourside private enterprise project in Darling Harbour, the Haysons were furious to find that in the leadup all their secret architectural formulas developed at great cost were given to the other applicants by the DHA, as part of the tender package.

These had been lifted from the first submission they put in to try to stimulate the Government. They included views from the promenade and all the things they had talked about at length with Rouse such as terrace cafes and other features based on what they had learned in Baltimore.

It all came out as control drawings and meant they no longer had a competitive edge over their rivals.

Tom Hayson then found himself on a short list up against the two biggest corporations in the business, Lend Lease and Westfield.

He knew they had the strength and wherewithal to beat the relatively small Hayson Group if they were serious about it, and it worried him. Indeed, it gave him nightmares.

He'd worked his guts out, eating, drinking and sleeping Darling Harbour and as the countdown approached to award the tender, he was exhausted and dreamt that Lend Lease had won it. He'd wake in a sweat, his bed moist with perspiration.

At other times in his sleep he would hear Wran, Brereton and the DHA chairman Alex Carmichael talking, and he was being denigrated.

In one vivid dream he heard Wran telling Brereton why they had to give the contract to one of the others. "They've got more money, better background and Hayson is small fry by comparison..."

Shortly before the winning announcement was to be made, Tom received an unofficial tip that he was the one and should make sure he was present.

He turned up on the day, dressed in his best, not sure if it was true. On this sort of occasion, with various Government officials present, he never pushed himself forward and tended to stay on the sidelines.

Before Premier Wran stepped up to the dais, Tom noticed Laurie Brereton in conversation with a leading DHA official. They looked towards him and he wondered what it was about.

Wran announced the winner, the joint venture partners Custom Credit together with CRI, the eminent Rouse Co of the US - and the Hayson Group. It didn't matter he was mentioned last, he was there!

At that moment there was no more relieved man on earth. He made a buoyant speech.

Tom had won the first private enterprise contract awarded in Darling Harbour. He expected to spend $80 million to build his Harbourside Marketplace but it would eventually cost $110 million. Under the terms of his consultant developer agreement, the Rouse Company now owned 7½ per cent of Harbourside.

To win it he had spent almost $1 million alone in fares and other costs flying people to and from Baltimore plus architectural fees.

Harbourside with its shops, restaurants and entertainment, would be the heart and key element in Darling Harbour to attract people. It would be the catalyst, a major part of the proposed overall development that would make the place "explode as a critical mass" - a term architects love to use.

In the midst of his elation he was brought down to earth with a thud by information passed on to him in a well-meaning way by the general manager of the DHA, Hank Laan, who in his short term of office always treated the Haysons with respect.

Tom was told that just before the Premier spoke, a top bureaucrat had said to Brereton: "No, we don't want Hayson to speak. What do you want him for? He's out."

Brereton had replied: "If Hayson doesn't speak, the Premier doesn't speak. And neither do I." Tom always respected Brereton after that.

The lease cost the Haysons $11 million and a generous share of gross takings from Harbourside. They won the tender on all aspects. Tom felt that the others were not serious because they had the resources to come up with better submissions, offering more money and a good technical design, and could have won it.

What Tom didn't know while making his application was that Lend Lease and Westfield were dragged kicking and screaming to take part in the tendering process. Neither could see how they could make any money out of the Marketplace project.

Brereton had actually pleaded with them to take part after they said they could not possibly risk their shareholders' money. After putting in bids in the interests of maintaining good relations with Government, each corporation said privately they were pleased they had not won.

If Tom had known that at the time, he would not have offered such generous terms to the Government. So much for alleged favouritism.

Attitudes towards the Haysons and their architects didn't change all that much, even after they won the bid. Architect Barry Young and his associates in the MSJ Keys group in charge of overall planning were sort of gritting their teeth having to deal with the young Hayson architects.

Young said to Bob Perry one day: "You know, there are a lot of professionals around town who are very concerned about this project."

"Why is that?" asked Bob.

"Well, they're just concerned at the calibre of the people on it. This is a very important world-scale project and frankly, the people on it are not qualified to do it."

On that basis the teaching of Jim Rouse and his planners in working with Perry's group had apparently not meant anything. Perry just laughed it off.

Tom had a similar experience attending a meeting with some members of the DHA. Chairman Carmichael said to him in the presence of some of Tom's own staff : "You've only been used to doing residential blocks. You wouldn't have got this unless you were associated with Rouse."

The attitude was quite different from Wran and Brereton. Tom wasn't aware of it then, but they had already developed a healthy respect for him and it was growing. On his part, he knew that if both of them had not got behind the Darling Harbour concept, it wouldn't have happened.

With the first battle over, Tom thought it a good idea to tell the public what was going on in order to create some positive interest in Darling Harbour.

The Hayson Group held a lavish promotional function at the Regent Hotel and invited the press. When Tom said up to 20 million people a year would visit there after the whole Darling Harbour project was finished, a senior woman journalist called out "bullshit! bullshit!"

A long way to go still.

Just after winning the Harbourside contract, Tom and his team were looking forward to the return of Mort Hoppenfeld to oversee the entire Darling Harbour plan.

It could only help them because, although he was still working for the Government, he understood their part of the project intimately and if they ran into trouble with any of the planners, he could straighten it out.

Besides, less than three years remained before the proposed opening for the bicentennial year of 1988, and everyone was anxious to get cracking.

Mort was preparing to return when, as usual, he went jogging near his home one morning in March 1985 in the rural surrounds of Columbia.

When he failed to turn up for work at Rouse's Enterprise Development Company, they went looking for him. A jogger on the road said some runner had collapsed and had been taken to hospital.

Mort was already dead of a heart attack, aged 56.

The news stunned the Haysons and everyone else in the project. Tom wept as he pulled out of his top drawer a copy of Mort's original plan which had been done in secrecy. Neville Wran too shed tears, wondering what would happen now to the new commercial concept he'd approved, described by the *Daily Telegraph* as the most exciting community development project in Australia this century.

Tom recalled discussing heart attacks with Mort in Sydney after Mort mentioned having his arteries ballooned. After talking to his friend Dr Chang about it, Tom advised him vainly to have a bypass operation.

Suddenly Darling Harbour was without its masterplanner.

A scramble occurred among architects and planners to gain credibility and power. Tom's bankers became nervous because Mort was no longer there to support his young architects. Rouse stuck up for them, telling the bankers it was important for the architects of Harbourside to have no previous experience in retail designing.

But the uneasiness remained and Tom tried to bring in Benjamin Thompson, a top architect who had done Harbourplace in Baltimore and the Quincy Markets in Boston, but he had ongoing allegiance to the Rouse Company.

Then the Baltimore architectural firm of RTKL was hired to work with Tom's Architecture Oceania group in Sydney and Baltimore on the Harbourside design. They didn't last long on the job but it held the line while the Nervous Nellies were showing skid marks on their underpants.

Professor Morton Hoppenfeld was *the* designer of the Darling Harbour concept.

Without detracting from the detailed work of the planners who took over from him and implemented it all, many involved in the Darling Harbour project agreed it would not have happened the way it did without him.

Supporters of Mort said they doubted if the Australians on their own would have come up with the right combination to make the place work.

It entailed not only technical skill but the knowledge of how to implement the genius of Rouse in being able to visualise how the public would react when they walked into Darling Harbour, where they would want to walk to next, the relationship of all the places in there to one another and how to put that necessary aura into the design.

Yet, in a quite disgraceful episode, Morton Hoppenfeld would be written out of the history of the new Darling Harbour.

He would be remembered by his colleagues in Columbia on the city's 20th birthday in 1987 with an illustrated address of one of his sayings: "To build a better city is to work at the heart of civilisation."

The measure of the man's ability and integrity was seen in an address he gave shortly before his death when he criticised his fellow architects for the "common grimness, uniformity and sterility that had come to pervade the new public places of so many American cities."

Modern sterile streets and places, he said, seemed designed merely to carry people to and from their work place, ignoring the tradition that city streets and urban places also were meeting grounds where people could gather and share their lives.

He expressed disappointment at the work of famous architects who put up giant buildings, pleasing their clients but forgetting about people in the cities by designing blank walls of concrete or marble-lined sidewalks aimed only to accommodate people walking from place to place. Even the not-so-famous architects tried to emulate the rich and famous ones, spreading the curse of urban sterilisation.

He called for a reassessment of values to serve the needs and aspirations of ordinary people.

Mort Hoppenfeld said one way to humanise and vitalise a downtown area in a more civil approach was through the "festival marketplace."

That's exactly what he planned in Darling Harbour.

After a few months the Haysons decided to buy out Custom Credit's half interest in Harbourside. To do so they borrowed the money from Citibank. They now had a banker in there providing the finance for full ownership rather than owning just a half share.

They felt they could do better on their own without partners and the constraints they imposed.

Also they had other ventures in mind.

20

THE BATTLE OF DARLING HARBOUR

NEVER in Sydney's history was there a more controversial project than Darling Harbour.

By comparison, the row over the Opera House and its designer Joern Utzon was a mere stroll in the park.

Darling Harbour became a political football of grand-final intensity right from kickoff, booted in all directions by people with their own selfish agendas.

The main motivation was sheer grubby, points-scoring politics.

Some of it was irresponsible in the way it financially affected Darling Harbour at crucial stages of development.

The Labor Party and Neville Wran were boosting Darling Harbour as something good for Sydney, therefore political opponents had to knock it down. Didn't *have* to but that's the way the game is played.

Opposition Leader Nick Greiner and his Liberal Party colleagues frothed at the mouth as they tried to tear it apart.

They said it was a waste of Government money, the millions being poured into this railway goods yard should be going into hospitals and other public infrastructure, corruption and wastage were seen in every pile being driven and the squandering of public money on such a white elephant would be regretted for decades...

Nick Greiner got up in the NSW Parliament and, shaking with political indignation, delivered these historic words: "What will we do with the windswept empty canyons of Darling Harbour after the bicentenary?"

The press, which in Australia runs on controversy, sensation and dissension, went into overdrive criticising the project. Reporters and leader writers fairly quivered with excitement as they dumped pessimistic phrases on the place.

One leading Sydney newspaper, not in the Murdoch Group, was the leading knocker. When they couldn't find out anything, they condemned the Government and the DHA, alleging "a veil of secrecy."

At first it was more of an irritation to those trying to plan and build the facility, doing their best to roll with the punches, but it quickly became serious, causing everything about Darling Harbour to be political.

Even many planners and architects in the institutions, perhaps because they weren't part of it, jealously took a political rather than a professional stance over the issue.

The whole protest movement had the effect of causing a difficult working environment, those in management and entrepreneurial roles feeling they had to perform under the gun in what was a short and difficult time frame even before any natural complications arose.

Worst of all, it created doubts among many minds, including some on the DHA, whether the Government was right by introducing "vulgar commercialism" into the project.

The diehards, like most of the City Council, were still whining that low-cost public housing should go in there, although obviously housing and places for people to gather for entertainment and relaxation do not mix.

Building Darling Harbour was not only difficult in terms of normal political opposition, but there was a great deal of pain within the Government's own ranks. A strong school of thought believed the money being spent there should have gone into essential public works.

Many heated deputations went to Wran about it and there was always blunt talk. That pain would eventually erupt inside the Labor Party.

Labor Party members repeatedly said behind the scenes there were no votes in Darling Harbour. And they were right. But there were votes in *knocking* it and their lack of enthusiasm for it contributed to the situation.

It made Labor politicians continually nervous thinking of the next election.

Indeed, the Philistines would have stripped Darling Harbour to the banal, bare and mediocre if people like Laurie Brereton had not moved quickly to get things done in the short timetable before the bicentenary.

At one stage Wran nailed his critics in Parliament by pointing out that doom-sayers had used the same cliches trying to stop the Harbour Bridge being built in the late 1920s.

Just about everything concerning Darling Harbour was controversial.

People worked themselves into a lather over the Monorail, portrayed as the "Monsterail" with buckets of oil supposedly dripping on hapless city victims walking underneath. The knockers were so feverish that Darling Harbour would be called Snarling Harbour.

Certainly there were union troubles on the site and overruns of the original budgets as things were added, but nothing to justify the allegations of corruption and wastage that reverberated around the place and which were proved to be unfounded by various committees of inquiries.

Tom Hayson, after winning the tender to build Harbourside, had gone into an unkempt little church in Pyrmont, got down on his knees and given thanksgiving in prayer that the battle had been won.

But news for Tom - the battle had only just begun.

For instance, he was supposed to be in partnership with the Government in building his Harbourside Marketplace. That was certainly pretty much the case as far as Neville Wran and Laurie Brereton were concerned.

But it never worked out that way. The bureaucrats saw to that, destroying the idea behind the scenes.

Tom felt there was never anything but a master and servant relationship in the way he was treated by the planners and the DHA. He believed he was always treated as a tenant and told what to do, although on a 99-year lease which had cost him a fortune. The freehold was owned by Her Majesty's Government, so stay in line, lightweight!

They needed private enterprise in there but this was a Government job and he'd be shown who was boss.

He did not feel negotiations were done in a proper way, by prior consultation or in a convivial fashion that indicated they were dealing with people of equal stature. He and his team deferred to the board of the DHA because they had the voting power, but he felt the more they went out of their way to co-operate the less the board responded.

One of the big problems, he believed, was that they didn't understand the concept of what he was trying to do. Most were not chosen for their expertise or experience, especially in a development on that large scale and, in fairness, nothing like what the Haysons were doing in there had ever been attempted by private enterprise in Australia before.

But the bureaucrats had their own fancies and prejudices on what should be done and that led to confrontation and disagreement.

Tom always felt the DHA chairman, Alex Carmichael, gave the impression that he was small fry and should not be in Darling Harbour.

There was rarely any hope of reaching first name terms, the atmosphere was never friendly enough for that. In fact, there was almost an air of hostility with some people when he went into the DHA offices.

The scene was similar when he went into the planning offices where MSJ Keys Young were working on the Darling Harbour plans.

They would stop talking when he walked in and he gained the distinct impression they didn't want him there. They looked at him with a condescending air. He just took the unfriendly attitude on the chin.

There was always that feeling that the Harbourside Marketplace was forced on the planners.

It appeared there was reluctance to accept the Rouse philosophy that his civic design ideas should go into the whole facility. The planners acted like policemen to note what ugly things the developer might do, and so the whip had to be cracked over Tom and his organisation. And with Mort Hoppenfeld out of the way, that was a hard attitude to get over.

Tom also thought that Carmichael adopted far too much of a penny-pinching attitude to his project, wanting to know every small detail and where every dollar was going and in Tom's view, not appreciating that the purse strings for such a new and radical development could not be held so tightly.

Against that, Carmichael was a tough bloke from a strong business and Government-body background who acted as if the Government money was his and should be spent carefully.

It reached the stage where Tom stopped going into the DHA offices.

They never invited him there anyway and if he wanted to discuss some obvious thing he had to make the approach.

Conferences were held that should have involved his planners, but at times they were not invited.

What hurt him most was that later as Darling Harbour was nearing completion and the Liberals came to power, the DHA never invited him to any of the social or official functions held there. Others of lesser stature went. He saw that as an affront to his dignity and a deliberate, calculated insult.

He had to fight for every point and defend everything he or his organisation wanted to do. The trouble he had in trying to get others in the Authority to work with him on making Darling Harbour an attractive people place alive with colour and movement, cost him a lot of heartburn and money.

In the words of one person who took part in the planning, if it had not been for Tom Hayson and the people he brought in, Darling Harbour would have finished up as a park with a picket fence around it and a convention centre inside which was there only because it had been talked about for the previous 25 years. Certainly, nothing there would have generated any revenue on a daily basis.

In other words, it would have been a joke and a disaster - not to mention the likelihood of standardised, unattractive public housing and the unsightly preservation of ugly old railway sheds as a "heritage" backdrop.

It has to be said categorically that nobody, in a whole range of dedicated people who put their efforts into finishing Darling Harbour on time, injected as much commitment into it as Tom Hayson - the only private enterprise person to put his money where his mouth was in the vital pre-planning and early stages when the development took shape.

That view was shared at the time by numerous people in a position to know, although not generally acknowledged, certainly not by most of the bureaucrats driving the work.

Those views, revisited now and considered in hindsight, make it all the more remarkable that he was not treated with greater respect at the time.

The following comments put Tom Hayson's role in perspective for that period when Darling Harbour was struggling to survive against trenchant political and press criticism, when there was only a small band of true believers and even before that, when nobody else would invest in it:

*When **Neville Wran** was asked for this book what he thought of Hayson at the time, the former Premier said on the record: "I say without question if it hadn't been for Tom Hayson's vision and guts, there may still have been a Darling Harbour, but it would have been a much reduced Darling Harbour.*

"And it would not have had the private sector element in it, the dynamism that the profit-making incentive brings with it which we needed and which proved to be the engine room for the growth of the area.

"The very fact that he was the only one who put his hand up gave us a peg to hang our hat on, and without his input and support, we had nothing. It would merely have been seen as another Government waste of money."

Gerry Gleeson, Wran's operations chief as Secretary of the Premier's Department, who at first meeting wrote Hayson off as a lightweight, said:

"Without Tom, Darling Harbour would have been like the Sydney Cricket Ground, where it is used on Saturdays for football, and there would have been a park where people could come.

"But we wouldn't have had the entertainment components, or the hotels. He attracted the hotels with his Harbourside as the drawcard. Look, if Tom hadn't started that, we would have been in real strife, no doubt about that."

Gleeson went further in his unstinted praise: "Tom's a great community man, and this wasn't just a question of him making a dollar.

"He actually felt he was building something Sydney could be proud of. He's a great enthusiast and wanted this city to be a city we could all be proud of."

Laurie Brereton, the Minister who grasped the nettle and pushed Darling Harbour through even against strong opposition in his own political party, said: "I gave Tom two enormous ticks. First, for the early enthusiasm and for steering us in the direction of the planning outcome we finally embraced and second, for having the guts and commercial courage himself to charge in and do the Harbourside Marketplace.

"Believe me, nobody else would go in there. They couldn't see any money in it. I've never made that public until now.

"Without him, we would have had an inferior development. Tom should be properly credited for putting his money in and introducing those commercial influences to give us the mix for creating a people place.

"He's responsible for that - a people place. It wouldn't have been a people magnet except for Tom.

"As a result, I'll always have time for Tom. I regard him as a great Australian."

Jim Rouse said in a letter to Hayson: "You are the real architect of Darling Harbour. Without you, it would not have happened."

Marty Millspaugh: *"Darling Harbour without Tom Hayson? No way.*

"Many people play roles but someone has to create the vision and ginger them up. I saw Rouse do it in America. Tom did it in Sydney."

Bob Blackmore, who saw it through as one of the Hayson architects: *"The catalyst or principal person who made Darling Harbour possible was Tom Hayson. No question.*

"I admired Wran too for giving the OK when Mort Hoppenfeld went to him with his plan. And I admired Brereton as the public works bloke who stuck to his guns, otherwise it would have bogged down in politics.

"Without Tom and these other people we'd have had public housing at Darling Harbour, destroying the area and taking it away from the city like Woolloomooloo."

Ian Hayson: *"When you're spending two or three billion dollars on a project, it's so massive that it's very unfair to claim to be the person who made it happen. But in this case in terms of original ideas, we can be sure.*

"Number one was Neville Wran. The first idea came from him in deciding to do his own Expo and wanting to put something in there. But number two, Darling Harbour as it is today came out of my dad's head. It's fair to say he's the one who ignited it and caused it to happen."

Bob Pentecost, a civil engineer by profession who was seconded from the Premier's Department in August 1985 to take charge of construction at Darling Harbour as chief executive officer of the DHA, had a lot to do with Hayson and his team in those days when the site was transformed from a mud heap to an award-winning world-class waterfront facility.

"Tom was always effusive and enthusiastic," Pentecost said, *"and full credit to him because it would have been real easy for him to have said this is too hard. But he never blanched once. He was exciting and forward thinking. And his enthusiasm was infectious.*

"There would have been something in Darling Harbour, but no Marketplace. That was a new concept which needed Tom's drive and energy to make it go. Without that, the place would not have had the size and energy. If Tom hadn't gone in there I don't think the level of funds would have been committed to make Darling Harbour happen.

"Without the commitment of Wran and Brereton and the finance and creativity of Hayson, it could still be a disused railway yard.

"I gave Tom top marks for his vision and energy. That's what was so terrific. He didn't make it dull and boring, he didn't come up with a

wimpy little shed and say well, I'll support you with this cheque for $5 million. He went in boots and all. Bloody marvellous."

After working closely with Tom Hayson, Pentecost was asked for his personal assessment of the man. "I found him to be just a lovely bloke," he said, "but he'd be a tough enemy. There are no flies on him.

"He cares about people and what's going on and I think that's why he can be tough, because he does care. I don't mean in a nasty, aggressive way but he has principles and if he believes in something, he'll fight for it.

"When it came to money he had to see the bottom line there but he had a broader vision than just thinking about the money angle of things. He had to believe in something as well as thinking of the profit motive.

"What I liked was he could see the funny side of things, too. Even going through the worst horrors, he still thought in an upbeat way. I regarded him as an uplifting person."

Pentecost was sent to China to negotiate the Darling Harbour Chinese Gardens, which Sydney's sister city in the province of Guanzhou gave Australia as a bicentenary gift. While there he had a revelation.

Visiting a large garden in Suchow and learning about the three noises of water and other mysteries that make up a good Chinese garden, he thought it a pretty big call when his guide said "this is the very best garden in China."

"Why?" asked Bob. "Is it the pavilions, the way the water moves...?"

"No, none of those things. Look at the **people having fun**."

"People having fun." For the first time he understood what Rouse and Hayson were saying, that Darling Harbour should be fun. He never had any difficulty understanding the Hayson concept after that.

Murray Sime, senior banking official: "I remember Tom Hayson explaining his vision for Darling Harbour to me in 1980 when dealing with the woolstores, and how he thought it would progress.

"Frankly, I think without him we wouldn't have Darling Harbour today, not as a great public place. He had a vision in the true sense of the word."

Even after the planners, architects and constructors started on Darling Harbour, the Haysons had to be watchful to prevent it from being turned into a concrete landscape.

But they had to be circumspect how they went about it, just as they had to be canny and resourceful to get Mort Hoppenfeld's early "masterplan" put in front of Brereton.

Much of the same battle for recognition involved in who came up with the masterplan and who designed the place, existed with the management of it.

Many of those connected with the DHA and the building of Darling Harbour saw it as a stepping stone to their future.

Once all the management structure was laid down and working, they didn't want anyone interfering. If seen to be successful, their bureaucratic futures and careers outside Government were assured.

If they did it well it could lead to promotion in Government, or they could step outside and write their own tickets in private enterprise jobs.

It wasn't every day you could say you played a key role in a multi-billion dollar project. Looked good on the CV!

So nobody really wanted to give any credit to anyone except themselves.

Tom wasn't just interested in building a new-style shopping centre there. He wanted to see the whole thing happen. Darling Harbour was something for Sydney and Australia and he wanted to see it done properly. That made his involvement emotional, not just commercial.

Whenever he saw something being done he thought was wrong, he was prepared to go in and fight to have it changed. But the last thing anyone wanted to do was to give any credit to a private enterprise bloke called Tom Hayson.

That's why it didn't take him long to get the message that he was in the way. But he continued the struggle, with management, Governments, anyone he thought was doing something that would damage the concept of a successful people place.

He even changed offices from Mosman to the city, where he could look down on Darling Harbour from his skyscraper balcony and see what was happening on a daily basis.

As more people became involved in Darling Harbour, they tried harder to keep him at arms length, grabbing credit for themselves.

One of the problems he confronted was trying to stop major changes to Mort Hoppenfeld's plan and attempts to revert to pre-Mort ideas by putting old things back in. If he had not stood up and been counted, some planning atrocities would almost certainly have occurred.

One example was an early determination to build a concrete wall around Darling Harbour. Can you imagine it?

Rouse had nagged the Hayson architects while they designed the Harbourside Marketplace to make a feature of the nearby water's edge, stressing that people had a fascination for it and there should not be any fence around it.

The Haysons were walking around the site with a representative group one day including Premier Wran in the early planning stages in 1985, when they stopped at the eastern waterfront.

Wran said: "We'll build a wall right around the waterfront to stop people falling in."

The wall was obviously in the pipeline. Both Tom and Ian spoke against it. But nobody took any notice of them.

Luckily James Rouse was in the group, on one of his four visits to Sydney. He spoke quietly but firmly: "Nobody will fall in the water. Take my word for it, I've done a few of these inner harbour things. If you put a wall around it, you'll make it like your Botanic Gardens.

"It'll be a physical barrier between the water and the people. All you need is a little low hob, where lovers can sit and read or watch the water. That'll be enough."

Wran issued a directive at once - no concrete wall.

The amount of planning in their own Harbourside building was immense, but the Haysons were able to influence other planning decisions as well.

To do so they had to go behind the scenes, circumspectly. That didn't make any friends but they considered it necessary.

Hayson was fortunate he had the support of the Premier, the head of his department and the Minister because their strength, even if only by their sitting in the background, kept at bay the ambitious mandarins who might have ridden roughshod over him on every issue.

Building the Haysons' Harbourside was incredibly complicated. So many different things were going on in Darling Harbour at the same time.

In the end it would be built at such speed that not all the planning could be put down on paper.

In the overall task of putting Darling Harbour together, priority was given to the planning, design and construction of the convention and exhibition centres. The Hayson architects were told to wait until priorities were worked out.

They were left sitting anxiously on the sidelines for months until their construction became urgent. As other jobs took precedence, they would be given just enough time to design and construct the Marketplace.

Darling Harbour was designed differently to Baltimore in that the green or recreation centre for people was in the centre, rather than on the side.

The roads instead of going down first would be built last outside the buildings on the edge of the site. The theme was much the same but the elements were in different positions, making it unique.

As think-tanking went on among the various planners, blocks of wood were being pushed around to allocate space on the plan, which was updated every few months. Bob Pentecost and his construction team bought time while definite plans were being crystallised by driving piles to prepare for a square-shaped convention centre.

Everyone knew Darling Harbour was a difficult site to build on because so much had to happen in such a short time. The service problems like power, water and electricity were something of a nightmare but were resolved early, with Minister Brereton's full help in dealing with the various authorities.

The first real snag for the Hayson Group came when John Andrews, designer of the convention centre, wanted to change the location of his building to the waterfront. That meant the Haysons would have to relocate their Marketplace to what they considered an inferior spot.

Mort Hoppenfeld had put the convention centre closer to where the Entertainment Centre already existed, where he thought it should naturally go.

In choosing the site for Harbourside, the heart and soul of the new Darling Harbour, he believed it was important that it should have a north easterly aspect and be in full line of sight of the waterfront and on the natural axis from the city. Jim Rouse agreed with the choice.

But somehow the planners had it ridiculously in their minds that the convention centre was some kind of national monument and had to be seen inexorably by people coming into the site.

Imagine a big, impersonal monolithic type of building, used only for organised functions, going into the natural place for the softer-edged

Marketplace, with its living, breathing, pulsating character aimed at attracting people every day?

It wouldn't have happened if Mort was still around and in charge. And it cast grave doubts that the planners understood the magical quality to make Darling Harbour work.

The Haysons opposed the move because it would create serious problems for their own development. But John Andrews had his way because the Authority decided it would happen.

With the approval of Tom and Ian, Bob Perry and his architectural colleagues reluctantly backed down, realising it was inevitable.

It meant the Harbourside Marketplace when built had to be shoved around almost to the Pyrmont Bridge.

Suddenly Harbourside had lost its prime connection with the city.

The new orientation also meant that instead of being bathed in sunshine from morning until late in the afternoon by facing east at an angle, a large part of the Marketplace would be in shadow from around lunchtime. Also Jordon's, planned to be one of the largest seafood restaurants in the world, had to be greatly reduced in size.

To fit in with the new design and location of the convention centre, the DHA planners then asked the Hayson planners to redesign their Marketplace from two buildings as in Baltimore, to one.

That was another planning blow because one separate Marketplace building was intended to feature food only, a concept shown to have worked well in Baltimore.

The convention centre had started out as a square building, but now late in the day while plans were almost no longer fluid it became semi circular, requiring new piles to be driven.

The convention centre would continue to slow the whole project down although they'd had an early start. The toughest building on the site to construct, it was tight, jammed and complex and that's where the unions gave the DHA its biggest caning.

Behind the scenes the Haysons helped solve the indecisions over internal requirements of that building, as they did on many other issues that arose in Darling Harbour.

Having to redesign the Harbourside Marketplace wasn't the only major problem caused by the convention centre change.

Rouse rang Tom Hayson from the US to say he feared the Marketplace could go broke because people could not easily get to it now.

So they had to arrange some transport to get people from the city into Harbourside.

That's how the Monorail was born.

A "people mover" for anything from trams up had been talked about and expressions of interest called for by the DHA, but nothing was definite.

After expensive research overseas, Tom took the bull by the horns and decided the Monorail was it.

The Hayson Group did costings and Ian personally took the scheme to Sir Peter Abeles of TNT, saying "here's a costing, 40 million. This is something you can do for Australia's bicentenary."

Sir Peter had put his hand up to do an international-type village but it was tossed out for lack of interest. A few days later he rang Ian and said: "I've decided to do the Monorail. I don't agree with your costs, it will be more than 40 million dollars. But I'm going to do it anyway. And I've already rung the Minister and told him."

Ian nearly fell on the floor. That was Sir Peter and TNT's bicentenary gift to the people of Sydney.

From a migrant, who had come from war-ravaged Europe with little to recommend him except some business experience, ambition and faith in himself, plus a love of his adopted country.

Nothing would stir up more controversy than the Monorail, bringing protesters out in force.

But Tom Hayson wasn't about to spend $110 million on pioneering a new building and stand by to see it go broke without a transport system to get people from the city into Darling Harbour.

But while that was reverberating in the press and on talkback radio, other hot issues on Darling Harbour were filling the air.

Apart from the simmering internal convention centre difficulty, there were brawls going on over the lack of marketing for Darling Harbour, on whether the Monorail should run down the side of the Pyrmont Bridge, and whether there should be a casino.

The casino was the tragedy of Darling Harbour.

Eventually it would be lost as part of the initial project and hundreds of millions of dollars with it, which could have paid for the convention centre. It should have remained in the spot where Mort Hoppenfeld placed it on his plan, on the eastern side of Darling Harbour right next to the city, drawing on the city infrastructure of hotels and theatres and so on to support it.

That site was taken over but not because of anything the DHA planners did. It was lost due to the relentless campaign of the State Opposition in white-anting Darling Harbour and alleging corruption.

But first, the convention centre.

It was clear to the Haysons from their travels and studies abroad that something was seriously amiss with plans for the convention and exhibition centres, that Australia had no experience of such facilities with their special requirements. Nobody would admit to problems, but the Haysons knew they existed.

Indeed, one of the major problems holding up the works was how big to make the convention centre. Planners sat around trying to decide. Should the exhibition halls be 15,000 or 20,000 square metres? Nobody thought above 20,000 or how many delegates to expect.

Ian Hayson fixed that one. From skiing in the US he'd made a good friend of Tom Pritzker, a member of one of the world's wealthiest families who among other things owned the Hyatt Hotel Corporation throughout the world.

They also owned Facility Management Group, which managed convention and exhibition centres around the world, including the vast Mosconi Centre in San Francisco and the Superdome in New Orleans.

While Darling Harbour was being built, Ian went to the US and was invited by Pritzker to have a look at his operation and be his guest at a Superbowl football game in the Superdome.

The stadium was so big he flew around inside it in a small plane. A small TV ad that day cost Hyatt $25 million. He noted that one light globe lighting up the place was as tall as three people.

On to San Francisco and his friend invited him to the Mosconi Centre to see how they could provide 10,000 hot dinners all at once for a convention of travel agents.

After seeing the Hyatt's Star Warsy advertising stuff from the VIP table, Ian went back-of-house to be shown how it was done with such efficiency.

Back in Sydney, Ian rang Brereton. "We've got another Jim Rouse for you," he said, "to help you out with that problem of the convention centre..."

Brereton never did anything special for the Haysons but he moved on things if convinced, living up to his nickname of The Bulldozer.

They liked him because if they rang and asked if he could help, he'd say yes or no on the spot. And when he said yes he'd add: "You know why I can help? Because it's helping me as well."

Brereton wanted to meet the Americans and Ian arranged for the president of the Facility Management Group to fly out to Sydney. Brereton did a consultancy deal with them to advise on the exhibition and convention centres.

As a result of one change the size of the convention centre was increased to 25,000 square metres - and it still turned out to be not enough.

If that hadn't been done, it's anyone's guess what might have happened.

As it was, the convention centre would not be delivered on time to meet its 1988 convention bookings schedule, creating a poor reputation for Sydney in the international convention market which took years to overcome.

That action by the Haysons caused some aggravation at the time and stirred up the people in the DHA. Tom and Ian didn't receive a cent for introducing the convention group but did it to help generally, first, because Tom had his dream and wanted to see it fulfilled and second, because they thought a successful convention centre would bring more customers to their shopping centre. After all, it wasn't a benevolent society.

Right at the beginning the Haysons had become similarly involved in saving the Pyrmont Bridge from being pulled down and later in the way the Monorail was routed across it.

In the early planning stages there was a serious risk of the bridge going.

Tom believed it should stay because there would be nothing to connect Pyrmont with the city, and they wanted it as a pedestrian connector for their woolstores and then, Harbourside and Darling Harbour.

Learning that a little residents' action group had been formed to save the bridge, Ian contacted the lady committee head and privately gave them $25,000 to fight the cause.

The residents employed a PR, had leaflets printed and kicked up such a stink that Wran announced the bridge would be preserved.

Next came the Monorail hassle.

It was an epic in its own right, requiring every ounce of Tom Hayson's energy and creative skills. Getting it through was so tough it seemed he needed to be a genius or have extraordinary luck - whatever came first. He settled for persistence and plain hard work.

His company spent almost $200,000 looking at various systems in Europe and the US before deciding the Monorail was best - it was almost silent, didn't interfere with the traffic and would work on a narrow raised platform in Sydney's narrow streets. The Haysons thought that by helping the Government, they were helping themselves.

After Sir Peter Abeles agreed to pay for it, the Hayson architects designed TNT's plans and TNT put in a tender to compete with other bidders.

Originally the "people mover" concept was to run from Central Station to Kent Street in the city but the TNT bid was to go along Pitt Street to link up with the tourist precinct there.

Just as well the Government's legislation gave it the right to include any area it liked in its Darling Harbour plans because the City Council would have stopped the Monorail forever from running along Pitt Street. In any case, the council would remain antagonistic.

Within days of the tender going in TNT was targeted by the City Council, the Institute of Architects and the Light Rail Association.

Some bureaucrat from the DHA, knowing that TNT was the one to beat, had leaked to the press details of their submission in an attempt to nail the Monorail and probably the Haysons and their architects. And with the press howling, that started the whole contentious issue.

The Hayson architects had suggested to Rolly Hoy, a director of TNT who would build the Monorail, that they should set up an urban design committee and invite various people to contribute ideas.

At the first meeting with Hoy after the tender was publicised, he asked: "Are these people who are bad-mouthing us in the press the ones you suggested we talk to?"

Told yes, he said: "If that's their attitude, they can get stuffed."

As a result, an urban design study was never done. The engineers just ran with it after TNT won the tender.

The architects admitted among themselves it could have been done better, even the colour specifications, but it just got away from them because of collective immaturity by the main critics, whose views would otherwise have been considered.

The architects just did the audio visuals, designed the stations and tried to ride it out.

The route was intended to be longer, running down to the Quay and along Hickson Road to Darling Harbour to give tourists something to see and enjoy and maybe do their shopping, but it was shortened due to the pressure put on the Government. One main complaint was that it "disfigured" Pitt Street and politicians were too nervous to extend it.

The controversy became so heated the architects had to run their audio visuals an unbelievable 55 times to the Government and others to get their message across that they could solve the problems that were raised.

Most of the allegations in the papers were bullshit anyway - that the Monorail would be noisy, drip oil all over the place, would stop firemen getting into buildings, look like the Cahill Expressway.

The campaign began to upset the architects. No new staff would come to work for them. Bob Perry and Bob Blackmore decided to do something about it and went to the PR person at the DHA to say they were sick of the distorted allegations which were affecting their reputations.

The PR sat them down and said: "Look, I know it must be frustrating for you. I understand it and so does the Minister. But he wants the Monorail controversy to go on exactly the way it is.

"There are lots of things going on over on the western side of Darling Harbour that are more controversial than the Monorail, like acquiring land. The Monorail controversy is acting as a decoy for that. If you do anything to stop it, the Minister will be bloody annoyed."

Walking out of there they said to each other: "How naive are we?"

So they shut up and pressed on. But months later it was still going on and getting worse. People marched in the streets against the "Monster Rail" handing out pamphlets with monster shapes on carriages.

It was really only a small group but they were so vocal it seemed like nearly all the community opposed it.

While that was still going on, the casino row was in full swing.

The Wran Government had always intended that the proposed casino would be a big funder for Darling Harbour and everybody in Government agreed the ideal site for it was where Mort Hoppenfeld had placed it on his plan - on the eastern foreshore right at the foot of the city.

Wran and his advisers were expecting to receive $300 or $400 million in upfront licence fees for the casino to help pay for Darling Harbour expansion plans, certainly the convention centre.

After expressions of interest were called for, DHA Chairman Carmichael drove a hard bargain to get the best deal for the Government.

State Opposition Leader Greiner was anti-casino and the spectre of corruption reared its head, as it usually does with casinos. He was against it, full stop.

In order to show the Government was pure in relation to the casino, Wran imposed the most stringent conditions for the successful tenderer.

He was too tough on himself because it turned out to be a mistake, playing into the hands of his opponents and other forces.

Naturally the tenderer had to pass several tests, including finance, honesty and reputation. The mistake was in making it conditional that every member of the consortium had to pass the probity test, meaning not only the equity holders but also the builder.

And that's where the tenderer came unstuck.

State Opposition members weren't the only ones against it.

There were elements in the NSW police force who did not wish to see a legal casino in Sydney. Plenty of illegal casinos were still operating, in spite of a Government crackdown. Hey hey!

The issue bogged down in politics and Sydney would not have a legal casino for about six more years, causing an imbalance in planned Darling Harbour activities. It was ludicrous and farcical because every other State already had legal casinos and NSW would lose hundreds of millions of dollars in revenue just for the heck of it.

When it was obvious the ideal Darling Harbour site would be lost and replaced by boring commercial buildings owing to the delay in casino decision making, the Haysons thought they would have a go at finding another site.

Showing a fine touch, Tom and Ian took a two-year option on private land at Pyrmont which was part of the site where the Star City Casino would eventually be built.

They drew up plans and Tom brought out leading Las Vegas casino operator Steve Wynne, owner of the Mirage, Golden Nugget and other casinos, with a view to forming a consortium, but in the political morass later gave up the idea after the option ran out.

As the Monorail rumpus rolled on, Bob Blackmore and Bob Perry enjoyed a rare coup.

The DHA instructed its engineers to run the Monorail along the side of the Pyrmont Bridge at deck level, on the inside of Darling Harbour. The rail was to sit on huge pylons with ugly big caissons around them to stop ships hitting the Monorail. Tourists inside Darling Harbour would look right on to this eyesore.

To enable the bridge to open still, a section of the Monorail track would be clipped on to the side of the swing span - an historic piece of engineering gear.

The architects went to TNT's Rolly Hoy and said: "We know we're not consultants to the Darling Harbour urban designers, but this is crap."

Rolly said: "My job is to build the bloody thing. I put it where the Government tells me."

So they took it on themselves to make an appointment with Barry Young, the DHA chief planner, telling him where he was wrong.

Young said: "I hear what you're saying, but it's our decision. Anyway, the Minister won't hear of your suggestion. His instructions are that it goes down the side of the bridge."

Still not accepting it, they went to see Bob Pentecost, an aggressive, pragmatic type of bloke whose job as CEO was to get Darling Harbour constructed on time. He said: "The Minister has spoken. I don't want to hear another word about it. Bugger off, it's nothing to do with you guys."

They went back to Rolly Hoy and harangued him. "So Pentecost said the Minister has made the decision, did he?" he asked.

Hoy reached for the phone and got straight through to Brereton, saying "I'm sitting here with architects Bob Perry and Bob Blackmore and they tell me..." Brereton said he wasn't fixed on the idea at all and after Hoy argued the position, Brereton said he'd get back to him.

Next day Pentecost rang the architects to say the Minister had given them 10 days to present two options - their idea of running the Monorail on a single spindle above the top of the bridge, or down the side.

They worked flat out on drawings and written submissions, bringing in an expert from Canberra who said apart from the visual pollution, clipping it to the swing span would probably throw the span's bearings out of balance.

Five days later down came the edict: Stick it down the middle.

It taught the architects a lesson on how the bureaucracy worked - decisions were sometimes made on what others *thought* Ministers wanted.

The mixup might have irritated Barry Young but to a bloke like Pentecost it was the type of jolly good stuff that came out of all the collective thinking and co-operation that went on among Darling Harbour groups. He didn't mind a donnybrook as long as the job was done.

Intriguingly, someone had stolen vital control components which operated the bridge swing span. Without them, the span could not be opened.

While this was being viewed with dismay, an anonymous male rang the DHA construction office and said: "No names, no pack-drill, but look in a bag at the western side of the bridge."

They were the missing parts.

Then Channel 9 entered the fray with a yes-no phone poll to see if people wanted the Monorail. Tom heard on the grapevine that Monorail opponents intended swamping the "vote no" phones, so he organised 40 or 50 people from TNT and his friends and relatives to ring in and vote yes.

He sat at home dialling the yes number continuously until his index finger hurt, ringing his friends in between to exhort them to keep going. His determination paid off - the yes poll won by 51 to 49 per cent.

The *Sydney Morning Herald* then organised its own poll. He rose early on the day of the result, relieved to see the poster outside the newsagent's: "Sydney wants the Monorail."

He thought that might end it but there was still more to come.

Meanwhile, as some construction went on, still being planned were the shape of buildings, layout of the gardens and roads and it wasn't until March 1986 - 22 months from the bicentenary opening - that the overall plan began to look like its final shape. The plan would not be complete until February, 1987.

The unions played it hard, demanding new occupational health and safety regulations and keeping strictly to the rules on wet weather, causing delays. The slightest sprinkle and they stopped work. Pentecost had a tough job keeping them up to the mark.

With only 20 months to go to opening, the DHA finally got around to the Hayson needs of designing and building their Harbourside Marketplace.

It was a difficult concept for Tom's architects, breaking with convention by interweaving art and entertainment with retail.

But because of its new location, Harbourside had to become one instead of two pavilion buildings as originally planned.

It needed something to make it stand out and change what could be a monotonous colonial-style mass. Tom's Architecture Oceania team came up with the specific details for his Crystal Galleria over the top as a gateway to the water and a landmark when viewed from the city.

Although incredibly monumental and statuesque from a distance with its huge Galleria, the building was also friendly because of its transparency and openness.

It also diminished in scale as you approached it. The closer you were to the building, the smaller it seemed. That was the clever thing about it.

The Marketplace was not alienating, not a monumental statement by the architects - Jim Rouse and Mort Hoppenfeld had wanted their buildings to be colourful, diverse and friendly, not officious or self reverential, with vague boundaries of what was private and public inside them. It was fate that Mort lived long enough to pass on his inspiration to Tom's architects.

Tom came under strong pressure from his marketing arm to reject the Galleria. They considered it too big, thinking of the bottom line in wanting the space taken up by extra shops. But he liked it and backed his architects.

His decision paid off because there would be no finer sight in Sydney at night than the silhouette of thousands of coloured lights from the Galleria lighting up the inner waters of Darling Harbour, known as Cockle Bay.

Even more important, the Galleria would become the symbol of Darling Harbour. Oddly, Harbourside was a name that would not catch on, but when people said "Darling Harbour," they would be thinking of that Galleria and the Marketplace - dominating the skyline as a monument to the man who built it.

The convention and exhibition centres would always be dead unless something was happening inside them, but the Marketplace would be the main event, going day and night - 365 days a year.

The Marketplace needed a big city presence from various vantage points and most people agreed later that Tom's young architects got it right, the building reminding them of the old Royal Easter Show and the Showground - not too serious but a bit jaunty and full of life and colour.

Bob Perry thought that building Harbourside was one of the bravest things he ever saw Tom Hayson do.

No pattern of movement or history of pedestrian traffic had existed there to indicate it would work and the whole atmosphere and operation of the place had to be created.

In a development sense, it was as big a gamble as might come along. It was also outside Tom's normal experience as a developer, which he recognised by partnering with Rouse.

Apart from designing the Harbourside building, the Architecture Oceania team was commissioned to do the interior designs, the audio visual communications for marketing, the decorative arts and making them happen, then supervising and designing all the tenancies along Rouse principles.

That meant each shop had to be individually specialised and themed to go with the produce. The speed and deftness of all that being done in such short time was possible only by a direct Hayson style of management.

The Marketplace plans called for 230 boutiques, classy restaurants and terrace cafes, 47 food bars and pushcart vendors, a section offering food of all nations, market stalls selling fresh bread, pies, roasting coffee, flowers, fresh fruits, a food hall with the best hamburgers, waffles, quiches and salads.

Specialist shops would sell everything from glassware to fashion, perfume, jewellery, accessories, sporting goods, books, newspapers from around the world, gifts, health foods and homewares.

From terrace cafes, people would gaze on to the city skyline.

When Tom tried to arrange for tenants to go in there and pay the rent later, the building was still a skeleton, without walls.

They all had to wear hard hats. As Tom did a presentation trying to enthuse them, you could hear some of the potential restaurateurs and shopkeepers exclaiming "oh shit" as they looked around in disbelief.

Darling Harbour still looked like a wasteland of half-finished buildings.

The convention and exhibition centres were only shapes. Bricks or pavings had not been put down and unfinished roads were churned up by concrete trucks.

After Tom spoke, construction boss Bob Pentecost told them confidently: "We will build this Darling Harbour, we're the Authority and it will rise out of this mud and concrete heap you see here today."

Architects had always been snobby about retail centres, regarding them as a lesser form of architecture. Most designers sterilised them and took the fun out as they tried to tidy them up and make servicing easy.

Harbourside was the opposite. As an artificial marketplace, trying to revive a social tradition, it had to be a bit anarchic with organised chaos.

Tom and Ian gave their architects their heads and didn't limit their spending. They spent $2 million on decorative arts, not in extra spending but as part of the normal budget. That was done for the first time in Australia, not as an afterthought but as part of the scenario from day one.

Sure, it was the Rouse formula, but it took courage to do it then because Australian developers and bankers thought it madness.

For a year the Hayson Group had a team of talented artists at work under artistic directors David Humphries and Rodney Monk, including Aboriginal master craftsmen Thancoupie and Banduk Marika, creating an extraordinary range of bright designs in their Harbourside Studios set up on a huge floor of one of their nearby woolstores, which the Haysons were refurbishing as luxury offices.

That spawned a new industry and the artists they engaged, including Zig Moskwa, Suzanne Holman, Peter Ellis and Lino Alvarez, were in keen demand later as similar decorative arts went into other developments.

Designers would later climb all over Harbourside, photographing, sketching, copying the arts and other innovative features of the building.

Lend Lease, who originally declined to go into Darling Harbour, were among the copiers, reproducing similar ideas in their Penrith Plaza.

Other new shopping centres would also introduce Harbourside-type colour, light and entertainment as standard features.

Unusually for a developer, Tom also backed a highly creative piece of sculpture to decorate the Galleria. Called Oceania Globe, it cost $100,000. The Galleria cost $2 million and a fountain, several hundred thousand dollars.

Bob Perry had the idea for the Oceania sculpture while waiting at Sydney Town Hall one day with colleague Bob Blackmore. Studying a magnificent stained glass window, he saw in it the figure of a woman holding a merino ram's fleece aloft, depicting agriculture. But she also held a miner's lamp and a trident, depicting mining and the oceans.

She was Britannia, with a Union Jack on the bodice of her dress, surrounded by waratahs and flannel flowers, standing in a globe under the word "Oceania," alongside "Advance Australia - 1788 to 1888."

Another window at the Town Hall showing Captain Cook was done by Lucien Henri, deported from France for being a political stirrer. Bob knew he'd had a big influence on Australian art, maintaining we should promote our own culture rather than trying to be European.

Delving into his knowledge of political history, Bob thought he'd come up with a bicentennial version of the Oceania window. He always thought Australia should be the capital of Oceania, a beautiful description of our place in the world, rather than a spot in Asia.

He created flying dolphins to symbolise Sydney as the water city.

The best view of the city from Darling Harbour would be from the Galleria, a loved symbol that would be photographed by millions of visitors and tourists.

If pressures had been tough enough generally at Darling Harbour, they became worse half way through 1987.

Neville Wran decided to retire from politics after a long innings as Premier and become a merchant banker.

Barrie Unsworth, who succeeded him, was a strong supporter of Darling Harbour. But dissidents in the Labor Party took advantage of Wran's departure to flex their muscles in the new atmosphere, trying to cut back funding to Darling Harbour and reduce the extent of development there.

For instance, they tried to cut the size of the Chinese Gardens in half.

An election was due in March 1988 and they were worried over all the bad publicity.

Brereton came under strong attack in Cabinet. One of the first things they focused on was the Monorail.

Brereton went to Tom and said: "The Government is going to scrap it. They're afraid it's going to cost us votes."

Tom galvanised into action. He took out full-page newspaper ads supporting the Monorail and called a press conference in which he said he would sue the Government for $100 million if they failed to go ahead with it. That seemed to put a bit of stiffness into some of the jelly backs.

He also brought out at his expense the chief of the Seattle transport system to explain to the Government and the public how successful a monorail had been in that city for many years.

At the same time architects Perry and Blackmore held a press conference in which Perry took the fight to the journalists, answering all the Monorail criticisms.

That crisis passed, to be quickly replaced by others.

The casino was back in the news. The Wran Government had awarded the casino licence to the Hookers-Harrah consortium but that was cancelled because Federal Hotels were not considered appropriate - although acceptable in every other State.

Police decided a shareholder from Asia who held only two per cent of the hotel group's equity could not pass the test.

On a rebid going to Hookers-Harrah under the Unsworth Government, the shareholder had withdrawn but police decided Federal Hotels were still not appropriate because he *had been* associated with them!

Also, there was a problem over George Herscu of Hookers, who had been involved in alleged corruption over building a house for union boss Norm Gallagher in Melbourne.

Herscu would later be jailed in Queensland on a corruption charge. With the election pending, the Government withdrew the licence.

[But later, the new Greiner Liberal Government would repeal the legislation altogether instead of leaving it in the bottom drawer and dusting it off down the track. When the Greiner Government changed its mind in favour of the casino, legislators had to start all over again, further delaying the process].

Sniffing electoral victory for the Opposition in the leadup to that 1988 election, Nick Greiner ran hard on the corruption angle, with his Liberal Party claiming Darling Harbour would be a failure.

A nervous Unsworth State Labor Cabinet then put enormous pressure on Laurie Brereton to redesign Darling Harbour and to curtail the contracts that had not yet been let.

Incredibly, Ministers wanted low-cost housing where the parks were intended to go in the middle of the Darling Harbour site!

What a shemozzle.

Brereton was able to say there could be no turning back because he had committed every one of the projects to contract.

If the bicentenary had not been looming and Brereton had not been so efficient in pressing ahead trying to get the main elements finished in time, the Philistines would definitely have got at Darling Harbour, pulled it apart and destroyed it.

But he paid the price for being a strong executive.

Officially, he resigned soon after from Cabinet. But in fact he was sacked. Gerry Gleeson was the executioner, carrying the Premier's message to him and moving him to another portfolio.

But he showed guts and refused to accept it, going on to the back bench to preserve his self respect. Later he left the NSW Parliament to go into Federal politics.

Brereton had given 100 per cent support to the project, often ducking into the site on weekends to check on things. Pentecost had two phones on his desk, one a direct line from Brereton. Almost every afternoon around four or five o'clock Brereton rang and asked: "How's it going, mate?"

"On schedule," said Pentecost. Brereton would say: "You bastard, you always tell me that."

He was that sort of down-to-earth bloke. And if ever the construction boss wanted him, he would walk out of Parliament to take the call and his approach was always "how can I help you?"

After that, under new Minister Peter Cox, the pressure went on the DHA to cut back, although the "soft" opening of Darling Harbour for the bicentenary was only about two months off.

In a situation of turmoil, with the press braying anew, Darling Harbour could have been in deep trouble at that stage. Pentecost, a prime force at that critical point, refused to walk away from his commitment in spite of intense political pressure.

He told DHA Chairman Alex Carmichael what he needed to finish the job and Carmichael proved himself a strong character by backing him fully.

For about the first half of 1987 Tom Hayson had not been seen in Sydney. Many wondered why, although Ian was leading the charge.

He was in London quietly organising behind the scenes for the Hayson Group to go global.

A strong personal friendship had developed with James Rouse and because of the association Tom wanted to spread his wings. He could see numerous opportunities for the marketplace concept in rundown cities.

In a complicated and time-consuming deal, he'd gone to London to arrange a merger with two UK property groups and Rouse's Enterprise Development Company (EDC) to form a giant international property consortium.

For the Haysons to leap from a relatively small aggressive private company to a high-profile colossus, he needed equity finance.

To obtain it, he paved the way to go public and list on the London and Sydney Stock Exchanges. It would put them into the big time.

Reaching that point did not happen overnight. Tom had been friendly for several years with Dursley and Bryan Stott, prominent in real estate and banking on the Isle of Man, whom he'd met through the Australian representative of the Nat West Bank of London, Leon Roberts.

He'd noticed how dilapidated English waterfronts were and suggested to the Stotts they should do something together on the English mainland.

So he bought one third of their Isle of Man company called Manx Overseas as a jumping off base.

The Stott family was keen to expand too, and they agreed to start a new company to do developments in the UK. Looking for an exciting name, Tom and the Stotts settled on Merlin, a small northern hemisphere bird of prey.

The name also had other connotations. Merlin was a magician in the Court of King Arthur and that tickled Tom's fancy.

Keen to expand also was a British developer, Peter Jevans, introduced to Tom by a leading UK financial organisation. His private UK retail development company, Abbeygate Securities Ltd, had just lifted its annual turnover to $400 million.

They formed a joint company and Rouse, who had never put a cent in anything outside his own companies, had such respect for Tom that he decided to become an equity partner and director.

The restructured Merlin UK with the Hayson Group, the Stott interests and Abbeygate on board, completed its internationalisation by acquiring one third of Rouse's Enterprise Development Company of the USA.

The Haysons put their Australian assets in the international group, including their stake in Harbourside and a new proposed $300 million retail and office development called Skygarden in the heart of Sydney's CBD, adjacent to the Pitt Street Mall. That gave them a 30 per cent interest in Merlin UK and effective control of the company.

They had two seats on Merlin's board in London, with Ian running the company from Sydney as chairman and joint managing director and Tom as deputy chairman. They thought it best to have Britisher Dursley Scott as Chairman. A stock broker by profession, he was highly regarded by Tom and Ian.

The Merlin group had $1 billion worth of projects with more in the pipeline after the Haysons transferred an estimated $500 million worth of their building projects into it, combining with Rouse projects in Las Vegas and Philadelphia and the English additions.

Through Tom's efforts the group had also been invited to tender for a huge $200 million urban redevelopment project on about 27 acres in the heart of Manchester. Other opportunities for urban regeneration were being identified. The Haysons, through their renamed Merlin company in Australia, were also looking at other projects in Australia.

They obtained approval to list on the London Exchange in record time to become the first truly international company dominated by an Australian property development group, offering something exciting and colourful to brighten English people's lives.

The name Rouse was revered in England and by association with him and through the energetic plans he generated, Tom gained enormously in prestige. The *Sunday Times* for instance, wrote up Rouse and Hayson as two "Harbourmasters" using their skills to refurbish the waterfronts.

Hayson was suddenly seen in Britain as somebody big. What pleased him most was his ethnic background didn't come into it, only the quality of what he could do. He felt a lot freer there and wanted to show his fellow Australians back home what he could do.

The company's London headquarters, five-storey Merlin House, was in upper crust Mayfair just off Grosvenor Square beside the American Embassy, surrounded by magnificent hotels and apartments.

Tom didn't dine in the classy restaurants there patronised by Princess Di and other trend setters, preferring a sandwich and dining with the pigeons and other birds in the park, watching life go by. He walked around London or took taxis or trains, keeping his feet on the ground.

Although Tom and Ngaire in their flat near Berkeley Square lived amid oil-rich Arabs and other fabulously wealthy folk, they maintained their normal simple lifestyle. They certainly didn't live frugally but preferred to cook their own meals and enjoy their own style of food.

They just enjoyed being together, going to theatre shows around Piccadilly Circus and Leicester Square, or to Harrods. In a way they wished they still owned their first simple little flat on top of a 15-storey building in Soho just off Carnaby Street, from where they could look out over London and see the time on two faces of Big Ben.

They were invited to be members of a group called the Mayfair Society and went to a few functions but didn't fancy getting dressed up like toffs, although Tom for the only time in his life would don the clobber of top hat and tails for a Buckingham Palace garden party, laughing at his appearance.

Ngaire and Tom loved the feeling of being anonymous as you can be in London. Now and then they enjoyed popping across to Nice on the French Riviera where they'd also bought a flat.

Tom had built a huge organisation. They were winning big projects by the dint of their own skills, not by manipulating on the stock market or stripping assets from company takeovers and leaving shells. The money they invested and capital they raised was going into worthwhile things.

The Haysons were flying high. But Tom was conscious of great responsibility. As he sat at peace in the park he wondered if he was overpowering himself with all of this. And he thought about it as he walked home past the big banks, magnificent offices and apartments.

Was it too good to be true? He had a young team around him and wondered if he should apply the brakes. But it was exciting, brilliant, exhilarating and so promising.

He was then in the late stages of middle age, advancing to the elderly. What if God wouldn't let him enjoy all of this, if suddenly something physical went wrong with him?

He prayed each night that nothing unforseen would affect his or Ngaire's health so they could enjoy this fulfilling stage of their lives.

Although he didn't like to admit it even to himself, he was a little frightened that at this level of business, it was easy to make mistakes and one mistake could lead to a series, which could be disastrous.

But that didn't stop him on waking each morning looking forward to grasping opportunities that might present themselves.

Before returning to Australia for a stint, Tom and Ngaire farewelled the First Fleet Re-enactment ships out of Portsmouth, due in Sydney for the bicentenary celebrations at Darling Harbour on January 26, 1988, coinciding with the "soft" opening of Darling Harbour.

The Hayson company was a major sponsor of the fleet, due to anchor on time in Cockle Bay right in front of his Harbourside Marketplace.

He and Ngaire were in the official party at Portsmouth and were presented to the Queen and Prince Philip, chatting to them at length and later dining with them. That was a big thrill for the boy from Barraba.

Opening Darling Harbour was next. Would it be ready?

21

"THE DUKE" TAKES A BOW

A remarkable thing happened just before Darling Harbour's so-called "soft" opening.

It was never intended to be finished in time for January, 26, 1988. But enough of the main elements were to be in place by then to put on a reasonably good unofficial show for the Bicentennial celebrations.

Indeed, Neville Wran had been careful to point out in Parliament that it would not be finished by 1988 and would probably not reach its maximum development until the year 2000. He was right.

And with good reason, because even the Opera House is simple by comparison. What you see there is what you get. But Darling Harbour is the type of urban planning that has been a living, growing, expanding thing, a continuing development not expected to reach its full impact until some time beyond the year 2000. You saw it happening gradually.

But getting it to look the part for that unofficial opening was a nightmare. Without an opening then, the whole project would have been regarded as such a joke it could never have recovered in the public mind.

Unfortunately people generally could not be allowed into Darling Harbour before then because as a building site, things were just too tight.

Viewing platforms were erected on the perimeter, but it was considered too difficult and dangerous to have the public in while work went on.

From all the adverse publicity it seemed there was always some trouble going on in there but the public couldn't see for themselves.

Darling Harbour, and activity on the site, was something of a mystery and by the time people were finally allowed in to see for themselves, keen expectation had built up.

As the clock ticked down to the bicentenary, it was obviously touch and go if enough buildings would be finished to make it worthwhile.

The schedule was so critical that in the last few months construction chief Pentecost inspected all works every day. He put someone in charge of every section and checked personally every day by walking to that area to examine progress.

The DHA had to have Darling Harbour ready for Saturday January 16, the day when the 16 Tall Ships were due to arrive from around the world and anchor in Cockle Bay just opposite the Haysons' Marketplace.

The magnificent sailing ships were on schedule, so there had to be a Darling Harbour by then. The DHA decided to let the public in on that day and on the Sunday too.

The First Fleet Re-enactment vessels would also be in Darling Harbour in readiness for January 26.

The big risk for the DHA in this critical timing was Christmas 1987.

Normally the workers would go on three weeks annual leave then. But if they followed normal arrangements, the DHA's opening was dead. Darling Harbour would still have looked just like a construction site when the public came in for the first time.

The remarkable thing that happened was that the workers, who had had more than a fair go at playing up on the site with phoney bomb scares and the like, not only recovered some pride but also decided they'd had enough of the knockers.

They were sick of seeing the place criticised. They knew that what they were doing was good and finally they'd had a gutful.

They woke up to the fact, before the newspapers and other critics did, that through their efforts the recreation habits of Sydney people were about to change forever and that Darling Harbour was about to become an exciting and worthwhile place.

The people on the Authority, the contractors and builders and the construction workers themselves responded to being told "we've got to have this finished prior to the opening."

And in comments among themselves, they said: "You bastards, we're going to prove all you knockers wrong."

So they worked through Christmas to finish essential work, and they worked well.

They proved that Australians could do the job when the chips were down. They could be quick, innovative and motivated - even if every now and then in the lead-up they liked to drag it out and go on strike.

Nobody ever expected the workers at Darling Harbour would win a construction award but because of the compressed time, they often had to work in an atmosphere that created unreasonable pressure.

From a blank piece of paper, they went to a fair degree of completion in four years - by comparison, it took 15 years in Baltimore. And in construction terms that was generally regarded as a great achievement in the time frame, setting standards for other big jobs in Australia.

To help in the overall countdown, all leave was cancelled for the 40 or so workers in the DHA one year ahead of the public opening. Pentecost told them: "No weddings or babies."

One young lady was married in the period, apologising profusely and asking for one day off, a Friday, so she could be back at work the following Monday.

On the night before the Saturday opening, the site was as busy as a stirred-up ants' nest. The construction team worked throughout the night.

Not all the brick paving was down and, to give the public area a finishing touch, they had to use red-brown bitumen which looked similar to bricks. That material wasn't readily available and it took a juggling and balancing act to locate enough of the stuff in time.

At some stage of the night the workers had to stop laying paving bricks and start pouring the red asphalt. When bricks are laid like that, you have to pour sand over them and sweep the sand across the tops of the bricks to put it in between them.

That work was being done by members of the Builders Workers' Union, wearing hard hats and hard shoes. At midnight they pulled down the safety fence and effectively Darling Harbour stopped being a construction site and became an open public area.

That was done to enable the DHA to bring in the cleaners to start cleaning up the mess for Saturday morning. The cleaners were members of the Miscellaneous Workers' Union. So at midnight they came streaming into the site.

Clearly there was an overlap of unions. But as they went on constructing and cleaning like mad, the guys were happy. It was an exciting, confusing, exhilarating sort of atmosphere. Kegs of beer came rolling down the hill and in between a foaming flagon or two, the boys worked with a will.

Joe Owens, the main industrial advocate on site who could be a bit of a problem, had gone to the Teachers Club for dinner and a few snorts, as he usually did on Friday nights.

About 1 am Bob Pentecost received a call to go to a spot on the site: Joe was playing up and he was needed. Bob went and found Joe, with a head of steam up, carrying on because he'd found Miscellaneous Workers doing builders' work by sweeping sand into the bricks. A fine line if ever there was one, and impossible to avoid as they swept the tiled area.

Bob and Joe began yelling at each other, and Bob suggested it was a bloody dry argument. Joe agreed. So they stormed off to the site sheds which were well out of the way. "For Chrissake buy me a couple of beers," Bob told the staff there.

Hardly any ambrosial fluid was left but it duly arrived. And they began arguing the issue. Work proceeded outside while the beer held up in the shed. Then it ran out and searching around, Bob found a bottle that had been sitting on top of a filing cabinet for about two years.

He handed it to Joe. He took a sip, pulled a face, tried another mouthful and said: "For Chrissake call me a cab. I'm sick of sitting here drinking your lousy, flat warm beer." They put him in a cab and home he went.

Beer diplomacy had won the day, or rather the night.

Pentecost was back on site at 6am to check on things before the party began. Marching bands and celebrations were planned for 10 am when the public came in. Security guards were among the first to arrive, allowed in for the first time as a group. Photos were taken of anybody and everybody.

At 8 am the party began for those involved in the development of Darling Harbour, about 200 of them, all invited to a champagne breakfast in Tumbalong Park near the waterfront. All happy, swapping yarns, yet sad that the great experience had come to an end.

Bands played, kites flew, balloons soared and suddenly good times were rolling as the public began streaming in by the thousands. Premier Barrie Unsworth and his wife Pauline were rockin' and rollin' in the sit-down area outside the Harbourside Marketplace under the Galleria.

Construction workers, there socially for the first time, were standing around just gawking at the scene. They no longer had to go through the old security arrangements to get on site and it was different finding their way to the buildings they'd worked on for years - the public had taken over.

As Bob Pentecost looked around, Joe Owens came up to him, grinned and said: "You did it, you bastard. Have you got a cold beer *now?*"

To stop the crowds milling around to see the First Fleet sailing ships and causing unmanageable congestion, staff moved them one way from the north east around the bay to the Pyrmont Bridge and into the city.

Once having done a full circuit, they could not turn back unless starting all over again. Several hundred thousand turned up on the day.

As Tom Hayson walked across the Pyrmont Bridge with Ngaire, mingling with the crowds, standing there looking at the excited throng and joining in the gaiety, he felt an overwhelming sense of exhilaration.

In that moment, he saw his vision, his dream come true. And he wept quietly. The feeling was greater than owning all the money in the world.

Ian Hayson was there too, in time for the early morning party in Tumbalong Park. His feelings were mixed.

He was like all those other people who had worked there for four years straight. Although basically only concerned with the Marketplace, he had attended up to seven meetings a day on Darling Harbour even on minor things, like the hydraulics of the place or how to move the garbage out.

He'd seen people working there for something like 18 hours a day and he knew how much it had taken out of him.

Like the others, Ian was emotionally involved. Now, seeing the public strolling all over the place, he suddenly realised Darling Harbour wasn't *his* any more. And it wasn't *theirs* - those who'd worked so hard.

Quickly coming to terms with his disappointment, he was able to let go. He wasn't so sure Tom could do so because of his greater emotional attachment and the titanic struggle he'd had trying to see things done the right way.

Ian believed he could understand the feelings of all those people on the management side of Darling Harbour who were distorting the truth a little in not wanting to give Tom the credit he deserved.

They probably didn't even realise it. They had been so involved and their commitment so intense they thought they'd done it all themselves.

But Ian and others were pleased to see people using Darling Harbour the way they'd wished to see it happen.

Within an hour of the opening, kids were paddling in the fountain on the promenade, some joined soon by parents who could be arrested doing that in other Sydney fountains. Ian and his associates didn't care a damn.

Darling Harbour now belonged to them and they could please themselves. But accepting it was a bit of a wrench.

For weeks after that, DHA employees would take time off just to stroll around among the crowd, taking in the atmosphere.

Princess Di, in town with Prince Charles for the January 26 celebrations, also had a good informal look round, meeting up with such fun characters as Kev Koala.

In the first year Darling Harbour would have 16 million visitors, more than Disneyworld in any one year, and better than Baltimore.

Nick Greiner had run a shrewd political campaign leading up to the NSW State election on March 19, 1988.

As a white elephant man, his denigration of Laurie Brereton and continuous knocking of Darling Harbour were strong factors in his winning the election and becoming Premier.

His campaign against Brereton was significant. Confidential polls obtained by the Labor Government in country areas showed that Darling Harbour was a big vote winner in the bush for Greiner and a big negative for Brereton. That's why Premier Unsworth had removed him from his Public Works portfolio.

Laurie had made himself unpopular too by having his name put up on all sorts of Government works and being dubbed the Minister for Signs, although an over-zealous staff man was blamed for that. But in the end the election result was a straight reflection of the polls.

However, having won the election, Greiner should have embraced Darling Harbour.

After all, it was a reality and so much Government money was committed there. But instead, the new Government squeezed it and gave more support to developing The Rocks area of Sydney. Many saw that as political immaturity.

But having verbally knocked the hell out of the place, how could he suddenly turn around after taking it over and say it was great?

Normally a Liberal Government would be expected to support big business, at least to encourage other investors.

Clearly, the Premier had trouble getting his mind around supporting something that a Labor Government had built. Also, there was the problem of coming to terms with the allegations of corruption that had been made.

It also probably troubled Nick Greiner that after bagging the place so fervently, he could not see any quick way of gaining any kudos from it - a point made by some of his friends.

All those continuing negatives were a bitter disappointment to Tom Hayson.

He'd had Nick over to Darling Harbour when he was Opposition Leader pointing out the merits, he'd contributed to Liberal Party fund-raising, but it made no difference. And every time he had a function at Darling Harbour he invited Nick in the hope he could understand it better and associate himself with the project. But although seemingly impressed, Nick still went away and played politics.

It didn't help the only private enterprise fellow in Darling Harbour with people in his Marketplace shops having to pay rent and trying to survive, especially when the Liberals would logically be expected to support a project in which Government was heavily involved.

Perhaps, Tom reasoned, the impending visit of the Queen in May 1988 to officially open Darling Harbour would turn Nick around, and the brush with royalty might encourage him to shift ground towards a more realistic approach, realising that Darling Harbour should be non political.

To Tom, the Queen's opening of Darling Harbour would be important for many reasons, but mainly because it would be the culmination of one of the most vital periods of his life, justifying everything he'd ever done.

As he pondered on the visit, he went into the little church in Pyrmont, struggling because of the dwindling population there, and thanked God that finally the battle had been won.

He reflected on that battle. He realised that so many people had played a part in its development, the Government, the Authority, the planners, architects, the workers, but he knew in his heart that the concept was his and that he'd been the only one in it every step of the way. And he felt proud.

As he sat alone in the church in contemplation, he looked back on his life as one of adversity and struggle, not only for himself but for his dear mother and father and all they had gone through to rear him in what was then often a hostile environment, coming from a non-English speaking background. But he was grateful too that he'd had the strength and faith to overcome adversity.

More than anything else, he wished he could bring his parents back, if only for an hour, so they could see what he had achieved.

Tom did not expect to play any part in the official opening or to have the Queen visit his shopping centre.

That would be an occasion when the Government and the Authority were expected to take full credit and call the shots. And he would have bet London to a brick that his name was not mentioned in discussions taking place between protocol officials from the Government and Buckingham Palace to set down the opening ceremony procedure.

But all the same he would have his Harbourside Marketplace putting on its cheeriest face for the big day. At least the Queen and Prince Philip would see it as they strolled by. And he hoped to gain some kudos from the fact it was the only major building fully ready on time.

The Exhibition building was okay but Tom was sore that the Convention Centre was still dragging the chain, because he was relying on expected conventioneers to provide business for Harbourside's duty free shops.

Leaving Ian in control, Tom returned to London to round off some work for their Merlin international company.

In the period when he was preparing to list on the London Stock Exchange, he had become friends with the Queen's private secretary, Sir William Heseltine. He too was an Australian, but a stickler for protocol.

When Tom was to see him by appointment he would go to the big gates at Buckingham Palace and, with a sense of foreboding, give his name to the Grenadier Guardsman. Will I be let in? He always doubted it.

But it was as if the red carpet had been rolled out.

He would be allowed straight in to a Palace door and someone would be waiting to show him in. The first time, Sir William was just finishing a telephone conversation with the Queen, the intimate scene giving Tom a great sense of being somebody.

291

Sir William took him to lunch several times to an exclusive restaurant called the White House in St James. Tom never took any liberties to breach protocol or make himself unpopular by discussing private matters.

But one day over afternoon tea in the Palace he thought he'd try his luck.

He was aware that Palace officials would have to send a suggested programme to the Government protocol officers in Sydney for Darling Harbour's opening.

So he said to Sir William: "As you know, my Harbourside Marketplace is one of the buildings in Darling Harbour. I wonder if you could arrange on the day for Her Majesty to visit my building? It would be part of the official function but separate to the opening ceremony, which I understand will be held in one of the Government buildings."

"I'll see what I can do," said the Queen's secretary. Nothing more was said.

Later back in Sydney Tom's heart was in his mouth when he received a copy of the printed programme. "I hope he's really done something," he murmured.

Running his eyes quickly down the printing, he saw that the official opening was to be held near Tumbalong Park and in the partly-finished Convention Centre. A moment later he spotted it - the Queen and Prince Philip to do a 10-minute walk through the Marketplace.

Tom had written his own invitation to the Queen.

Fired up, he busied himself in preparation. Ngaire saw her dressmaker and also began getting down on one knee to practise the curtsey. Tom issued invitations to all the important people from abroad whom he wanted to bring out for the opening.

He invited the two Stott brothers from the Isle of Man and their wives, Jim Rouse and his wife Patty and Marty Millspaugh and his wife Meredith. That left one other person they felt deeply about, the late Professor Morton Hoppenfeld.

Ian tried to negotiate with the Authority to bring out Mort's widow, Jeanne. But nobody wanted to acknowledge Mort on the day or name some part after him and nobody would agree to bring out Jeanne.

It bitterly disappointed Tom and Ian that Mort was now a forgotten man, and it would continue to upset them that although some people would later travel the world talking about Darling Harbour, his name would never be raised.

They felt Mort deserved it as the man with the experience and intellect to provide the inspiration for the original plan, the one who had the ability and credibility to sit down in front of the Premier and other power players and say this is what I think you should do, giving them the confidence to go forward.

Sure, he was well paid for his concept plan which time had prevented him from finishing with definite form and shape. And necessary adjustments were made by other talented people like the MSJ Keys Young group who were generally considered to have done an exceptional job interpreting the overall design features and setting out the gardens and public areas.

They had dug deep in an emotion-charged, pressure atmosphere to finish what Mort had begun, converting his sketch plans into practical results in town planning terms, working in with other architects to give size, form and shape to the various buildings.

But without that original concept and commercial dynamism which was a huge initiating contribution, Darling Harbour on all the earlier evidence would not have become a successful fun or "people place" where Australians could go and celebrate with a sense of pride and excitement.

Darling Harbour without his guiding hand throughout was like the Opera House without Joern Utzon in at the finish - the same, but different.

Failing to acknowledge him was a blot on the history of Darling Harbour. For some reason it would remain a sensitive issue.

Tom and Ian Hayson paid for Mort's widow to fly first class to Sydney and stay in the best hotel so his memory was represented at the opening.

Their company also spent about $50,000 arranging an orchestra and entertainment on a specially-decorated barge on the waterfront in front of the amphitheatre at Harbourside, to leave more room for the public when the Queen and Duke of Edinburgh came out on the Marketplace balcony to acknowledge and greet the crowd below. Tom also flew in exquisite flowers from Melbourne for the occasion.

He had a special plaque set in place on the balcony to mark the opening.

The Queen and the Duke sailed into Darling Harbour in the royal yacht Britannia on May 4 and disembarked at 10 am. Thousands crowded around the promenade as the Queen did the opening ceremony before new Premier Nick Greiner and his wife, Kathryn.

In the presence of the Royals, Nick lauded Darling Harbour!

While that was going on Tom and Ngaire and Ian and his daughter Melissa, 18, were waiting at the Marketplace entrance to greet the royal party. All the shops in there remained open but for security reasons shoppers were cleared from the building.

Waiting up on the balcony were the Rouses and the Millspaughs, and Jeanne Hoppenfeld. Kathryn and Nick Greiner were to accompany the royal couple through the Marketplace and finish up on the balcony with everybody in the group who were waiting at the entrance.

The Queen and Duke duly arrived, met by Ngaire in a stunning new outfit and Tom wearing his best bag of fruit. Tom led off with the Queen, trailed by Ngaire and the Duke, followed by the Greiners, Ian and Melissa with the Secretary of the Premier's Department Gerry Gleeson and protocol head, John Miller.

First thing the Queen did was congratulate Tom on his floral display. She knew a thing or two about flowers, having seen a few flower shows in her time. And then some.

All the decorative arts were in place and these brought lively comments from the Duke who loved to joke about such things.

They certainly looked bright, the wall designs of waratahs and currawongs, terrazzo patterns of glass snakes, even of jelly beans and licorice allsorts on the doorsteps of specialty shops.

The whole place gave a sense of fun and fantasy, with huge brightly painted banners, one mural capturing the Harbour Bridge in a wreath of flame from Bicentennial fireworks, together with flocks of lorikeets, pelicans and parrots hanging from ceilings, vividly-painted tropical fish and all manner of Australian flora and fauna, hand-painted ceramic tiles with sharks, dolphins, sails and sailing ships.

Amid the Marketplace array of shops, bazaars, kiosks and carts representing Australia's multicultural life, their eyes caught one feature dominating the Oceanic theme - Bob Perry's colourful idea of a huge model of Mother Earth viewed from outer space, adorning the main atrium.

As Tom led the Queen around she was full of questions and he was full of chat, giving her a good summarised background to Darling Harbour.

"It seems, Mr Hayson, you've been in this right from the start?" she said.

"Right from day one, Ma'am, right from the concept."

"Well, you should be very proud of yourself. This building is absolutely marvellous. I'm so pleased I've been able to come here and see it."

As she asked about various things, Tom was ready with the answers. One, he said, was a marsupial platypus, another "a wallaby, like a small kangaroo."

"And what is that, Mr Hayson?" she asked, pointing to a black bird motif.

As he told friends later: "I didn't have a bloody clue but I learned one thing in my radio days - when you're uncertain about something, say it with conviction."

So he said: "Oh, that's a raven, Your Majesty."

"Hmnn, strange," said the Queen, "it's quite different to the ones we have in England."

In fact, it was a common old squawking crow. But at least he was in the ballpark because the Australian raven is the largest member of the crow family.

The minutes slipped by and the scheduled 10 minutes were shot to shreds. Tom thought he'd better explain what came next.

"Well Ma'am," he said, "there are a lot of people out there on the promenade below who've come to see you and according to the security people, we have to walk out there at the end of the corridor and on to the balcony so they can see you."

"All right Mr Hayson, let's go."

They looked around and there was no sign of the Duke. He'd taken a mischievous interest in the arts and having a penchant for beautiful women, was in fact at that moment chatting up some pretty shop assistants - a favourite pastime of his.

Tom stopped in the corridor leading on to the balcony of the southern pavilion and said: "Your Majesty, the Duke is nowhere to be seen. We'd better wait."

"Oh, don't worry about him. He's caught up somewhere. Let's go out."

So the Queen with Tom behind stepped out on to the balcony. As she appeared, Tom's friend, legendary entertainer Bobby Limb, the master of ceremonies for the entertainment below, announced at the microphone in his best circus voice: "Ladees and gentlemen, boys and girls. Your Majesty the Queen and his Royal Highness the Duke of Edinburgh!"

Thousands cheered and applauded, then laughed and cheered again as they saw Tom, bald pate shining, standing there with the biggest grin imaginable.

The Queen, in a smart white pillbox hat and a bright lemon full-length coat, enjoyed the joke too and laughed with the crowd who kept on applauding.

Tom thought of acknowledging the cheers and it was all he could do to stop his right arm from shooting up, but he managed to restrain himself, thinking it might be a bit too cheeky. But he nodded and grinned his appreciation.

When the crowd's greeting subsided, Tom introduced the Queen to his special American guests on the balcony, including Jeanne Hoppenfeld, the orchestra struck up and a colourful youth pageant began.

It was several minutes before the real Duke found his way on to the balcony. Tom didn't move aside. The Duke had to stand behind him and the Queen for the rest of the function - having to play second fiddle to a commoner for probably the first time while the Queen was taking a bow with her "royal consort" beside her.

Tom had accidentally stolen a march on those bureaucrats who had treated him with scant respect. Hard to keep a good man down!

They chatted away as the pageant continued, Tom saying he hoped to open something like the Marketplace in Manchester and Birmingham. "Oh do you?" the Queen remarked. "Let me know when you're going to do it."

The Queen took a closer interest in the large group of children performing, asking what they were doing.

"Well Ma'am," said Tom, "this is a special presentation for you. It reflects all the multicultural aspects of our society, all the different races over here, and I'm one of them. Second generation Australian, my grandfather came from Lebanon..."

The children, looking beautiful, healthy and fresh in their different national costumes, then sang a rousing song called *Proudly Australian*, specially commissioned by Tom's company to the melody of *Click Go the Shears*.

Tom felt so thrilled his chest could have burst as the words of the chorus rang out: "Proudly Australian, proud proud proud..."

He studied the Queen's face as she looked and listened intently, and he felt sure she understood that all these different children were symbolic of the new Australia, a country now of all races, where being an Australian embraced many races and cultures.

As Tom gazed on all the earnest, happy faces, white, black, brown, they epitomised all that he had ever longed and striven for, notably acceptance for himself and all other ethnic races, living in harmony.

He felt that in this ecstatic scene before him, his longing had been realised, and in the best possible company.

It was the proudest moment of his life.

Amid his crowded thoughts and emotions, he thought fleetingly of his parents.

The Queen moved on to lunch and at once Tom became known as "The Duke."

The headline writers had a ball over the novel situation. In London the newspapers zeroed in on him as "The Duke of Darling Harbour" with big pictures of him and the Queen alone on the balcony, giving their readers a good laugh over his cheek, but for once in a nice way when dealing with a colonial.

Some of the other headlines were: "Shopping for a new man;" "My husband and I;" "Hayson consorts with the Queen;" "How Hayson became 'King' for the Queen;" "Duke's stand-in stands by Her Majesty."

Writers elevated him to the peerage, saying he was considered frightfully pukka by the Poms now as he walked tall among the Hoorays rejoicing in his recently conferred title of "Duke." Mock entries in Debrett's were quoted.

It was all a bit of good fun but when newsmen brought it up again on his next visit to London immediately after, he became worried that he might have carried on a bit and offended the Queen or the Duke and he wrote to her secretary expressing his concern.

But he was assured in a note from the Palace that the Queen had enjoyed herself immensely and neither she nor the Duke had taken any offence at press coverage that was flippant or derogatory.

In four hours at Darling Harbour, she'd put ceremony aside to spend more time at the Hayson's Marketplace than anywhere else.

One of his warmest memories of the day was the pleasure he and Ian had given to Jeanne Hoppenfeld. As they left the balcony she kissed him and said: "Thank you for being so kind. Words cannot describe my feelings. I'm so grateful to be here for Mort's sake."

Tom was delighted to receive a letter of appreciation from James Rouse a week or so later, saying: "Four years ago when we first met in my office, I remember very well your words of exhortation: 'Jim, this will be your crowning glory.'

"Well,, Tom, it truly was *your* 'crowning glory' - Darling Harbour (following Mort's plan which you entrepreneured through Laurie Brereton); Harbourside, the greatest festival marketplace; and then the presence of the Queen waving to the crowd - what a triumph!"

With that kind of support and admiration from great and powerful friends, there was no reason to suspect that "The Duke's" future would be anything but rosy.

22

TAKING DARLING HARBOURS
TO THE WORLD

TWO days after being Duke to the Queen, Tom left for London to pursue new opportunities.

His Australian company had gone public, Merlin having listed on the Australian Stock Exchange a few months earlier in February, 1988.

The big stock exchange crash of October 19, 1987, which put many companies under, had made little difference to them. Indeed, the London shares would go to five times their listed value.

Tom's first task was to resume lobbying in a hot field for redeveloping County Hall on the south bank of the Thames. And he wanted to wrap up his bid for the $200 million Manchester redevelopment.

Late on the scene for Manchester after his English competitors had a six-month head start, he had only two weeks for his architects to get his ideas on paper and lodge specifications.

Working his team around the clock, he produced a viable bid that was delivered only half an hour before deadline. It came out the winner.

The joint venture scheme was aimed at transforming a rundown inner city warehouse area with a marketplace regeneration having all the Hayson/Rouse trimmings - specialist shopping, food stores, restaurants, a hotel and leisure and entertainment facilities.

While that was still being considered, Tom was already moving on a development in Birmingham, 27 hectares at the junction of three smelly and depressing canals. He ran into stiff competition from British groups but in a smart move joined forces with one, Shearwater Properties, and won the right to do part of a $1 billion contract. His Darling Harbour effort won them over.

Hearing that in the centre of Glasgow they wanted to restore the historic old Sheriff's Court building, he put in a plan for that too, telling officials his wife's mother had been born in Glasgow and he'd like to give something back to the community. Merlin received planning consent to do that, dressing it up with retail accommodation.

Next, Merlin won the tender to restore Brighton Pier, one of Britain's most famous landmarks, at a preliminary cost of $20 million. Although final plans were still to be drawn up, the restoration would include shops, boutiques and restaurants in a mini Darling Harbour style with a view to making it once more the seaside playground of Londoners who in Victorian and Edwardian days "took water" there long before packaged tours to foreign places like Majorca became fashionable.

Just after that success Tom was briefly back in Sydney to greet British PM Maggie Thatcher when she visited Darling Harbour. Nick Greiner didn't miss out on being there, either.

Showing the flair of an old ham, Tom arranged for a group called the Harbourside Barbershop Quartet to serenade her with the song, *"When You and I Were Young, Maggie."* Corny, but she loved it.

Returning to London he saw the opportunity to develop a decaying landmark building known as the Trocadero between Piccadilly Circus and Leicester Square, joining a John Elliott company with plans to turn it into an entertainment complex. But he was only the second highest bidder and lost that to an Irish group - who copied his ideas from Darling Harbour!

It took time and money with architects and other experts to prepare their plans and more than $1 million was spent on leadup work.

Ian was still running the Merlin day-to-day operations from Sydney, jumping on a plane every two months for a London board meeting.

His leap to corporate status gave him a great deal of responsibility because of the overseas connections, but that didn't worry him. Being a true entrepreneur, he missed the hands-on control, having to sit in an office more than before instead of going out and doing the deals himself.

He had to rely on other people to run various group aspects and now when spending his and Tom's own money, he had to accept the judgments of others rather than call the shots himself.

Ian had never had any formal training in running a big corporation and it meant that to keep on top of things he had to work hellishly hard. He proved an effective chief executive but the long hours affected his personal life, in particular his often-rocky marriage to the Red Bikini Girl.

Lillian was unhappy at not seeing enough of him. They liked to go travelling together but that became difficult. She hated Sydney's hot dry climate, saying she couldn't breathe, yearning for the damp air of Europe.

Lillian blamed herself for her parents' breakup and wanted Ian to go and live in Europe with her. He said it was impossible and she complained more often about them not spending enough time together. That situation had become serious just before Darling Harbour was due to open.

"Look," said Ian, "wait until we open Darling Harbour and then we'll take off for a long trip to Europe."

The last straw was in the weeks leading up to the opening when Ian was flat out with last-minute arrangements and entertaining.

Although they lived just across the Harbour Bridge in Mosman, he was under such a strict time schedule that he moved into a suite at the Intercontinental Hotel in the city to be nearer the action.

Lillian said "I'm out of here," and took off for London.

What should have been a time of joy for him as the Queen opened Darling Harbour, was one of sadness. That's why he was accompanied by his daughter Melissa instead of his wife.

It was the second time Lillian had taken off and this time as far as Ian was concerned, it was for keeps. They never got back together again.

The truth was that for a high-spirited young woman who liked to disco at the drop of an eyelid and live life as if it were about to end, Lillian had too much time on her hands in which to meet other attractive men and with her fatal charm she found herself another admirer, a South African.

Ian had no regrets over the time he and Lillian spent together and retained good thoughts about her. She kept in touch by ringing from London.

Lillian was such a free soul without hangups that while married to Ian she still rang her former photographer lover in Ian's presence. One day she said to Ian: "That's the last time I'll be talking to him. He has just asked me to please not call him any more. His new wife has told him there'll be trouble if he speaks to me again."

Lillian proved one thing: She was no gold digger, as Ian well knew. She always told him that if she decided to leave, she wouldn't ask for anything, and that's how she played it in the end.

But some months after the parting, Ian generously arranged a property settlement with Lillian as part of their divorce, including establishing her in a Knightsbridge shop selling Russian art. She later remarried.

Later, reflecting on his past, it would become clear to Ian that his two marriages were due to the foibles of a young man who had twice been smitten by captivating beauty, that his partners had been totally unsuitable for a lasting relationship and what he thought at the time to be love, turned out to be infatuation.

His experience of those two misguided marriages, combined with a few more years of maturity to bring steadiness to him, would prepare him for a relationship of mutual love and respect for Miss Right when she came along, making it third time lucky.

Her name was Natalie Fegan, one of nine children. Unlike his previous European city wives, Ietstje and Lillian, Natalie was a country girl of Australian birth, born and bred on the land. Her parents owned a sheep and cattle station in north-west Queensland.

A beautiful brunette, tall and slim with a no-nonsense approach to life, Natalie was a real home-maker with a sensibly frugal attitude to money, and a workaholic when it came to the welfare of her home and family. This writer was impressed with her directness and natural personality.

At the time of writing, Natalie and Ian would have three young children produced almost in quick succession - Jack, four, Max, three and Ruby aged eight weeks.

Ian's hard work was justified by Merlin's performance in its first year.

In October 1988 he announced that Merlin's net profit for the year ended June 30 was $18.1 million, saying the good result was due to a lift in performance. He talked of quality developments and plans to expand in Britain and the US, exporting Darling Harbours to the world.

The company's peers, he said, and people abroad were describing their Harbourside Marketplace as the best of its kind in the world.

Directors of Merlin from Sydney and London celebrated by holding their next meeting in a top hotel in Geneva, Switzerland, where they considered what they might do in Europe, and Japan too.

Outlining the company's assets in his announcement, Ian said that apart from winning the tenders for Manchester and Birmingham, Merlin had Harbourside, a multi-million redevelopment of Manly Wharf, was tendering for a $120 million hi-tech entertainment area called Darling Walk at Darling Harbour and also for the air rights of a development over Melbourne's Flinders Street railway station.

Work had just begun on the $300 million Skygarden specialty retailing and commercial complex in the heart of Sydney's CBD.

In addition, with an eye to the future, the Haysons through Merlin had bought two large car parks with 2,600 spaces and were adding another 1,000 to one of these at the Entertainment Centre.

No wonder the lovely, sexy Lillian had felt a little neglected with all those corporate goings-on taking place.

The Darling Walk entertainment area was specially interesting because like the woolstores and Harbourside, it reflected Tom's vision for Darling Harbour and showed his confidence in the overall development when hardly anyone else thought it would be a goer.

Darling Walk was a flat area of land of more than two hectares beside a lake, which the Hayson Group had built. It was the last parcel of Darling Harbour land to be developed, right on the eastern or city edge, adjacent to where Mort Hoppenfeld had planned as the original hotel/casino site.

Having been in at the beginning, Tom wanted to see it out to show that his concept for Darling Harbour was right.

The site went out to tender. At his company's expense, Tom flew out first class from Denmark an old friend, Nils Jorgen Kaiser, and his wife, Kirsten. Nils was director of Copenhagen's famous Tivoli Gardens, one of the world's premier people places. He was introduced to the Government and plans were drawn up for a Tivoli Garden for Sydney.

But the DHA knocked it back. That was a pity because at the time Tom could arrange the finance and later it would be judged that without it, Darling Harbour didn't have enough greenery and flowers.

The tender went to Perth entrepreneur Kevin Parry who submitted a grandiose, costly scheme in association with Luqman Keele, one of the businessmen present at the meeting when Premier Wran first raised the possible development of Darling Harbour.

But the Parry Corporation, fresh from an attempt to win the America's Cup, collapsed in the wake of the October 1987 stock market crash. The site went out to tender again and although nobody else wanted to invest in

Darling Harbour in tight new economic times, it cost the Haysons a high price as the DHA extracted the last drop of blood.

After paying Parry $5 million to take over his interests, they then had to pay the DHA to buy in. It cost the Hayson Group about $20 million before they could even draw up new plans to do anything there. Darling Walk went into Merlin's international assets.

What had brought about this burst of general activity by the Haysons after concentrating so completely on Darling Harbour?

The explanation lay in the background to how they became involved in the Skygarden development in Sydney's Pitt Street Mall.

After his heart attack Tom was supposed to be taking it easy, but that was a myth. He *had* handed over the daily running to Ian, although still taking part in the big decisions. And in Ian and his fellow director Roger Kohler, he had two young Turks keen to build an empire.

But in getting the Harbourside project up and running, Tom had taken on a team of highly-paid specialist people like builders and engineers and they were keen to do other things. When the Skygarden opportunity came along, they said let's do it.

It came about after Ian and Roger went to Tom and said they thought they could get a sensational site which had the gilt-edged tenet of property dealing - *location, location, location*. Slap bang in the middle of the city's retail area, passed by a million people a week. The best site in Sydney.

Normally Tom would have said no, even to such a tempting project. At that stage they were starting construction of Harbourside, they were still trying to do something with the woolstores and had plenty on their plate.

But something else was niggling at their judgment.

What if Darling Harbour was not successful? The relentless criticism in Parliament and the press - but not Murdoch's News Limited group - had created serious, widespread doubts. It caused misgivings even in Tom.

There was no way anyone could be sure the place would work when finished. Indeed, there was no guarantee Darling Harbour would ever be finished given the political dogfight still going on.

It was all so hard and uncertain. The Monorail was another downer. Tom also found it depressing that the DHA did so little to counter the constant carping against Darling Harbour and it sapped his energy having to be the only one taking the fight to the media.

It posed the question, in spite of Tom's dream and determination, of whether they were wise in having all their eggs in one basket, tying up all those millions in Darling Harbour?

They could see other opportunities for their creativity, too, through the new understanding that came from their association with Rouse.

Perhaps it would be smarter to diversify in case Darling Harbour came a gutser. The knockers had made negative inroads in all areas.

Tom agreed to do Skygarden. It would be a fateful decision.

They paid almost $12 million to amalgamate four properties on the site.

Tom and Ian, wanting quality, planned to use the best materials to create an atmosphere of "leisure and lifestyle" on six levels, with an atrium and soaring glass roof and restaurants on the top floor.

Artists were called in and plans drawn up to make it one of the most prestigious retail, office and restaurant complexes in Sydney. Tom and Ian wanted to create a centre that people could be proud of, where they would feel something special when they walked in there. People deserved that.

It took an agonising 18 months to get the plans through the City Council.

Then, with the plans approved, an insurance and investment group offered to buy the project. It meant that at that stage without going to the trouble of building it - flicking it on, as they say in the trade - Merlin could make a profit of $10 million.

But senior Merlin executives were keen to build it. They said to Ian: "If we build it ourselves, we can make $80 or $90 million profit. You're crazy to take the smaller profit now when there's a larger profit there for the taking."

Tom was away from the action in London but he and Ian wanted to take the $10 million, although the property market was strong then and banks were happy to lend Merlin the money to build. But before deciding, the company took another precaution by obtaining a finished valuation on the property and future market prospects from the most reputable firm of valuers in Sydney.

Armed with all that positive knowledge, the board at a meeting in Sydney decided to go ahead and build Skygarden. Ian was the only one at the meeting to oppose the move.

Once that decision was made, others followed.

The NSW Government for a long time had wanted to see the wharf facilities upgraded at Sydney's famous Manly beach resort.

It was a mark of Tom's enthusiasm that he wanted to make his city's environment better and, knowing the wharf was in such an awful state of disrepair, he went in there on what many considered a risky enterprise spending more than $40 million on international food outlets and shops to make it attractive for visitors.

Ian and Roger found another site at suburban Parramatta, epicentre of Sydney to the burgeoning west. The idea was to build a shopping centre bigger and better in competition to Westfield's big centre at the other end of Parramatta, which was little more than a dust bowl by comparison with Ian's site by the river. David Jones's department store was to be part of it.

Tom went along with it because it was a fantastic location and he could see how it would uplift people's lives there. In Texas he'd seen a lovely area in San Antonio where the river ran through the shopping centre and he could see how the Parramatta setting could be garnished with waterfalls and riverside facilities. The Hayson Group proposed a $250 million development.

Merlin then won a tender against all comers to develop Flinders Street railway station, the most historic site in all Melbourne used as a favourite rendezvous, where a million people passed by each day. They planned to make it a people place even better than Darling Harbour.

With imagination they beat their opponents, including Lend Lease, Bond and the John Holland group, by obtaining a forgotten 100-year-old plan for the station which showed the original scheme had never been completed. They embellished it in the Rouse/Hayson way.

All those assets, including Harbourside, were transferred to Merlin's international operation in London.

At that stage the Haysons, with Merlin's assets and successful tenders, controlled an international group with a projected $2 billion worth of real estate.

They had reached a pinnacle.

Only time would prove the most tantalising of all real estate challenges - could a visionary with pioneering spirit succeed in the long term in the face of unpredictable cycles?

23

VISION VERSUS COMMERCIALISM

IF Tom Hayson thought it difficult at times dealing with the Darling Harbour Authority under Premiers Wran and Unsworth, he was in for a shock under Premier Greiner.

Having spent its time in political opposition criticising Darling Harbour, the Greiner Government squeezed funding to finish off the job after coming to power early in 1988, although Ministers enjoyed the occasional brush with super celebrities there like the Queen and Maggie Thatcher.

For one thing, Darling Harbour needed a major marketing effort.

Precious little was forthcoming from the DHA or the Government in funds or knowhow and the Greiner Government didn't want to spend any money on marketing or anything else in there, wanting it to pay for itself.

In the words of Neville Wran, expressed privately, nobody in Government understood marketing or how to run shops or entertainment - one reason why he came to respect Tom Hayson so much for his single enormous contribution.

Relations became so strained between the Liberal Government and the old DHA board that six months after the opening, Alex Carmichael and his fellow directors resigned en masse. They gave no reason except "pressures" from Government decisions.

The Government then put a broom through the place and nearly all the people who had done the work were cleaned out. In came a new board of political appointees and management staff.

Only one or two of them knew anything about the contribution that had been made by the Haysons and others. The situation was just highly political.

Nick Greiner would eventually change his mind about Darling Harbour, but for some time after his election it was tough for those trying to put the finishing touches to it and change its image.

The Government and the new DHA gave every indication they didn't understand the value of what they had in Darling Harbour.

The public increasingly appreciated its worth and enjoyed what it offered long before acknowledgment by the Liberal Government or media.

One irritating by-product of the new Government was the number of inquiries it fostered into Darling Harbour by the Auditor-General, management consultants and a Parliamentary public accounts committee. None found evidence to justify earlier claims of corruption.

Indeed, the public accounts committee "found no evidence to support claims of gross mismanagement by the DHA, the Board, senior officers or staff."

But the committee did go as far as claiming that industrial strikes and "highly irregular" work practices had delayed Darling Harbour and cost taxpayers an extra $50 million, with 37 per cent of available man-hours lost or wasted in less than three years - in an estimated $3 billion project.

However, DHA executives who controlled the purse strings always hotly denied Darling Harbour ran over budget. They said it was always within budget and contingencies, except when something new was added.

The report said many contractors and sub-contractors in the peak on-site workforce of 3,000 allegedly lost money on the site and significant industrial relations processes were abused.

But many people prepared to offer information informally would not give evidence at the committee's public hearings for fear of recriminations by the construction industry.

The DHA had to deal with problems so complex that it operated in an atmosphere of "urgency management."

The committee found the DHA was put under great pressure by the short timescale set down for the project, by the volume and complexity of demolition, construction and on-site services needed, the special nature of fast tracking the work and "a peculiar industrial climate on a large, high profile public project in an overheated construction industry."

In spite of those difficulties, the parliamentary committee criticised the DHA for not always meeting the demands placed on it, although acknowledging it worked hard to manage the project.

Above: Proudly Tom displays his Order of Australia with NSW Governor Sir David Martin, Ngaire and Paul Hayson.

LEFT: After his investiture at Government House, with Ian and Paul.

ABOVE: Work begins on the Haysons' Harbourside development at Darling Harbour (April, 1986).

BELOW: The old derelict buildings demolished, developers start pushing earthworks about on the Darling Harbour site.

ABOVE: The Haysons' Harbourside development, showing the huge Galleria to full effect - the symbol of Darling Harbour. Harbourside became the heart and soul and drawcard of the vast waterfront complex.

ABOVE: Even the rain didnt stop them from pouring in by the hundreds of thousands to celebrate Darling Harbour's opening. Suddenly Sydney had a vast celebration centre where huge crowds could assemble, like the Mall in London or Times Square in New York. Visited by millions each year from all around Australia.

LEFT: That cheeky shot again of Tom Hayson upstaging The Duke at his Harbourside opening.

ABOVE: Setting new standards, the Haysons assigned teams of artists to work in this warehouse studio producing colourful art designs which they incorporated in their Harbourside development in Darling Harbour - an innovation seen in a shopping complex for the first time in Australia.

ABOVE: Yippee! Members of the public let themselves go in Darling Harbour. They simply relax and enjoy themselves. Lonely people go there to feel alive and part of the world. Visitors walk more slowly and talk to one another, just as they did during the 2000 Olympics. All are equal.

ABOVE: Australia's Ashes - winning cricketers in Sydney's first ticker-tape welcome at Darling Harbour - another "first" by Tom Hayson.

LEFT: The Monorail, introduced by guess who?

BELOW: Revised (second) secret Darling Harbour plan by the Haysons' American architect Mort Hoppenfeld.

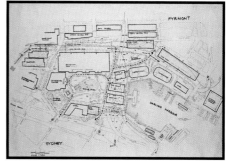

LEFT: Happy days for Tom and Ngaire as son Paul graduates in law from Sydney University.

RIGHT: Princess Di meets up with a few characters at Darling Harbour.

LEFT: Christmas pageant sponsored by the Haysons to help make Darling Harbour the celebration centre it is today.

BELOW: Family shot of Tom and Ngaire with daughter Rosemary and Tom's mother Lavina, having a swell time at the Sahara in Las Vegas.

ABOVE: Intrepid travellers - Tom and Ngaire at Jungfrau, the top of Europe.

LEFT: One of many visits to New York.

BELOW: Honolulu, a favourite stopping off spot.

LEFT: Ngaire takes in the Cedars of Lebanon and some family history.

BELOW: Brighton's famous pier - Tom successfully tendered to develop it.

BOTTOM: On the boardwalk of Atlantic City.

ABOVE: Tom wanted to turn a part of Sydney's Parramatta into a beautiful river centre like this scene in San Antonio Texas. But a parochial, shortsighted Parramatta Council knocked him back.
Result: the area still looks like a dust bowl.

BELOW: Tivoli Gardens, Copenhagen. Tom proposed a version of this famous entertainment garden for land he leased at Darling Harbour, but the Darling Harbour Authority knocked it back.
Result: the area still doesn't have enough greenery.

ABOVE: Tom and Ngaire on the balcony of their luxury home on famous Manly Beach.

LEFT: Ian and Natalie Hayson christening one of their two sons, Max.

RIGHT: Paul and Anne Hayson christening one of their four children.

ABOVE: A nostaligic Tom visits the home site in the mountain village of Aitou, North Labanon, from where his grandfather, old Tannous Elhessen, emigrated to Australia in 1886.

BELOW: At the museum and tomb of Kahlil Gibran, Lebanon's greatest poet - part of Tom's journey to discover his family's history stretching back to the ancient Phoenicians.

ABOVE: Tom and Ngaire ceremoniously turn on the street lights in the Lebanese village of Aitou, a facility which Tom installed and paid for as a gesture to his ancestors.

BELOW: Photo of a brass plaque presented to Tom and Ngaire for "turning on the lights." The villagers cried, "God bless you."

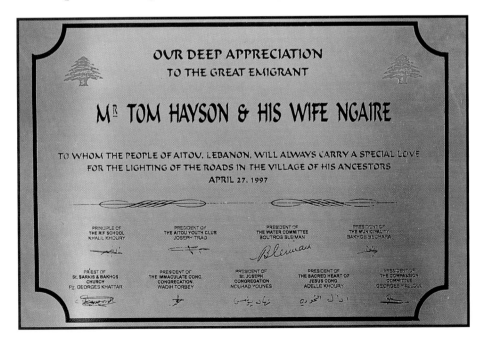

OUR DEEP APPRECIATION
TO THE GREAT EMIGRANT

M͞r TOM HAYSON & HIS WIFE NGAIRE

TO WHOM THE PEOPLE OF AITOU, LEBANON, WILL ALWAYS CARRY A SPECIAL LOVE
FOR THE LIGHTING OF THE ROADS IN THE VILLAGE OF HIS ANCESTORS
APRIL 27, 1997

PRINCIPLE OF
THE RIF SCHOOL
KHALIL KHOURY

PRESIDENT OF
THE AITOU YOUTH CLUB
JOSEPH TRAD

PRESIDENT OF
THE WATER COMMITTEE
BOUTROS SLEIMAN

PRESIDENT OF
THE MUNICIPALITY
BAKHOS BECHARA

PRIEST OF
St. SARKIS & BAKHOS
CHURCH
FLr. GEORGES KHATTAR

PRESIDENT OF
THE IMMACULATE CONC.
CONGREGATION,
WADIH TORBEY

PRESIDENT OF
St. JOSEPH
CONGREGATION
NOUHAD YOUNES

PRESIDENT OF
THE SACRED HEART OF
JESUS CONG.
ADELLE KHOURY

PRESIDENT OF
THE COMPASSION
COMMITTEE
GEORGES KALSOUL

ABOVE: When Ngaire's health degenerated, Tom encouraged his life's partner to tick off her checklist of wishes unfulfilled. Here they enjoy the famous mountain scenery of Guilin, China. Note the cormorant.

ABOVE: Thrilled to be a bikie.

ABOVE: Tom's son Paul, a solicitor, with wife Anne and Daniela, Matthew, Luisa and Luke at their Clifton Gardens home.

LEFT: Ian and wife Natalie, at their Palm Beach home.

ABOVE: Studying the old ways in the land of Tom's forefathers in the ancient city of Byblos, where the alphabet was invented.

LEFT: Daniela Hayson, granddaughter of Tom on the trail of Ngaire's family history at Tillicooltry, Scotland.

BELOW: Justin Hayson, a grandson of Tom's, following in the family's real estate footsteps.

Among other criticisms were that the DHA suffered from the length of time to get key managers in place, crucial early decisions were rushed, insufficient attention was given to marketing planning and public relations, the system for handling contracts was inadequate and it relied too heavily on general management to cover specialist areas.

"The Authority," said the report, "failed to protect the interests of the project by not countering effectively the barrage of negative publicity and often misleading or simply inaccurate figures relating to costs and claimed 'budget blowouts.'"

Tom found the opinion of the committee's Liberal Party chairman, Phillip Smiles, a bit hard to accept.

Tom had spent many hours on the phone and fax using his friendship with Rouse, Millspaugh and others arranging a VIP tour of Baltimore's Inner Harbour for Smiles and his committee members, so they could be fully briefed. Tom couldn't believe it later when Phillip Smiles in effect put the boot in with his comments.

Smiles said in a dissenting foreword to his committee's report, published at the end of 1989, that in the previous five years $2.163 billion had been spent by the private sector and $1.093 billion by Government on Darling Harbour in building "what may well be a white elephant in 25 years."

Although his report described the difficulties in fast-tracking Darling Harbour as a complex "industrial relations nightmare" in rushed time, the words mostly seized on by the media were "white elephant."

Published everywhere and repeated by Smiles on radio and TV, it fuelled new doubts and caused enormous damage to Tom's efforts to attract shoppers and give confidence to his Harbourside tenants, some of whom were battling to survive. Tenants who couldn't make a go of it ran to the press and complained about high rents.

Other big developers in Australia had just as many problems with tenants in their shops, but nobody bothered about that. Darling Harbour was attacked because it was in the spotlight.

The chairman drew attention to the fact that this huge redevelopment was done without a cost benefit study or environmental impact statement and without anywhere near final plans prepared at the beginning of construction.

Heavens above - if those things had been done, we'd still be waiting for the first pylons to be driven.

But he certainly got it right in saying the initiating Labor Government had been electorally crippled by issues raised over Darling Harbour.

And he was no doubt right in saying that "a Board of outstanding NSW citizens who gave much for minuscule, if any, financial reward, were publicly humiliated with a very public sacking/resignation."

But Phillip Smiles also raised the tired old cry that future historians might ask why the site wasn't used for public housing of 6,000 people as originally planned. Hell!

This "white elephant" prophet disappeared from politics without further trumpeting, expressing the hope in an afterthought on behalf of NSW taxpayers that his forecast would be proved absolutely wrong.

That annoyance aside, Tom couldn't find any common ground with the new DHA Chairman, merchant banker James Graham, or his board. He found it difficult to converse with him, and had the feeling that he and Ian were regarded as lowly tenants while the board was lord of the manor.

He invited the board to his offices one day to discuss plans for Darling Walk, bringing in a special chef and treating them to a superb lunch, but they seemed indifferent and he felt it was all a waste of time.

Tom always talked the place up, believing if it could be made attractive, everybody would benefit. But he received little support from that board and felt he could not get his message through.

He received no sympathy towards rental concessions or the like in difficult times when many people were still doubtful about the future.

Marketing was a major problem. Building the place was one thing, but without "selling the product" properly, it could well have fallen in a heap.

A brilliant marketer, Tom knew if it was to succeed, Darling Harbour must reach out and work closely with other promotional bodies, using showmanship to generate a happy, friendly atmosphere.

But the idea ran into resistance, even from the previous DHA board. They didn't understand marketing and didn't want to spend money on it.

So in one hit the Haysons put in $2 million and for the first two years after Darling Harbour opened, the bulk of marketing was funded by them and managed by their marketing man, Michael Miller.

They were really suckers to fall for it but were so keen to see it all happen that ultimately it would cost them several million dollars, not only to market their own Harbourside activities but also the rest of Darling Harbour.

The Government's miserly attitude was one reason why Darling Harbour languished after its opening.

Tom and his company began the Christmas Pageant, which became an institution. He employed top producer Mary Lopez to organise numerous functions, promotions and entertainments such as the annual Dragon boat race and historic train rides.

He spent $150,000 launching the Manly-to-Darling Harbour marathon swim in which Shelley Taylor-Smith beat the men. It made every front page but the DHA, having to pay for it after that, didn't continue it.

But trying to get the idea for a permanent floating stage through the marketing troglodytes at the DHA almost drove teetotaller Tom to strong drink.

After he staged the successful youth pageant on a floating barge before the Queen at the Harbourside opening, he and his producer Bobby Limb decided to create a permanent stage.

Bobby managed to interest the Prudential Assurance Company and Tom arranged for renowned architects Philip Cox Richardson and Partners to do a design, with all technical details. He hit on the name Aquashell and approached the DHA.

The idea met a cool response, a DHA woman board member saying privately "over my dead body." She wanted the place kept bland.

That put his hackles up and he threw himself into the campaign, spending at least $100,000 just to get them interested.

Every obstruction was put in his way, even through decibel tests. Finally he received a terse letter saying it would be approved depending on final plans - but it could only be used infrequently.

In desperation he went to the then Transport Minister Bruce Baird, who was supportive but wanted an independent committee to evaluate it. That done, the Minister gave him a permanent mooring place on the Parramatta River.

The Opera House used his stage for a brilliant symphony concert out on the main harbour, and only then did the DHA accept final plans - after 2½ years! - welcoming it with open arms for all their big functions, allowing a permanent mooring where they at first refused, right in Darling Harbour's Cockle Bay.

But for all he'd done, Tom was never invited to any of the official functions held in Darling Harbour by the DHA, nor to any social event or international waterfront convention held there to honour the development.

And when later, in 1991, Darling Harbour would receive a top honour from the world authority for waterfront developments - the Waterfront Centre in Washington DC - he had to wait to be told about it from Martin Millspaugh in the US.

Millspaugh, new President of Rouse's Enterprise International Development Company, wrote to Tom saying: "I am enclosing a copy of the citation, which I think should make you feel extremely proud - having been for all effective purposes the originator and in many ways the driving force that launched the Darling Harbour redevelopment on its way."

It was interesting to note that the award had been presented to Barry Young of MSJ Keys Young and T.W. Jones, the then General Manager of the Darling Harbour Authority.

No mention of the talented young Hayson architects, Clarke, Perry, Blackmore who designed the Harbourside Marketplace.

Or Mort Hoppenfeld.

Or indeed, of Tom Hayson who made the place "sing."

The citation said in part: "The transformation of the Darling Harbour area in downtown Sydney is one of the most dramatic in the world.

"Dedicated by Queen Elizabeth in May 1988 as part of Australia's bicentennial, the combination of attractions carved from an abandoned rail depot and wharves, now receives an estimated 16 million visitors a year.

"It thus belongs with Baltimore's Inner Harbour as a bold, popular and commercial-cultural success. The resemblance is furthered by the presence of a festival marketplace within the Darling Harbour project..."

In between jousting with the DHA in Sydney, Tom was going great guns in London.

Apart from projects already in the bag, he was actively discussing other developments. Largely through his efforts, Merlin was the front runner to manage regeneration of the Covent Garden Market and surrounds.

The UK's largest insurance group, Prudential, controlling £2.5 billion worth of property and Forte Hotels, Europe's largest hotel group, discussed joining Merlin in specialist shopping projects.

Talks had also begun with Harrods and the House of Fraser with a view to Merlin buying some of their department stores for redevelopment as specialist shopping centres.

They had also been invited to join an international consortium for a £400 million redevelopment of the huge Royal Victoria Dock area. Other big groups wanted to joint venture with them too, including the Rosehaugh Group and the huge John Laing construction and development group.

The English Tourist Board chief, Miles Collinge, asked them to advise on a masterplan for regenerating inner areas of UK cities.

One good idea ended in a minor disaster. Tom and his Isle of Man partners had formed a company called Dolphin to acquire new businesses and had gone into outdoor advertising. They had erected signs from one end of England to the other when a freak cyclonic storm hit Britain, destroying nearly every sign, even uprooting trees in Hyde Park near the Mayfair flat where Tom and Ngaire rode out the storm.

Oh well, said Tom, let's move on to something else.

The connection with James Rouse had helped greatly in opening up development opportunities and things had begun with great promise.

But after a while all was not well below the surface.

Tom and Ian finally decided the merger was unlikely to work. Although their English partners were honest and acted with integrity, their style of doing business was in sharp contrast to the more open Australian give-and-take way.

Tom realised he should have done what Rupert Murdoch did when he moved into England and later America - taken Australians with him and put them in charge. Tom had talked to Murdoch about that in London in 1981 after he took over *The Times*.

Rupert wrote to him thanking him for the "nice thought" in advising him to buy an American television network, saying he was barred by American foreign ownership laws (that was before Murdoch became an American citizen and bought Fox TV).

Tom had made all the running in the early stages, negotiating big projects while the Englishmen were inclined to move much more slowly.

Tom and Ian believed that if they were to get any real benefits out of all the Australian properties they had put into the public company - discovered and worked up by themselves - they needed to control those assets. That meant taking them back.

The path was made easy because banks in Australia were keen to lend them money. Property was holding up well, in spite of Federal Treasurer Paul Keating's thoughtless 1986 comment that Australia was likely to become a banana republic, wiping $2.5 billion off the value of the share market. Investors had boosted property after the 1987 crash by taking their money out of the stock market and putting it into real estate.

Losses from that crash could have triggered a major recession but the banks, anxious to avoid the mistakes of the 1930 Depression when they restricted credit, extended credit into the economy to compensate for a lack of business confidence .

Many borrowers and corporate raiders were buying businesses with bank funds but in the case of the Haysons, banks were lending to buy real estate. The banks simply loved lending to them because funds would be secured by real estate, backed up by the Haysons' successful track record and faith in property.

Ian Hayson was approached in early 1989 and told plenty of bank money was available to enable them to buy back their assets from the UK company. Things looked good generally and no downturns were predicted.

To buy in and obtain their controlling 30 per cent shareholding of the UK international group, the Haysons had paid some cash and put in their Australian real estate assets.

As a sign of goodwill they told other shareholders they would not sell any of their shares for at least three years. They could have sold some shares and comfortably stashed away £5 million without losing control, but didn't.

In business, the English can be as hard as anyone and they made it tough for the Haysons to withdraw their assets. Merlin's English directors took the view that they weren't going to sell back the assets at a figure below their real worth.

The deal would have to stand up to any scrutiny. So they made the Haysons pay what they thought was an excessively high price.

The Haysons' bankers carefully checked out the assets before committing loan funds to complete the deal, and all were looking good - Skygarden, the River Centre at Parramatta, Harbourside, Flinders Street Station and Manly Wharf. The Darling Walk entertainment project was included too.

To do the deal, the Haysons had to take on an extra $100 million debt - the debt associated with buying back the properties and the existing project financing to develop each asset. Against liabilities, their assets were considerably higher.

But being astute, and with unpredictable circumstances in the back of their minds, the Haysons didn't want to take on all that responsibility.

They offered to pay the bank a higher fee out of profits to take some of that risk so the Haysons would have less risk personally, and the bank was prepared to do that.

Once more the Haysons became a private company in Australia, the bank calculating that Tom and Ian would probably make $100 million on paper when everything was developed.

To show its confidence in the future and in the Haysons, the bank then wanted to tell the world and ran a full-page newspaper ad about the deal.

Sydney had never seen anything quite like it.

The party to open Tom and Ian Hayson's luxury $300 million Skygarden shopping complex was hailed as one of the city's best. If there was subtle talk of recession and gloom in the air, you'd never have suspected it.

More than 700 of Australia's heavyweight VIPs and best-known celebrities, dressed to kill, made it a memorable night as champagne flowed non-stop, choirs and a symphony orchestra performed and solo musicians like jazz trumpeter James Morrison gave a jolly air to the gala affair.

The glitterati jostled one another as they rode the escalators and wandered through five levels of elegant brightly-lit shops offering everything from imported evening wear to fine art.

In one novel feature to the charity black tie show, producer Mary Lopez had members of the Police Rescue Squad dressed as waiters abseiling down the central "well" of the building, balancing trays of chilled Veuve Clicquot.

The celebrity knees-up, which the newspapers said in good round figures cost $400,000, showed once again that when the Haysons did something, they did it in style. Not even the most ardent cynic could grumble on the night.

315

Skygarden, with its decorative arts, parquetry and terrazzo floors inlaid with motifs of Australian flora and fauna, its unique designs and glamour shops, set new standards in Australia.

Even the dining concept broke new ground with its extensive array of food under a huge glass conservatory in a rooftop garden atmosphere. Everyone agreed the whole place was five or 10 years ahead of its time.

The archway entrance was spectacular too, adorned outside with a large $250,000 marionette clock, a gift to the people of Sydney from Tom Hayson and Seiko.

To top it all off, Tom had a real live duke on deck to add a bit of couth to the opening ceremony - the Duke and Duchess of Wellington, no less, whom he flew out from England.

The Duke and Duchess, also known as Valerian and Diana Wellesley, looked on happily as Premier Nick Greiner, with wife Kathryn at his side, did the opening honours.

Among the rows of celebs were Neville and Jill Wran, John and Caroline Laws, Sir James Hardie and assorted bankers, TV stars and politicians. Socialite Lillian Frank led the Melbourne brigade.

Valerian was the eighth duke of the line. His forebear the Great Duke was the man who ended 20 years of Anglo-French fighting by giving Napoleon a hiding at the Battle of Waterloo in 1815, after which a grateful nation bestowed so many honours on him he became the most decorated man in England's history.

The current Duke, kicking up his heels a treat on the night by dancing with many of the bright young things, was no slouch himself when it came to doing his bit for his country. After leaving Eton he had a lark in the Royal Horse Guards, held a few royal-type posts but when the chips were down he served out the war in the Middle East, Italy and Germany.

Escorted around by Tom and Ngaire, the Duke and Duchess mixed in as if they were born to the relaxed Aussie way of getting together over a drink or three.

At the end of the night, marked by an indoor fireworks display, Tom presented the Duke with a cheque for $35,000 for the Royal Alexandra Hospital for Children, rekindling for Tom and Ngaire memories of illicit and voluptuous nights there among the physiology skeletons nearly 50 years before. Of course they remembered!

Sydney social lioness Di "Bubbles" Fisher voted it the bash of the year.

It didn't end there. The Haysons and TNT's Sir Peter Abeles staged a fun weekend for the Wellingtons at Hayman Island, joined by well-heeled Melburnians and Sydneyites who forked out generous charity bucks.

After returning to his grand ancestral estate of Strathfield Saye House in Hampshire, the Duke wrote thanking Tom for the wonderful time he'd given him and his wife, and for his gifts, especially the opals.

"Australians are a warm and friendly people," he wrote, "and it was moving for both of us to find that life is really very similar in many ways in Australia, especially in people's attitudes.

"Australia has an enormous future. I do hope it will continue to maintain that certain Britishness that it still has at the moment."

It would be no surprise that Skygarden the following year would win the coveted international design award from the US-based International Council of Shopping Centres, beating dozens of competitors on four continents for its innovation.

That was the first time the accolade had gone to Australia and would be handed over to golden-tonsilled Tom at the Las Vegas Hilton.

After so much experience, so many ups and downs on the way to the top, Tom Hayson knew by instinct all the unwritten rules and traps in the property game.

Most people can never work for themselves, no matter how high they climb, but property is one area in which they can fly free like the swallow as Tom did. Although it was a gamble like casinos, horses and the stock market, a developer could still have a fair degree of control.

Tom was not a greedy entrepreneur but when a degree of risk was justified, he was prepared to "gamble" on his judgment.

He knew that in doing so, more than losing his shirt, he could quickly be made destitute if he failed to follow the rules and a deal went wrong.

One of the most basic of the Hayson survival rules was not to go into a deal unless you could leave something in it for someone else.

In Tom's experience an investor or developer could prosper only by adopting a prudent approach. By exercising prudence all the way when assessing a deal, you were less likely to make mistakes.

That was the normal Hayson way, and always the ideal. But some deals would never work out as planned.

When advising people who asked him the rudiments of property dealing, Tom always suggested they look at one of the richest companies in the world, the Prudential Assurance Co. Their symbol? Miss Prudence (a beautiful girl wearing a flowing scarf).

Owning property worth billions of dollars throughout the world, the company could put AMP in its back pocket.

He advised them to read the synonyms for *prudence* over and over before entering or getting out of any property deal to help overcome the tendency for greed, rashness and wrong judgment.

Prudence meant caution, care, commonsense, presence of mind, cool judgment, shrewdness, acumen, calculation, discretion, tact, vigilance, weighing up all the possibilities and assessing one step at a time...

Exercising those qualities, Tom believed, made a successful property person. But easier said than done. And the bigger the deal, the more important it was to adhere to those principles.

When it didn't work out, *cutting one's losses* was essential. Better to get out with some losses than losing the lot. Knowing when to get out and how much you could save by cutting those losses, was vital.

He knew all the subtle variations of the rules in the big league. But even with his gift of being able to see so far ahead through a highly creative mind, there was always the risk that vision could get in the way of commercial considerations.

And as usual, time, with all its unknown factors, was likely to beat vision in a long-term project, just as time conquers all in the human field.

Few people in Australian corporate life, prominent bankers and finance journalists among them, predicted what was around the corner when the Haysons arranged the financing to buy back tens of millions of dollars worth of property.

Indeed, most of the corporate world was taken by surprise later when Federal Treasurer Paul Keating suddenly clamped on his "recession we had to have."

Many people expected the 1980s boom times to end at some stage, but nobody believed after the cycle began that it would become as severe or last as long as it did.

Certainly nobody then in 1989 predicted that it would develop into Australia's worst recession since 1930.

As the Federal Labor Government moved with indecent haste to rectify an overheated economy, disaster reverberated through the business world.

Some banks had lent so indiscriminately that when the recession hit, many companies were heavily geared and had developed their own liquidity crisis. Bond was the prime example, although there were hundreds of others.

Bank panic buttons were pressed and those fair weather friends, who will lend you an umbrella on a sunny day and take it back when it rains, then reacted to the situation by going the other way, calling in loans left, right and centre.

The credit squeeze by banks generally had a snowballing effect. One result was that by 1991 the bottom had fallen out of the property market, with values halved. Properties that had been worth $300 million a year before, were worth only $150 million.

Some values went down by 70 per cent, others even more.

Along with thousands of other companies, the property downturn affected all of the Haysons' equity and their ability to develop and sell their projects, and that triggered some losses. Property companies around the world ran into the same problem.

But when the crunch came Australia, being a small market on a global basis with not many players but a lot of competition nonetheless, as usual stayed down longer than other countries, led by the nose by what happened abroad. Australia is simply not big enough to control what happens elsewhere and probably never will be.

The severity of that recession would last for about five years in Australia, less elsewhere. One by one many of the best business people, among them the best contributors to Australia's wealth, went under.

No longer was Australia the lucky country.

Apart from the cowboys who had taken advantage of the boom times, some of whom went to jail for stealing or simply took off with the dough like Skase, tens of thousands of good businessmen went bust.

Thousands chose to go bankrupt rather than face the stress of dealing with probably the most difficult situation of their business careers.

The recession caused the biggest string of corporate disasters in Australia's history. Banks lost about $30 billion in bad debts.

Property, dictated by supply and demand like any other commodity such as wheat, sugar, barley or foreign currency, proved to be not very liquid in a falling market. Everybody dealing in property found it difficult.

The Haysons knew by 1990 they would have some losses, although even in such a serious recession they also had properties that would be profitable. They needed time and more funds to finish off their projects but when the crunch came the banks were unwilling to lend.

The long established investment development companies like Lend Lease and Mirvac managed to ride through the recession because they were able to keep intact the capital they had invested over the previous 20 or 30 years, but the Haysons were new in that long term field and did not have the same huge equity base.

If they had kept on trading or turning over their projects, they would have sailed through the recession untroubled.

But they had tied up their equity in long term development, wanting to build some of the best shopping centres in the world in Darling Harbour and Parramatta and the best office and shopping complex in Sydney, Skygarden.

They then had the bad luck of running into probably the second worst recession of the century.

To resolve their problems, they entered into a workout situation with their bankers to get the best possible price for their assets, most of which were sold at large profits. With time on their side they could have held on and finished their projects, but the recession didn't allow for that.

However, they were able to trade right through on a low profile.

With the co-operation of their bankers, they restructured the group and closed down loss-making ventures, allowing an orderly sale of assets without any receiverships or liquidations. That enabled them to market their properties at the best possible price and keep their names up.

Some assets were sold to minimise losses, others were held for sale until the market began to rise again. Where projects were sold off quickly, as with Manly Wharf and Flinders Street Station, there were losses and the Haysons saw their equity evaporate.

But where they had time to work on projects and profits came out at the end, their bankers received all their capital and interest and made money.

It could be said the Haysons lost a large amount of their equity in the best possible way - by putting it all into bricks and mortar. No assets were stripped or shareholders' funds raided.

Their difficulties were caused basically by accumulated interest on projects that had been funded in a high interest atmosphere. With Skygarden, for instance, they began by paying about 8-10 per cent interest but as the Government quickly applied the screws and the recession deepened, they finished up paying more than 20 per cent, even 27 or 28 per cent at one stage.

Ironically, the Harbourside Marketplace which the doomsayers had written off all along with Darling Harbour as an albino jumbo, was the crown in the Hayson property portfolio.

It cost $110 million to build, went down in value like everything else in the recession, but eventually sold coming out of the recession for more than it cost, justifying the confidence Tom and Ian always had in it.

The woolstores also justified their judgment.

By the time they had worked their way through the early frustrating period with the City Council refusing to change the zoning and reached the point where they were ready to develop their two biggest woolstores, the banks would not finance them, wanting only to build something traditional and "safe" like an office block.

That was sheer bad luck.

With Council approval they could have sold their proposed apartments so cheaply that they would have begun the trend to live in the area several years before Darling Harbour became the Great Generator for the Pyrmont-Ultimo area and the western fringes of the CBD.

But in spite of reluctant bankers and an early lack of commercial interest, they still turned the Pitt Son and Badgery store into tasteful hi-tech office space and two other woolstores into carparks to provide much-needed parking for Darling Harbour, also converting one or two other buildings.

With a bit of luck and co-operation from their Hong Kong partners, the Haysons could have held on to the whole western facade of Darling Harbour, selling at the right time if they wished for a fortune. Those woolstores were the only freehold land in the whole Darling Harbour plan.

Their judgment was to hold on to the woolstores but their partners could not see it, panicked in the recession and insisted on selling for the short-term benefit of recovering their investments.

Tom even flew to Hong Kong trying to persuade the partners to hang on at least for another year or two, telling them they would make more money then. But they only wanted to sell quickly.

All the stores sold for profits, which would have been much larger if they'd held on for a while until Darling Harbour took off.

In the case of the AML & F store, bought by the Haysons for $1.1 million, they sold it to a Japanese consortium for $11.5 million. Less than two years later it was resold for $21 million.

The giant Goldsbrough Mort woolstore was an even bigger profit earner.

An Australian consortium, including Mr Ian Joye and Mr Dennis O'Neill, bought the front section for about $14 million, converting it into 520 residential units. The Haysons, who had turned the back section into car parking, had bought both buildings for $1.9 million.

The new owners of the Goldsbrough Mort store were believed to have made something like $50 million by developing the front half after the DHA approved their plans. Chinese fleeing Hong Kong bought many of the units.

Once again, the Hayson vision had been right. The Darling Harbour factor was now kicking in, as Tom and Ian had predicted.

But after the Haysons saw the big picture and did all the hard yards, others who came in later made the big profits - due to the lack of foresight and nerve by the Hayson partners.

One project Tom and Ian reluctantly had to abandon was Tom's dream of taming the Parramatta River at Parramatta in western Sydney.

They envisaged transforming a part of Parramatta, often a "dust bowl" in high summer, in a similar way to the remarkable achievement by American authorities in redirecting the course of the San Antonio River virtually through the centre of San Antonio, Texas.

They planned to redirect the river where it flowed under the Lennox Bridge at Church Street as part of impressive plans to complete a new-style shopping complex to rival Westfield's at the other end of Parramatta.

The Lennox Bridge, where the river narrowed as it passed underneath Church Street, was in the heart of their development. A back-up of water occurred there when the river was in full flow.

The Haysons had spent millions of dollars putting properties together, drawing up plans and arranging bank and other feasibilities for the complex.

Then, out of the blue the NSW Government released the result of a survey by the Water Board saying that every 50 or 60 years there was a big risk of that part of the Parramatta River flooding as water rushed along under Lennox Bridge.

The Haysons offered to carefully pull down the bridge block by block and rebuild it up the river in Parramatta Park, where it could not be affected by flooding.

But, influenced on the surface by a few bellowing objectors, and an obviously orchestrated campaign by some groups whose interests would be affected by such a project, Parramatta Council repeatedly knocked back their plans on "historic grounds."

For more than three years Hayson experts, engineers and architects addressed the council on every aspect but they would not shift, even though the State Government favoured the bridge removal.

On that basis, the banks would not fund the project.

The council's decision stank. It smacked of falsehood and did not benefit their district. A small but overpowering coterie of people seemed to collar the local press, banging a hollow environmental drum and convincing people that the area would lose part of its heritage. What crap!

The people of Parramatta were the losers.

They missed out on an alternative shopping centre with life and colour similar to San Antonio, with pleasant shops by the river bank, a delightful recreation area where people could enjoy leisure and cultural activities on and beside the water day and night and in all weather conditions.

Instead, they were left with a lifeless rundown area, having to travel to Darling Harbour to sample the lifestyle they could have enjoyed permanently in their own locale.

The Haysons relinquished their hold on Flinders Street Railway Station when Melbourne became an even worse economic disaster area than Sydney, the project being bought by Jamie Packer and his business partner, Theo Onisforou.

They also sold Manly Wharf on which about $40 million was spent in what was overwhelmingly a labour of love and sense of community.

Tom had just gone to live on the Manly beach front and had noted the syringes left in the toilets at the wharf and the dilapidated, ramshackle condition of the wharf visited by people from Australia and abroad.

Wanting to do something decent there, he refurbished it with elegant shops, restaurants and an international food hall.

The severity of the recession in the UK destroyed their dreams there too as companies went under by the hundreds in rapid succession.

Merlin UK survived, while bigger companies crashed. The recession destroyed some of Merlin's venture partners who were much longer established, but the relatively small Australian-inspired company was able to hang on with its big Manchester project "in the bag," although unfortunately it relinquished all other successful tenders such as Glasgow, Brighton Pier and the vast Birmingham project.

Adopting a low profile after delisting from the London Stock Exchange, Merlin UK continued to trade profitably mainly by retaining its hold on the Manchester development in partnership with another property group.

Finally winding up their holdings in exchange for the full buy-back of their Australian assets, Tom and Ian resigned as directors and no longer had any equity in the company, although keeping in touch with its directors and watching progress with friendly interest.

With Skygarden, the Keating recession destroyed one of the great property myths held to be sacred down the years. The Haysons thought they would be safe even in a down cycle if they adhered to the market maxim by building on a site that spelled *location location location.*

Sir Les Hooker, the longtime Sydney property magnate, used to say that waterfront property around Sydney Harbour, especially with uninterrupted views, might stand still in a recession but would never go down "because God ain't making any more of it.".

But he was wrong. So was everybody else.

That truism went in one puff a year into the recession. Even the prime Sydney waterfront mansion Paradise Sur Mer of Sir Frank and Lady Susan Renouf at Point Piper dropped down from about $19 million to less than half.

Skygarden, on the best commercial site in Australia, was a beautiful building, judged by New York experts to be the best in the world, its quality shown in written comments by property and business leaders, including:

Nick Lucas, *Managing Director of Ballieu Knight Frank, one of the world's biggest real estate agencies: "Sydney is considerably richer for the addition of this marvellous property;"*

Lester D.J. Martin, *director of Richard Ellis, international property consultants: "In every way, professionally, practically and aesthetically, Skygarden is undoubtedly one of the most exceptional retail complexes that I have visited world wide."*

John Singleton, *the advertising tycoon: "Your foresight with Skygarden deserves massive success. Anywhere else in the world, you Ian and your Dad would be national heroes."*

However, quality wasn't enough. Soon after its glittering opening, Tom and Ian sold Skygarden by contract to an Australian property trust group.

But they dropped out at the beginning of the Great Recession when their financing fell through. The Haysons held on to it at high interest until the cycle began to move up again.

In hindsight - hindsight being prognostication with the errors removed - the Hayson Group could have sold the development with its approvals and made a profit of $10 million without building it.

At the time the property market was still roaring along and investors were knocking one another over to buy good properties in the city. When everyone else is "punting the ranch," it's not easy to go against the tide.

Harbourside figured prominently in the Haysons' recession strategy of changing their operation from developing properties to managing assets, a strategy they would continue to follow successfully.

Tom and Ian survived that traumatic recession experience, believing the most important outcome was to preserve their good names.

Their chief bank found they had put everything into bricks and mortar. It not only supported them, treating them as partners through the ordeal, but gave glowing references on them as honest and reliable people.

And as soon as the deep recession was over, banks were willing to lend to them again on the basis of their reputation, honesty and skill.

One senior executive, Murray Sime, said when asked to go on the record for this biography: "We respect and admire Tom Hayson for what he tried to achieve and the way he came through this with his name intact.

"Usually you end up in a huge legal brawl but not in this case. Tom and Ian co-operated in every possible way in difficult times. Tom has never tried to hide from his obligations. I think he was unlucky to encounter the worst recession in 50 or 60 years."

In the washup Tom and Ian lost most of their equity and personal wealth estimated at about $50 million each.

Tom's dedication to his business was such that he never took a large salary or director's fee as other big businessmen did. Although handling huge sums, he'd only ever taken out what he needed to live on comfortably, paying himself what his junior executives earned, $100,000 or $200,000 a year.

He felt he had let his wife down by adopting such a high-minded, non-acquisitive attitude and choosing to put every possible dollar back into the business. Ngaire too had worked hard and he regretted she should have been given cause for concern when things turned tough.

He was a big shot, handling tens of millions, and if he'd done what other top executives in the big time had done, he could have justifiably paid himself millions over the years. But he just wasn't built that way.

In fact, he was so meticulous in meeting his liabilities in the recession that he even cashed in substantial shareholdings put away for a rainy day.

Given the co-operation of the banks, it was a pity then that the Darling Harbour Authority didn't extend the same courtesy to the Hayson Group in its attempts to develop the Darling Walk land in which they had already invested millions of dollars.

It was always recognised that the wide eastern promenade or front of the site facing Cockle Bay in full view of the city was the best part of the land. The rest was under the freeways, bordering on the Chinese Gardens.

The Haysons had spent many millions buying into the full site on a 99-year lease, in excavating and putting down footings.

If they'd invested such a high amount with anyone other than the Government, they would have owned it as freehold. Yet, the DHA dictated harsh conditions.

After the recession hit, nobody would come within a bull's roar of investing in Darling Harbour. But the DHA threatened to take the best part of the Darling Walk land from them unless they developed the back end first. Tom went to Premier Greiner, pleaded their case and was granted a year's extension to produce a worthwhile plan.

Tom scoured Australia and twice went abroad but was unable to find investors. Nobody wanted to know Australia.

The second time around Tom was forced to deal with the head of the Premier's Department, Ken Baxter, whom he found to be brusque and unco-operative.

Finally, the DHA board unflinchingly stuck to the fine print and strict wording of the original lease made in far better times, and seized the best part of the Darling Walk site - the head, about half a hectare, right on Cockle Bay, leaving Tom with the then isolated stomach and tail.

The DHA couldn't do anything in the recession either on that choice piece of land.

They spent nearly two years before they found someone to build an IMAX Theatre there. Ironically, those people used the same IMAX camera that the Haysons had arranged to use from the Powerhouse Museum for their planned IMAX theatre in Darling Walk.

As well as that slap in the face to a private organisation whose money and efforts had created the concept of Darling Harbour, the DHA action also put the rest of the Darling Walk site into limbo for years.

If the DHA had allowed the Haysons to start at the front or develop the back and front together, they would probably have succeeded in developing Darling Walk.

When the Haysons requested more time until the economy improved, the DHA demanded that they pay $5 million to provide temporary sports facilities on the remainder of the site - as a penalty for extending the lease.

That action caused much public anguish and media-created controversy later when the sports facilities had to be removed.

But even worse was to come. Despite the recession, the DHA refused to bend even slightly the original conditions which were tough enough to satisfy any hanging judge of the Old Bailey last century.

Trying to make the rest of the site viable in the tough circumstances of the time, the Haysons came up with a novel idea that should reasonably have been accepted by a public organisation that was supposed to know what was needed to complete the finest waterfront development in the world - a description given to it publicly by James Rouse and other experts.

The DHA refused an imaginative 21st century computerised entertainment-type family hotel on the top of a big traditional entertainment centre which the Haysons planned for the site.

Tom and Ian had performed a minor miracle in rugged times by finding the finance for the hotel venture, convincing the worldwide Holiday Inn group and two other leading hotel groups to express serious interest in funding the complex, subject to development approval.

Not only did the hotel idea provide the entertainment aspect insisted on in the DHA zoning and lease conditions, but it also meant that thousands of visitors a year would be accommodated in Darling Harbour itself.

Fancy bringing extra people into Darling Harbour! Too radical!

They knocked it back, although they had no alternative offer in the middle of a recession. For head-in-the-sand thinking, that rivalled the decision of a previous DHA board in knocking back an Australian-style Tivoli Gardens on the site.

Concrete before camellias!

Tom had wasted his time in flying in at his own expense the Director of world famous Tivoli Gardens from Copenhagen to help mastermind a similar type of development for Darling Harbour.

And also, on the other side of Darling Harbour, the hotel principle he favoured was already established, with the Ibis and Novotel Hotels and a big home unit block allowed on top of car parks. And later other hotels would be allowed inside Darling Harbour.

The hotel proposed by the Haysons, linking up on computer with all other entertainment in Sydney, could have paid for the entertainment area below it.

That treatment by the DHA was the biggest let-down Tom and Ian ever had.

The Hayson Group, because of the tight economic times, were then forced to sell their interest in the Darling Walk lease to a consortium containing the giant Sega entertainment group and a few Sydney investors.

After all the Haysons had done for Darling Harbour, all the money they'd spent, for the inspiration in providing the concept and for their help in kick starting it and promoting it at their own expense, that was shabby treatment.

Tom didn't feel like going to Darling Harbour any more after that. Nor did Ian.

Tom was driving along in Sydney one morning thinking of his problems, his old radio station 2UE playing in the background, when a news item suddenly caused him to listen in disbelief.

His close friend, leading heart surgeon Dr Victor Chang, had been murdered on his way to St Vincents Hospital during a scuffle in Lang Street, Cremorne - just around the corner from the office where the Haysons had started out.

His mind racing, he drove at once to Dr Chang's northside home at Clontarf on Middle Harbour. Police cars were parked outside, people stood around.

He went in to find Victor's wife Anne and daughter Vanessa in distress.

He embraced them both. A weeping Vanessa said: "He loved you Tom."

They knew little more about the shocking incident except that he'd been shot after fighting with two men.

Anne, trying to hold back tears, told him how fate had intervened that morning. "We were supposed to be in Singapore today," she said.

"Victor was to attend a patient there with a dodgy heart, but he couldn't be operated on because he developed a disease. So at the last minute Victor didn't go. As a result, he didn't have any operations this morning at St Vincent's.

"He was more relaxed than usual. While chatting over breakfast we planned a trip to Melbourne where he wanted to see a motor car collection. He nearly didn't attend the hospital today but thought he'd better go in to check on something. He took his time leaving, which again was unusual... "

A policeman politely intervened. Would she go to the City Morgue to identify Victor's body?

Dr Chang had saved Tom's and also Ngaire's life with a heart bypass.

The Cardiac Kids, he called them. What began as a formal patient/doctor relationship became one of warm friendship and close affinity. Victor Chang was born in Shanghai of Australian-Chinese parents and worked hard to become one of the world's leading heart transplant surgeons.

He and Tom spoke the same emotional language, had the same sensitivities and were confidants. Victor discussed the most personal aspects of his busy life. Tom felt they mirrored each other in that they shared feelings of ethnic inferiority.

Probably nobody else suspected that of Victor because he often gave an impression almost of arrogance, was self-assured, in control and was a full-on aggressive, assertive person. But he talked to Tom about the struggles in his life, especially in an Anglo-Saxon world.

He liked to play down the importance of his work, referring to it as "just plumbing." But like all cardiac surgeons he thought he was God in the operating theatre.

After examining Tom at times, he would say: "I am terribly worried about you." Nobody else had ever said that to him, although obviously Tom was putting on too much weight in the wrong places.

When finishing an operation he often rang Tom just after pulling off his surgical mask to talk about a property he'd seen and wanted to buy. Tom would steer him off. But he helped him buy waterfront land at Sydney's ritzy Palm Beach once in unusual circumstances.

Victor was in Adelaide to operate, Tom knew another party was to sign a contract on the Monday, so he drove with Anne to Palm Beach on the Saturday night before and she signed the contract at midnight.

He died at the hands of two lowlife Asian thugs bent on kidnapping him for ransom. His bizarre, unreasoned death caused Tom and millions of others to reflect on how unjust fate could be.

On behalf of all Dr Chang's patients, Tom joined Vanessa to give the eulogy at his funeral in St Mary's Cathedral. He spoke without notes, from the heart.

More than two thousand in the cathedral and millions of TV viewers heard him say: "Dr Chang held my heart and my wife's heart in the palm of his right hand, and with great skill and loving care he performed an operation that gave us both a new lease of life."

At the end of his eulogy, Tom made the first call for funds that helped start a responsive public appeal for the now renowned Victor Chang Cardiac Research Institute.

The best thing to come out of the struggle of Darling Harbour arrived as a bolt from the blue.

Tom and Ngaire at the time were living at *Toft Monks*, an exclusive apartment block in Elizabeth Bay, just before moving to Manly.

Strolling to the mail box one day he pulled out a letter with the Governor-General's emblem on it.

Opening it, he couldn't believe what he read: Would he accept the Order of Australia?

He went to a quiet corner and wept with elation. He had no inkling of it, no idea who had initiated the honour, although Premier Nick Greiner had formally recommended it.

Tom walked around for the next few days with the letter in his pocket, just thinking about it, touching it now and then for reassurance. He knew he would proudly wear the Order in his lapel every day that he lived.

When the announcement was made on Australia Day, the plaudits flooded in. One of the first letters was from former Premier Neville Wran.

Congratulating him, Wran said there was no doubt at all about "the seminal role" Tom played in developing Darling Harbour.

Stuart Hornery, Chairman of Lend Lease Corporation, sent his congratulations. "You have made a tremendous contribution and it's a real pleasure to see it recognised," he said.

Laurie Brereton rang. "You shouldn't be just a Member of the Order of Australia - you should have got the highest award, Knight Commander of the Order of Australia."

Many high profile MPs wrote personal notes. Bob Carr, then NSW Opposition Leader: "Australian society now more than ever needs people who strive for excellence, as you have done."

And from Bryan Stott on the Isle of Man: "In all my life I have never met anybody who is such an enthusiastic and great communicator for his country."

Doug McClelland, ex Australian Senator and former High Commissioner to London: "I don't know anyone who is more Australian than you Tom, or a greater ambassador for your country."

Tom was happy. He only ever wanted to be known as a good Australian.

When as a kid at Barraba he'd gone to school thinking he was just the same as any other Australian youngster around him but was wrongly and unfairly called a black bastard as well as a dago and a wog, the hurt and doubt and confusion it caused had stayed with him, sub-consciously shaping his life.

Now the Order of Australia, for services to business and commerce, might soothe the residue of those emotional scars in the remaining years.

He needed that lift for the Hayson resurgence.

24

THE RESURGENCE

IAN Hayson stood at the ruins and contemplated the past.

Several men with him respectfully moved aside, leaving him to his thoughts. He turned away, thinking they would not see the tears trickling down his cheeks.

It had begun here just over a century ago. From this spot in 1886 his great grandfather Tannous had begun his journey to Australia. Not normally so emotional, Ian looked around at the scattered stones and the remains of two low wall sections that were once part of the Hayson ancestral home.

He gazed down towards the blue Mediterranean and noted the northerly direction old Tannous and the others would have taken to Tripoli. Somehow he felt at home.

That night nearly 500 of the Aitou villagers turned out for a feast in his honour. They made welcoming speeches in English and to his surprise one told how he'd noticed Ian weeping when visiting his roots at what they called "The Rocks."

He spent several weeks in Lebanon, visiting historic places, seeing the Cedars and skiing in the mountains.

The 20-year civil war that began in 1975 had just ended, costing more than 150,000 lives and devastation that would need $25 billion to repair. It seemed that when anyone wanted to start a war in the Middle East, they went to Lebanon to do it.

As always, it ended in poverty, tragedy and exhaustion for so many.

Following his soul-destroying effort with Tom to save the Hayson name and reputation in the Great Recession after doing everything so well, Ian felt the need for a break to restore his vitality and prepare for the future.

He took a year off to visit Europe, looking in on Lebanon and Scotland. Strangely, he had that same feeling of belonging when he visited the birthplace of Ngaire's maternal ancestors near Glasgow.

Then Tom and Ian began rebuilding their business towards pre-recession heights, at least from the point before Darling Harbour so radically intervened in their lives.

In setting out to recreate their fortunes, they vowed things would be different this time. They would not go out and do it on their own by borrowing and leaving themselves open to cycles, they would do it through shrewdness and prudence, looking for special opportunities, taking in a partner and putting together deals on sites that stood alone.

At his venerable age, Tom would now be more in the role of the wise counsellor to his eldest son, with Ian finding the projects and carrying them through design and council approval stages for either sale or development.

Other businessmen wanted to go into partnership with them because they had confidence in their ability.

Investment adviser and accountant John Leece had already seen their survival ability and tenacity to rebuild from difficult situations.

He had observed previously that this was due to Tom's courage, vision, foresight and strength of character to talk to people, open doors to create opportunities, put aside the negatives and build on any available positive. Ian had inherited those same talents.

A senior bank executive early in Tom's career, talking to him one day at the Hayson Neutral Bay home during a bad economic downturn, had looked across at the submarine base and said: "See that submarine there? You're like that. You're under the water but still flying the flag."

By now Ian too was a more mature operator, wiser and shrewder for having been through the wringer. James Rouse had been impressed with him, saying he was in his father's mould. But whereas Tom had come up through the middle end of town, Ian had gone straight into the big end of town and had not had the same grinding experience. He was a quick learner, though, now fully blooded in the vicissitudes of the market.

The Haysons intended returning to their core business - trading. The old Phoenician way of life. Among property developers, the traders who moved in and out quickly knew the market in the short term but probably couldn't pick where it would be in six months.

The other main type, the long term visionaries, tried to anticipate what the market would be in say a year's time.

The long term developer had to be like the farmer who knows that basically a drought is likely every seven years or so.

Ideally he has to keep down stock numbers in his paddock to carry him through the drought, just as a developer has to keep his borrowings at a low ratio to carry him through a bad cycle when it hits. Return on assets was always the thing that counted long term.

Then there were the lucky ones.

Many property developers who survived the Keating recession were simply lucky enough to actually sell just before the crash and become cashed up. Without that luck they would have gone broke.

Kerry Packer had been lucky in pulling off the deal of the decade, although he certainly wouldn't have gone broke without it. He sold his Nine TV Network to Alan Bond in 1987 for $1 billion before the crash and bought it back for less than half the price three years later when Bond collapsed.

The Haysons could have made an absolute fortune if they'd stuck to trading and inner city development, the trend which they began.

The truth is they would have done that if they had not digressed into Darling Harbour, a gut-wrenching venture beset with controversy and interfering bureaucrats and politicians - all for the privilege of risking large sums of their money.

But if they too had sat back like everyone else and done nothing about it, Darling Harbour would *never* have happened.

They wanted to be the pacemakers, the adventurers, the pioneers doing something worthwhile for the community. They wanted to build their dream. As a result, being ahead of their time, they made it all happen for other people to come in and make a lot of money at their expense.

Even the parking stations that Tom and Ian built after noting Baltimore's Inner Harbour parking problems, became gold mines for their new owners.

To see his grand visions accomplished, Tom had had to bring in dozens of experts, sometimes hundreds, to see the work through - bankers, financiers, project managers, artisans of every type, people with skills to deal with a multiplicity of government authorities in taking over large areas of land, technical advisers to draw up leases, solicitors, marketers, planners and designers.

They produced landmark developments, but it cost more.

In future the Haysons would not take those long term risks, exposing themselves to the sorts of things that could go wrong with long building lead times such as spiralling interest rates, fractious unions or refusals and indecision from recalcitrant bureaucrats or councillors.

No longer would they develop exotic, ground-breaking edifices, but neither could they bring themselves to build rubbish. The quality would still be there but the developments would not be too radical.

Tom had finally learned that vision and profitability were too hard to combine in the long term. But he had never really been a routine developer in it just for the profit, unfailingly watching the bottom line all the time, putting up an ordinary-type building so that money came first in any eventuality.

He was innovative, had the ideas and could have sold his vision and services, letting someone else try to put it into bricks and mortar.

He and Ian had been satisfying their consciences by fulfilling the dreams they had for their city, thinking they would make money at the same time.

By all standards they had developed some wonderful buildings, ones that would remain as monuments to their efforts, from the Golden Gate through to Harbourside and Skygarden. Now it was someone else's turn to contribute selflessly to the facilities and character of the city.

Apart from Darling Harbour, the Haysons started the movement that brought the whole of the inner city of Sydney to life. Like most other world cities, the heart of Sydney died as huge regional shopping malls sprang up in the suburbs.

They were the first to focus on inner city living by renovating existing buildings rather than tearing them down in rundown suburbs close to the city like Surry Hills, Darlinghurst, East Sydney, Kings Cross, Alexandria, Paddington, even out to Bondi and on the lower North Shore. The Haysons were first in the world to use "inner city living" as an advertising slogan.

They were first in with loft apartments after Ian saw small groups of people banding together to buy whole empty floors inside warehouses in Greenwich Village in New York and converting them into the rough forerunner of loft apartments.

In real estate terms, their pioneering of the inner city living concept and office and unit strata titling will go down as one of the great contributions to Australian commercial and residential living.

Through others copying their revolutionary work in Darling Harbour, they also put colour, light and entertainment into otherwise dull and mundane shopping centres.

After seeing their work, no longer could anyone think quick, cheap and nasty when the word "developer" was mentioned. People had even come from abroad to study the colour and variety Tom had pioneered in Australian shopping centres. It gave him a sense of reward.

Tom had not been chasing money in Darling Harbour like the other developers and leading businessmen who were invited in by Premier Wran, but who stayed out because they couldn't see any financial return.

As someone said at that meeting, the only thing Darling Harbour had going for it was that the Government would be paying for it. Nobody else would touch it.

The difference was that Tom could see it in its finished form with millions of people enjoying themselves, transforming an area two-thirds the size of Sydney's central business district that had been lying there for years forgotten, unsuspected and decaying. He was looking at it as an achievement for his city, to give the city a heart.

Achievement. *That's what made Tommy run.*

All because he was made to feel inferior as a sensitive boy in a predominantly Anglo-Saxon society when they called him a dirty dago.

Darling Harbour had knocked the stuffing out of him mentally and physically, mentally because he'd had to put so much effort into it, physically because it gave him a heart attack with high blood pressure for the rest of his life.

Month after month running into years he'd been pinned to his desk, feverishly pounding phones to enlist support, marshalling his inner strength to talk up all the negative attitudes surrounding what he wanted to do, with friends and even some of his own planners saying forget about it, it's just a dream, it won't happen.

But they never broke his spirit, which emerged as strong as ever.

And through it all, when flying high and routinely handling millions of dollars, he never changed his lifestyle, remaining the same simple but enthusiastic bloke.

Many times he'd had the opportunity to amass a fortune and keep it, but he saw money as something that only allowed a person to indulge himself. He found no need to surround himself with the trappings of wealth when he could gain far greater satisfaction from achievement.

Tom realised he should have been ruthless. But ruthlessness didn't come easily to a man who, if he saw an injured dog or bird in a public place, would take it to a vet and pay for its treatment, a man who in earlier days would go to the chemist to pick up medicines for his elderly tenants.

However, he knew he could have been tougher in selecting some of the people around him for their skills in certain areas. And he should not have delegated so much. No longer would the heart rule.

That problem would be rectified. In future they would focus on tighter, hands-on control.

Tom made the vow that he would be extremely reluctant to ever deal with governments again, no matter how good the project. They were too acquisitive, just too tough without heart or compassion.

He would never forget how a Liberal Government through the DHA had taken the best third of his Darling Walk land on which he'd paid dearly for a 99-year lease.

At one stage he'd brought in a Disney executive who wanted six months for a feasibility study before Disney would decide whether to build a leisure complex on the whole site, but he could not obtain the necessary extension of time.

Whenever he gazed on that site, he felt it was morally his and had been filched from him. He could perhaps have understood it if the DHA had had an alternative at the time.

Eventually, on the inferior part of his Darling Walk site that was left, Tom arranged with Sega Enterprises for a $100 million hi-tech theme park to be built there.

But control and the financial return passed to a local group and two South African businessmen. Tom helped them in every way.

At that stage a Labor Government was back in power with Premier Bob Carr, and money was once more being spent on Darling Harbour.

At Sega World's retail launch of the theme park before 200 leading citizens in October 1996, the new Chairman of the DHA, Gerry Gleeson, made the first public acknowledgment of Tom Hayson's role in Darling Harbour.

Gerry, who had known from the start what Tom Hayson had done and respected him for it, lauded him for "the principal contribution" he had made in the overall planning and development of Darling Harbour. Pressmen were there but nothing appeared in the papers.

The new Minister, Michael Knight, who was not then aware of Tom's major contribution, made no reference to him but welcomed "the architect of Darling Harbour, Neville Wran and the builder, Laurie Brereton."

However, after Knight's remarks, several people came up to Tom and said things like "we know this place wouldn't be here if it wasn't for you."

As the speeches ended and the drinking began in earnest, he slipped away quietly, pausing in his car as he approached the Harbour Bridge to look back on the sparkling scene of Darling Harbour lit up at night.

He wasn't bitter, just disappointed and a little angry still that he had not been given more of a fair go over the Darling Walk land by the previous Authority.

His feeling of injustice would not be eased in the near future either when his earlier predictions of "platinum in them thar hills" came true and Darling Harbour became the greatest residential and commercial generator in Sydney's history.

Billions of dollars were being poured in by leading developers like Lend Lease and billionaire tycoon Harry Triguboff to redevelop the western fringe of the city behind Darling Harbour, with hotels, restaurants apartment blocks and new waterfront communities such as Jacksons Landing on the Pyrmont peninsula, showing views to the Harbor Bridge, the Anzac Bridge, the city, Balmain, even over to the Opera House and to the Heads, vistas of one of the most beautiful harbours in the world.

The once dirty backside of the city had shaken off its stigma and was now buzzing with new life as a waterfront renaissance took place - from Cockle Bay, beyond Sussex Street to the harbour fronts of Ultimo and Pyrmont and to the Haymarket.

All because of one thing - the new Darling Harbour.

What Tom had started there when nobody else in the commercial world would risk being involved was now adding not millions but hundreds of millions of dollars to the State coffers in rates and taxes, stamp duties and various other development earners.

Where was that pale-looking elephant?

Where indeed were the knockers? Eating their words and presumably choking on them. Unfortunately many Australians tend to be a race of knockers, somewhat insular and reluctant to accept radical new ideas until these have passed muster first somewhere else in the world.

They also like to pull down anyone who tries to better themselves. That's where the Americans are different, admiring those who get ahead, using it as a spur to improve themselves.

Even the Fairfax press had now joined in the party, having its offices in the 27-storey IBM Tower in Sussex Street on the eastern shore of Darling Harbour - Mort Hoppenfeld's original site where the casino was supposed to have been built - Fairfax's staff and executives enjoying the view of a vibrant Darling Harbour and beyond.

If the Haysons had been able to hold on to all their land in and around Darling Harbour, by the year 2000 it would have been worth $1 billion. That's how much the values had soared.

But like many other top-drawer Australian property entrepreneurs, they didn't cry over their losses. They were soon back, with a re-invigorated Ian leading a hands-on operation and Tom, at 81, as patriarchal chairman.

As the property market improved they were entertaining new speculative projects again, minimising risk through joint venture partners and reducing lead times to a maximum of 12 months.

Essentially the Haysons moved back into inner city living development, their natural environment where they had so much expertise.

In early ventures Ian quickly developed 160 new home units in the inner city, bought sites for another 1,000 units and sold them at a profit.

But he was not straying far from the Haysons' special skills in dealing with existing properties and developing their potential.

With profits from speculative ventures they branched into income-producing properties or businesses such as hotels, buying sub-regional shopping centres that showed further development scope.

One purchase was the Kogarah Town Shopping Centre, containing Woolworths and Franklins and 35 speciality shops, another was the Hillsdale Shopping Centre near Maroubra with Woolworths, Franklins and 42 specialty shops. Partners were later secured for both ventures.

They also bought the Metropole Hotel at Cremorne partly for unit conversion, refurbishing its shops and supermarket, renaming it the Cremorne Town Centre and improving the image of the area. In another move they also bought the Top of the Town Hotel at Kings Cross, again for units, sharing the risk with two other asset-rich partners.

They did something similar with the former Her Majestys Theatre site near Central Railway. After negotiating its purchase, they gained approval of development plans and sold it on to others.

They soon built up high income-producing assets, showing a strong level of assets over liabilities.

Tom had fulfilled his pioneering desires with the Harbourside Marketplace. At the time his thinking was 10 or 15 years ahead of the average Australian in his field, probably because of the creative talent he was born with, strengthened by his journalistic and broadcasting experience and vast travel, opening up possibilities by seeing different things abroad which he adapted for Australia.

Now it was for Ian to return to more basic ventures.

It wasn't the spectacular, high flying headline-grabbing stuff of dreams like Darling Harbour, Skygarden or The Golden Gate, but nonetheless it was a safe and solid type of business.

The type on which a new empire could be built.

25

THOUGHTS OF A DINKUM AUSSIE

THE flowers on the altar were fresh and beautiful.

What seemed like thousands of small electric candles lit the statues inside the church.

The Stations of the Cross with their delicately carved figures in marble and stone adorning the walls were illuminated by chandeliers.

Two immaculately robed priests and several attendants were in place and the organist, a teenage boy, was seated ready to play. A choir assembled in the wings.

All was in readiness for the special mass.

Outside the Maronite Church of St Sarkis and St Bacchus it was almost dark. The big church on the hill, named after two saints who had been Roman soldiers, was the newest of the four Christian churches in Aitou. It overlooked the Lebanese shore and the hazy Mediterranean far below.

As Tom and Ngaire arrived at the church by car, villagers were crowded around outside near an enormous oak tree. They immediately called out their name in English and Arabic: "Hayson, Hayson. El Hosn El Hosn."

Swarming around, they wanted to touch Tom. Some of the ladies kissed and hugged him, patted him on the back and warmly shook his hands. Several of the men kissed Ngaire. Finally they were led into the church.

Tom and Ngaire were mentioned all through the mass in their honour.

Hearing their names was the only part of the service they understood because it was in Aramaic, the ancient Semitic language still used in parts of Lebanon. The music and singing made Tom feel highly emotional.

When they filed outside, it was dark. Suddenly the lights came on. The cheers and applause were ear splitting. Below in the village the yellowish glow of street lights could be seen for the first time.

The churchgoers, joined by more people from the village, talked excitedly to Tom and Ngaire in English, French and Arabic. Speeches were made, flashlights popped and one English speaker pointed to a big light over the church entrance lighting up the scene like day and said in a raised voice: "One of your lights, one of your lights, God bless you."

Tom and Ngaire were then ushered to the oak tree. They pulled a cord to unveil a plaque officially turning on the village street lights.

Expecting just a simple church service, he was overwhelmed that people had turned out in their finery to pay homage to him.

It was the second time Tom and Ngaire had been back to Lebanon since the war ended. On his first postwar visit he'd returned to the village and wondered what he could do for Aitou as a gesture to his forefathers.

They had electricity in the houses but no street lights. The villagers couldn't afford it and the Government, burdened with a huge rebuilding programme after the civil war, would not do it.

It cost Tom $80,000 but gave him great pleasure.

After the mass and ceremony they were taken to a French restaurant in the village where 250 people feted them. Tom felt like a conquering hero returning to the fold. Leading citizens made speeches in Arabic, including one by the Mayor, Bakhos Bechara, Tom's fifth cousin.

They presented him with a brass plaque mounted on polished wood, signed by village leaders and inscribed with the words: "Our deep appreciation to the great emigrant. Mr Tom Hayson and his wife Ngaire. To whom the people of Aitou, Lebanon, will always carry a special love for the lighting of the roads in the village of his ancestors. April 27, 1997."

A Beirut businessman and Aitou summer resident, sitting next to him, said: "We could probably have put the money together over time, but we didn't think of it. It's strange that it takes an outsider to do something selflessly like this for the village."

Tom and Ngaire spent a week in and around Aitou before visiting other parts of Lebanon. He was surprised how Westernised even Aitou had become.

Although the villagers were still poor, they were clean, wore Western clothes and like the rest of Lebanon, their lifestyle was that of a Western enclave in the middle of an Arab Middle East. "Modern" Aitou had a huge radio and TV communications tower known all over Lebanon.

Rocky but a little greener than he remembered it, Aitou epitomised the rest of the Christian parts of Lebanon, abounding with religious symbols.

Christian Lebanon, especially here in the north, had more memorials, tabernacles, churches and shrines than any other part of the world. Every few hundred metres appeared a shrine to Jesus or Our Lady.

Down in the Valley of the Saints they saw where the hermits and the early Christians had hidden from their Turkish oppressors, ancient caves that mostly had now become small churches.

This was hallowed religious territory, where Christianity had come immediately after it began in Palestine.

They listened to the stories of local historians but took with a grain of salt their claims that it was here in North Lebanon where Jesus first revealed to his disciples that he was divine.

They also didn't believe another piece of folklore which said 11 of the disciples of Jesus came from Lebanon. The Lebanese are fond of telling such tales but scholars refute them.

However, there was no doubting that Jesus and some of his disciples visited Southern Lebanon or that the religious fervour of Christian Lebanese went right back to the beginnings of Christ.

Tom also visited the spot in South Lebanon where Jesus according to the Book of St John performed his first miracle by turning water into wine. For extra true believers, the containers said to have been used at the time, still lay in the ground.

He thought it unbelievable that two major religions, Christianity and Islam, could exist side by side, so close yet so far apart.

Snow still covered the peaks of Mount Lebanon and the fir trees above Aitou, although winter had not yet set in when Tom and Ngaire drove further up to see one of the few visible monuments to the Phoenicians, the Cedars of Lebanon.

The stand of 400 or so cedars at Becharreh was among the finest remaining from the huge forests which the Phoenicians cut down and hauled to the coast to trade with the Pharaohs or to build their own ships for trading and fighting. They covered the bows of their fighting galleys with bronze for ramming.

Tom climbed over a fence and touched one patriarch which incredibly was between 6,000 and 8,000 years old, going back to the time when man first settled in the area. This ageless giant, representing the emblem on the nation's flag, had survived from the dawn of Lebanon's history.

The Phoenicians had lived all through these mountains felling the cedars in pre-Christ times of antiquity. Historians could not be sure but believed Aitou was so old it was probably founded by the Phoenicians as a camp or staging post.

In his quest to trace the ancestors of the Lebanese people, Tom visited the National Museum in Beirut, a city older than Rome, to view the ornaments of a Phoenician civilisation lasting more than 1,000 years.

There, apart from pottery and carvings, gold-leafed figurines and gold necklaces, he saw carved on a marble coffin of the King of Byblos one of the earliest known examples of the Phoenician alphabet going back more than 1,000 years before Christ.

The 22 symbols which the Phoenicians gave to the world were far simpler than any other attempted form of writing, each representing a distinctive sound.

From Beirut Tom drove north along the coast to Byblos, believed to be the oldest inhabited city in the world where archaeological diggings have traced Lebanese history for almost 7,000 years. Here, man settled one of the world's first known urban communities.

To come to grips with its past, one had to imagine a town lived in for 70 centuries. London could count only 10 centuries, New York less than four.

To reach there he travelled the route that is probably the most historic in the world on which the great empires of the past, including the Romans and Egyptians, marched their armies.

All those civilisations, founded on force, had disappeared but the Phoenicians who traded from ports on the same coast were still around, their identity preserved through the Lebanese.

In Byblos Tom and Ngaire were lucky enough to see French and Lebanese archaeologists just unearth a Phoenician bath, with evidence of running hot water having been used thousands of years ago.

Returning to the south, they studied two other great Phoenician coastal cities, Tyre and Sidon. From Tyre, which dated back to the third millennium BC, Phoenicia pioneered navigation by the stars and extended its empire to do business all over the Mediterranean, sending its ships to found Carthage on the African coast, sailing completely around

Africa, to Spain and Atlantic ports and as far north as Cornwall and Wales.

It was also from Tyre that the alphabet, invented in Byblos, was introduced to Greece.

Here too the Phoenicians held out for 13 years in one of history's great sieges against the bloodthirsty King Nebuchadnezzar of Babylon, with the defenders supplied in their island fortress by Phoenician ships.

Finally Alexander the Great took the heroic city after building a causeway to the island.

Confronted by so much history, Tom could only marvel at the exploits and achievements of his distant Phoenician ancestors, who in their trading were past masters at diplomacy and deal making.

Before leaving Aitou, Tom spent some time at "The Rocks."

From here he could look up the hill and see the Church of St Sarkis and St Bacchus. Nothing was growing on the disused land except an olive tree, two or three fig trees and a withered old lemon tree.

After Grandfather Tannous had left there, his younger brother Bechara the Dumb continued to live in the house until his parents died. Then he went to live with his sister Sarah, who had married John Jabrin Slaimen from a neighbouring village. At that point, in 1906, half the land was given to John Slaimen and the other half still belonged to the El Hessen family.

They told Tom the land was now his. But he didn't want it, feeling it didn't belong to him. Then the Mayor told him the family owned some nice land further down the mountain in the valley.

"We'll give you that and you can build yourself a good house and even if you don't want to come back here to live, it will remind you of your family," said the Mayor.

Tom was tempted. But he had mixed feelings. These were his people and he felt at home among them. He thought about it again when he stood at The Rocks. He picked up two stones and held them in his hands.

Then he put them down on one of the low walls, rested his palms on top of them and felt them lovingly.

Suddenly an overwhelming feeling came over him.

He said to Ngaire: "I'm an Australian. I don't want to push my roots too far into the village. The past is past."

It was as though the baggage of the years was cleared from his mind in that moment.

No longer was there any tug of war between two different cultures, two distant places.

For the first time he realised and accepted fully that he was of Lebanese descent but was 100 per cent Australian.

No matter where he ended his days, he wanted to return to the little town of Barraba where he was born, where he lay on the river bank looking up into the sky, dreaming. Barraba was where he wanted to be buried.

Before visiting Lebanon this time he'd gone back to Barraba to look around and reflect on the past. Among those he met was a former school boy who used to taunt him.

"Why did you call me 'Licorice' at school?" Tom asked, quietly.

"Oh," the old man said, "it was because you were always eating licorice."

Tom knew it wasn't true, of course, but thought it was nice of him to put it that way. Racism was no longer in the man's mind and to pursue it further would be embarrassing and pointless.

Besides, it reflected a change in attitude wrought by time.

Coming to terms with his demons in Aitou gave him a good feeling. It seemed to erase the angry thoughts he'd harboured all through the years against some Anglo-Saxons. He could see now how foolish he'd been to feel inferior, but it had been something tangible beyond his control, something that went deeply into his soul.

He told himself: "If someone calls me a dago now, I'm not going to feel hurt as I did when young. I'm going to say listen, I'm probably more Australian than you. How long have you been here? Don't forget, you're a migrant too from somewhere along the line."

It had not come as a revelation, nor did it mean he felt any less loving or proud about Lebanon. The understanding had come slowly, only just crystallising on this visit.

He saw Lebanon as a place of many different races, some dark, some with olive skins and many with fair skins and even red hair. But in spite of their many differences, especially in religion, the one basic thing that stood out in all their troubles was their belief in themselves as Lebanese.

He thought of all the things that had helped bring about his different attitude - the changes in Australia, the diversity, the mixture of races now from 150 different countries with one in four of the population being born outside Australia and 40 per cent of Australians having at least one migrant parent, and emanating from it all the greater degree of tolerance towards non-Anglo immigrants.

He felt more at home now in Australia than at any time in his life.

Tom looked back and thought about the tough times his grandparents, parents and their relatives had been through and his own experiences at school and as a youth.

Australia was then a racist country, predominantly white Anglo-Saxon, isolated and insular and largely ignorant of other cultures and races.

In the days of late 19th century when his grandparents emigrated from Lebanon, the Australian community was afraid of losing jobs to the newcomers and afraid of other changes the migrants might cause. That was always at the centre of racism anywhere - the fear of change.

But old Tannous and his brother and Tom's grandparents on his mother's side had gone out into the bush, carried their worldly wealth on their backs, toiled and mixed with Australians and earned respect. Tannous quickly became an Australian citizen.

They had little choice if they wished to survive and be welcomed in a strange land. And they did it hard compared with later generations of migrants who had the benefit of social services, community support groups, free English language lessons and anti-discrimination laws. Tom's grandparents had only the help organised within their own groups.

But if prepared to work and be good citizens, they always believed they could make it. Tom's forebears had made it because they supported themselves and went out into the community joining in with Anglo Australians.

His brothers Claude and Bill and sisters Joyce and Pauline had become patriotically and emotionally Australian in every sense because of his mother's wisdom in putting her Lebanese background behind her and insisting that they embrace Australian values and lifestyle.

That was still in the days of bigotry when more than 90 per cent of the population was of Anglo-Saxon stock, when Australia was an insular British outpost in what was basically an Asian region.

Although viewed with suspicion and often hurt by name calling, in retrospect they assimilated fairly easily into Australian society.

The tolerance and understanding Australians developed for the Haysons, for other Lebanese, for Greeks and Italians, came about because they integrated into the Australian community.

That acceptance then extended to other ethnic groups as second generations married into Australian families.

To Tom the wonderful thing about Australia was that someone like him could come from such poor and humble beginnings and, with nothing to recommend him except hard work and faith, make it to the top and earn the respect and friendship of his fellow countrymen.

Any poor migrant could still carve out a decent future with hard work, a bit of ability and a good attitude, because Australian society gave every newcomer that opportunity.

But Tom hoped that in the more enlightened atmosphere existing in the new millennium year of 2001, others would not have to struggle as he had done because they felt racially inferior. That was too hard, too corrosive of one's soul. He often prayed for goodwill on all sides.

If they could succeed by working and striving, both giving and receiving goodwill and understanding, Australia had every chance of remaining an oasis in a generally racist world.

Returning home, Tom was still in reflective mood.

He thought about the changes immigration had brought since he worked as a junior clerk in a Sydney foundry, discussing it with friends and family.

Australia was now a better place compared to that time when he had his nose broken trying to resist racist remarks.

The country was more tolerant and interesting due to the fusion of different cultures and ideas, the varied cuisine, the blending of different races.

His fervent wish was to see Australians treat one another for their contributions and for what they were as individuals, rather than where they came from or what they looked like, as in the colour of their skins.

There was still a way to go, but Australia was potentially, if not already, the best example of a multi-racial society in the world, even more diverse than the United States, and so far without its extremes.

Tom was proud that in his own family, through his union with Ngaire and the marriages of his children, there were 11 different nationalities -

Lebanese, Australian, English, Scottish, Irish, Polish, Dutch, German, Spanish, Russian and Italian.

At family gatherings he was particularly proud of the fact that many of his 12 grandchildren had blonde hair and blue eyes.

Such diversity, reflecting the changing face of Australia, suggested the old practice of wog calling should surely be over.

The mono culture that existed in Tom's youth had been diluted forever by intermarriage and gradual change. Australia had clearly gone well past the point of no return as an immigrant society.

Tom also looked forward to the day when the words "ethnic" and "multiculturalism" would not need to be used at all.

When that point was reached, migrants could take their place naturally in the Australian community, hopefully accepted without reservation by the Australian-born population, as long as they were decent law-abiding citizens.

As the product of a migrant family, he had reservations about the word "multicultural." He could understand why many of his fellow Australians didn't like the word.

Theoretically, multiculturalism has a lot going for it as a policy aimed at creating social cohesion, to give everyone a sense of belonging and to be treated fairly and equally. That is the Australian ideal.

The new policy of multiculturalism seems a natural progression from the dismantling of White Australia. But labels like that often create a false impression of consensus.

In practice, it can have undesirable consequences. If it means forming separate cultures or ghettoes, rather than a blending of cultures as had occurred gradually in Australia over previous years without the use of labels, then the wonderful intention behind it will fail, and that policy can be divisive and go against the interests of the majority of Australians.

In extreme cases, it can even lead to violence, racism and discrimination - the last thing any true Australian wants to see.

Tom dearly wished to see people in the country he loved regard themselves as Australians first and foremost, rather than ethnic entities, just as Americans put their nationality as Americans before anything else.

He admired the patriotism of Americans under their flag and hoped one day to see the same feeling of pride and unity by Australians under their national flag, for which Australians had bravely fought and died.

The United States as the biggest immigrant society on earth, was probably the most successful, in spite of some serious black/white difficulties. They didn't call themselves multicultural but simply multi-racial. Migrants were expected to become Americans and live up to their nation's ideals.

Australia saw the first positive national advantages of people from different cultures working together in the Snowy Mountains hydro-electric scheme, just after World War 11.

About 80,000 migrants from 30 countries formed the bulk of the 100,000 workers who toiled together in freezing conditions to achieve one of the world's great engineering feats.

They worked, frolicked, drank, gambled and made love together in rugged terrain to drill through mountains and build 16 dams, seven power stations, 145 km of interconnected tunnels and 80 km of aqueducts. That was the real beginning of multi-racial Australia under mass migration.

Fifty years later, in October 1999, about 15,000 of them reunited in the Snowy in a flood of memories. As one "now proud Australian" said on television: "We didn't call it multiculturalism or any other ism. We just got together and did the job and it worked well."

Those workers became good Australians under the then broad policy of integration and assimilation. It worked well just as the Snowy experiment had.

President Clinton, while addressing migrants at a graduation ceremony in Portland, Oregon in June, 1998, had a word on the subject for racially mixed America that had a strong lesson for Australia.

He said: "Ethnic pride is a very good thing. But pride in one's ethnic and racial heritage must never become an excuse to withdraw from the larger American community. That does not honour diversity, it breeds divisiveness. And that could weaken America."

The president also said: "You must honour our laws. Embrace our culture. Learn our language. Know our history and, when the time comes, you should become citizens."

If he'd said that in Australia in the climate of absurd political correctness that grew up by the 1990s, he'd have been branded a racist.

Tom hoped that something else the President said on the speed of change through migration would be understood too by all non-migrants in Australia.

President Clinton said: "When Americans hear the new accents, see the new faces, they feel unsettled. They worry that the new immigrants come not to work hard, but to live off our largesse. They are afraid that the America they know and love is becoming a foreign land.

"This reaction may be understandable, but it is wrong."

Dr Stephen Fitzgerald, a former ambassador to China commissioned by the Hawke Labor Government to study immigration policy, noted in his three-volume report released in Federal Parliament in 1988 that there was disquiet about the way immigration was thought to be changing Australia.

"Multiculturalism," he said, "associated in the public mind with immigration, is seen by many as social engineering which actually invites injustice, inequality and divisiveness."

Dr Fitzgerald urged an open debate on Asian immigration, saying if it was out in the open, like so many other immigration issues, it might not seem so threatening. But in the ridiculous atmosphere that had grown up in which public discussion was seen as racism, the Government buried the report to avoid criticism.

John Howard, when Federal Opposition Leader in 1988, tried to get a debate going on immigration in what he called a new One Australia policy.

Called upon to explain his attitude, Howard said that regardless of a migrant's ethnic or racial background, he wanted to see at the end of the day a situation where loyalty and commitment to Australian values, Australian traditions and institutions should take precedence over everything else.

He said: "I think the objection I have to multiculturalism is that it runs the risk of promoting separate cultural and political development, also the risk of promoting dual loyalty.

"I don't want somebody who is, say, Greek-born or of Greek ancestry, to forget Greece, the Greek language or Greek customs. But what I do want is an Australia, one Australia, where the ultimate commitment to Australian values takes precedence."

He too was accused of "racism" and stepped back from the question. Australia has still not had its rational immigration debate, not even after Pauline Hanson raised the subject rather more nakedly in connection with her One Nation policy 10 years later.

But, in spite of the stifling of public discussion, it became obvious that a majority of the Australian population was concerned that Australia was becoming a country divided into minority ethnic groups, moving away from fostering the idea that Australians should form one homogeneous society.

There was a clear feeling that all Australians were not being treated equally, that we were in danger of becoming an amorphous mix of ethnic groups, many looking for special advantages.

That division threatened the development of harmonious relations between new migrants, indigenous people and most of the older established population.

A perception had grown that the Labor Governments under Prime Ministers Hawke and Keating were pandering to ethnic minority groups to woo their votes. It became irksome that anyone who criticised or even questioned immigration policies was branded racist and howled down , even if their concerns were genuinely felt.

This general attitude was accurately summed up in author Paul Sheehan's 1998 book, *Among the Barbarians - the Dividing of Australia*, where he said:

"The central fantasy of the multicultural industry is that Australia should be a cultural federation.

"But Australia has a distinct, dominant, cohesive, assimilative, blended culture that has been painstakingly built through trial and error.

"There is an enormous difference between the self-evident diversity of Australia's multi-racial society and the big protective tent under which this diversity is thriving. Take away that big tent - Australian culture - and this diversity curdles into state-sponsored tribal animosities."

Most Australians, for instance, have genuine concerns over ethnically-based crime gangs.

The problem is that many of the young new migrants have known little other than violence and civil war before emigrating to this country and, unlike earlier migrants, have no respect for Australian institutions.

This is particularly galling to the older migrants who have worked hard and made successful lives for themselves in this country, contributing substantially to its culture and well-being.

A soft attitude from authorities towards the gangs is seen as weakness by the young criminals, and a placid, easy-going community is regarded by them as something heaven-sent to be exploited.

Authorities need to sharpen up to stop foreign criminals and those of questionable character entering this country, and to deal more forcefully here with young criminal gangs of all and any origins.

Professor Marie Bashir, the NSW Governor and Australia's first Governor of Lebanese descent, has spoken out courageously against this "disappointing, anti-social trend" among sub-sections of the Lebanese community.

Speaking at the Australian Lebanese Association's annual youth awards in July, 2001, Professor Bashir said direct evidence indicated that the good name of Lebanese Australians was under threat. She said the first generation of Lebanese migrants were law-abiding and had developed pride in their new home.

The fine legacy of Lebanese migration was being undermined by the trend. She suggested the best way of handling it was to identify the reason for the alienation and get down to solving it.

It also worries Australians, including all those of migrant backgrounds who have found happiness in Australia, that some self-interested minority groups are trying to push their cultures to the exclusion of all others.

If that flourishes, the degree of tolerance needed to make Australia's great experiment work in the long term, is unlikely to be forthcoming.

Even many migrants are unimpressed at the attitudes of some of the more recent migrant arrivals who want to rapidly change the existing order, after living here just a short time.

Migrants who have settled in, and natural-born Australians, believe that change should evolve naturally over time, as it has in the past, not by decree or through pressure groups.

Australia is a new country and it's not unreasonable to expect that those who come here to take advantage of what the country has to offer in the way of security, harmony, social benefits and lifestyle, should respect its customs and laws. That's why many migrants chose to live here in the first place.

Old ethnic arguments and bitterness abroad also have no place here and should not be imported.

Violence in "peaceful" street protests should not be tolerated as it has been, and offenders should be punished by law, especially those disrespectful and mindless enough to burn the Australian flag.

Our politicians, instead of being gutless and uncommitted on these issues as they have been, should strongly support the police and give them whatever powers and resources they need to see that the law is upheld.

Certain values must, or at least should, stand at the heart of the present nation as a basis for the future, otherwise the cohesive society which all migrants and other Australians hope and pray for, will not be achieved.

Tom Hayson loved Australia and its new cosmopolitan, richly diverse way of life, an achievement that had been shaped and moulded by the struggle and contributions of all newcomers over the years, and with the co-operative spirit of the Australians who accepted them.

He'd seen the earlier lack of understanding and insularity of Australians towards migrants begin to change in his manhood, eroding in the years since.

He realised his suffering at the hands of many Anglo-Saxon bigots in his early days had been due to ignorance and isolation on their part, and too much sensitivity on his. He would never forget it but he'd forgiven his tormentors long ago, having come to understand that Australians were the most tolerant and well-disposed race of people in the world.

Tom deplored the attempts by all those in Australia who were trying to artificially submerge the dominant British Anglo-Saxon traditions and heritage on which the European society in Australia was based. The New Australia was adapting, being varied and shaped by the way those traditions and indigenous values blended in with new minority cultures.

There can be no argument that Australia has a right to preserve its essential character and values.

For instance, for the record, English should be proclaimed the official language of this country.

Why not, when the Malaysian Prime Minister, Dr Mahathir, complains that Chinese Australians here are "oppressed" because they are expected to speak "foreign" English?

It's a poor show when English is regarded as a foreign language in this country, and time to do something about it.

One worry is that some ethnic groups seem not to want to blend their cultures, seeing their religion or ethnicity as some kind of political philosophy that should assert itself in a superior way.

The future Australian now in transition will emerge naturally in time, just as Tom's own family, in all its multi-racial hues, has developed over a century into proud Australians from their humble Lebanese village beginnings and Anglo-Saxon and European links.

Tom often thanked God he was born in a country that stemmed from English traditions - for no other reason than in all his worldly travels, he had not seen any better form of democracy.

He hoped that that background didn't disappear from Australia's language or way of life, or was broken down or over-simplified too much, because he genuinely believed the traditions inherited by migrants in Australia were the best available and a proven model, based on decency, fairness and as good a system of justice as existed anywhere.

There was room for every culture here, but he believed others should merge with Australian values and traditions to enhance what mainstream Australia offered, showing understanding to all, rather than being self-assertive.

That's how he idealistically saw the Australian of the future, giving and receiving tolerance.

Having such a polyglot racial mix was essentially risky, but the most promising thing Tom observed was that, unlike in his youth, children from various cultures were now playing happily together at schools and sharing different foods without any sign of prejudice over race or colour.

I went with Tom one day to a number of schools in inner and western Sydney to see this new attitude in operation at play and in the classroom, and the natural happy way it was occurring indeed engendered a feeling of warmth and hope for the future.

Australia's uniqueness as an island continent, distantly separated from other countries and having it all to ourselves, is blessed with every chance for our great race experiment to succeed.

With a bit of luck, and vigilance, we can become an inspiration to the rest of the troubled world.

But vigilance is not enough. Clearly the wider Australian community is now looking to the Federal Government for urgent leadership and action to curb ethnic tensions, which are likely to increase in the future, particularly in cities like Sydney.

These racial problems are not confined to any single ethnic group, so I will not mention a group. The newspapers and broadcaster Alan Jones have responsibly brought these problems to public notice.

But I offer a vital observation. Australia has had a massive immigration programme since WW11, but at no stage has any Federal Government seen fit to consult the Australian people on either the nature, extent or character of our immigration policy, or the source from which Australia should draw its migrants to establish the ethnic mix of our population.

It has been social engineering on a gigantic scale from our elected Governments without any mandate from the people, and it affects our future.

The Federal Government is seen as too liberal in identifying people outside the Christian religion as suitable migrants.

Suggested solution: I propose two courses of action: First, the Constitution should be amended at once to declare English as Australia's one and only official language.

Second, there should be a referendum seeking the approval of the people of Australia to write into the Constitution, as a broad principle, that Australia's ethnic mix or composition in the future shall be determined by the current mix as at the last Federal Census taken in August, 2001.

Such a fixed and non-manipulated quota system here would save us suffering some of America's racial problems. The US for many years had a quota system but then opened the floodgates, and Hispanic migrants have now become a major force - causing serious tension with the Negro population.

We don't want that sort of tension.

26

STRIKING OLYMPIC GOLD

THE applause was deafening and went on and on.

The distinguished guests from many parts of the world stamped their feet and yelled their congratulations to such an extent that the man at the centre of it sitting at the official table was embarrassed.

"Bravo" and "great work" shouted some of the foreign visitors. An obvious Australian in the crowd called out "you beauty!"

More than 160 world leaders in waterfront development were gathered at a dinner in Sydney to mark Darling Harbour's third International Waterfront Development conference.

They came from the US, England, Europe, South Africa, Asia and South America. The dinner, in the Star Room on top of the IMAX theatre in Darling Harbour, was a highlight of the conference. The date was September 25, 1998, just 10 years after Darling Harbour was initially opened by the Queen.

A new-look Darling Harbour Authority was host. Two similar conferences had been held before by earlier authorities but tonight's main guest had not been invited then.

A radical change had followed the election of a Labor Government again in NSW. The new Premier, Bob Carr, had appointed Gerry Gleeson, Neville Wran's former departmental mandarin, as chairman of a revamped Darling Harbour Authority.

Until his retirement Gleeson had been the State's most powerful public servant and keeper of secrets. He'd been at that meeting in Wran's office 14 years before when Wran tried to interest Australia's biggest entrepreneurs in helping the Government develop Darling Harbour.

One of the first things Gleeson did on his appointment to the DHA was to issue a directive: In future, Tom Hayson was to be invited to all important functions held by the DHA.

At the conference the delegates had been lavish in their praise of Darling Harbour, seeing it as one of the best examples of waterfront development in the world and a main reference point for any city wanting to regenerate a waterfront area.

On this night Gleeson took the microphone and thanked a number of people for their contributions. He pointed to Tom, saying "and of course, sitting there is my old friend and colleague Tom Hayson, who played such a principal role in establishing Darling Harbour."

A polite round of applause.

Then Gleeson introduced the keynote speaker, Neville Wran.

The former Premier said: "I'm probably speaking against myself here when I say this but for the first time I'm telling the truth tonight about Darling Harbour."

He told how in 1981 when it was suggested Sydney should try to get World Expo for 1988, he'd negotiated with Prime Minister Fraser but the cost was going to be $1.9 billion to build something that would have to be pulled down later.

Wran described how he offered to hold a scaled-down version for half the cost but the French organisation running Expo wouldn't have a bar of it, insisting on all or nothing. You wouldn't believe it, said Wran, but three weeks after his scaled-down version was refused, Expo went to Premier Bjelke Petersen in Queensland on an even more reduced basis than he'd suggested, supported by Fraser.

"So," said Wran, "we decided to hold our own Expo by building something permanent at Darling Harbour. We called a meeting in Sydney of all the leading businessmen, the nation's biggest companies and entrepreneurs. And among them was this little Hayson outfit. I don't know how they got into the act but somehow they were there.

"We despaired because we couldn't get any help from anyone at that meeting, except for one person. This man, Tom Hayson, he was the only one to put his hand up and tell us positively we could do it and further, he put his money into it."

And he turned to Tom seated at the official table and said, slowly and with emphasis:

"If it wasn't for you, Tom Hayson, there would not have been a Darling Harbour."

That's when the applause broke out. Loud and long. It took Tom by surprise. Ngaire sitting beside him couldn't believe it either.

After the years of tension and struggle over Darling Harbour, it had all ended in disappointment for them - until this moment.

Wran went on to tell how Tom had brought out Jim Rouse and a team of other American experts who suggested all sorts of things, exciting him with the prospects: "They even drew us a plan, which we changed a bit, but they showed us the way and that's how Darling Harbour got going, that is the result you see today."

Tom never thought he'd hear anyone give him the credit for what he'd done. He could not have wished for a greater tribute, especially before this distinguished audience in Darling Harbour, and by the former Premier.

It was the first time he'd been fully acknowledged in public. Some people had said things in private, but never to such an extent publicly.

Gerry Gleeson had invited him to a DHA Christmas party earlier and told them "Tom is the man responsible for this - without him there wouldn't have been a Darling Harbour," but that was a private function.

When the applause died down from Wran's remarks, those at the official table were profuse in their attention and praise. Sam Fiszman, director of Tourism in NSW and a member of the Gleeson DHA Board, said with genuine admiration: "That's how important you've been to Darling Harbour."

Others came up and congratulated him.

One guest, a leading architect, was especially gracious to him. Tom remembered that the architect, who had had a say in the planning, was negative at the time he brought out Rouse, saying Tom's scheme for Darling Harbour would never get off the ground.

After Wran's ringing endorsement on this celebrated night, the architect shifted ground and said to him: "I remember all this at the time. You had such fervour for Darling Harbour and you knew it would go."

"Yes," said Tom, quietly, "I also remember giving myself a heart attack."

Barry Young of MSJ Keys Young was there and also joined in the congratulations.

Tom went home a happy man that night. Ngaire too was happy. She said in the car: "At last someone has done the fair and decent thing. I never thought I'd hear it."

In his heart Tom knew the truth of what Wran had said.

Without him and his $200 million investment, Darling Harbour would not have happened. No Government would dare have started something so radical and costly without private enterprise money.

Of course it could not have happened without Wran's political courage to make the decision, or Laurie Brereton's drive to bulldoze it through the Nervous Nellies.

But Tom also knew that without his vision and the experts he'd assembled, Darling Harbour would have finished up a low-grade housing settlement with a park surrounded by a picket fence.

Now it was Sydney's celebration and relaxation centre, attracting visitors from every State. Apart from winning architectural and tourism awards, the attractions and restaurants of Darling Harbour were now generating revenue of about $600 million a year for Sydney.

All he'd received for his efforts and investment was the AM.

But that was enough. It represented achievement. Darling Harbour was his monument.

He hadn't realised why he'd gone into property but now he knew.

He'd wanted to build monuments. They'd called him a dago and he wanted to say to them by inference "all right, I've put up this building. What have you done? "

It was his way of saying to his racist detractors that he was just as good as them.

He recalled the private words of his old friend, John Laws: "When I retire what have I to be long remembered for? You are the builder of monuments that will last for generations."

As we all know, Darling Harbour was the inspiration Premier Greiner needed to give him the confidence to say go for the 2000 Olympics.

It was the second most important Games venue to the main Games stadium of Olympic Park at Homebush Bay in Sydney's west, hosting six Olympic sports, boxing, judo, wrestling, fencing, weight lifting and volleyball.

And as such Darling Harbour was the meeting place and celebration point for tens of thousands of competitors and fans who were able to "let their hair down" along the attractive harbourside promenades and top-class restaurants of Harbourside and Cockle Bay.

Olympic officials chose a Darling Harbour hotel to stay in, the Olympic press communications centre was in adjoining Pyrmont and many festivities directly linked to the Games were held in Darling Harbour.

Since the Games, judged the best ever by the International Olympic Committee, the last remaining doubters of Darling Harbour's worth - some politicians, jealous architects and planners and certain City Council members - are nowhere to be seen or heard.

In their wake, Sydney is proud in the knowledge it has one of the world's most celebrated public places where people of all ages and from all spheres of life and of all races and faiths can mingle in harmony every day to relax and enjoy themselves.

Visitors from around the world are drawn to Darling Harbour, almost irresistibly, to rub shoulders with Sydneysiders and other Australians.

As Darling Harbour's fame has spread, its effect on the previously "forgotten" adjacent areas of Ultimo and Pyrmont have been incalculable in monetary terms, as thousands of well-heeled and middle-income Australians and others have realised that this peninsula at the very foot of the CBD, practically surrounded by the Harbour, promises a new and different lifestyle with captivating views, second to none in Australia and the equal of any residential waterfront area in the world.

Tom thought it appropriate that one of the three men who supported him from the early days, Gerry Gleeson, should now not only be in charge of Darling Harbour but also the whole surrounding area as chairman of the Sydney Harbour Foreshore Authority.

Nick Greiner, before becoming Premier, always claimed Government money should not have been used in Darling Harbour - the main reason for his criticism - but to his credit he later acknowledged the importance of the facility after beginning the Sydney bid for the Games in 1991.

Indeed, Nick changed his mind to such an extent that he said: "I would not have bid for the 2000 Games if Sydney hadn't had Darling Harbour as a first class venue. It was crucial."

Darling Harbour became an integral part of the Sydney submission to the International Olympic Committee, showing not only that the city had a world class venue but also Australia could do large-scale projects on time.

Bruce Baird, who was Minister in charge of Sydney's Olympic Bid, said on the record to this writer that having Darling Harbour was an important part of the decision to bid.

"We were short of venues and sporting infrastructure at the time and Darling Harbour became an important and integral part of the process," he said.

"The IOC members whom we brought out were very impressed with Darling Harbour. I remember Juan Antonio Samaranch being more impressed with Darling Harbour than Homebush Bay, given that there wasn't much at Homebush then. He thought Darling Harbour was terrific.

"In my view we would not have won the bid if we hadn't had Darling Harbour."

Mr Baird wasn't alone in his views.

Nick Greiner told this writer: "I agree with Bruce Baird. Darling Harbour represented the only facilities in place prior to the bid being made and it obviously was crucial to the bid. Otherwise we'd have been bidding on spec."

Rod McGeoch, Chief Executive of the Sydney Olympic Bid, said: "I remember when Juan Samaranch visited us in 1993 with some IOC members, I personally escorted him around and he actually said to me firstly that he thought Darling Harbour was fantastic and secondly, he said he found it much more impressive than what we were beginning to build at Homebush.

"When we started our bid, the Darling Harbour facilities were all we had to inspect. It gave us a sound basis for bidding.

"On the basis that we had Darling Harbour, our feasibility study in 1990 showed only a modest projected profit from the Games of $70 million. So you can see that if Darling Harbour had not existed, it would have been much more difficult financially to stage the Games."

Kevan Gosper, Vice-President of the IOC and Australia's most senior IOC official, said on the record: "Without Darling Harbour, given the paucity of other facilities in Sydney at the time, we would have been in difficulty winning the 2000 Games.

"What we were able to do while Homebush was being built was show Samaranch and the IOC members Darling Harbour, and these were facilities that could deliver a substantial percentage of the Olympic programme, giving us credibility for putting on many indoor sports in this great space in the centre of the city. The existence of Darling Harbour was very persuasive for visiting IOC members, including Samaranch.

"If we'd brought IOC members out to look at Sydney after Melbourne's defeat at the hands of Atlanta, they could well have said hang on a minute, you're talking about Homebush Bay, we can't see much else around Sydney in the way of facilities. That is, without Darling Harbour. And I think Beijing would have looked more attractive.

"Darling Harbour was also there for other forms of entertainment associated with the Games and an influx of visitors - for cultural and social activities, even accommodation for IOC members. It meant we didn't have to deliver up new facilities for these other activities. Yes, Darling Harbour was a very important factor in winning us the Games."

On that basis, Tom Hayson not only was the man who gave us Darling Harbour, he was also responsible for bringing the 2000 Games to Sydney and Australia. The experts at the centre of the action have spoken and few, if any, would deny him that accolade.

Gerry Gleeson also said publicly that Darling Harbour was the generator for the Olympics. He did so before 850 guests at a lavish dinner in 1999 at which Premier Carr opened extensions to the Convention Centre as Darling Harbour was officially declared finished - 11 years after its opening, 15 years from the start.

At that dinner, Tom, with Ian beside him, was once more accorded a burst of applause as Gleeson retold the story that he was the only man among Australia's entrepreneurs to put up his hand and spend his money to enable the Government to start Darling Harbour, which he described as the world's most praised waterfront development.

Tom and Ngaire had attended several Olympic Games since she accompanied him when he covered Mexico City as a broadcaster in 1968. Naturally he arranged their tickets for Sydney's 2000 opening and closing ceremonies.

But sadly for Tom, Ngaire would not be with him this time.

His beloved wife, unwavering friend and loyal supporter, died in August, 1999, a year before the Sydney Games were held, and before the story of his life, which they shared for 57 years, could be published.

In the last few months of her life, he was beside her every day and night at their beautiful home on the Manly beach front. Nurses, including her friend and confidant Belinda Scott, cared for her around the clock, doctors Joe Galati (the family GP) and Peter Moore (in charge of palliative care at Mona Vale Hospital), called daily as the home became a hospice.

One morning while standing beside her bed with Ian's 25-year-old son Justin, who was very tall, Tom said to Ngaire: "He makes me look small, doesn't he?"

"You've never been small," said Ngaire. "You've always been a big person. Remember that."

It was typical of Ngaire, always building him up, sensing although never commenting on the reason why under it all, he had felt inferior.

In those last weeks she told friends including Violet Stedman, then aged 98, she'd had a wonderful life with Clem - her preferred name for him - and would not have changed a thing. She had been around the world with him 37 times and seen and done more than she ever dreamed of doing.

At her funeral service in St Andrew's Presbyterian Church, Manly, sons Ian and Paul paid warm and personal tributes to their mother and several grandchildren read prayers, while her daughter Rosemary held a heartbroken Tom together. Tom's sisters, Joyce and Pauline and brothers Claude and Bill, lent family support.

A soloist sang the emotive *Maori Farewell* in honour of her New Zealand birthplace and as family members slowly bore her casket from the crowded church, the *Amazing Grace* lament sounded from a lone piper, evoking memories of her Scottish heritage and strong qualities.

Neville Wran and Gerry Gleeson were there to pay their respects, Bob Pentecost, architects Bob Perry and Bob Blackmore, faithful secretary Andreé O'Toole and many others from the Darling Harbour days, rekindling memories of lively deeds and exciting times. John Laws left his 2UE morning radio programme to be there with his wife Caroline.

Tom Hayson walked slowly over the Pyrmont Bridge, the bridge he and Ian helped to save, and gazed across at the Harbourside Marketplace he'd built and once owned, nodding to himself with satisfaction as he saw the crowds strolling about enjoying themselves.

He looked across to Pyrmont and Ultimo where billions of dollars were being spent, all because of Darling Harbour sitting like an oasis between there and the CBD.

Developers who hadn't shared his faith in Darling Harbour were now competing madly to cash in on the new commercial and residential precinct spawned in the city's near west.

There *was* gold in them thar hills. Platinum too.

Most of the old buildings on the city side of Darling Harbour around Sussex, Kent and Clarence Streets had been built with their backs to the industrial eyesore that was once Darling Harbour, as though turning away from a slag heap.

Now the new apartment and office blocks springing up in those once-derelict streets cheerfully faced Darling Harbour, acknowledging it, wanting to be part of it, begging to be in its orbit.

Everything he'd predicted for the decayed Pyrmont and Ultimo area was now happening. He'd often said that once Darling Harbour was developed, the rest would follow.

Tom had foreseen it before anybody else, buying those big old woolstores well before Neville Wran met Prime Minister Fraser in February 1981 with a view to putting Expo into the ramshackle Darling Harbour railway yards.

His friends in the property world who'd laughed and joked about his dream, were looking a little foolish as reality stared them in the face.

The old money people, the traditionalists, were still in the city to the east, but the new ideas people like the Asians and other newcomers, were in this flourishing City West where it was more mixed, varied and cosmopolitan, a reflection of the New Australia.

He felt rich and proud, knowing how it all came about.

As he crossed the bridge and went down into Darling Harbour, he thought of people like Mort Hoppenfeld and Jim Rouse. The Great Rejuvenator had also passed on, aged 81.

Shortly before his death Rouse wrote to his friends in Australia urging them not to be saddened by his imminent departure.

Expressing the faith that had made him so successful after a tough early life as a teenager, he wrote: "I am just taking another step in my life, entering something new and exciting."

Even after all the money Rouse had spent in housing the poor through his Enterprise Foundation - a gesture to his conscience for having built up so much personal wealth - he still died a multi millionaire.

He too had been a vital player in the Darling Harbour saga, helping Tom convince the politicians and bureaucrats to "dream wildly" before the constraints of budgets and unimaginative minds took over.

Tom walked around the waterfront promenade listening to people talk, looking on as visitors from Japan, America, England and elsewhere snapped pictures to take home and show their friends and families the exciting, unique meeting place they'd just visited in Sydney.

Nobody took any notice of him as he strolled anonymously among them, at times standing beside them, gazing about like everyone else, appearing to take it all in for the first time.

None suspected he was the person who would become known as "Mr Darling Harbour."

When he heard their comments, he relived in his thoughts some of the dramas that had occurred as Darling Harbour evolved.

And sometimes as the sun came up, workers and other early morning people saw a well-dressed elderly man strolling in the streets on the ridge just behind Darling Harbour, a small gold badge in his left lapel, his shoulders drooped a little with age as well as the weight and turmoil of battles fought and won.

Nobody took any notice of him then, either. He could have been a resident from one of the big new apartment blocks, or a guest in one of the international hotels there.

But those who happened to glance at him as he passed had the same puzzled feeling.

They wondered why he was looking towards Darling Harbour and smiling.

EPILOGUE

I sat over a cup of coffee with Tom Hayson and a migrant of European background one day, talking about the future Australia.

"I'll tell you why I came to live in this country," said the migrant.

He pulled out a 20-cent coin, tossed it in the air and slapped it on the table between us.

"There," he said, pointing to the head of Queen Elizabeth 11, "that's why. To me, it symbolises freedom and democracy.

"That's why I've made my home here, and I don't want to see the system change, through a republic, agitation in the streets or anything else. I want to see Australian democracy stay the way it is."

The migrant, an Australian citizen, was obviously sincere. I'd heard others say similar things. From that experience, it's reasonable to assume that many others among the four million migrants who were born outside Australia, also thought along similar lines when deciding to call Australia home.

The man's passion and conviction set me thinking. Precisely what was this *democracy* he talked about? And what were the dangers?

As a longtime working journalist and author, who has observed our democracy at work over the years, I've come to know many solicitors and barristers, regarding some as personal friends. I put it to them and did some research.

As a result I came away with some firm views which I consider worth throwing into the ring on the subject of Australia's future.

Our democratic society is based on the rule of law. And our basic law is contained in the Australian Constitution - the legal instrument which brought us together as a federation of States on January 1, 1901.[1]

The Federal Constitution is binding on the courts, judges, and people of every State and part of the Commonwealth, notwithstanding State laws.[2]

The High Court is the keeper of the Constitution, interpreting its meaning and enforcing its observance in a changing society.

The Federal Constitution defines and limits the power of the Commonwealth Parliament to alter that law - which I hope to show, is where potential dangers lie.

Our Federal Constitution was negotiated over 10 years of trials and tribulation in Australia by the Fathers of Federation between 1890 and

1900, to iron out competing differences before the then six Australian colonies could agree to unite under a written constitution.

The colonies were independent and self-governing, the only thing in common being the sovereignty of the Crown. That was the common bond, or glue, which bound them together in a vast continent.

After 10 years, without any participation by the UK, Australia drew up its own Constitution and agreement to federate in the relevant Act, and each colonial parliament passed the legislation. Then the people in each colony unanimously approved the proposal by referendum.

The draft bill for the Act, containing the Constitution and the federation agreement, was taken to London and, after a short period of negotiation, approved by the UK Government and the UK Parliament with only minor amendments.

That is believed to be the first time such individual action was taken by a group of colonies in the then British Empire. Australia is also the only nation whose Constitution went through such a democratic process.

It was aptly described as "The People's Bill" by leading conservative Adelaide barrister, Sir Josiah Symon, on January 17, 1900. A King's Counsel, he was later a Senator for South Australia in the first Federal Parliament. In a letter to the Earl of Selborne, Under Secretary of State for the Colonies, he said the Bill was unlike any other propsed legislation ever framed in an English community, in that it owed its existence to the people themselves.

"They chose a special Convention to frame the Federal Constitution and to bargain between the Federated Colonies, refusing to entrust this solemn task to any Parliament," Sir Josiah wrote. "They insisted on having the Bill sumitted at large to themselves for acceptance or rejection. So it became the People's Bill in a very literal sense - unalterable without their direct consent."

Our Federal Constitution is contained in the Act of the United Kingdom Parliament called the Commonwealth of Australia Constitution Act, 1900. For simplicity, I'll call it "the 1900 Act."

That constituted "Australia's sovereign act of national self-determination" - acknowledged by the Hon Murray Gleeson, Chief Justice of Australia, when he said in his (2000) Boyer lectures: "In the contemplation of the law, the Australian nation came into existence on 1 January, 1901, when the Commonwealth Constitution took legal effect."

To take the background a bit further - before coming to the punchline - Australia became an independent sovereign nation through that 1900 Act, proclaimed by Queen Victoria at Balmoral on September 17, 1900 (her successor, Queen Elizabeth 11, was declared Queen of Australia by an Act of our Federal Parliament).[3]

The six Australian colonies then became the six States of Australia, united under the Crown, in one federal commonwealth called The Commonwealth of Australia.

The 1900 Act is sometimes referred to in legal circles as the "Australian Federal Compact" because first, it expressly records and sanctions the agreement (inspired and forged in Australia) between the six colonies to unite in one indissoluble federal commonwealth under the Crown, and second, the agreement between the six colonies on the one hand and the UK on the other.[4]

The UK Parliament was the only power on earth that could legally bring this about. The Australian colonies acting on their own could not do it.

It's fair to say that to have the UK Parliament enact the 1900 Act was a small price to pay to peacefully create an independent federated Australia, armed with a Constitution drafted by Australians and designed to serve the needs of Australians for all time (subject to the power of alteration).

Due to the wisdom of our founding fathers, the 1900 Act entrenched the sovereignty, or ultimate power of the Australian people over our basic law and our various parliaments, Federal and State.

Under the Constitution, the *legal* sovereignty is vested in the Crown and effectively held in trust for the Australian people, and the *political* sovereignty is vested in the people.

That fact was reaffirmed recently by the Chief Justice of the High Court, the Honourable Murray Gleeson, AC, who said "the sovereignty of our nation lies with the people, both as a matter of legal principle and practical reality."[5]

In an ABC Boyer Lecture, the Chief Justice said it was the special duty of the High Court to uphold the words and meaning of the Constitution "precisely as framed."[6]

Under the 1900 Act, each of the unified States preserved their self-governing identity, while the Constitution provided for the government of Australia as a whole.

[Later events have removed the power of the UK Parliament to make laws affecting Australia.

The Australia Acts (Imperial and Commonwealth) were passed by the UK Parliament in 1986 at the request of all Australian Parliaments, in order to strengthen Australia's international position as an independent sovereign nation. Under the Australia Act, the UK Parliament can never again pass laws relating to Australia, including our Constitution].

Back to the 1900 Act. It consists of several parts.

The first three paragraphs are the "preamble" to that Act. Briefly, it says the various States from 1901 onwards will "unite in one indissoluble Federal Commonwealth under the Crown of the United Kingdom..."

Then follow sections 1 to 8, referred to as "the covering clauses."

Section 9 of the 1900 Act embodies our Federal Constitution. That is divided into various chapters dealing with issues such as Parliament and its powers, the office of Governor-General, finance and trade, the States and so on.

It also sets out section 128, providing for the Constitution to be amended - by national referendum approved by a majority of the people of Australia, and also by a majority of people in four of the six States.

[Where an amendment affects certain key rights of the States, a majority in every affected State is also required].

That is the only way our Federal Constitution can be amended.

It's interesting to note that the fundamental democratic process of referendum (to ascertain the will of the people), does not exist in the UK or the US under the US Federal Constitution. To that extent, our Constitution can properly be claimed to be more democratic than theirs.

Australia adopted the "referendum" idea from Switzerland, where it still forms an important part of the Swiss Federal Constitution.

But, there's a catch. Section 128 does not authorise any amendment to anything except the schedule to the Act in section 9 (the Constitution).

You cannot use section 128 to amend the preamble or the covering clauses of the 1900 Act because the structure of the Act renders them incapable of being altered or repealed under Australian law. The power of alteration by referendum under Section 128 is confined to the Constitution itself, embodied in section 9 of that Act.

The people's right of referendum was considered so important that, when the UK Parliament passed the Statute of Westminster in 1931 to give all independent Dominions in the British Empire equal status with the UK, our Federal Parliament insisted on a special clause being inserted in the statute to protect the referendum aspect of the Australian Constitution.[7]

Clearly, any alternative process attempting to alter the Constitution would be illegal and unconstitutional - and in legal terms destroy the Federation, plunging Australia into constitutional crisis.

The sovereignty of the Crown is entrenched in the covering clauses 1 to 8 and the preamble of the 1900 Act, and as such, it is also entrenched in the Federal Constitution.

How do I know? Well, some of Australia's best legal brains since Federation have said so on the record.

Any proposed legislation to remove the Crown from the preamble and covering clauses to the 1900 Act, would create an immediate legal conflict between those provisions of that Act and the Federal Constitution (in section 9).

That was what the Federal Government's proposed constitutional alternations threatened to do in the 1999 referendum, if passed, by aiming to make Australia a republic.

The proposed legislation purported to remove all references in the Federal Constitution to the sovereign, or Queen, replacing them with "the President."

For one thing, the "republic law" would have destroyed the legal status of every Australian citizen in being subjects of the Queen of Australia.

But the preamble and covering clauses of the Act would have prevented this from taking legal effect, even if the referendum had succeeded.

Why? The proposed alterations would have been legally invalidated because they are inconsistent with the preamble and covering clauses, as well as the Federal Constitution, in the 1900 Act.

However, that constitutional conflict and dilemma has never been debated or explained to the Australian people.

Yet, based on some of our best legal authorities (quoted below), the 1999 republican legislation was unlawful and unconstitutional because, the constitutional authorities say, the Crown cannot be removed from the 1900 Act under existing Australian law.

That was the third major grab for power by an Australian Government.

The Scullin Labor Government in 1930 tried unsuccessfully to pass a bill called the "Constitution Alteration (Power of Amendment) Bill" to give Federal Parliament the right to alter the Constitution at will without going to a referendum.[8]

The second attempt was made by the Curtin Labor Government in 1944 in seeking to amend the Constitution to give Parliament the right to interpret laws without reference to the High Court, and the people rejected it at a national referendum.

The founding fathers of Federation, being wise old blokes, looked around the world at federal systems first, before deciding to deliberately frame our Constitution to stop radical governments and power-greedy politicians from taking the law into their own hands.

The Commonwealth Royal Commission on the Federal Constitution in 1929, which held 198 sittings and examined 339 witnesses over a period of two years, considered in detail the extent to which the powers in the Constitution could be used to amend the covering clauses or the preamble to the 1900 Act.[9] The commissioners said it could not be done.

Owen Dixon, King's Counsel, later knighted and still recognised here and abroad as one of Australia's most eminent jurists ever (who became a Justice of the High Court in 1929 and Chief Justice in 1952), gave this evidence to the Royal Commission:

"The covering clauses prevent any complete and fundamental change in the parliamentary nature of our government. You could not get rid of the King as head of the Executive, or do anything of that sort...".[10]

Dixon repeated that evidence to the Law Council of Australia in 1936, saying the sovereignty of the King in Parliament over the law, was *"indestructible."[11]*

The Commonwealth Solicitor-General, Sir Robert Garran, one of the founding fathers of the Constitution, said in evidence to the 1929 Royal Commission that we did not have power to amend the covering clauses, only the schedule to the Act (the Constitution itself).[12]

Sir Edward Mitchell, then a King's Counsel and leader of the Bar in Melbourne, told the same Royal Commission: "Those covering clauses, I think, are quite clearly incapable of alteration under the provisions of section 128 of the Constitution.

"Power to alter the Constitution does not commence until you get to the words 'The Constitution,' *after* the covering clauses."[13]

Speakers in Federal Parliament went further when the Scullin Government, in 1930, tried to gain power for the Federal Parliament to change the Constitution without a referendum.

Even the Federal Attorney-General, Frank Brennan, whose Government was trying to push it through, agreed with Sir Edward Mitchell by admitting in Parliament that the covering clauses could not be changed by a section 128 referendum. Mr Brennan said:

"Sir Edward Mitchell's opinion affirms several propositions. One is that section 128 of the Constitution extends only to the amendment of the Constitution itself, and not to the covering sections which constitute an Act of the Imperial legislature. That is certainly admitted; indeed, it may be accepted as a truism."[14]

Among other speakers to condemn the proposed constitutional alterations were the Opposition Leader and Member for Kooyong, John Latham (later knighted and who became Chief Justice of the High Court), and Senate Opposition Leader, Sir George Pearce. Both said it would destroy the federation and bring an end to the Constitution.

Latham said: "This is more radical than any other amendment that could be conceived. It really means the abolition of the Constitution.

"It is a proposal to confer unlimited power upon any party which may control this Parliament and to deprive the people of any voice in the matter by way of referendum.

"Parliament will have the power or right to govern the whole of Australia from Canberra.

"The inevitable result will be either that the States will be suddenly killed, or they will wither away as their functions are diminished and their powers and prestige decreased."[15]

Sir George Pearce, Senator for Western Australia, told Parliament the bill was the most extraordinary, audacious and revolutionary ever conceived. He said it would enable Parliament to alter the Constitution almost from day to day as it thought fit, without consulting the people.

It would centralise power in Canberra, cause absolute confusion, enable the Federal Government to take part of one State and add it to another, or carve up Australia in any way it liked. States would not have entered into a federation if they had known they would end up without a constitution.

Sir George made it clear that if the unconstitutional alteration was allowed, it would destroy the Commonwealth of Australia as a Federation and democracy as we knew it.[16]

The proposal in the 1999 republican referendum - to remove the sovereignty of the Crown by using section 128 of the Constitution - would have had much the same effect, if successful.

It was nothing less than a calculated attempt to override the 1900 Act - Australia's fundamental law and therefore, the Constitution.

However, as the quoted authorities say, it can't be done because the Crown's sovereignty is entrenched in the preamble and covering clauses of the 1900 Act and they cannot be abrogated by a section 128 referendum (or otherwise).

Okay, if both the Federal Government and the Opposition in 1930 were agreed that the preamble and covering clauses of the 1900 Act were untouchable by referendum, why was it suddenly considered proper and legal by referendum in 1999 to toss out the sovereignty entrenched by those clauses and the Federal Constitution?

The answer is I don't know. But I can speculate.

I'd say the hunger for power over the Australian Constitution by the present Federal Government and Opposition - with the conservative parties having a so-called "conscience vote" on the republican issue - is far greater than was that of the Scullin Government in 1930, despite the serious problems it faced over the Depression.

In the leadup to the 1999 republican referendum, the Commonwealth Parliament published a comprehensive bibliography of the major constitutional reviews to "assist community debate." But it excluded the recommendations and findings of the 1929 Royal Commission, which said the covering clauses of the 1900 Imperial Act could not be amended.

The reason given? The findings were considered "likely to be of diminished relevance."[17]

Yet, the High Court of Australia obviously thinks the 1929 Royal Commission findings are still relevant since, in 1999, it published a judgment in a highly important constitutional law case (Sue versus Hill) quoting verbatim directly from the 1929 Royal Commission Report.[18]

I invite you to draw your own conclusions on that.

All the constitutional jiggery pokery we have gone through in the last few years emanated from a speech in Parliament by then Prime Minister Paul Keating in June, 1995, when he championed a republic, equating it to having an Australian as Head of State.

Among other things, he said: "Sooner or later we must have an Australian as our Head of State. That one small step would make Australia a republic."

The Australian people have been deceived into believing that, as an independent sovereign nation, we cannot have our own Head of State unless we become a republic.

They have also been led to believe that the only way of having our own Head of State by law, is to amend the Federal Constitution.

So say members of the republican movement. Both claims are incorrect.

The 1900 Act (also containing the Federal Constitution), is completely silent on the so-called title of "Head of State of Australia."

This means such a title can be created by an Act of the Federal Parliament, provided it does not contain any provision inconsistent with the 1900 Act, including the sovereignty of the Crown.

Therefore, a short Act could validly declare for example, that the person holding office as Governor General, also holds the honorary title of "Head of State of Australia."

That new title could also be designated "President of Australia" - as long as the relevant Act expressly provides that nothing impinges on the powers, duties or functions of the Governor-General under the Federal Constitution, or affects the sovereignty of the Crown.

The Governor-General's position as representative of the Queen of Australia would be unaffected under the Federal Constitution .

We need not go as far as "President of Australia." The title "Head of State" might fill the bill. In any case, the Australian people should be consulted on this by a national plebiscite (not a referendum), as was done to select Australia's national song.

Such a question - within the law - to avoid confusion with other plebiscite questions finding their way into Australian newspapers, could be along the lines set out in the appendix at the end of this epilogue.

That would be much cheaper and less controversial than a referendum and could be held at the same time as a general election.

Interestingly, as an alternative, we would not need to appoint the Governor-General as Head of State. A law could be passed by a majority vote of both Houses of Federal Parliament appointing anyone they liked as Head of State, provided it did not affect the Constitution or sovereignty of the Crown.

It would not convert Australia to a republic.

But, at the stroke of the Governor-General's pen, it would remove the key element in the propaganda issued by the republican movement.

Such an Act would be truly a symbolic measure without changing the Constitution. After all, Federal Parliamentarians have already legislated to give us a national flag, flower and song, so if a "Head of State" is considered important enough, the solution already lies in their hands.

The exercise of going through the constitutional convention and the 1999 referendum was estimated to have cost Australian taxpayers $800 million - just to make what we were told was a "symbolic" change to the Constitution - "one small step."

Who's kidding who?

The Australian people were led to believe they were voting on a purely symbolic change to our constitutional arrangements, which would have no underlying or substantial effect on the way our Constitution operates.

That was untrue.

The legal mechanism for purely "symbolic change," without destroying the Constitution, has always been available to Federal Parliament by conventional legislation.

As the law stands the Government and Federal Parliament have no legal or constitutional power to convert Australia to a republic, since that involves setting aside the 1900 Act and destroying the sovereignty of the Crown - impossible under the "rule of law."

So how did the Government intend to overcome the obstacle of the covering clauses and the preamble to the 1900 Imperial Act, which makes it clear you can't throw out the Crown and become a republic?

The only public discussion on this issue has been in the 1929 Royal Commission, which ruled it out completely. These historic facts weren't controversial then. Fashion may have changed, but the law hasn't.

And as Sir John Latham indicated in 1930, you can kiss goodbye to the Australian Federation if you try to change the Constitution without going to a referendum - and even then, you could not make the necessary changes to the preamble or covering clauses to the 1900 Act to remove the Crown.

Although it has never been spelled out in detail to the Australian people, the Federal Government now claims it can remove the preamble and covering clauses of the 1900 Act - something the 1929 Royal Commission and various constitutional experts of the time said could not be done.

The explanation of how this can allegedly be done was technically placed on the record, but you need to be a bit of a Sherlock Holmes to find it.

It was contained in an explanatory House of Representatives memo, circulated with the authority of Prime Minister John Howard, to the proposed 1999 bill to insert a preamble to the Constitution (one of the two proposed laws submitted to the 1999 national referendum and rejected by the people).

A paragraph in the memo claimed that if in the future it was considered desirable to change the preamble or covering clauses in the 1900 Act, "this could be done by the Commonwealth Parliament at the request of the States under the Australia Act 1986, or by a further contitutional referendum."

A similar phrase, circulated with the authority of the Federal Attorney-General Mr Daryl Williams, was contained in a revised Senate explanatory memo to the proposed bill to establish a republic (the second proposed law submitted to the 1999 referendum and also rejected).

If the 1999 referendum questions had been passed, both bills would then have been put before Parliament and no doubt enacted.

In simple terms the Federal Government, if requested by the States, believes it can remove the preamble and covering clauses to our Constitution through the Australia Act, 1986 - without a referendum.

That's not what the Attorney-General Lionel Bowen said when introducing the second reading of the "Australia Bill" to Parliament on November 13, 1985 and in his address in reply on November 25. First, he said **"nothing in the legislation will impair the position of the Queen as Queen of Australia."**

Then to Opposition concerns expressed about the Bill's effect on the Constitution, Mr Bowen said: **"Nothing can happen to the Constitution of Australia unless the people of Australia agree that it should happen."**

In other words, no changes can be made to the Constitution, through that Bill or any other, without the people approving it by referendum.

Well, it now emerges that the Federal Government claims to possess more power than the Scullin Government tried and failed to get in 1930 - namely, the power to amend the Constitution at will without reference to the people, removing the preamble and covering clauses.

By what magic wand has this been achieved? What battles have been fought, what constitutional conventions held, what Parliamentary debates played out to obtain this power without telling us?

Surely we would have heard about it if the politicians had been able to usurp the exclusive sovereignty or power of the people over their own Constitution and transferred it to Federal Parliament?

As they have not told us of these revolutionary developments, we can only assume that the politicians had a hidden agenda in the 1999 republican referendum, using it as a smokescreen to cover their true intentions ie, to grab power to alter the Consitution in the future without going to the people on the issue.

[In 1930 the Scullin Government sought only to alter the Constitution itself (section 9 of the 1900 Act) without a referendum, not the preamble and covering clauses 1 to 8. Indeed, Prime Minister Scullin admitted in Parliament on 14 March, 1930 that the Commonwealth had no power to amend clauses 1 to 8 of the 1900 Act.]

Constitutional lawyers to whom I have spoken recently insist it can't be done under Australian law, including the Australia Act 1986.

For one thing, they say that when the UK Parliament passed the Statute of Westminster Act in 1931 (basically giving Dominions equal status with the UK Parliament), our Commonwealth Parliament insisted on a clause in the Statute to preserve the Australian people's rights under the Constitution, including exclusive control by referendum over any changes. That was later written into our Statute of Westminster Adoption Act of 1942.

That clause overrides anything in the Australia Act. Appearing in the 1942 Act as clause 8, it is referred to in the Australia Act (section 5) under the heading "Commonwealth Constitution, Constitution Act and Statute of Westminster not affected."

So where is the Federal Government coming from?

The only way to throw out the Crown would be by revolution, or *coup d'état*. If that happened, the "rule of law" in Australia would be treated with ultimate contempt.

That would lead to anarchy, not necessarily riots in the streets, but an absence of law and effective government.

The Australian Constitution is substantially based on the American Constitution. The US Supreme Court has upheld the principle that the Union of the USA is complete, perpetual and indissoluble, with "no place for revocation or reconsideration except by revolution."[19]

Our founding fathers intended our Federation to be indissoluble too.

Indeed, the High Court of Australia handed down a judgment in 1907 (Baxter v The Commissioner of Taxation), in which Chief Justice Griffith and Justices O'Connor and Barton (previously our first Prime Minister) said: "The Constitution was not intended to provide merely for the exigencies of a few years, but was to endure through a long lapse of ages."

As a result of the wisdom of our founding fathers, it is one of the most successful national constitutions anywhere in the world (even against the US Constitution, the fragility of which was shown up in the delayed Presidential election of George W. Bush).

We are talking about things that could threaten the stability and integrity of the whole of the Commonwealth of Australia. It may be no exaggeration to say that if we allow politicians to grab power by tampering with the Federal Constitution, we could end up in the same position as the USA in 1861 - facing civil war as some States resorted to armed conflict in trying to withdraw from the Union.

A Federal Labor Government will no doubt try to put a "republic" in place. When that happens, there will be one almighty constitutional row in the High Court.

If the republican referendum had succeeded in 1999, the High Court would have faced a similar dilemma to that which confronted the Fiji Court of Appeal after the Speight rebellion of May 19, 2000 - what happens when a nation's constitution has been overthrown?

The Fiji Court of Appeal (constituted by a panel of judges from NSW, New Zealand and New Guinea), was called upon to determine whether Fiji's 1997 Constitution was still in force.

The Court ruled that it was, saying in its judgment that when a Constitution was purportedly overthrown but leaving the Court system intact, the Court had only two options.

One was to say that the usurping government had succeeded in permanently changing the previous legal order and the new order was legally valid; the other was to declare the usurpation invalid - and that is what the Fiji Court of Appeal found.[20]

Fiji remained in anarchy after the rebellion, with profound public uncertainty as to its Constitution and rightful Government. It was only due to great restraint by the population that, by 2001, wholesale civil war had not broken out.

When Australians voted in 1900 to unite their six colonies, they decided the exclusive power to change the Constitution should only be done through the people by referendum, and not entrusted to any Parliament.

By taking that action, they unanimously adopted a constitutional instrument (the 1900 Act including the Federal Constitution), which provided that the proposed Federal Parliament would be one of strictly limited legislative power, ie, it would not have full sovereign power, as does the UK Parliament.

Just as our Federal Parliament is controlled by the 1900 Act and the Australian Constitution, so too is the US Congress (the equivalent of our Federal Parliament) subject and subordinate to the US Constitution. That control is one of the essential features in a federal system of *democracy*.

Those essential features are put in place to keep meddling politicians and other power mongers at bay. The features have been referred to often down the years, including being outlined in a speech in Federal Parliament in 1902 by Sir Alfred Deakin, then Commonwealth Attorney-General and soon to become our second Prime Minister.[21]

The famous British constitutional lawyer, A.V. Dicey, summed it up neatly in the 19th century when we were still separate colonies.

Abbreviated, he said that a federal constitution must be "written," it must also be "inflexible" or "inexpansive," and the law of the constitution "must either be legally immutable, or else capable of being changed only by some authority above and beyond the ordinary legislative bodies existing under that constitution."[22]

That's the way we went. The Australian people determined that the powers of their Federal Parliament would always be subject and subordinate to the terms of Australia's fundamental law, as set out in the 1900 Act - including that the sovereignty of the people be preserved under section 128 of the Constitution, making a successful referendum necessary to approve any change in the Constitution.

It was done to protect the rights of ordinary people like you and me, like Tom Hayson and everyone else.

That power, or reservation, has never been surrendered by the people of Australia, and never should be, knowingly or voluntarily.

It's a cause for vigilance when politicians want to snatch more power by changing our Constitution - especially when the Government doesn't fully explain its intentions or the consequences of proposed constitutional changes.

Fortunately, when Australians smell a rat, they vote no.

Finally, a few points that may "assist community debate" when the republican issue revisits us.

As a group, the founding fathers who drafted our Federal Constitution (the 1900 Act), represented Australia's most eminent constitutional lawyers.

They included Mr Andrew Inglis Clark (later a Justice of the Tasmanian Supreme Court), a recognised expert on the US Constitution who travelled to the USA and kept in touch with the leading American jurists and statesmen while serving on Australia's Constitution drafting committee.

Mr Clark, ironically a republican, believed the US founders had solved the fatal flaws of republican government by combining popular control with constitutional safeguards against abuses of power.

Our founding fathers incorporated into the 1900 Act the best features of the three leading Federal systems of government of the day - from the constitutions of the USA, Canada and the Swiss confederation.

When it was finally adopted, Australia could justifiably claim to have the world's most advanced democratic federal constitution.

In recommending a (federal) constitutional monarchy, as opposed to a republican system of government, the founding fathers did so with their eyes wide open, considering it in Australia's best interests

So Australia's Federal Constitution is based mainly on the US Constitution combined with the British system of constitutional monarchy, incorporating both "representative government" (where members of parliament are democratically elected) and "responsible government" (where the executive government is carried on by ministers responsible to parliament).

It should be remembered that the British system of government was forged in the fires of a lengthy civil war and revolution in the 17th century (in which King Charles 1 was publicly beheaded).

That was followed by 10 years of republican government under Oliver Cromwell, the Lord Protector of England - a system abandoned on Cromwell's death.

Recognised for its democratic foundations, the British system which we adopted, has therefore been developed over several hundred years.

Those foundations basically are the Crown, which represents every citizen in the land; the legislature, being Parliamentarians who make our laws; and the judiciary, who interpret and enforce the laws.

Like the surveyor's tripod, remove any one of those legs and the whole thing falls over.

Anyone who imagines Australia could be converted into a "republic" and still have a workable Constitution and system of government by removing references to the sovereign in our written Constitution and replacing them with "the President," demonstrates an ignorance of the Constitution (our fundamental law), including the unwritten conventions and civil rights of Australians that go with it.

In this context, the views of Mr Harry Evans, the Clerk of the Australian Senate, are worth noting.

He said in a Parliamentary paper in September, 1994,[23] that the problem with Australian republicanism was that it saw a republic as simply the absence of the monarchy, without understanding Australian constitutional history.

There were two popular misconceptions - first, that federalism was regarded as a "brake on efficiency" rather than a restraint on central government power, and second, the process of changing the constitution by referendum was "a tiresome barrier to reform."

Mr Evans said: "Constant propaganda along these lines may brainwash the public into thinking that these elements of the constitution must be jettisoned with the monarchy. There is a conspiracy to conceal the republican nature of these institutions and their value."

He added: "The danger of the republican movement is that it will result in centralised and unrestrained government."

Instead, he warned, further safeguards were needed against the centralisation and abuse of government power.

It may well be that, after a century, our Constition needs updating in part, that some time in the future Australians may wish to change to a republican form of government and remove the Crown.

But my point now is to alert people that these things should be done strictly according to the rule of law, not subject to the whim of a passing parade of politicians who do not put their cards on the table and seek power they were never intended to have.

I rest my cup. This mixed brew, served up by a concerned migrant sipping a cappuccino as he tossed a coin, needs to be well stirred before it settles.

APPENDIX

AUTHOR'S PROPOSED PLEBISCITE QUESTION.

"Do you favour Australia's Federal Parliament (Canberra) using its existing legislative powers to enact a law to provide that the person holding office as Governor General of Australia shall also hold the new, purely symbolic and ceremonial title of:

"Head of State of Australia"

on condition that such new law (and title) shall operate and have full effect without in any way altering or affecting -

- our existing Federal Constitution;

- the (existing) powers, duties and responsibilities of Australia's Governor General, under the Federal Constitution;

- the constitutional and legal position of the Queen as Australia's Sovereign [holding the title of "Queen of Australia" (in accordance with the Royal Style and Titles Act, 1974 (Commonwealth of Australia)]?"

END NOTES TO EPILOGUE

1. Commonwealth of Australia Constitution Act 1900 (United Kingdom), (covering) section 5;

2. Gleeson M. "The Rule of Law and the Constitution" (p.8);

3. Royal Style and Titles Act, 1974 (Australia);

4. Baxter v Commissioner of Taxation (NSW) (1907) 4 CLR 1087 (at 1104-5);

5. Gleeson M. "The Rule of Law and the Constitution" (p.6) (quoting Sir Gerald Brennan, speech   upon swearing in as Chief Justice of Australia);

6. Gleeson M. "The Rule of Law and the Constitution" (p.53);

7. Statute of Westminster 1931, s 8 (UK); Statute of Westminster Adoption Act 1942, (Aust);

8. House of Reps Hansard (14 March 1930; Mr Scullin, Prime Minister (at p.177);

9 Royal Comm on the Constitution 1929, Government Printer, Canberra (pp.16-17; 228);

10. Royal Comm on the Constitution, Minutes of evidence, Part 3, 13 Dec 1927, p.776, at p 794-5;

11. "Jesting Pilate" and other papers and addresses by Rt Hon Sir O. Dixon (at p.87);

12. Royal Comm on Constitution 1929. Evidence of Solicitor-General (Pt 1, p. 41 (at p.64);

13. Royal Comm on Constitution. Minutes of evidence, 12 Dec, 1927. Pt 3 (p.754);

14. House of Reps Hansard, 10 April 1930 (at p. 1146);

15. House of Reps Hansard, 10 April 1930 (p.507-515);

16. Senate Hansard 1 May, 1930 (at p.1288-1292);

17. "Constitutional Change - select sources on constitutional change in Australia 1901-97."House of Reps Standing Committee on Legal and Constitutional Affairs, Feb 1999 Canberra (p. 1);

18. Sue v Hill (1999) 199 CLR 462 (at 496);

19. Texas v White (1868), 7 Wallace 700; Boyd's Const Cases, p. 552; (at 556);

20. Australian Law Journal, May 2000, Vol 75, at p. 277-8;

21. House of Reps Hansard, 18 March 1902 (Judiciary Bill, 2 r), at p. 10966-7;

22. Federal Government, A.V.Dicey (1885), Vol 1, Law Quarterly Review p. 80 (at p. 83);

23. Papers on Parliament No. 24, Sept 1994. "Essays on Republicanism: Small r republicanism." Harry Evans - Dept of Senate, Parlament House, Canberra.